THE CIVILIZATION OF THE AMERICAN INDIAN SERIES

The Spokane Indians

THE SPOKANE INDIANS

CHILDREN OF THE SUN

By ROBERT H. RUBY
and JOHN A. BROWN

WITH A FOREWORD BY *Robert L. Bennett*

UNIVERSITY OF OKLAHOMA PRESS : *Norman and London*

By ROBERT H. RUBY AND JOHN A. BROWN

Half-Sun on the Columbia: A Biography of Chief Moses
(Norman, 1965)
The Spokane Indians: Children of the Sun (Norman, 1970)
The Cayuse Indians: Imperial Tribesmen of Old Oregon
(Norman, 1972)
The Chinook Indians: Traders of the Lower Columbia River
(Norman, 1976)
Indians of the Pacific Northwest: A History (Norman, 1981)

The Spokane Indians is Volume 104 in The Civilization of the American Indian Series.

LIBRARY OF CONGRESS CATALOG CARD NUMBER: 79–108797
ISBN: 0–8061–1757–5

3   4   5   6   7   8   9   10   11   12   13   14   15   16   17   18   19

Dedicated to

Henry
and
Janet

Foreword

The history of the Spokane Indian tribe, as related in *The Spokane Indians*, is a microcosm within the macrocosm of Indian–white relationships. It is the story of the American Indian buffeted by massive cultural changes, seeking to accommodate to, then to resist, the tide of white encroachment, but in the end succumbing.

It is a story sometimes heroic, sometimes ludicrous, but always familiar in its humanity. It presents a vivid panorama of the ordinary people—their hopes, ideologies, and conflicts, from which the American West emerged.

The Spokanes, whose legends predicted the coming of the white man, consistently courted the friendship of the newcomers, except for one brief but bitter encounter. The outcome was preordained, resulting in the tribe's relocation to reservations on lands the white settlers considered too worthless to covet. There, by the beginning of the twentieth century, the remnant Spokanes had descended into a pervasive poverty.

As early as the 1880s, there were those who voiced angry criticism of the policies that had reduced these once proud and independent people to abject poverty. A few at first, then many, began to urge remedial legislation, and this became the pattern of the twentieth century.

When the Spokane Reservation was first established in its present location, its thickly forested slopes offered little to the agriculturally minded settlers. Today, however, timber is one of the tribe's greatest assets, with an allowable annual cut of eighteen million board feet. Two modern mills on the reservation process a portion of this harvest.

The Spokanes own thirty-five miles of valuable lake-front property on Lake Roosevelt, considered of primary importance because of its tourism income potential. Orchards, strongly opposed around the turn of the century as being too innovative, flourish now in the rich bottomlands on the reservation.

Formal education, when first introduced on the reservation, was haphazard. Truancy was the rule rather than the exception. The present decade, however, has seen the Spokanes outpace their neighbors, with a greater percentage of students graduating from high school than the national average.

With the discovery of the richest uranium-ore producing mine in the United States on Spokane land, the tribe's progress into the contemporary world was accelerated. Recent judgments in the U.S. Court of Claims, authorizing reimbursement to the tribe for lands taken during the period of westward expansion, have further stimulated their advance toward total self-sufficiency— now within the forseeable future.

The Spokane Indians, with its wealth of documented detail, is an important addition to the written history of the Columbia Plateau. More noteworthy, however, is its contribution to the understanding of the American Indian as he is today—an individual, an American citizen, and an irreplaceable part of our treasured heritage.

ROBERT L. BENNETT
Commissioner of Indian Affairs

Preface

A white man once said that, were he to drop a twenty-dollar gold piece among a group of Spokane Indians, he would more likely get it back than were he to drop it among his own people. Very complimentary. Yet not so the words of another white man, who described the Spokanes as a "lazy indolent tribe." These diverse statements perhaps tell as much about the white men who made them as they do about the Spokanes. We are not unmindful that, in attempting to present an ethnohistory of these people, we will tell more of ourselves than we would like to admit. Nevertheless, it is still true that groups of men, at any time and any place, present a complexity of patterns for those who would study them—a task filled with equal complexity. This has been not only our problem, but our challenge.

Like other students of the American Indian, we have had to examine much of Spokane history through the eyes of white men. The Spokane Indians of the interior Salish peoples left few, if any, written records; and the records they left buried in the sands of time have, on discovery, been interpreted by white men. We are thankful that a thread of Spokane folklore spun out from earliest times has remained, but there are signs that, in the heterogeneous white American society into which the Spokanes have been forced, this lore along with other aspects of their culture may be swept away. The realization of this danger has given an urgency to our study. Despite the limitations under which we have approached our task, we have tried, but never with as much success as we would wish, to view the Spokanes from "inside the tipi."

Throughout much of their known history, the Spokanes—despite a measure of geographic and cultural homogeneity—have been a house divided. They comprise two or three groups (as white men have tended to divide them). Spokane separation carried over into the contact and postcontact eras, when the imposed reservation system perpetuated, rather than diminished, division among them. In this book we have made no comprehensive effort to trace the amalgamation of Spokanes with other Indians of the Flathead, Coeur d'Alene, and Colville Reservations, where some of the Spokanes removed around the turn of this century. Nor have we endeavored to present in depth the story of Spokane Indians who have recently moved to white communities. Instead, we have concentrated on the story of those Spokanes who went to the Spokane Reservation, where today a remnant keeps alive Spokane tribal entity and name.

Having previously written a biography in this series, we were tempted to permit a biographical approach to our study. We have tried to resist this temptation, although in narrating the story of Spokane development, it has been difficult to write without giving embodiment to specific types—chiefs, prophets, shamans, warriors. Thus, personalities will break through, such as Chief Spokane Garry, whom we attempt to portray as neither all saint nor all sinner, as he has been pictured by previous writers. We have sifted many sources for our information, some of it statistical. We have attempted to humanize cold facts wherever possible, and in so doing, may cause raised eyebrows in the belief that we have occasionally included inconsequential materials. Yet we believe that little things have meaning.

In the preparation of our manuscript, we received help from many whose kindness we would acknowledge. From the Federal Records Center in Seattle we received valuable information on the Colville and Coeur d'Alene Indian agencies, for which we expressly thank Archivist Elmer Lindgard. We would also thank, for their assistance, Marjorie M. Halpin, instructor in anthropology, Office of Education and Training, Smithsonian Institution; Jane F. Smith, director, Social and Economic Records Division, National Archives and Records Service; in that same agency, Garry D. Ryan, assistant director, Old Military Records Division; and Elmer O. Parker, chief, Army and Air Corps Branch.

From the Bureau of Indian Affairs we would thank Sally Rosenberg of its Correspondence Office; Erma Walz, chief, and Guy W. Louell, acting chief, Tribal Claims Section; LaFollette Butler, assistant to chief, Branch of Real Property Management; Earl R. Wilcox, assistant area director. We are especially indebted to personnel of the Colville Indian Agency—Superintendent Elmo Miller; Acting-Superintendent Stanley T. Poch; Leo J. Wolfe and C. V. Nelson, who provided us with materials and valuable suggestions. For their assistance we are also indebted to tribal leaders of the Spokane subagency—Alex Sherwood, Dave Wynecoop, George Lowly, and Glenn Galbraith. We would also thank other tribal members who supplied us with information of their peoples' past—Ella McCarty, Ignace Pascal, Sadie Boyd, Albert Sam, and Tom Cornelius. We would also thank Harold D. Roberson, superintendent of the Flathead Agency, and Bill Bryan and Daniel H. Olney, acting-superintendents of the Northern Idaho Indian Agency, for supplying us with information. Other government servants who supplied us with information were Paul Lemargie, field solicitor of the Department of Interior; Stephen G. Wade, chief technical liaison officer, Corps of Army Engineers; Mrs. Lee Prochaska, administrative assistant to the project manager of the Bureau of Reclamation; and Tom Mutch of that agency.

We especially thank personnel from other government agencies and institutions who provided us with so much assistance: Col. Virgil F. Field, archivist, State of Washington Military Department, Office of the Adjutant General; Fred O. Anderson, Outside Property Supervisor, Office of the Spokane County Assessor; David Davis, Lincoln County engineer; Paul W. Heritage, Stevens County engineer; O. T. Hansen, inspector of mines for the state of Idaho; Arthur D. Welander, professor of fisheries, University of Washington School of Fisheries; and Jack Forbes of the department of history, University of Nevada.

We also wish to thank the governor and committee of the Hudson's Bay Company, by whose permission we include from their archives portions of the reports of Chief Factor Alexander Kennedy, and of John Work. Of inestimable assistance to us was Hazel Mills, research consultant of the Washington State Library, as was Miriam Allen, documents librarian of the University of Washington; also, personnel of the Eastern Washington Historical Society, Archivist Betty Bender and Assistant Librarians Hilda Schlicke and Edna Reinbach. Also valuable was assistance given us by Mary Avery and Earle Connette, archivists of the Holland Library, Washington State University; Archivist Wilfred J. Schoenberg, S.J., of Crosby Library, Gonzaga University; Mildred Sherwood, northwest librarian of the University of Washington Library; John Barr Tompkins, head of public services, Bancroft Library; Haydée Noya, cataloguer, Department of Manuscripts, Huntington Library; and Virginia Rust, assistant in manuscripts of that institution; staff members of the Newberry Library; Priscilla Knuth of the Oregon Historical Society; and Willard E. Ireland of the (British Columbia) Provincial Archives. In addition we owe a debt to C. M. Drury of the San Francisco Theological Seminary; M. Jeanne Gulick of the Penrose Memorial Library, Whitman College; and from the Presbyterian Historical Society, Assistant Secretary William B. Miller, Research Historian Gerald W. Gillette, and Records Researcher Catherine H. Thomas. Other archivists and librarians to whom we owe so much are Flora Wester of the Board of National Missions of the United Presbyterian Church in the United States of America; Ruth Bryant, secretary to archivist, The Church (Episcopal) Historical Society; Mary and Florence Johnson of the Spokane Public Library; Annie

Preface

Koinzan, Marie Kennedy, Mrs. Lawrence Bingham, Pearl C. Munson, and Irma McKenzie of the North Central Washington Regional Library; Audrey Kolb, Betty Jean Gibson, and Arvilla Scofield of the Wenatchee Valley College Library. From the newspaper profession we wish to thank Lavonne Carter and Joseph Baily of the *Spokesman-Review*, and Walt Wilbur and Norman Nelson of the *Davenport Times*.

We owe much to a host of other individuals: the Honorable Thomas Foley, U.S. House of Representatives; the Honorable Sid Flanagan, Washington State House of Representatives; John Hudson, professor of sociology, Harvard University; Warren Avery, Pat and Sylvester Hubert, George and Ruby Wiltz, Harold and Alice Bryant, Guy Ramsey, Edward Arnold, Leonard Ekman, Edson Dow, Bruce Mitchell, Ruby Babcock, Cora E. Schaffner, Ella and Frank Evans, A. M. Denman, Dennis Norman, George W. Patterson, Helen Peterson, Leroy Ledeboer, Linda Brown, Jerry Haaland, Elsie Elder, Mary Morris, Jerome Peltier, Sallie Probst, and Shari Gurnard. We would acknowledge our gratitude to Elizabeth Racy, who translated documents from the French, and would especially thank Angie Debo and Anne Briley, who read our manuscript and offered suggestions. Just as people were vital in the history we herein present, so were they in its preparation. Without their kind assistance, this effort would have been impossible.

ROBERT H. RUBY
JOHN A. BROWN

xv

Contents

Illustrations

xix

A group of Spokane Indians
A group of Spokane Indians at Old Agency
Indian children at the school at old Fort Spokane
Indian bead work at the all-Indian fair in Wellpinit
The Colville Agency
The chapel building at old Fort Spokane
The dining hall at the Indian school
The laundry room at the Indian school

MAPS

The Spokane Indians

CHAPTER ONE

Ashes to Ashes

An ancient lake once stretched from western Idaho into eastern Washington; around its rim, some sixty-six hundred years ago, a scattering of Indians had settled. One day the earth convulsed, a volcano spewed ashes, and the Spokane River took on its present shape.[1] It was an overflow of the receding lake, which is present-day Lake Coeur d'Alene, lying just east of the Washington-Idaho border.

The riverbed was formed long before. Spokane mythology tells of a giant dragon who created it. He had invaded the land, gorged himself, and fallen asleep where the Columbia River today receives the Spokane. When the Indians discovered him, they fastened him to trees and rocks, as Swift's Lilliputians had bound the sleeping Gulliver; then they assaulted the dragon. But he was invulnerable to all their weapons. He roused himself and lumbered off to the east, dragging along the trees and rocks to which he had

[1] The ashes were from Mount Mazama in central Oregon; Crater Lake now fills the erupted cone. Robert Butler, *Contributions to the Prehistory of the Columbia Plateau: A Report on Excavations in the Palouse and Craig Mountain Sections*, 4.

been fastened, until he settled at Lake Coeur d'Alene. In this way, according to folklore, a channel was plowed to carry the waters of the lake to the west.[2]

Since the Spokane River flows in a smooth channel, it was necessary for the mythmakers to tell another tale to explain the falls, where the river drops 130 feet over a half-mile course of sudden plunges and rapids, further broken by upthrusts of basalt. So Spokane Indian mythology tells of Chief Mosquetquat's daughter, who was married to a lesser chief, Moxnoose, but whose heart strayed to the Okanogan chief's son, Stinging Bee. The lovers met at a hill south of the falls, and each told the other of being warned by spirits not to come. They decided to poison Moxnoose to rid themselves of the oppressive spirits. Moxnoose soon died, in great pain, at the hands of his wife. When next the lovers met, they were confronted by the ghost of Moxnoose. This terrible apparition turned Stinging Bee into a mass of rocks, so that he became the falls of the river. Into the pit beneath the falls was cast Mosquetquat's daughter, so that she would ever after bear upon her shoulders the weight of the water pouring over Stinging Bee. The apparition then turned himself into a second mass of rocks, so that he could continue to watch the punishment of Stinging Bee and Mosquetquat's daughter.[3]

Geology tells another story.

The Spokane River flows to the west along the Columbia Plateau. This plateau is a huge gentle decline from the Rocky Mountains to the Cascade Mountains. At a point almost dead center on the Columbia Plateau between these two great mountain ranges lies the city of Spokane at the falls of the Spokane River. To the north is the Colville River valley, to the northwest the Okanogan, to the west the Yakima, to the south the Walla Walla. To the east, across the open plain of the Washington-Idaho border, is Lake Coeur d'Alene. Here, toward the end of the eighteenth century, white men came and found Indian tribes of the intermontane plateau: the Spokanes, the Colvilles, the Okanogans, the Yakimas, the Walla Wallas, the Coeur d'Alenes, along with near-

[2] The Spokane *Spokesman-Review*, Mar. 15, 1896, p. 15.
[3] *Ibid.*, Dec. 7, 1895, p. 7.

ly twenty other tribes who shared the same culture. This culture
was at first peripheral to that found on the Pacific slopes of the
Cascades. But after the introduction of the horse to the region,
c. 1730, the plateau tribes ventured to the east beyond the Rockies
onto the Great Plains to hunt buffalo. This opened up a wide cor-
ridor to Plains Indian culture. The principal languages spoken on
the intermontane plateau were Salish and Shahaptian.

During the Miocene and Pliocene periods, lava, erupting from
fissures in the earth, spread over the Columbia Plateau to form its
unique basalt-covered topography. On reaching the Spokane area,
the lava was checked by hills. Later flows spread over ridges in
rimrock fashion. Still later, deep valleys were eroded; then new
lava flows poured into the valleys. One rimrock flow oozed down
to form the falls of the Spokane River. During the Pleistocene
period, glacial ice lay over much of western Canada and northern
Washington. The ice sheets receded from northern Washington
about fourteen thousand years ago, except in the Puget Sound
area, where they disappeared as recently as eleven thousand years
ago.[4]

When Spokane Indians were asked where their ancestors had
come from, they answered, "Up north." This is in agreement with
the generally accepted theory that early man came to North
America twenty thousand to thirty thousand years ago in many
separate migrations, pulsing south through Canada. At any rate,
it is known that Indians lived on the Columbia Plateau between
eight thousand and thirteen thousand years ago.[5]

[4] For a description of the dams and lakes formed during the periods of glacia-
tion, see Gerald M. Richmond *et al.*, "The Cordilleran Ice Sheet of the Northern
Rocky Mountains, and Related Quarternary History of the Columbia Plateau," in
The Quarternary of the United States, 231–41.

[5] Richard Daugherty, *Early Man in Washington*, 11. A scientific team from
Washington State University in 1968 recovered near the confluence of the Palouse
and Snake rivers remnants of a human skull and other bones in undisturbed
sediments beneath distinctive series of deposits dating it up to thirteen thousand
years of age. Radiocarbon age determinations of mollusc shells in sediments over
the sediment in which the bones were found date ten thousand to eleven thousand years. Recent analysis suggests that the "emergence" of Columbia Plateau
culture (as ethnographically known) can be placed at about the time of Christ,
instead of about A. D. 1200–1300, as previously hypothesized. David L. Browman
and David A. Munsell, "Columbia Plateau Prehistory: Cultural Development and
Impinging Influences," *American Antiquity*, Vol. XXXIV, No. 3 (July, 1969), 249.

The earliest Indians in the Spokane region were hunters; game was apparently plentiful, for the land was then covered with conifers, as revealed by pollen studies of the earth strata.[6] But in time the bison and antelope the Indians hunted left the region. The forests appear to have thinned out a good deal. The Indians became increasingly dependent on roots, berries, and fish. Some scholars claim that the Spokane Indians of the interior Salish-speaking peoples are directly descended from these early hunters of the Columbia Plateau. Others see their origin on the Great Plains, believing that in historic times the Salish-speaking tribes crossed the Rocky Mountains and spread along the major river valleys all the way to the sea.[7] The Shahaptian-speaking peoples occupied the lower Columbia Plateau, with considerable Salishan encroachment about the late eighteenth century. The Spokanes seem to have taken little part in these territorial changes.[8]

The Spokanes explained the origins of the world and of themselves in their native folklore, which clearly reflected the biblical matter that had been impressed upon them by white missionaries. Amotkan, the Creator, made light only after all the animals had congregated to create it for themselves. The animals first erected a high pole and sent Woodpecker up it, but the pole was too hot for him. They next sent Coyote up the pole. But he was too noisy, all the time shouting down to his children. Bear volunteered, but he found it too cold atop the pole. The sound of thunder shattered their efforts then. It loosened a piece of red rock, which

[6] Henry P. Hansen, *Postglacial Frost Succession, Climate and Chronology in the Pacific Northwest*, 79.

[7] George Gibbs, "Tribes of Western Washington and Northeastern Oregon," 224–25. Hereafter cited as "Tribes of Western Washington."

[8] Authorities disagree in their explanations of the ebb-and-flow movements of these peoples. See Albert Buell Lewis, *Tribes of the Columbia Valley and the Coast of Washington and Oregon* (hereafter cited as *Tribes of the Columbia Valley*); Verne F. Ray, et al., "Tribal Distributions in Eastern Oregon and Adjacent Regions," *American Anthropologist*, Vol. XL, No. 3 (July–September, 1938), 395–96; Verne F. Ray, *Cultural Element Distribution: XXII Plateau*, 226–28; Douglas Osborne, et al., "Archaeological Investigations in the Chief Joseph Reservoir," *American Antiquity*, Vol. XVII, No. 4 (1952), 313; Leslie Spier, *Tribal Distribution in Washington*, 1–23; Verne F. Ray, *Cultural Relations in the Plateau of Northwestern America*, 1 (hereafter cited as *Cultural Relations in the Plateau*).

turned into a handsome red man. He wanted a brother, so Amot-kan gave him one made from the root of an herb called *spowaunch*. The two brothers went to a lodge occupied by a witch, Lady Bullfrog. She became so enamored of the brother formed of the root that she leaped onto his face—and stuck there. In pulling loose, she tore out one of his eyes. He then volunteered to ascend into the sky to be light for the earth, for he did not want people to see his face, now missing one eye. Thus, he became the sun, and when people looked at him, they had to close one of their own eyes. The other man joined his lonely brother in the sky. But before he did so, Lady Bullfrog had jumped onto his face, too. He became the moon. Today, if one looks carefully at the moon, one can see Lady Bullfrog clinging to his face.[9]

Because he was lonesome, Coyote, after several failures, made Spokane man. In his first failure, he molded a man of pitch, who melted. He tried clay, but the rains washed the clay man away. He sculpted a man out of hot rock; it cracked. He wove a man of reeds; but this man caught fire and burned. Coyote then mixed all these elements together and—adding berries, smoke, and fire—created Spokane man. With these same elements, he created Spokane woman, and Amotkan, the Creator, gave her life. Man and woman soon became wild, caring little for the safety of the others who had sprung from them. A flood came then and covered the land, destroying all except a few people. The survivors banded together for safety, elected a leader, and multiplied. In time, the leader divided the people into small groups. They became the various tribes.[10]

Equally Adamic in nature was the Spokane explanation of the tribal name. They say there was once a hollow tree. When an Indian beat upon it, a serpent living inside made a noise which sounded like *Spukcane*, a phonetic sound without meaning. One day, as the chief pondered the sound, vibrations radiated from his head. Eventually, the word *Spukcane* came to have the

[9] Tom Cornelius interview, Wellpinit, Washington, July 3, 1965.

[10] Ella McCarty interview, Spokane, September 21, 1966 (hereafter cited as McCarty interview); A. Diomedi, *Sketches of Modern Indian Life*, 13.

vague meaning "power from the brain." When white men found them, the Spokanes called themselves *Spukanee*, which is translated as "Sun People," or "Children of the Sun." They called their chief *Illim-Spukanee*, or "Chief Sun." No one knows exactly how, why, or when *Spukcane* (power from the brain) came to be replaced by *Spukanee* (Sun People), which was rendered in English as Spokane. (Thus, Illim-Spokanee.) The similarity to the ear of the two words, *Spukcane* and *Spukanee*, suggests a possible reason. Some maintain that the word *Spokane* was originally the name of the head chief and of nothing else.[11]

The Spokane tribes came to rest along the banks of the Spokane River. The falls appear a third of the way down the river's mildly meandering ninety-mile course west from Lake Coeur d'Alene, against a prairie background. Below the falls, the river joins Latah Creek from the southeast. Then it bends northward to join the Little Spokane River (*Senahomana*, "The River of the Salmon Trout") from the northeast. Swinging westward again, it receives Tshimakain (variously spelled) Creek from the north

---

[11] McCarty interview; "Uncle Dan" Drumheller, *Uncle Dan Drumheller Tells Thrills of Western Trails*, 111. Another meaning given the name is "Wheat fields," or *Spokaine*. Also see Thomas W. Symons, *Report of an Examination of the Upper Columbia River and the Territory in Its Vicinity in September and October, 1881, to Determine Its Navigability and Adaptability to Steamboat Transportation*, 129. William S. Lewis, *The Case of Spokane Garry*, 11.

[12] (A) Verne F. Ray, "Native Villages and Groupings of the Columbia Basin," *Pacific Northwest Quarterly*, Vol. XXVII, No. 2 (April, 1936), 116. Hereafter cited as "Native Villages and Groupings." (B) James A. Teit, "The Salishan Tribes of the Western Plateaus," in *Forty-fifth Annual Report of the Bureau of American Ethnology*, 1927–28, 298. Hereafter cited as B.A.E. *45th Ann. Rep.* (C) McCarty interview. (D) John R. Swanton, "The Indian Tribes of North America," in Smithsonian Institution Bureau of American Ethnology *Bulletin* 145, 444. (E) Major R. D. Gwydir of Spokane, as related to William S. Lewis, corresponding secretary of the Spokane Historical Society, Spokane. (F) James Mooney, "The Ghost-Dance Religion and the Sioux Outbreak of 1890," in *Fourteenth Annual Report of the Bureau of American Ethnology*, 1892–93, 732. (G) Edward S. Curtis, *The North American Indian, Being a Series of Volumes Picturing and Describing the Indians of the United States and Alaska*, VII, 54. Hereafter cited as *North American Indian*. (H) W. P. Winans, Annual Report (1870), Winans Papers, Box 4, no. 34. (I) Secretary of the Interior, *Annual Report*, 1870–71, 41 Cong., 2 sess., *House Exec. Doc. No. 1*, Pt. 4, p. 486. (J) Alexander Kennedy, Spokane House Report 1822–23. (K) Secretary of War, *Annual Report*, 1854–55, 55 Cong., 2 sess., *House Exec. Doc. No. 1*, Vol. I, Pt. 1, p. 428. (L) Spier, *Tribal Distribution in Washington*, 8–9.

Designations and Locations of Spokane Bands.[12]

AUTHORITY	UPPER	MIDDLE	LOWER
(A) Ray	"Up River People," "People of Steel-head Trout Place." From Spokane Falls to Tum Tum.	"Middle River People." Tum Tum to 10 miles from mouth of Spokane River.	Last 10 miles of the lower river only.
(B) Teit	*Senxomê'* "Salmon Trout." Little Spokane Valley eastward.	*Sntutuū'li,* "Pounding."	*Stsêkastsi',* "Running fast." Near mouth of Spokane River.
(C) McCarty	"Lake People." Present city of Spokane to Lake Pend Oreille.	Mouth of Little Spokane.	"Big River People."
(D) Swanton	Little Spokane and valley.	Latah Creek and east.	
(E) Gwydir		Country west of Spokane, the Deep Creek group.	Country along lower Spokane.
(F) Mooney	*Sineegunomenah.*	*Sintootoo.*	*Chekisschee.*
(G) Curtis	*Sintutuuli,* "Muddy Creek People." Post Falls to Latah Creek.	*Sinhomene,* "Salmon Trout People." Little Spokane to Tum Tum area.	*Tskaistsihlni.*
(H) Winans	*Sin-ce-quo-men-ah.*	*Sin-too-too.*	*Che-kis-chee.*
(I) Dept. of Indian Affairs	*Sin-ee-guo-men-ah.*	*Sin-too-too.*	*Che-kiss-chee.*
(J) Hudson's Bay Co.	*Sintatoluh,* "Up River People." At Upper Falls.	*Sinohomenish,* "Middle Way Indians." On Little Spokane.	*Scaite Cuthinish.*
(K) War Dept.	*Sin-too-too-lish,* "Upper River Indians."	*Sma-hoo-men-a-ish,* "Middle River Indians."	*Skai-schil-t'nish.*
(L) Spier	From Tum Tum east.	Latah Creek area and Spokane Falls.	Tum Tum to south.

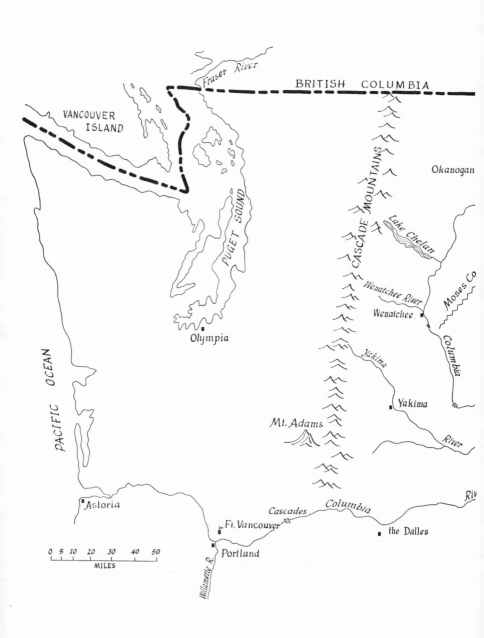

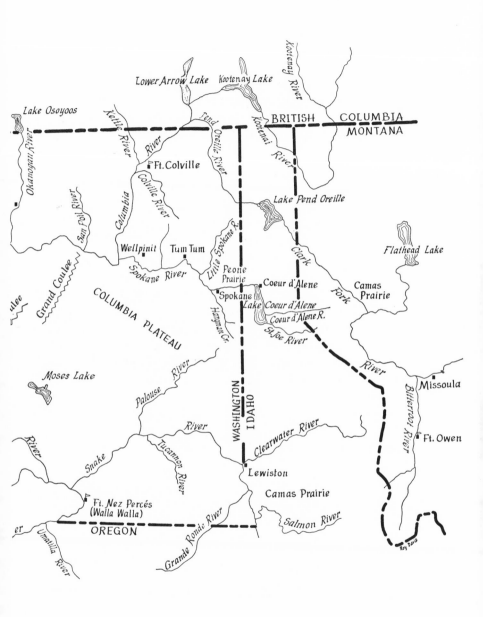

The overall area in which the Spokane Indians lived.

before tumbling over Little Falls to lose itself in the Columbia River.

It is believed that the Spokanes were composed of several bands loosely grouped into two or three divisions, although they have been divided into as many as eight.

1. *The Lower Spokanes*, the most homogeneous group, had social and economic ties with Salishans to the west—the San Poils, Nespelems, Columbias (Sinkiuse, Rock Islands or Isle des Pierres), and other scattered peoples.

2. *The Middle and Upper Spokanes* had ties with Salishans to the east and north—the Coeur d'Alenes, Kalispels, Pend Oreilles, Flatheads, Kootenays, Chewelahs, Colvilles, and others.

Geographic proximity produced rather close association among all the Spokane peoples. Yet defining their precise locations is not as simple as the geographical designation of their names would suggest. Parents often came from separate groups. In interviews with anthropologists of the early twentieth century, children often identified themselves with one group while living within the geographic confines of another. This was particularly true of the Middle and Upper Spokanes who, as the nineteenth century progressed, were increasingly referred to by several authorities as a single group, Upper Spokanes.

In the precontact period, the basic Spokane unit was the autonomous village band composed of several families.[13] A band was often formed by a male on acquisition of wealth, which consisted of wives and, later, horses. The larger numbers of women occasioned by the exposure of males to greater hazards encouraged polygamy. The band leader took his group to a nearby site to settle it. A band could be dissolved as easily as it was formed. There was mobility between bands. Members and families of a band might spend one winter with one group, and the next winter with another. Sometimes a woman came to live in her husband's band, but more frequently he went to live with her people.

[13] Ray, "Native Villages and Groupings," *Pacific Northwest Quarterly*, Vol. XXVII, No. 2 (April, 1936), 121–37. See also Ray, *Cultural Relations in the Plateau*, 14.

Mothers named their newborn according to circumstances at birth. As the children grew up, they were given other names. Affection was tempered with discipline, which sometimes took the form of whipping. Women taught their daughters domestic pursuits and, when they reached puberty, to set themselves apart in the special hut for menses. Training of the boys gradually passed, with their increasing years, from mother to father. Parents did not interfere with the courting patterns of the young and, as a rule, did not arrange marriages. Husbands and wives sometimes divorced each other without ceremony; it was usually the man who left, often for the lodge of another woman, leaving the children with their maternal relatives.

In times of trouble, bands coalesced into tribes. Emergencies required stronger leadership than usual. Spokane chiefs normally held tenuous power; it was based to a small degree on lineage, to a greater degree on wealth. In later days, knowledge of the white man's ways became an equally important factor. The trend toward tribal organization increased during the nineteenth century as more and more whites came to the region.

The Spokanes, typical of the Salishan central Columbia Plateau tribes, usually fought neither long nor hard, except when defending themselves from attack.[14] This was particularly true of their latter eighteenth-century wars with the Blackfeet. This did not alter the fact, as anthropologist James Teit has observed, that the Salishans went raiding and carried on small feuds.[15] Sometimes groups of Spokanes went raiding to break the rhythmical patterns of their lives and to bring new blood into the tribe (women). Gambling arguments and misunderstandings involving women occasionally erupted into open conflict. The outcome was settled by furious combat or, just as often, by arbitration and payment of blood money. Hostilities did not necessarily prevent trade between tribes.

Slaves were reported to have been taken by all Salishans in

[14] The Blackfeet were an Algonkian-speaking people of the Great Plains, composed of three groups: Piegans, Bloods, and Blackfeet proper, although they are often lumped together under the designation "Blackfeet."

[15] Ray, *Cultural Relations in the Plateau*, 35.

early times, but the Spokanes appear never to have forced captives into slavery.[16] This did not mean no class among the Spokanes was regarded as inferior. There were, for instance, the *Semtaussee* (meaning literally "dugout home"), a backward band dwelling on the south side of the Spokane River near Little Falls. Refusing to adapt to mat houses, they lived in domestic carelessness in earthen homes.[17] Although they were held in low esteem, they were not slaves.

In about 1700 the Middle Spokanes fought the Coeur d'Alenes while the Upper Spokanes remained friendly, thus effecting some ill feeling between the two Spokane groups. Sometime before 1790, the Spokanes presented one of their maidens to a Coeur d'Alene chief. He came to regard her as the cause of his own ill fortune and soon killed her. The Spokanes fought for two years to avenge her death. At last the Coeur d'Alenes gave the Spokanes a woman to kill to even the score.[18] Again, in about 1799, the Coeur d'Alenes, angered at harsh treatment of one of their women by her Spokane husband living in their country, made war against the Spokanes.[19]

The Spokanes frequently allied with the Kalispels, who were known as good fighters, having sharpened this skill in many brushes with the Blackfeet. War-minded Kalispels put white earth upon their heads to signify their warlike intentions. If other Kalispels were similarly inclined, they formed a war party, chose a chief, and sent an invitation to allies to join them.[20] The Spokanes sometimes allied with the Kootenays and the Flatheads.[21] They seldom if ever fought the Flatheads,[22] and in later days allied

[16] The Flatheads kept slaves, and the Coeur d'Alenes also kept a few. That there may have been female slaves in the upper Columbia is supported by Hegler, who showed that frequently the blood type indicated in female skeletal studies was variant from the usual for the area. Rodger Hegler, "A Racial Analysis of Indian Skeletal Materials from the Columbia River Valley," 73.

[17] McCarty interview.

[18] Rowena Nichols, "Items Collected at the Mission."

[19] Ross Cox, *Adventures on the Columbia River*, II, 151–52. Hereafter cited as *Adventures*.

[20] Richard Glover (ed.), *David Thompson's Narrative 1784–1812*, 331–32. Hereafter cited as *Thompson's Narrative*.

[21] B.A.E. *45th Ann. Rep.*, 360.

[22] Curtis, *North American Indian*, VII, 45.

with them against the Blackfeet. The Coeur d'Alenes warred against other Salishan tribes and the Nez Percés, a Shahaptian people of the southern plateau.[23] Occasionally, the Spokanes skirmished against the Nez Percés.[24] Generally, the Salishans and Shahaptians did not engage each other in sustained conflicts, as did Shahaptian and Shoshonean peoples living below the plateau. In the nineteenth century, when mounted Spokanes had greater mobility, they frequently warred against the Shoshonean Bannacks. At that time, Spokane conflicts with Salishan neighbors as well as the Nez Percés were greatly reduced because all were forced to join together to meet their common enemies, the Blackfeet.

The San Poils and Nespelems, occupying river valleys of the same names, were more peaceful than the Spokanes, a trait mistakenly interpreted by both whites and Indians as laziness. Their peaceful inclinations and immobility subjected them to raids. If legends have any basis in history, the Spokanes at an early time attacked the defenseless San Poils.[25] Tradition also has it that the Spokanes raided the Okanogans many times, once near present-day Okanogan, where all the Spokanes but one were killed on the spot, and he, in the end, was killed, too, trying to escape. Another time the Spokanes were said to have raided the land of other Okanogans, the Conconullys (Konkonelps). In that raid the Spokanes were said to have been wiped out to a man, after which their Spokane brothers returned and in revenge killed many Conconully women and children.[26] War was certainly not the prime activity of the Spokanes; they spent less time struggling against man than against nature for survival.

For centuries peoples of the central plateau had relied on salmon for the mainstay of their diet. So well known were the Spo-

---

[23] B.A.E., *45th Ann. Rep.*, 119.

[24] Alvin M. Josephy, Jr., *The Nez Perce Indians and the Opening of the North West*, 20. Hereafter cited as *The Nez Perce Indians*.

[25] This is revealed in a legend explaining the name of Hellgate Rapids of the Columbia River, a treacherous boulder-layered constriction downstream twenty-two miles from the mouth of the Spokane River. These rapids are now inundated by waters behind Grand Coulee Dam.

[26] Walter Cline, *et al.*, *The Sinkaietk or Southern Okanogan of Washington*, 79–80.

kanes as salmon eaters, and their river as a salmon stream, that when they met others whose language was unfamiliar, the Spokanes identified themselves by moving their hands to suggest the movement of the tail of a salmon in the act of spawning. They also put their hands to their mouths, then complacently patted their stomachs to indicate what they did with the fish.[27]

Like others living along the inland fresh-water routes, through which salmon flashed their way from the sea, the Spokanes had their own fisheries. To trap the salmon of these runs, the Spokanes constructed a rock barrier part way across the stream from each shore just below Little Falls, at their first big fishery on the Spokane River. Upstream from the barrier, they built a weir of slanted willow poles. At intervals they closed off the weirs, speared the fish, and threw them ashore to the waiting women. They stilled the wriggling of their prizes with deft knife slashes, separating entrails and backbones from flannel-red flesh. Then they draped strips over scaffolds to dry for about a month before carrying them, in woven baskets, to rock-covered caches in the ground to protect the strips from moisture and marauders.

News of the arrival of the salmon was spread to surrounding tribes. Sometimes as many as a thousand natives responded—besides Spokanes, mostly Coeur d'Alenes, Kalispels, Colvilles, Palouses, San Poils, and Columbias. Although they were guests of the Spokanes, as the Spokanes were often guests at their fisheries, they considered the salmon communal property to be distributed according to the numbers present and the work contributed. The tribes enlivened the fishing season with potlatches (gift-giving ceremonies) where the Indians danced, gambled, and traded (later on, horses and even wives) in an atmosphere of a county fair. A fair with its own smells, too, particularly the permeating stench of discarded fish entrails. The festivities were carried out under a ceremonious salmon chief, or *seepays* (chief of the waters).

As the river receded, the Spokanes moved about a mile downstream to a cross-river barrier, where they trapped as many as eight

27 *Spokesman-Review*, March 15, 1896, p. 15.

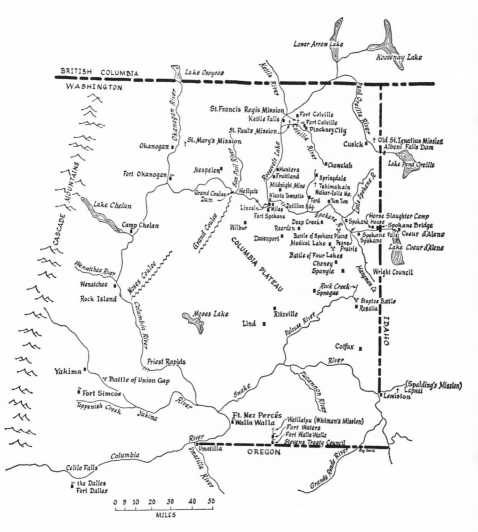

Territory occupied by the Spokane Indians from the Cascade Mountains to the Idaho border.

hundred fish daily, each weighing up to forty pounds. Farther downstream, close by the mouth of the Spokane River, were fisheries visited mostly by Spokanes, San Poils, and Columbias. At this spot in later days pitch torches were used at night to attract and snare fish.

Upstream from Little Falls the Spokanes maintained another fishery, where the Little Spokane River leaves its peaceful valley to join the Spokane. Immediately to the south camped one of the largest Spokane bands. The natives constructed a barrier across the Little Spokane, placing it at an oblique angle so that the current would not wash it away. From this obstruction, they placed funnels leading into basket-work traps on the upstream side. When the traps filled with salmon, the natives closed the funnels with brush and speared their catches with points of horn and bone laced to the ends of poles. The women dried the salmon on sun-exposed scaffolds and shaded tree limbs. Visiting tribes baled and packed the meat away in parfleches. The Spokanes packed their meat in baskets and placed it in large caches dug into hillsides south of the Little Spokane.

Salmon escaping the Little Falls and other fisheries near the village clusters lining the bluffs of the Spokane, to the mouth of Latah Creek, reached (the big) Spokane falls. There a small fishery was operated for about six weeks under the supervision of the salmon chief. Below the river bar, the Indians built a wall of loose rocks across one arm of the rock-divided river, leaving a space in the rock extremity where they placed nets. To catch the last finny migrants, the fishers built on the bank a trestlework where captive salmon were laid until cut and dried. Ownership of the falls fisheries was claimed not only by the Spokanes, but by the Coeur d'Alenes as well. These latter peoples, at the tail end of the runs, could not catch all the salmon they needed for winter use. They supplemented their diets with trout caught from their lake. Frequently, they traded dried salmon, dentalium, abalone, and other shells (obtained from the coast) to eastern tribes for buffalo robes.

The largest fisheries in the area were at Kettle Falls of the

Columbia River. Fishing began there later than it did on the Spokane, about mid-July,[28] and lasted about two months. The falls were double, a few hundred yards apart. There, the Spokanes and other fishers of the area joined the Colvilles and Kettle Falls people. At Kettle Falls, the ceremony was reminiscent of that of the San Poils on their river, with the salmon chief in complete charge. No one was permitted to spear a fish before the season formally began. The salmon chief, seeking to discover whether the catch would be heavy or light, went to a lodge to receive an omen, a vision of a certain animal at some particular spot.[29] If, on coming from his meditative seclusion, he saw what had been revealed to him in his dreams, the season augured to be a good one—provided no fragment of bone was thrown into the river or no fisherman came upon the skull of a dog.[30] Should these ill omens occur, offenders had to purify themselves with a bark concoction. When proper propitiation was made, a ceremony and dancing marked the arrival of the salmon.

Despite heads battered by rocks, and shrinkage of as much as a third of their size, the salmon expended their remaining energy in astounding leaps to clear the falls—only to drop short of the crest into large baskets which the Indians suspended from the rocks. These baskets, averaging ten feet long, three wide, and four deep, were sometimes built with backstops to keep the salmon from leaping over them. One might suppose the baskets to have been lifted and emptied, but such was not the case; in most instances it would have taken a machine to hoist them, so heavy did they grow with fish. Instead, the Indian fishermen jumped into the baskets and threw the salmon ashore. Baskets were emptied from three to eight times daily. Sometimes two hundred fish were in a single haul, and an excellent day's catch reached two thousand.

The Spokanes not only extracted nature's gifts from the water but from the land. Waking from its winter slumber, the warming earth beckoned them from their permanent villages along the

[28] Paul Kane, *Wanderings of an Artist Among the Indians of North America,* 311–12. Hereafter cited as *Wanderings.*
[29] Curtis, *North American Indian,* VII, 78.
[30] Glover, *Thompson's Narrative,* 336–37.

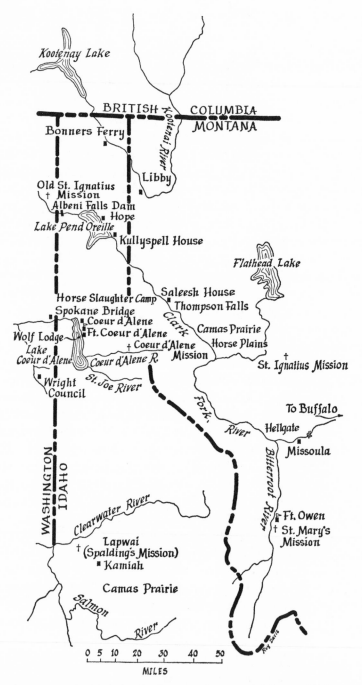

Territory occupied by the Spokane Indians in Idaho and Montana.

Spokane and Little Spokane rivers[31] to the root grounds. Unlike the Indians of the Plains, the Spokanes little used their dogs for packing as they trudged to and from the root grounds; starvation and inbreeding had deprived Spokane dogs of much size or strength. In the coulees and meadows rimming their rivers, the women dug for camass bulbs, using three-foot deerhorn-handled thornbrush or other hardwood sticks.[32] The Spokanes shared camass meadows with Kalispels along the Pend Oreille River, with Coeur d'Alenes in grounds south of the falls, and with Nez Percés and Yakimas in their respective countries. Beginning in March, they dug *Camassia quamash*, and later, *Camassia leichtlinii*. In one day, with an early start, a woman in a good field could dig a bushel of camass to fill her woven bags. She also harvested the balsamroot, the bitterroot (often called *"spetlum"*), the wild onion, and the wild carrot or parsnip.

Early in the season the Spokanes held their first root ceremonies to thank the Great Spirit for adequate food. They then fasted a day or more as a test, after which they piled up heated rocks and threw them into water, believing that, if one had kept the fast, he would not get his fingers burned.[33] Ceremony properly observed, the women baked the camass in grass-lined earth-pit ovens six to eight feet wide, by covering the bottoms of the ovens with flat stones on which they built fires. After the stones were very hot, the fires were removed and the stones covered with a two- to three-inch layer of broad green grass. They then placed the camass six to twelve inches deep on the grass and covered it with another layer of grass, then with six inches of earth. They let the camass steam for a day or two, then pounded it into a pulp, which they shaped into small cakes. Those not eaten on the spot were placed in caches in the ground for winter use, along with stores of berries and salmon. During the spring season, as the women processed the camass, the men reveled in

---

[31] Ray, "Native Villages and Groupings," *Pacific Northwest Quarterly*, Vol. XXVII, No. 2 (April, 1936), 133–37.

[32] Albert Sam interview, Wellpinit, Washington, July 2, 1965.

[33] Charles Wilkes, *Narrative of the United States Exploring Expedition During the Years 1838, 1839, 1840, 1841, 1842*, IV, 449. Hereafter cited as *Narrative*.

gambling and other games, particularly horse racing. This helped to limber up the slightly stiffened joints of their ponies, which were pretty much covered with shaggy hair from winter.

From summer through early fall, the Spokanes gathered berries. After the first fruit ceremonies, like those attending the gathering of roots and salmon, the women scurried about the hills gathering the serviceberry, blue elderberry, wild currant, golden currant and squaw currant, hawthorne, gooseberry, Oregon grape, chokecherry, and huckleberry. The latter two were dried for winter use. The women also gathered grasses and herbs, one species of which they used to keep blowflies off salmon. Another was used for catarrh, and a third, called "*ngagaleunt,*" they boiled for tea.[34] In the collecting and processing of foods in season, women's work was seldom done. Among the Spokane Indians, women were the final authority over the disposition of each family's winter food stores; their husbands had to seek their permission to take any food from the stores. Only through the diligence of the women was there any food left at all.[35]

In fall and winter, the natives held large hunts. In one prehunt ceremony, they threw old moccasins into the fire, retrieving them partially burned. These they hung on trees along the trails at strategic positions on the periphery of a seven- to eight-mile circle as huntsmen converged toward its center, driving before them the timid creatures who had caught the human scent on the moccasins. In the center of the circle, the Indians made their kill.[36] They also fired portions of the plateau, driving the game before them in encircling movements, as in their woods hunts. In the spring, the men also drove their prey over cliffs, like one near Little Falls.[37] The women found pleasure in eating deer-bone marrow scooped

[34] Tom Cornelius interview, Wellpinit, Washington, July 3, 1965.
[35] Wilkes, *Narrative,* IV, 449; A. N. Armstrong, *Oregon: Comprising a Brief History and Full Description of the Territories of Oregon and Washington,* 133 (hereafter cited as *Description of the Territories of Oregon and Washington*).
[36] Diomedi, *Sketches of Modern Indian Life,* 19–20.
[37] Arthur Jones, "Minnie-Wah-Wah," *The Overland Monthly,* Vol. XXIII, No. 134 (February, 1894), 195.
[38] *Spokesman-Review,* March 28, 1957; Titian R. Peale, "On the Uses of the Brain and Marrow of Animals Among the Indians of North America," 370 (hereafter cited as "Uses of Brain and Marrow").

with wooden spoons from split bones; these had been roasted in pots over hot coals.[38] The men ate only of the warm marrow fat; the women scooped the cooled fat from the top of cook pots, packed it in animal bladders (sometimes intestines), and stored it for winter. After hunting came the winter purification rites.[39] When the men carried on their social activities, they partook of meat previously cut into long strips, hung on scaffolds, smoked, sun dried, and cured. It also was a nourishing and convenient food to carry on long trips.

The Indians knew many lean winters when their salmon supplies were low, stolen, or destroyed by fire. When there were few deer and poor root and berry harvests, they did not abandon their old and young, as the Kalispels and Coeur d'Alenes sometimes did,[40] but subsisted on black moss gathered from pine trees to tide them over.[41] They boiled the moss until it had the consistency of glue, and from this they then molded a cake, which they flavored with bits of meat and wild onions.[42]

To prepare clothing, Spokane women first softened deerskins by soaking them in solutions of deer brains and, sometimes, of rotten eggs.[43] Next, they stretched the skins and cleaned them of hair. Then they started fires in their usual way, by spindle twirling a dry stick of wood between the palms of their hands until friction on another piece of wood caused it to burn. On coals they placed rotten cottonwood whose smoke gave the buckskin a brown yellow hue and kept it from becoming hard when moistened. The smoke smudge also kept horseflies away.[44] With this processed buckskin, they made shirts for both men and women (longer for women),

39 Curtis, *North American Indian*, VII, 87.

40 *Reports of Explorations and Surveys to Ascertain the Most Practicable and Economical Route for a Railroad from the Missouri River to the Pacific Ocean*, I, 23 (hereafter cited as *Pacific Railroad Reports*); May Arkwright Hutton, *The Coeur D'Alenes or a Tale of the Modern Inquisition in Idaho*, 26.

41 Ignace Pascal, "Spokane Root Festival."

42 Gabriel Franchère, *Narrative of a Voyage to the Northwest Coast of America in the Years 1811, 1812, 1813, and 1814 or the First American Settlement on the Pacific*, 279. Hereafter cited as *Narrative*.

43 Peale, "Uses of Brain and Marrow," 390; Samuel Parker, *Journal of an Exploring Tour Beyond the Rocky Mountains*, 236 (hereafter cited as *Journal*); Albert Sam interview.

44 Albert Sam interview.

leggings, and moccasins.[45] They made their footwear with short tongues and with seams down the front, a style rare among other tribes.[46] Their clothing was ornamented with fringes, beads, shells, bear claws, elk teeth, and feathers.[47] For a very short time, Spokane women wove grass caps,[48] but they seem to have abandoned them when they augmented their woven baskets with buffalo-skin pouches. They used buffalo hides for winter wrap-around robes, but seldom for clothing.

Perhaps nothing altered Spokane patterns of living more than horses, as these animals had also changed the lives of other western tribes since the sixteenth century, when the Spaniards introduced them into the New World.[49] After Indians of the Southwest acquired horses, they passed them on through trade, theft, or payment of gambling debts; the animals eventually reached the Shoshones, the main suppliers of horses to northwestern tribes.[50] Had the Spokanes acquired horses earlier, they might have traveled more frequently to hunt buffalo. As it was, they seldom went to the buffalo grounds until after the first decade of the nineteenth century. Hides were obtained before then indirectly from the Great Plains through trade with other tribes.[51]

The Spokanes acquired horses originally from either the Nez Percés,[52] the Kalispels,[53] or the Flatheads.[54] According to tradition the first Spokane to have a horse was a Middle Spokane named Coyote (not the legendary Coyote).[55] No one remembers pre-

[45] Wilkes, Narrative, IV, 447; Lewis, Tribes of the Columbia Valley, 187; Parker, Journal, 236.
[46] B.A.E. 45th Ann. Rep., 334.
[47] Wilkes, Narrative, IV, 447; Lewis, Tribes of the Columbia Valley, 187.
[48] H. K. Haeberlin, et al., "Coiled Basketry in British Columbia and Surrounding Region," in Forty-First Annual Report of the Bureau of American Ethnology, 1919–24, 139. Hereafter cited as B.A.E. 41st Ann. Rep.
[49] Franchère, Narrative, 270; W.P. Clark, Indian Sign Language, 306; Clark Wissler, "The Influence of the Horse in the Development of Plains Culture," American Anthropologist, Vol. XVI, No. 1 (January, 1914), 1–25.
[50] Francis Haines, "How the Indian Got the Horse," American Heritage, Vol. XV, No. 2 (February, 1964), 80; Pacific Railroad Reports, I, 404.
[51] B.A.E. 41st Ann. Rep., 141.
[52] Cox, Adventures, I, 200.
[53] B.A.E. 45th Ann. Rep., 351.
[54] Gibbs, "Tribes of Western Washington," 221.
[55] McCarty interview.

cisely when, but it is believed that by 1800 the Spokanes were accumulating herds.[56] Their horses came, not through local breeding, but from trading principally with the Nez Percés[57] and other Shahaptian tribes, as the Cayuses and Yakimas. The Nez Percés particularly excelled in horse raising through selective breeding; they gelded inferior horses.[58] Francis Haines, an authority on the western horse, describes a sale on the flat near the mouth of the Little Spokane River, one of the leading horse marts of the Northwest:

> The Nez Perce lined up on one side, each man holding the lead rope of his "trading" horse. Each Spokane came forward and placed his pile of trade goods in front of the horse he liked. If the Nez Perce was satisfied, he handed over the lead rope and took the goods. If not, he might try for an extra article, or he might lead his horse to some other pile which interested him. It might take all of a pleasant summer day to trade forty horses, but this seemed to worry nobody.[59]

Nez Percé selective breeding produced rather small animals—cayuses of about seven hundred pounds standing about thirteen hands high, with small hooves, broad foreheads, and walleyes. Their prevailing color was white and gray, but spotted horses became sought after.[60] When the white man came, he brought larger horses, which the Indians called "Frenchmen's horses." Although they did not practice selective breeding, the Spokanes were selective in the use of their animals. They prized the swift sleek ones they raced, each worth several pack animals in trade.[61] They equally prized their fleet buffalo horses, well suited for chasing down the shaggy beasts of the plains.

Horses helped shift tribal boundaries and break village isolation, altered warfare patterns, and permitted their riders to widen

---

56 Gibbs, "Tribes of Western Washington," 221.
57 Cox, *Adventures*, I, 200.
58 Haines, "How the Indian Got the Horse," *American Heritage*, Vol. XV, No. 2 (February, 1964), 80.
59 *Ibid.*
60 *Pacific Railroad Reports*, I, 404; Wilkes, *Narrative*, IV, 458.
61 Diomedi, *Sketches of Modern Indian Life*, 8.

their searches for food, particularly to well-watered meadows. They helped the Spokanes frequent the Dalles of the lower Columbia and the lands of the Nez Percés and Yakimas for goods which now could be easily transported home. North of the Dalles, they traveled to the huckleberry meadows near Mt. St. Helens[62] and, toward the mid-nineteenth century, as far afield to the south in California as they traveled eastward to the Great Plains.

In winter, the Spokanes turned their cayuses out to forage for themselves on Spokane Prairie and in the plateau near Four Lakes southwest of the falls.[63] The animals came through mild winters in good shape, but poorly when winter snows robbed them of nutritious prairie grasses, such as bunchgrass, forcing them to eat cottonwood bark and brush. The Indians kept an eye on their herds, for they were the measure of their wealth, helping them to purchase wives. The herds were even used to "square the debt" in murders. The Indians lassoed free-running wild horses in narrow defiles, or from mounted steeds after saddles with pommels came into use.[64] Women straddled the horses in riding, just as the men did. The Spokanes loved to ride at full gallop, hair flying, yelling at the top of their lungs. Thrill-seeking young Spokanes spent hours breaking in their cayuses. They tied ropes around the animals' bellies to restrain them and sometimes blindfolded them, also tying down their ears.[65]

The young Spokanes found their greatest pleasure in racing their horses, a reward for their efforts at breaking them. Their elders found theirs in betting on favorites to win. They threw their possessions onto high stakepiles and won or lost them (and their economic status, too) on the outcome of the contests. They had many opportunities to recoup or lose a stake, because they raced and bet wherever and whenever they congregated. Terrain and weather permitting, this was done often on the flat between the two Spokane rivers and on Spokane Prairie, near present-day

[62] Anonymous, *Sketches of Mission Life Among the Indians of Oregon*, 178–79.

[63] William S. Lewis, "Spokane House, the History of an Old Trading Post," 7.

[64] Franchère, *Narrative*, 269; *Pacific Railroad Reports*, I, 405.

[65] *Ibid.*

Hillyard just east of Spokane.[66] Mounted bareback—and later on saddles, even before the advent of whites—they raced as many as thirty horses in heats as long as five miles.[67]

All was not play. The Spokanes worshiped their creator, Amotkan, with dancing. Praying dances were held without drums to acknowledge Amotkan's favors. The Spokanes also began formal ceremonies with purifying sweatbaths.[68] Believing the sun to be the master of life, they humbled themselves in the Sun Dance by acknowledging their weaknesses.[69] This dance, unlike the Sun Dance of the Great Plains, was practiced beyond the mid-nineteenth century; it was held at the solstice. Later, the Sun Dance and praying dances were combined, gradually losing their original reason for being held.[70] Spokane scalp and buffalo dances were similar to those of the plains. The Spokanes believed that, besides the force of good aiding them in their quest for sustenance, there was a counteracting force of evil. Below, in the ground, was hell, ruled over by the Black One, probably akin to the old woman sorceress of the Kalispels, whose influence produced ill fortune.[71]

The Spokanes believed in a soul which left the body at death.[72] They believed that, in mythological times, there were neither men nor guardian spirits. Then there were only beings having the physical and psychological attributes of animals. They appeared in the guise of men, taking animal form in emergencies.[73] After true men appeared, the earlier spirits became visible, taking human form only when communicating with men. Prepubertal children first learned to communicate with the spirits by setting out alone

[66] Cox, *Adventures*, I, 200; Roger Durheim, "History of Peone."

[67] A saddle was made of a stuffed pad of buffalo, deerskin, or buffalo hide with attached stirrups. Women used a saddle with pommel and cantle.

[68] Leslie Spier, *The Prophet Dance of the Northwest and Its Derivatives: The Source of the Ghost Dance*, 57. Hereafter cited as *Prophet Dance*.

[69] "Exploring Tour of Reverends Eells and Walker 1838," 6, Elkanah Walker Papers, Box 4, No. 25.

[70] Spier, *Prophet Dance*, 57.

[71] *Pacific Railroad Reports*, I, 297.

[72] Ray, *Cultural Relations in the Plateau*, 83; Armstrong, *Description of the Territories of Oregon and Washington*, 134.

[73] Spokanes, as other Salishans, have legends of tribes of dwarfs and giants inhabiting hills and mountains. When man came on earth, these beings, in Spokane lore, became spirits.

on quests lasting from one to several days and nights. On these quests, they sought visions in which their tutelaries (animate usually, inanimate infrequently) appeared, sometimes in human form, to leave the novitiates with special songs and, frequently, dances. Occasionally the novitiates held vigils in their search for tutelaries. They forgot these experiences until maturity, when, during the Spirit Dance, a shaman called upon the spirit to visit an individual. These dances were usually held in mid-January.[74] The dances were never repeated in a single winter at the same villages, although villagers during a winter season often attended dances elsewhere.

It was at these ceremonies that each Indian sought to identify with his spirit. Those with Bluejay power, which played a dominant role among Salishans, identified so strongly with this conceptualized form of the mythological being that spirit seekers often removed their clothing in midwinter, and for as long as two months they conversed and ate with others, but scavenged leftover scraps, as did Bluejay.

Medicine men and, in later years, medicine women, did more than practice medicine; they were shamans, advisers, prophets. They conducted the all-important winter Spirit Dance. They were obliged to obtain success for their people in gathering food, fighting wars, and warding off evils (such as illnesses). They were expected to relieve sickness by ceremonials and herbs; they extracted invisible evil-spirit darts from their believers by sucking, blowing, and uttering incantations. Their medicine was also preventive, for they were expected to forestall a foreign spirit power from interfering with that of their own people. They had been commissioned for the profession during youthful vision quests,[75] or they may have decided later in life to become shamans, in which case they had to prove their ability before an aged, well-seasoned practitioner of that art. Either way, their life was one of disciplined training.[76] Their profession was hazardous, too; should a shaman

[74] Ray, *Cultural Relations in the Plateau*, 119.
[75] *Ibid.*, 80.
[76] Willard Z. Park, *Shamanism in Western North America: A Study in Cultural Relationships*, 8–10.

fail to heal a sick believer—for which services he was often paid heavily, sometimes at least one horse[77]—the bereaved family could take the shaman's life, unless he escaped to the sanctuary of another band.

These medicine men faced their severest test in the smallpox epidemic of 1782. When it passed, Spokane population, estimated by anthropologist James Mooney to have been fourteen hundred in 1780 (and somewhat excessively by Teit at about twenty-five hundred), was reduced by half.[78] The disease was said to have come from the plains to the Columbia Plateau. It unleashed great ravages on the Spokanes, who, like other Salishans, had no previous exposure, and hence no immunity, to virus diseases. Whole bands were wiped out. In some places lodges were so full of victims that the dead could not be buried and dogs ate the bodies.[79] Even a small offshoot of Spokanes who went down to live on the mid-Columbia were all killed off, for the disease spread downstream.[80]

Many funeral customs must have gone unobserved in that time of sudden mass death. Normally, the deceased would have distributed their possessions before death had they an indication that they might die. Sometimes their possessions were distributed after their burial during celebrations in their honor, in the donation feasts or potlatches. Even after white contact, until the state laws forced on Indians, their possessions were handed down through no regular descent pattern and without benefit of anything resembling a will. Wives designated the recipients of their deceased husbands' properties, knowing that certain items were cherished by others. Sometimes friends and relatives stole the deceased's property, usually horses.[81] In later days, speakers at feasts lamented the dead, a practice of native origin reinforced by the Christian practice of eulogizing at funerals. After feasting and celebrating,

[77] Diomedi, *Sketches of Modern Indian Life*, 5.

[78] James Mooney, *The Aboriginal Population of America North of Mexico*, 15 (hereafter cited as *Aboriginal Population*); Swanton, "The Indian Tribes of North America," 444.

[79] B.A.E. *45th Ann. Rep.*, 316.

[80] McCarty interview.

[81] Wilkes, *Narrative*, IV, 448.

no one mentioned the names of the deceased, for to have done so would have brought their spirits close by. Even wives on these occasions changed their names.[82]

It may have been about the time of the big epidemic that the Spokanes began draping horse hides over sticks and trees to mark graves at the burial ground just west of the village, near the confluence of the Spokane and Little Spokane rivers. By the early nineteenth century, this custom was well established. The Spokanes also hung moccasins, buffalo robes, weapons, and, later, kettles and pieces of gaily colored cloth on poles as grave markers. Under Christian influence, they marked graves with crosses, but alongside these symbols they continued to place what to them were these more practical tokens.[83] Either way, the trail of the deceased led to the happy hunting grounds. Graves at a large burial ground at the mouth of Latah Creek were not so profusely marked with possessions.

Although the Spokanes appear not to have feared death,[84] the passing of a male occasioned much crying, shouting, and beating upon breasts, arms, and faces,[85] until chiefs called for quiet among the people and a four-day ban on painting their faces. Women in mourning cut their hair to the shoulder, and men bobbed the tails of their horses.[86] A member of the same sex as the deceased washed the body and painted its face red. All garments about the deathbed were placed with the corpse and wrapped in mats and hides. The body was laid to rest usually in an upright or sitting posture, a common burial position among the Upper Spokanes.[87] The Lower Spokanes placed bodies parallel to the river with their heads downstream,[88] burying with them (as did other Spokanes) bone carv-

[82] Curtis, North American Indian, VII, 76.

[83] Sir George Simpson, Narrative of a Journey Round the World, During the Years 1841, 1842, I, 142. Hereafter cited as Narrative.

[84] The Reverend Elkanah Walker to the Reverend D. Greene, October, 1841, "Letters Concerning Elkanah and Mary Walker," (hereafter cited as "Walker Letters,") 115, Walker Papers, Cage 57/276.

[85] Armstrong, Description of the Territories of Oregon and Washington, 122.

[86] Curtis, North American Indian, VII, 76.

[87] David Douglas, Journal Kept by David Douglas During His Travels in North America 1823–1827, 173. Hereafter cited as Journal.

[88] Collier, et al., Archaeology of the Upper Columbia Region, 16, 35–36, 46, 55–56.

ings, pipes, and stone tools.[89] On slopes they sometimes piled rocks on graves to protect them from predators. The Spokanes did not follow the same procedure with graves on prairies or plains away from the river camps; rockpiles there would have revealed the graves to possible enemies, as the Blackfeet in buffalo country. Instead, the Spokanes disguised them by building fires or staking horses over them.[90]

The Spokanes were not given to the practice of tree burials, although their neighbors were, for a number of such graves were found near the mouth of the Okanogan River soon after whites came to that area. As in coastal burials, the bodies were wrapped in skins and tied upright to tree trunks, high enough to keep them from animals.[91] Two such burials were discovered in 1911 in trees in Greenwood Cemetery near the city of Spokane.[92] They could have been placed there by visiting Nez Percés, who sometimes laid their dead to rest on scaffolds in trees, or they could have been placed there by diehard Spokanes who wished to spare their dead embalming and interment in vaults and caskets. With the advent of the white man, some Spokanes, like their close neighbors the Chewelahs and Coeur d'Alenes, began covering their dead with small log and, later, frame houses capped by flags, pennons, and sometimes even timber crosses. These structures occasionally covered five or six bodies.[93] The Spokanes seem to have built such burial shelters to cover the dead before they built them to cover the living.

A fresh Spokane grave in the plague year 1782 held the remains of the little son of Yureerachen ("the Circling Raven"), a shaman brother of the chief of the Upper Spokanes. Yureerachen, anguished at the death, blasphemed the Creator. "Why," he sobbed to his chieftain brother, "did He take my son, who has committed no crime, and leave bad people on earth?" One day his chieftain

[89] Louis R. Caywood, *Archeological Excavations at Fort Spokane 1951, 1952, and 1953,* 1–84. Hereafter cited as *Archeological Excavations.*

[90] Ray, *Cultural Relations in the Plateau,* 61.

[91] Lewis, *Tribes of the Columbia Valley,* 190; *Pacific Railroad Reports,* I, 413.

[92] *Spokesman-Review,* July 23, 1911, Pt. 4, p. 2.

[93] E. Barnard Foote, "An Indian Burying-Ground," *The West Shore,* Vol. XIV, No. 9 (September, 1888), 471; Durheim, "History of Peone."

brother told him, "All right, we will be as animals; we will disband our laws. First, you must go to the top of the [Spokane] mountain and fast four days and nights, then come back the fourth day just before noon. If you find no proof of our Creator, we will then disband our laws and live like animals." Clad only in a breechcloth, Yureerachen went to the top of the mountain. He built a fire, prayed, beat sticks, cried, and sang. On the fourth day, before dawn, in a burst of light, he heard the voice of the Creator. "Look down the mountain into the future of your people," spoke the Creator. Overwhelmed, Yureerachen knew in an instant that he had to bring word of this vision to his people. But he also knew the time to do so was not at hand, for in mourning the recent loss of their loved ones, they would never believe him. What should he tell them?

Yureerachen raced down the hill to affirm to his chieftain brother and the other people his own faith in the Creator. The rest of his story, a prophecy, he kept to himself until the time should come to reveal it. One day, about the year 1790 (approximately, for the Indians had no calendars or written records), there was a deafening blast, the air clouded, and the ground became covered with a flour pumicite. The people, well versed in stories of the earlier volcanic catastrophe, were stricken with fear by the "dry snow" mantling the earth. It was as though an evil hand were completing a sinister cycle on earth, from ashes to ashes. They thought that the end of the world was at hand.[94]

Yureerachen felt that it was the proper time to prophesy. First, he calmed his people with assurances that the Creator was not ending their existence on earth. "Soon," he said, "there will come from the rising sun a different kind of man from any you have yet seen, who will bring with them a book, and will teach you everything, and after that the world will fall to pieces." When the people pressed him for details, he said white men would come.[95] He told them they had to accept the white men, that they would

[94] Walker to Greene, September 12, 1839, 82; Spier, *Prophet Dance*, 57–58; *Pacific Railroad Reports*, I, 298.
[95] Some believe he told them that both white and black men would come, the latter being Negroes.

be friends to the Spokanes. They would be the *chipixa* ("the white-skinned ones") and would be called the *Sama*, something sacred, because it was an "unbelievable" thing.[96] The Spokanes, assured by the words of their prophet, awaited the *Sama*.

[96] McCarty interview.

Skins for the *Sama*

When the *Sama* came, it was from a source no more super-natural than the Northwest Fur Company's Rocky Mountain House, established in 1788, at the confluence of the Saskatchewan and Clearwater rivers.[1] From that place David Thompson, a Northwest employee (or a Nor'Wester, as they were called), de-cided, in late 1800, to send two French Canadian trappers, Le Blanc and La Gasse, to accompany a party of Upper Kootenay Indians to the Indians west of the Rocky Mountains. Their mis-sion was probably to explore the country for furs, to teach the natives the techniques of trapping and preparing furs, and, finally, to return with a catch of furs themselves.[2]

[1] The Northwest Company, organized in 1787 by the partnership of several traders in Montreal, had sent Alexander MacKenzie within six years to two oceans, the Arctic and the Pacific, in hopes of finding a shorter and cheaper route to supply the company's Athabaska Department.

[2] Another version has it that the two were preceded by a white man covered with hair and nearly half-starved. *Wenatchee Daily World*, January 26, 1943. Information about the two is from McCarty interview and from Claude E. Schaef-fer, *Le Blanc and La Gasse Predecessors of David Thompson in the Columbia Plateau. The Colville Examiner* of February 22, 1913, p. 4, reported the death on

Spokane tradition tells of the coming of the first *Sama*, two men, very possibly Le Blanc and La Gasse. If the Spokanes had expected something miraculous of them, they were in for a disappointment, for the two came dressed in leather and furs like Indians, on mounts "smaller than horses" (possibly mules), each leading another animal. They brought buffalo robes with them. They appeared very hungry and unable to prepare food. The Spokanes treated them kindly, as the prophet Yureerachen had told them to do. The Spokanes put the *Sama* up for the winter on Blue Creek in the Colville River valley, where they brought them food. The Indians soon learned the mission of the two *Sama*— the securing of furs, which appeared to the Indians rather selfish. One of the two *Sama* was bald. The Indians dubbed him "Nelekualsha," or "Noweaquanoore," a more descriptive name meaning "Face Upside Down," as he was not only bald, but had a beard. To add further to their disillusionment, they found the other to be a poor camp maker. They called him "Chekualkua," their first impression of him, as he "couldn't figure things out for himself." He may have been the one the Kootenays called "Bad Fire," because he liked a small fire in contrast to the other, who preferred a large roaring fire. The Spokanes learned that the two had brought no big medicine, for Spokanes went right on dying all through the winter of their stay and even after they left. The Spokane hosts learned only that the *Sama* were willing to exchange strange new gifts, like a metal knife, for furs, and that before long more of the *Sama* would follow.[3]

About the time the two *Sama* left the upper plateau, other white men appeared in its lower reaches. In 1805, runners from tribes

the Colville (Washington) Reservation of Alexander Daylight who, at a reported age of 114, claimed to have talked with David Thompson and with another white man "many moons" before, possibly Le Blanc, La Gasse, or their predecessor.

[3] McCarty interview. In Lewis, "Indian Account of the Settlement of the Spokane Country," 2, six Spokane Indians on October 20, 1916, told Lewis that the earliest traders showed their people a pocket knife with two blades—one open and one half-open—telling them that if they did not listen to them or do as they said and give them furs, the knife would cut out their lives. Lewis' informants also said that another scheme the traders used was to show the Indians a doll, claiming it to be an evil spirit, and telling them that if they didn't obey, the evil spirit, on their deaths, would throw them into the fire.

to the east brought word to the Spokanes that a party of white men was moving west, approaching the Columbia River. The Spokanes immediately sent two runners down to meet them. It was the Lewis and Clark expedition. The two Spokane runners returned with a "look-at-self" object (probably a mirror), and an ornament not made of sea shells or bone (probably glass beads or copper buttons).[4] Apparently these were not the only Spokanes the famed explorers met, for they tell of meeting others at the Long Narrows of the Columbia at an ancient village, Echelute (Wishram Village), at the head of a three-mile channel worn through hard black rock, from fifty to one hundred yards wide, through which the water swelled and boiled. Lewis and Clark discovered this to be not only a place of swirling waters, but of swirling populations, where interior Indians came with horses and skins to traffic with lower Columbia River peoples. When not trading, the Indians engaged in wrestling and racing their horses and themselves.[5] Visiting the village were members of the Lartielo (Upper Spokanes)—six hundred souls who lived in thirty houses at the falls of the Lastaw River (the Spokane River) and below the great Wayton Lake (Lake Coeur d'Alene) on both sides of the river. On their map, Lewis and Clark placed their number at nine hundred, more than the number recorded in their journal text, a difference of three hundred, possibly because they included the Lower Spokanes in the numbers on the map. The nine hundred figure, if reasonably accurate, would indicate that in the quarter century since the smallpox epidemic of 1782, Spokane population had decreased to about half its estimated pre-epidemic numbers.[6]

[4] McCarty interview.

[5] William Cameron McKay, "Early History of the Dalles," William Cameron McKay Papers, 1839–92.

[6] Mooney in *Aboriginal Population*, 15, estimated the Spokane *Lartielos* to have numbered fourteen hundred in 1780, just prior to the plague. Mooney estimated the *Highenimmos* (the San Poils and Nespelems) at eight hundred. Possibly included in these *Highenimmos* were the Lower Spokanes who were associated with these two peoples. If this were the case, the numbers of Spokanes would have been larger than the fourteen hundred estimate of Mooney. For the enumerations of these tribes, see James K. Hosmer, ed., *The Expedition of Lewis and Clark*, II, 506. The map appears in volume I. For other enumerations of the tribes, see Elliott Coues, ed., *History of the Expedition Under the Command of Lewis and Clark*, III, 990–91.

Lewis and Clark had been instructed by President Thomas Jefferson to investigate the possibility of shipping Pacific Coast furs eastward from the headwaters of the Missouri River. Scarcely had they reported back to the President when David Thompson, whose company was not unaware of the American expedition, slipped across the Rocky Mountains through Howse Pass (present Jasper National Park) in June, 1807. He moved past the fierce Piegans, who had opposed his westward projects because they did not wish their western enemies, the Kootenays, to be supplied with powder and ball. Following the Blaeberry River, Thompson reached the Columbia River. But since it ran north, he did not recognize it. He named it the Kootenay. Moving up the Columbia, he stopped near present-day Invermere on Windermere Lake and erected a stockade and building, the first known post in the upper Columbia River country. In that area he spent the winter of 1807–1808 with a clerk, Finan McDonald, and six servants.

In the spring of 1808, Thompson followed waterways south to a point near present-day Bonners Ferry, Idaho. He spent the winter with the Flatheads and took their furs back east in the spring. McDonald descended the Kootenay River to a point near present-day Libby, Montana. Here, he set up two lodges and a log house and traded during the winter of 1808–1809. In August, 1809, Thompson returned with some of his men to the Flathead villages in northern Idaho. Purchasing horses, he rode overland to Lake Pend Oreille. At its eastern end, near present-day Hope, Idaho, he began constructing his next post, Kullyspell (Kalispel) House. The Kalispels (Lower Pend Oreilles) were pleased to have traders among them, if for no other reason than to obtain guns, ammunition, and iron-headed arrows to be on an equal footing with their enemies. Also trading at Thompson's house were Flatheads, Coeur d'Alenes, Spokanes, and other Salishans. Thompson pressed southeastward to build Saleesh House, near present-day Thompson Falls, Montana. In the summer of 1810, he sent the faithful Finan McDonald and one Jacques ("Jaco") Raphael Finlay to build a post among the Spokanes.[7]

[7] Glover, *Thompson's Narrative*, i–xcviii, 274–333; T.C. Elliott, "The Fur

The Spokanes welcomed McDonald and Finlay, as they had welcomed the previous *Sama*. The Spokanes called all Frenchmen "*Sama*," because the French had been the first white men in their lands. Finlay did little to change this illusion, for he spoke French, carried Indian blood in his veins, and took an Indian wife. Mc-Donald, the "pugnacious Celt," was built to be noticed, standing six feet four inches. His bushy beard and flowing red hair, which matched his temperament, had a somewhat frightening effect on them. But this was lessened when he took to wife the daughter of an Indian chief (believed to be a Nez Percé). There were children from this union. No one knows which of these two men selected the site of the post, about a half-mile up the Spokane River from its junction with the Little Spokane, situated in the land of the Upper and Middle Spokanes.

In the spring of 1810, Thompson ordered that a supply of trade goods be brought to the Spokane site and that the building of the post begin. Jaco Finlay was the likely builder of the post, which, like him, was unpretentious, consisting of not more than two or three cabins, a warehouse to store trade goods and furs, and one or two structures for living quarters. In all likelihood the buildings were not much different from those of Kullyspell House, hurriedly built of logs chinked with mud or clay, since tools and such materials as nails were very scarce.[8]

Thompson came south by way of the Kootenay and Pend Oreille rivers from the headwaters of the Columbia with trade goods to supply his posts. He thanked heaven for a safe arrival at Spokane, where he reported finding Jaco with about forty Spo-

Trade in the Columbia River Basin Prior to 1811," *Oregon Historical Quarterly* Vol. XV, No. 4 (December, 1914), 241–51; Kent Ruth, *Great Day in the West: Forts, Posts, and Rendezvous Beyond the Mississippi*, 52. For a definitive analysis of Thompson's journeys in the Pend Oreille country, see Allan H. Smith, "An Ethnohistorical Analysis of David Thompson's 1809–1811 Journeys in the Lower Pend Oreille Valley, Northeastern Washington," *Ethnohistory*, Vol. VIII, No. 4 (Fall, 1961), 309–81.

8 There is considerable literature on Spokane House. Three significant studies are: Jerome A. Peltier, "Neglected Spokane House," *The Pacific Northwesterner*, Vol. V, No. 3 (Summer, 1961), 33–41; Lewis, "Spokane House, The History of an Old Trading Post"; C. S. Kingston, "Spokane House State Park in Retrospect," *Pacific Northwest Quarterly*, Vol. XXXIX, No. 3 (July, 1948) 181–99.

kane Indian families. There was little about this quiet, "singular looking person," as J. B. Tyrell of the Geological Survey of Canada characterized Thompson, to indicate to these Spokane families or anyone else that he was the foremost land geographer of the British Empire, having surveyed and mapped well over a million square miles in Canada. With only a compass, watch, and crude artificial mercury horizon, he would set latitudinal and longitudinal locations to within approximately one second of present-day calculations.[9] Of more interest to the Indians at the time of his arrival was his short nose and black hair "worn long all around, and cut square, as if by one stroke of the shears just above the eyebrows."[10] Because of this style of cutting the hair, British traders came to be known among the Spokanes as "the long hairs" in contrast to American fur traders, "the short hairs," who were soon to come to their lands.

If the Spokanes had regarded Thompson's coming as fulfillment of a prophecy, as has been suggested, they appeared little impressed with his pleas to them and a band of Kalispels camping nearby to cease their war plans against the Teekanoggin (Okanogan) Indians. Proud of their newly acquired guns and iron-headed arrows, the Indians seemed eager to try them out. Thompson dissuaded them with small presents and the suggestion that they should vent their aggressions on the Blackfeet. About fifty warriors took this advice and went to the aid of the Kootenays and Flatheads against their enemies on the plains. The others went to the Columbia River to release their energies in salmon fishing.[11] Thompson descended the Columbia River in hopes of opening up a passage for trade to the Pacific, sailing away with the confidence that he had enlarged his company's fur empire by one more post, Spokane House.

The Spokanes had traded for generations, but trading with white men was a relatively new experience for them. Word of the post was noised about, and tribes living to the south and west

---

[9] Aubrey L. White, "Old Shrine Saved," *Spokesman-Review*, December 24, 1939.
[10] T. C. Elliott, *David Thompson, Pathfinder and the Columbia River*, 7.
[11] Glover, *Thompson's Narrative*, 333–38.

soon came to trade there. They brought beaver, bear, otter, and other skins to trade, and assurances for the traders that their countries abounded in many other animals. From their vast open ranges, the Indians also brought many horses, an evident surprise to the traders, who had seen few of these animals among tribes they had contacted in the more thickly wooded areas west of the Rocky Mountains. Not only did tribes come from the south and west, but also from the northeast. Spokane House fast became a mart and a mecca. The indefatigable Thompson returned to the Spokane area and traveled on over the Rocky Mountains for a new supply of goods for Spokane, Kullyspell, and Saleesh houses. In late November, 1811, he met John George MacTavish and James McMillan. They had fifteen men and ten horses, carrying about a ton and a half of merchandise for the trade. MacTavish and McMillan held down the post at Spokane House for the winter, while Thompson and Finan McDonald traded with the Flatheads. In early spring, 1812, the Spokanes saw Thompson for the last time. Accompanied by MacTavish, he set out on April 22 with a brigade of six canoes for Fort William, never again to return further west than Lake of the Woods.[12]

One day in late August, 1812, "the short hairs" descended on the simple buildings of Spokane House, with its ten men, all under the management of James McMillan. It was a party of Astorians, named after John Jacob Astor, the American fur king. The party was led by one of Astor's partners, John Clarke (a former Nor'-Wester). He had three clerks, twenty-one Canadians, six Polynesian Kanakas (Sandwich Islanders), and an Indian guide. Indian tradition has it that among the early traders on the Spokane, there was also a colored cook.[13] Missing from the party of Astorians was one of its clerks who got lost, Ross Cox. A fortnight later, rescued by Indians, he straggled to that place, his "clothes all

---

[12] For information concerning Thompson's journeys in the Spokane country, see T.C. Elliott, "David Thompson's Journeys in the Spokane Country," *Washington Historical Quarterly*, Vol. VIII, No. 3 (July, 1917), 183–87. Articles under the same title appear in the same quarterly, Vol. VIII, No. 4 (October, 1917), 261–64; Vol. IX, No. 1 (January, 1918), 11–16; Vol. IX, No. 2 (April, 1918), 103–106, and Vol. IX, No. 3 (July, 1918), 169–73.

[13] Lewis, "Indian Account of the Settlement of the Spokane Country," 4.

torn, his feet bare, and his belly empty." It took Cox about three months to recover.

Clarke chose a site for a post about a half-mile southwest of Spokane House, right under the nose of the Nor'Westers. He chose a site close to his rivals not so much from contrariness as from the need of mutual protection from the Spokanes and other Indians, whose attitudes he had not as yet tested. Having arrived from Astoria near the Columbia mouth with a string of some fifty Nez Percé horses, the newcomers were well supplied with goods, ammunition, spears, hatchets, knives, beaver traps, copper and brass kettles, white and green blankets, colored cloths, calicoes, beads, rings, thimbles, hawk bells, foodstuffs, and moderate quantities of spirits in kegs holding, on the average, nine gallons.[14]

The Astorians did not confine their competition to the Spokane country. Accompanied by six men, Francis Pillet went up to oppose Nicholas Montour and his Nor'Westers in the Kootenay country. Another group made a similar journey to the Flathead country. Besides company help, the Astorians employed freemen in the trade, former employees of the fur companies who continued to hunt and trap on their own, trading their catches to the same companies for goods. One early writer said of them: "Having passed their early youth in the wilderness, separated almost entirely from civilized man, and in frequent intercourse with the Indians, they relapse, with a facility common to human nature, into the habitudes of savage life."[15]

Under Clarke's direction, a snug and commodious house was built, more elaborate than that of the Nor'Westers. It contained four rooms and a kitchen, together with a comfortable bunkhouse for the men, and a capacious store for furs and trading goods. Surrounding this was a paling, "flanked by two bastions with loopholes for musketry."[16] The Astorians were now formally in busi-

[14] Not all goods carried in the bateaux flotilla which left Astoria on June 29, 1812, were destined for Spokane House. Some were taken by Donald McKenzie and his party up the Snake River. Some were taken by David Stuart and his men to the already established Fort Okanogan. Cox, *Adventures*, I, 118.

[15] Washington Irving, *Astoria*, 98–99. Irving tells of one of these freemen, Regis Brugiere, who trapped for the Astorians in the Spokane country.

[16] Cox, *Adventures*, I, 194.

ness among the Spokanes, in their "fort." They were in solid competition with the Nor'Westers, who operated from "houses." As soon as the fort was finished, Clarke, the former Nor'Wester, sought to outmaneuver his opponents. This tall good-looking man assembled the Indians and made long speeches to them. He promised much, to which they responded in like manner, as they were so fond of doing. Things augured well for the trade. On occasion, Clarke brought forth his silver goblet, or drinking cup, from "which he would drink with a magnificent air," much to the wonderment of the natives.[17]

The Spokanes, "a quiet, honest, innoffensive tribe," gave them no trouble, and the traders seldom had to close the gates of the post. Their chief, Illim-Spokane, set them a pattern of inoffensiveness. According to Alexander Ross, who came from Fort Okanogan to visit Clarke for three days that December, he had

frequent opportunities of observing the sly and underhand dealings of the competing parties . . . . When the two parties happened to meet, they made the amplest protestations of friendship and kindness, and a stranger, unacquainted with the politics of Indian trade, would have pronounced them sincere; but the moment their backs were turned, they tore each other to pieces. Each party had its manoeuvreing scouts out in all directions, watching the motions of the Indians, and laying plots and plans to entrap or foil each other. He that got most skins, never minding the cost of the crime, was the cleverest fellow; and under such tutors the Indians were apt disciples. They played their tricks also, and turned the foibles and wiles of their teachers to their own advantage.[18]

It was no accident that Illim-Spokanee and his people found it politic to keep the path well worn between the two posts.

In competitive settings such as this back in the East, Nor'-Westers and Astorians alike had plied the Indians with liquor; although diluted, it was still potent for the red man. Fortunately for the Spokanes, the two companies in their territory now compacted to abstain from giving them liquor, thus sparing both

17 Alexander Ross, *Adventures of the First Settlers on the Oregon or Columbia River*, 212–13. Hereafter cited as Ross, *Adventures*.
18 Ross, *Adventures*, 202.

traders and Indians the drinking bouts which often resulted in maiming and loss of life.[19] Most Indians whom the traders permitted a taste of liquor did not seem to relish it. But on one occasion, the Nor'Westers gave a few glasses to Illim-Spokanee. He returned to his lodge but was back in a few days, walking a straighter line, for a little more of the "strong water." Since it would never have done for a chief to set a pattern of drunkenness, the traders refused to give him any more, alleging that their stock was exhausted. No such restrictions existed on tobacco. More than once tobacco decided success in a bartering bout.

Trade from the Spokane and surrounding country was good for a few years. Some items traded to the Indians were trifling but showy, secured largely from Europe.[20] In that same Europe, gentlemen treasured fashionable hats made of beaver trapped in the Spokane country. From this region, the Astorians would soon ship the furs of the silver-gray fox down the Columbia and across the Pacific to China, where mandarins would treasure them, as they had treasured other furs gathered from the Northwest Pacific Coast for many years.

Many items traded to the Indians were by no means trifling—guns, pots, knives, axes, flints, and steels, the latter replacing the wooden spindles spun between the hands to start fires. Yet the profit on them was still great. Ross Cox tells us that

> The great object of every Indian was to obtain a gun. Now a good gun could not be had under twenty beaver skins; a few short ones we gave for fifteen: and some idea of the profit may be formed, when I state that the wholesale price of a gun is about one pound seven shillings, while the average value of twenty beaver skins is about twenty-five pounds! Two yards of cloth, which originally cost twelve shillings, would generally bring six or eight beavers, value eight or ten pounds! and so on in proportion for other articles;—but they were satisfied, and we had no cause to complain.[21]

[19] Gordon Charles Davidson, *The Northwest Company*, 224.
[20] Hiram Martin Chittenden, *The American Fur Trade of the Far West*, I, 1–5.
[21] Cox, *Adventures*, I, 199.

This mutual satisfaction depended on the fact that each party had strong desire for items which the other valued lightly.

The traders observed that Spokane women made good wives and affectionate mothers; an evaluation concurred in by some of the Canadians who took them for wives, having become impressed with their slavish and submissive traits. The freedom of these women from the "vice of incontinence" may have been a factor in their choice. The traders observed that Spokane men practiced a sort of free-enterprise system, since riches or poverty were "generally proportioned to their activity or indolence"—or, they might have added, to their success or failure in gambling. So taken were the Spokanes by this diversion that they wagered horses gained the hard way, by trading the goods they had received from the traders to the Nez Percés in exchange for furs.[22]

The fur trader was prone to see the worst in the tribes that fit poorly into the fur trade, and conversely, the best in those fitting into it well. There was a causative relation between furs and affection.[23] Traders found the Spokanes to be superior to the Indians of the coast and the lower Columbia River, particularly those given to stealing around the Cascades and Long Narrows, where the traders always found the going rough. They had even found the noble Nez Percés troublesome in their dealings with them along the Snake River. They found the Spokanes friendlier than the Coeur d'Alenes, and regarded both more highly than the San Poils, who sometimes stole their horses. The Spokanes, however, could never match the Flatheads in the eyes of the traders, who had been charmed by a "frank and hospitable reception"— and the furs they had received in the Flathead lands. The Spokanes were to suffer for some time to come by white men's comparisons between them and the Flatheads. The moving story of what were supposed to have been Flatheads, but were largely Nez Percés (the Flathead designation was at first incorrectly applied to interior tribes, Salishan and Shahaptian alike), who traveled to

[22] *Ibid.* I, 200.
[23] Lewis O. Saum has pointed this out in his study, *The Fur Trader and the Indian*, 46–49.

44

St. Louis in 1831 to seek the white man's "Book of Heaven," did still more in the eyes of white men to heighten the contrast between the two peoples.

The traders appeared little desirous of altering customs pertaining to the dead. They observed graves ornamented with horse skulls and skins, buffalo and deer hides, blankets, moccasins, leather shirts, and weapons of war.[24] But the traders could not resist suggesting certain changes in Spokane customs for the living. When the Astorians, in 1813, planted their first garden—of turnips, potatoes, cabbage, and other vegetables—they expected the Indians to follow suit. By the next year, the Indians had indeed acquired a taste for vegetables, but hardly enough to give them incentive to garden. They raised the following objection: Why should they garden when they could help themselves to the vegetables in the traders' gardens? They said that if they took to gardening, it would not only upset their hunting and fishing, but it would stop their women from collecting fruits and roots, thus making them lazy. The women seemed perfectly content to keep things as they were, "notwithstanding their laborious duties," which included collecting (and preparing) fallen game and other foods, firewood, and water, making clothes, and performing a hundred other chores.

The Spokanes were as unwilling to accept changes pertaining to their horses as they were to their women. They preferred their own horse gear—hair-rope bridles and deerskin saddles, both of which irritated their mounts. Nor did they favor suggestions in handling their mounts. They preferred to canter or gallop rather than to trot. Horse racing thrilled them and entertained the traders. The excitement of betting and competing with surrounding tribes—Coeur d'Alenes, Kettle Falls, and Flatheads—stimulated the racers and the onlookers as, from the blast of fired guns, they sped through gravel-peppered heats in the big plain between the Spokanes and the Coeur d'Alenes. The Spokanes never shod their horses. Since the fur traders had brought no smithies, the horses were put out of action in about ten years. They were good

24 Cox, *Adventures*, I, 200.

then only for transporting children. Sometimes horses' hoofs deteriorated when their riders made long trips, as to the plains. Then traveling on these animals became risky. If they did not know how to shoe their horses, the Spokanes still loved them. There was an indescribable affinity between an Indian and his horse. The Spokanes could never bring themselves to eat their mounts, although they were not averse to having horsemeat on the menu, provided the traders furnished the meal. One old Spokane living near the fort, Cholsumque ("Grizzly Bear"), sold bunchgrass-fed horses to the traders for their meat. Neither traders nor Indians could be choosy in their choice of foods, but in some respects, the Indians were choosier than the traders. The Spokanes seldom, if ever, ate dogs, which they saw die from eating offal at the fishing grounds. The traders bought dogs from the Indians, but not always for pets and pelts;[25] traders' stomachs became strong when they became empty. The common threat of famine facing both groups proved that the traders' greatest danger came not from the Indians but from nature.[26] The Spokanes also resisted suggestions from the traders to change their hunting methods, especially the tendency to overkill their game. On horseback, they continued the age-old practice of firing the tinder-dry grasslands to drive bewildered deer into ever-narrowing circles.

The Spokanes were quite loyal to the traders. On one occasion in November, 1813, ten young Spokanes offered to wage a war against Nez Percés who had been harassing Cox and three others because that spring Clarke had ordered the hanging of a Nez Percé who had stolen his silver goblet. The traders declined the Spokane offer, because the Nez Percés had not continued the chase and because it was their policy to discourage trouble between Indian bands. Just one month before the Spokane offer to help Cox against the Nez Percés, an agreement had been executed by which Astor sold his holdings in that region to the Northwest Company. Astor blamed the War of 1812 for his loss; in time, he would claim that his partners had sold him out. While Astor

25 Franchère, Narrative, 266.
26 Saum, The Fur Trader and the Indian, 43.

fumed at his losses, the Nor'Westers became fur kings of the Pacific Northwest. Astoria, the symbol of its namesake's fur dreams, became Fort George, through which the victorious company channeled its furs and received its supplies.[27]

How much of these developments the Spokanes knew about is not known, but they certainly knew something was afoot when the Nor'Westers moved from Spokane House to the more commodious Fort Spokane, which was, by comparison, a handsome establishment. They hauled down the American flag and hoisted the Union Jack in its place. These changes seem to have concerned the Indians little. When a party of Nor'Westers reached Fort Spokane the last day of August, 1814, the whole tribe assembled around the post; they excitedly viewed the powder kegs and tobacco bales as they were unloaded from the horses. A large circle was formed in the courtyard. The calumet was lit and a few rounds smoked to celebrate the meeting, after which a quantity of the weed was given to the Indians. Then the oratory began, a practice not the least bit offensive to the trader, who knew that it got bartering sessions off on the right foot. Illim-Spokanee delivered a long speech of welcome in which he revealed his people's dependence on the traders' goods, particularly tobacco: "The white men made us love tobacco almost as much as we love our children." (It is noteworthy that one of his children was destined to lead the Spokanes in difficult days ahead in their dealings with the white man, who would call him "Spokane Garry.") Illim-Spokanee also revealed that his men, in their dependence on the traders, had "broken their arrows," and had almost forgotten how to use them. He confessed that they believed the white man had deceived them when he failed to bring more guns and "fire powder" in the big canoes. He promised that the Indians would hunt all the harder. Then they all commenced dancing, jumping, and crying out:

---

[27] For a further explanation of events attending the sale, see Dorothy O. Johansen and Charles M. Gates, *Empire of the Columbia*, 133–41. A copy of the sale may be seen in B.C. Payette, *The Oregon Country Under the Union Jack*, xiv–xix.

The good white men, the good white men,
Our hearts are glad for the good white men.
The good white men, the good white men,
Dance and sing for the good white men.[28]

The next day, to show their appreciation, the Spokanes, better hunters of game than of furs, gathered a supply of grouse, geese, and duck for the traders' table. They were impressed with the animals the traders had brought with them, animals that did not have to be hunted—a cock and three hens, goats, and swine. The traders could have been among people less hospitable than the Spokanes. One day Finan McDonald, believing a chief had cheated him at gambling, challenged him to a duel. The Indian chief accepted, but only on his own terms: firing at his opponent from behind trees. Traders stepped in and calmed the Celt down; the duel was called off, a victory for the cause of good relations between the two groups.[29] Another disturbance involved one of the Spokanes' "nymphlike damsels." She became the wife of one of the younger clerks, who in all probability had been her dancing partner in the ballroom of Spokane House, where she had apparently exuded little of the "indescribable coldness" which Cox said marked the American Indian from "Chile to Athabasca, and from Nootka to the Labrador." The union was consummated in Indian fashion, with a generous supply of blankets, kettles, beads, hawk bells, and the like distributed to her people. At the post, she changed her native frocks for more appropriate clothing, and removed her paint and grease. Hardly had the week passed when a party of young braves galloped through the gates of the post. The bride hid out in an adjacent store, for her Spokane Indian husband was in the group. An interpreter assured the Indians that, had the clerk known the girl was already married, he never would have taken her as a wife. The Indian husband agreed to accept, as compensation, a gun, a hundred rounds of ammunition, three blankets, two kettles, a spear, a dagger, ten fathoms of tobacco, and a

---

[28] Cox, *Adventures*, I, 346–47.
[29] *Ibid.*, I, 350–52, has a lengthy, humorous dialogue between McDonald and the chief.

quantity of smaller articles. The calumet was smoked; the brave was satisfied. The price had been exorbitant, but it was a relatively small one for the company to pay to stay on good terms with the Spokanes.[30]

Women often carried on their work in wooded areas away from the camps; consequently "female violation [was] by no means uncommon among them." Once, in 1815, a Spokane wife discovered her husband in an intrigue with another woman; she inflicted such injury on him that he died the next day. This set off a blood feud in which her husband's brother killed her with an arrow. The traders effected a reconciliation between the feuding factions, but not before two men and two women lay dead.[31]

The traders continued to make peace among their hosts, a policy made easier since competition, the bane of harmonious trader-Indian relationships, had been removed when the Astorians left. Not so elsewhere. In Canada, Nor'Wester half-blood hunters, the *métis*, began a reign of terror which, in 1816, resulted in the murder of colonists who had settled on the Red River on lands which the Northwest Company considered their domain. The War of 1812 had impeded travel of company personnel to the West. There was jealousy and bickering between the wintering partners in the region. Lax and wasteful methods which had developed when the country was rich in furs had not been shaken off, and a general war psychology had engendered inefficiency and indifference. There were also difficulties in marketing furs. An arrangement with a Boston firm to carry company furs to Canton to bypass an East India Company monopoly at that port was of some help, but American trade on the Pacific Coast was an annoyance.[32]

Searching for means to rescue the floundering trade in the West, the company authorized the establishment of Fort Nez Percés (later, Fort Walla Walla) at the confluence of the Walla Walla and Columbia rivers, a place much closer to the Columbia River than Spokane and a gateway to the fur-rich Snake River

[30] Cox, *Adventures*, II, 35–40.
[31] *Ibid.*, II, 148–50.
[32] Frederick Merk, ed., *Fur Trade and Empire George Simpson's Journal*, xxiii–xxiv. Hereafter cited as *Fur Trade*.

country to the east. From Fort Nez Percés, which he built in 1818, Donald McKenzie went trading in the Snake country the next year, returning with 154 horses loaded with furs. The success shut down operations at Spokane in favor of Fort Nez Percés.[33]

The end of competition between rival fur-trading companies came in a London agreement in 1821. A merger was effected; the Hudson's Bay Company name and administration were retained. This gave new life to the Spokane post, although prospects for Hudson's Bay success in the region were dim. Not even a Parliament-approved, exclusive British right to the area could change that. Nevertheless, in the latter half of 1822 and early 1823, new palings were set, the large dwelling house remodeled, new buildings built—a store and new quarters for the men, capped by a two-story bastion with stairway to the topside of the palisades, so that guards could scan the surrounding area.[34] Security was tighter than it had been before. Since Indians continued filtering into the potato garden, which Indian wives of white men at the fort tended, palisades were planted to keep the marauders away. Finan McDonald, who had not been moved out in the reorganization, seemed to have caught the new spirit. In June, 1822, we find him urging the Indians to get out and get some furs rather than to dance and gamble their property away.[35] But he found it much easier to have the buildings at the fort whitewashed than to rid the Indians of bad habits.

As the trade fell off, so did the affection of the traders for the Spokanes, although the Indians' dependence upon the traders never abated. Chief Factor Alexander Kennedy, in his 1822–23 Spokane House report, stated that the 210 families of Spokanes (a more detailed census in 1829 reported their numbers at 704 people) were

> a lazy indolent tribe who do not bring us One hundred Skins in the Course of the Year, [and] they think us much beholden to them for allowing us to remain on their lands, and as the[y] generally

[33] Alexander Ross, *The Fur Hunters of the Far West*, 95–97.
[34] Caywood, *Archeological Excavations*, 75.
[35] *Ibid.*

reside near the House, we are at a great expense on their account by keeping an open House for them to smoke in constantly, besides supplying them gratis with Tobacco to smoke in their lodges.

Tobacco, he reported, was not the only item used to appease the 60 families living in the village nearby, but also provisions and ammunition. In fairness to the Spokanes, it should be said that they regarded these favors as rent for the use of their lands, an exclusive privilege not enjoyed by the other tribes who came to trade there. These tribes would depend more on the castors, or beaver, they could harvest, bartering with the pelts, which were used as a medium of exchange for the white man's goods at the store.[36] In the village, Kennedy gloomily added that there were three chiefs whom the company generally clothed once a year. Kennèdy did not identify the recipients of these bounties; in all likelihood one was Illim-Spokanee.

Kennedy also complained that parties from the numerous Spokane villages along the river were constantly dropping by to request tobacco, ammunition, and medicine. The company, he wrote, in order to keep on good terms with them, was obliged to satisfy their requests for nothing. It was a seemingly unfair exchange to him, since, with fewer beaver in that part of the country, even had the Indians been inclined to work, the traders had little to receive from them. Kennedy concluded that the post was badly located for the trade, not only because of a scarcity of furs, but also because the Indians "monopolized" the salmon, so that all food for the post had to be conveyed upriver from Fort George at great expense. The answer to the problem? Move the Spokane post to Kettle Falls.[37]

The man who would order its removal, George Simpson, the efficient governor of the Hudson's Bay Company, reached Spokane House on October 28, 1824, in company with three other em-

---

[36] For an explanation of this system of exchange, see Robert M. Ballantyne, *Hudson's Bay; or Every-Day Life in the Wilds of North America*, 38–40.

[37] Kennedy, Spokane House Report 1822–23; Robert C. Clark, "The Archives of the Hudson's Bay Company," *Pacific Northwest Quarterly*, Vol. XXIX, No. 1 (January, 1938), 3–13.

ployees.[38] Simpson appointed the capable McDonald to Spokane House and Peter Skene Ogden to supervise the Snake River operations, hitherto "considered a forlorn hope." That area, in 1823, had provided over half the nine thousand beavers caught in the Spokane district, and there were more available, provided they could be secured before the Americans took them.

Simpson believed the trade would increase if natives living in the lake and creek country of the Spokane and similar districts would apply themselves to the hunt during the winter months. Perhaps the Indians had been infected during that season by the indolent habits of the freemen, whom he characterized as "the very scum of the country," a "most unruly and troublesome gang to deal with in this or perhaps any other part of the World." He observed that the Spokanes, Nez Percés, and Flatheads occasionally raided the lower Columbia River country, carrying away scalps, women, slaves, and horses. As they acquired more horses, the Spokanes pillaged as far as the Willamette Valley, as well as in the vicinity of the Dalles and in the country of the Yakimas, who called the Spokanes "robbers."[39]

For Simpson to lay stress on these aggressions would have given an excuse to his superiors to press for greater security measures, in turn involving greater expense. Instead, he stressed the Indians' peaceful relationships with the company, because the elderly and incapacitated were becoming increasingly dependent upon the trader and his posts as places of "resort and refuge." The post, in Simpson's thinking, had to be the vital spot in trader-Indian relationships. Pillaging and hunting for game, he believed, would give way to hunting for furs, a distinction the Indians could not grasp as easily as Simpson could. To help sustain those on the Spokane House grounds, he advocated the planting of bigger gardens.

The Indians, he believed, could profit from missionaries who could instruct them in morality and religion at, of course, mod-

---

[38] Information on Simpson's first journey to the West is from Merk, *Fur Trade*, including the introduction.
[39] B.A.E. *45th Ann. Rep.*, 360.

erate expense, for a soul, like a pelt, should be secured economically. He talked over the prospects with the Spokane chiefs, who concurred in his thinking regarding the establishment of a mission station at Spokane House. (Simpson also suggested missions at the Cascades on the lower Columbia River and at the Thompson-Fraser River confluence.) He laid down qualifications for a missionary with the same calculation and coolness that he used in selecting a trader. The clergyman, who would be to a certain degree under the protection of the company, should not be too willing to find fault with what might appear to him a laxity of morals at the posts, where the facts of frontier life had produced families without marriage ceremonies, or "country marriages," as they were called. A clergyman should also realize that any attempt to change this uncivilized custom would be futile. These informal marital arrangements at the posts did little to minimize the involvement of personnel in intrigues with Indian women, "a lamentable fact" which Simpson claimed was the source of every difficulty the company faced in Indian country, and was the cause of nine out of ten murders committed by Indians on whites.

He saw Indian conversion as no threat to the trade, rationalizing that the red man, by accepting the white man's religion, would accept the rest of his culture and thus raise his own standard of living and the profits of the trade as well. Trader and missionary would complement each other. The missionary would profit by what the trader had already done to raise the living standards of the Indians. They already had fancier blankets, guns, kettles, scissors, and improved looking glasses in which the Indians enjoyed a better view of themselves, as they were made over in the white man's image. Simpson himself had observed the rapid rise in England of missionary, Bible, and other religious societies. These had created a Christianizing zeal, which not even the governor and committee had escaped, and in which, under terms of their license, they had fostered the establishment of missions for the instruction of the Indians. Not daring to overexert his independence from the London management, Simpson seemed to have been converted to its way of thinking. An important link between him and the company's mission policies was the Reverend John West, who arrived at the Red River settlement in October, 1820, under commission of the (Anglican) Church Missionary Society. By 1822, West had established a school for Indians and was casting an eye toward the Columbia River as a field of missionary endeavor. He had the ear of the directors in London, as did the Reverend David T. Jones, his replacement.[40] At this time the Kootenay and Spokane chiefs entrusted their sons to Simpson's care to be taken and educated at the Mission Society School at Red River, and he was entreated to send them a missionary or religious instructor.

It is not known how much religious instruction the Spokanes had already received from the traders. Iroquois trappers, brought from eastern Canada by the British companies to encourage the western tribes, by example, to do more trapping, had introduced Roman Catholic ceremonies among the Flatheads. They may have exerted some influence among the Spokanes in this faith, although there was a primitiveness about their religion, which, like their blood, was somewhat mixed. At any rate, it would appear they had at least as much influence in these matters as the clerks, whose religious backgrounds were orthodox Anglican, Presbyterian, and Catholic. The Indians quite naturally associated the religion of the mercantilists with material benefits, medicine for the body linked with medicine for the soul. About the time Simpson was visiting the Spokanes, they were in the habit of holding religious services in the lodge of the chief (possibly Illim-Spokanee). In these rites a religious picture secured from the traders was spread on the ground and the natives knelt before it. Illim-Spokanee began a prayer to *Quilentsatmen*, the Maker (literally, "He made us"), in a plaintive request for His protection, and to be taken to Him at last to be saved from the Black One down below. When Illim-Spokanee finished his prayer, others knelt, uttered shorter petitions, and then chanted a hymn and danced.[41]

---

[40] J. Orin Oliphant, "George Simpson and Oregon Missions," *Pacific Historical Quarterly*, Vol. VI, No. 3 (September, 1937), 213–48.

The Nez Percés held similar dualistic views of the universe, and while Simpson was at the forks of the Spokane and Columbia, some of their chiefs came to see if he were the son of the Master of Life, there to see if their hearts were good, or His war chief, there with bad medicine to see if their hearts were bad. In an act which seemed to have ceremonialized his new responsibility as protector of Indian souls, Simpson baptized the sons of the Kootenay chief and of Illim-Spokanee. The boys would bear the names "Kootenay Pelly" and "Spokane Garry." Pushing forward, he lined out the site of the new post, Fort Colville, on the banks of the Columbia about three-quarters of a mile above Kettle Falls.

By mid-April Simpson was on his way East, leaving to one John Work the responsibility for removing Fort Spokane to Fort Colville. Work had spent the winter of 1824–25 at the fort. He was well acquainted with the Indians and the problems to be encountered in such a move, not the least of which would be Indian reaction to it. A note he received from Simpson in late April warned that the Spokanes would not be pleased with the move; it was no news to Work. He may have felt that the "few gifts" and "fair words" which Simpson had suggested to bring the Spokanes around would be inadequate. They had to be brought around if, for no other reason, than to utilize their horses in packing all the removables from Fort Spokane to the new site. On July 22, 1825, Work officially broached the matter with the chiefs, along with a request for the use of their horses. The chiefs gave no definite answer to his request, but appeared to take the news better than he had thought they would, possibly after it was intimated to them that the fort and a few traders might remain, a promise they "seem to swallow . . . notwithstanding its improbability." Had most of the Indians not been down at the fish barrier below the post busily taking seven or eight hundred salmon daily, the leavetaking might have been more difficult. As it was, "the scoundrel Charlie," with some other Nez Percés who resented removal of the post

41 H. S. Lyman, "Reminiscences of Louis Labonte," *Oregon Historical Quarterly*, Vol. I, No. 1 (March, 1900), 169–88; Parker, *Journal*, 239.

seventy miles farther from their lands, made a disturbance, threatening to block off the horse supply from the Snake River.[42]

Moving the post to Kettle Falls was a slow process. In December, Work went to Kettle Falls to check on the progress of the new buildings, only to find that little had been made. With no fort at Colville and the one at Spokane in the process of folding up, some of the Spokanes took their beaver and other pelts to the Flathead post in the late fall and winter. There they found that liquor was an important item of trade. It had been customary at the Flathead post to reward chiefs and headmen on their arrival with a dram; it was weakened with water, but not enough to prevent some Indians from becoming tipsy.

In February, 1826, Work was back at Spokane. He engaged the Indians to furnish horses to transport the company properties—furs (collected at Spokane), provisions, and sundries—down to the forks. In March, one string of sixty-two horses and another of eighty were used in this task. Other cargoes came down in three boats. The Indians were paid for their help and the use of their horses. But they watched the process with regret, frequently complaining, as Work narrates it, that they would be "pitiful" when the whites left them.[43]

The spot of land between the Spokane and Little Spokane rivers was now a lonelier place than it had been for a decade and a half. As a final ironic act—especially since it happened on the first day of spring (1826)—the blacksmith and cook, the last employees at the post, busily collected all the iron from the place, even the hinges off the doors. Thus, the buildings, the hub of a once bustling trade, were now ready for the slow process of decay. Pack

[42] For events preparatory to the moving of the post, see T.C. Elliott, "Journal of John Work, June–October, 1825," *Washington Historical Quarterly*, Vol. V, No. 2 (April, 1914), 83–115.

[43] For John Work's activities from the fall of 1825 to the spring of 1826, see Elliott, "Journal of John Work, September 7th–December 14th, 1825," *Washington Historical Quarterly*, Vol. V, No. 3 (July, 1914), 163–91; Elliott, "Journals of John Work, December 15th, 1825, to June 12th, 1826," *Washington Historical Quarterly*, Vol. V, No. 4 (October, 1914), 258–87. For additional information on the role of John Work in the fur trade, see Henry Drummond Dee, "An Irishman in the Fur Trade: The Life and Journals of John Work" *The British Columbia Historical Quarterly*, Vol. VII, No. 4 (January, 1943), 229–68.

trains from the Snake River, on their way to Kettle Falls, would occasionally stop off here. The company would continue to winter its horses and carry on some trade in the area. Old Jaco Finlay— who, like other Canadians, Iroquois, Crees, etc., had married into the Spokanes—would remain at the post to beget a large family and enjoy the isolation, since the company had taken a dim view of his freeman activities of selling it furs he had bought from the Indians. In May, 1826, he repaired the gun of David Douglas, the botanist for whom the Douglas fir was named, whose search for plants and seeds had brought him that way. Douglas rewarded Jaco with tobacco. Harsh weather, which left nothing but pine moss for food, made that winter around the old post all the more gloomy for the Indians.

The Spokanes began bringing their furs into Fort Colville in 1827. John Work has left a record of the Spokanes' trade for the years 1827 and 1828: 68 and 88 beaver skins, respectively; 746 and 985 muskrat pelts. There were a small number of martens, foxes, otter, and mink. Much of the Spokane items brought to trade were food: salmon, venison, roots, and berries. The Spokanes also traded horses, packsaddles, pack cords, bags, and parfleches. To Work we are also indebted for statistical information pertaining to the Spokanes in the years immediately following the removal of the post from their lands. He tells us that the Scait[t]e Cuthinish (Lower Spokanes) consisted of sixty-six men, seventy women, forty-nine boys, and fifty-two girls. They lived at the lower falls under the leadership of their principal chief, Big Head. The Sinohomenish (Middle Spokanes) numbered ninety-four men, ninety-five women, forty-three boys, and fifty-four girls. They lived at the site of the old post under their principal chief, Illim-Spokanee. The Sintatoluh (the Upper Spokanes) had sixty-two men, seventy-six women, nineteen boys, and twenty-four girls. They lived around the big falls and on the plain toward the Coeur d'Alene under the chieftaincy of Tuwesilihkin.[44]

---

[44] "Some Information relative to Colville District by J. Work Ap[ri]l 1830." Chief trader at [Fort] Colville, John Warren Dease, in an 1827 report gave the number of Spokane men as 222.

For years to come the Spokanes would take their furs to Fort Colville, where the Hudson's Bay Company was not to terminate its affairs until 1872. After this, Spokanes would still bring pelts to frontier posts, but the heyday of the trade, particularly involving the beaver, was nearly over. Exploitation of that animal in Spokane lands marked time with the ascendancy in faraway Europe of the silk hat, introduced there at about the time the company moved its operations to Fort Colville.

CHAPTER THREE

Decade of Dedication

In 1829, after an absence of four years, Spokane Garry returned from the Red River school with a fur brigade. He was now eighteen, mature, short, and stocky. He and his schoolmate, Kootenay Pelly, came armed with truth from the Anglican Book of Common Prayer and a King James Version of the Bible, knowledge of which was to be kept sharpened by Christian prayers and ceremonials.

Their arrival may have been instrumental in the resurgence of the Prophet Dance, which spread from the Flatheads to other tribes of the interior. It was a religious movement of belief in the destruction and renewal of the world and of the resurrection of the dead.[1] The words of Garry and Pelly sounded similar to the teachings of the Indian prophets. To the Indians, one prophetic teaching complemented the other. The recent death of his father, Illim-Spokanee, gave Garry greater influence among his people than he would have had during his father's life.[2]

[1] Spier, *Prophet Dance*, 20.

[2] For information on the sojourn of Garry and Pelly at Red River, see Thomas E. Jessett, *Chief Spokan Garry, 1811–1892, Christian Statesman and Friend of the White Man*, 21–32. Hereafter cited as *Chief Spokan Garry*.

The Upper Spokanes considered Garry's youth an advantage over the age of their chief, Nahutumhlko ("Erect Hair"), and he became a nephew of the old man. Since he was also wise in the ways of white men, he became virtual chief of both Upper and Middle Spokanes.[3] Garry also received a good reception to the south. Since ties between the Spokanes and the Nez Percés were close, the Nez Percés would soon come under the influence of his teachings. A Nez Percé chief, Lawyer (Hallalhotsoot), heard Garry teach in the winter of 1829–30. He carried back to his people Garry's teachings, such as the observance of the "Sabbath." These teachings moved the Nez Percés to send to Red River two of their young men, along with others including Garry and Spokane Berens.

Garry returned home in 1831. With a bell someone gave him, Garry called his people together on Sundays. He had a tule-mat church built in the village where his brother lived, just across the river from the abandoned Spokane House. In his services, he taught his people prayers, hymns, the Ten Commandments, and right conduct from the Bible, so that when they died they might go up to see God. The church most likely doubled as a school. He also had the Indians build a tule-mat schoolhouse (in present-day Spokane) in and near which he taught children and adults the rudiments of English, agriculture, and Christianity.[4] In 1831, four Indians (three Nez Percés and a half–Nez Percé–Flathead), set out for St. Louis in search of Christian teachers.[5] It was a journey filled with ironies, and it is believed that only two of them returned to tell about it. In St. Louis, Clark, of expedition fame, an Episcopalian, took the visiting Indians to a Roman Catholic cathedral for baptism. But it would be Protestants who would send the first missionaries to the Nez Percés and Spokanes, in answer to their appeal.

[3] Curtis, *North American Indian*, VII, 55.
[4] William S. Lewis, "Statements of Nellie Garry, Susan Michel, Curley Jim," M.S. 1. A Spokane junior high school scheduled for completion in 1970 will bear Garry's name.
[5] Letter of the Reverend Asa Bowen Smith, August 27, 1839, in *Missionary Herald*, Vol. XXXVI, No. 8 (August, 1840), 326–29.

But first, the American trader Nathaniel Wyeth, passing through the Spokane country in late March, 1833, on his way from Fort Vancouver to the States, observed that near the Spokane River stood a lone bastion of the fort, the only part the Indians had not torn down for firewood, a palisades of sorts left by them to mark the final resting place of one believed to be Jaco Finlay, lying in a coffin buried beneath it.[6] Samuel Parker of the American Board of Commissioners for Foreign Missions, a body representing the Congregationalists, Presbyterians, and Reformed churches, spent the winter of 1835–36 at Fort Vancouver. In May, 1836, he came to the Spokane country. He visited Nez Percé and Spokane villages, whose inhabitants "manifested a perfectly friendly disposition," although they were "in want of subsistence." At last a missionary had come to the swollen Spokane River to view the remnants of the old trading post and its grave-marker bastion, above which thrushes, wrens, and warblers competed with the clattering notes of the magpie. The missionary visited a Spokane village and observed a garden planted with potatoes, peas, beans, and other vegetables, the first he had seen planted by Indians west of the Rocky Mountains.

Despite a meeting with Garry, Parker believed the Spokanes to be experiencing their first exposure to a minister and the Gospel. He was under the impression that the Spokanes returned to their village to establish a crude church, when actually Garry had built it some five years earlier on his return from Red River.

The next day, the missionary, accompanied by a number of Spokanes and Nez Percés, left for Fort Colville. On Sunday, May 29, 1836, he held services in English at the fort. The Indians attempted to convey to him what their religious beliefs had been and their desire to hear more of the Gospel—a request he felt unable to fulfill because of his inability to communicate with them. Of the problem of communicating with the Indians in general, he wrote: "The number of words and terms in their language expressive of abstract and spiritual ideas is very small, so that those

[6] F. G. Young, ed., *The Correspondence and Journals of Captain Nathaniel J. Wyeth 1831–6*, 186.

who wish to instruct them in these subjects are compelled to do it by means of illustrations and circumlocutions, and the introduction of words from foreign languages." On May 31, he set out to return to Fort Vancouver with two guides, one a Spokane.

In 1836, missionaries from Parker's American Board traveled from the East overland to Fort Vancouver. They were Marcus Whitman, his wife Narcissa, Henry Harmon Spalding, his wife Eliza, and layman William H. Gray. From Fort Vancouver, they backtracked to set up missions in the interior. The Whitmans established theirs among the Cayuses at Waiilatpu, some twenty-five miles east of Fort Walla Walla. The Spaldings located among the Nez Percés in a small valley, Lapwai, where a creek of that name flowed into the Clearwater, a Snake tributary.

On March 29, 1837, the lay worker, Gray, came to the Spokane River Valley. Three days later, he was joined by Spalding, who was on his way to Fort Colville for supplies. Spalding held a service for the Spokanes. The natives assured him their country was very poor, and that should a white man come to live with them and teach them how to live, they would look up to him as a father and do as he told them. Spalding and Gray left, but not before Spalding had given some religious paintings to Garry. Garry made a great impression with these pictures in his teachings, so much so that Lower Spokane Chief Big Head decided to go down to Spalding's Nez Percé mission to get some of them.

Spalding's enthusiasm for pictorial presentations is understandable. The American Board's certificate given to its missionary workers showed a rising sun shedding its rays on a tropical harbor into which rode a full-rigged ship carrying missionaries. It also showed natives with outstretched arms beneath palm trees on the shore, representative of the thousands who made up the vast harvest fields of souls.

Two missionaries of the American Board destined to labor among the Spokanes, the Reverends Elkanah Walker and Cushing Eells, with their wives Mary and Myra, might have been on such a ship had not war broken out among the Zulus of Africa and had Walker not suffered from seasickness. This turn of events helped to bring them from New England overland in the spring and summer of 1838 to a land of pines and red men. Traveling with the Walkers and Eellses were the Reverend A. B. Smith and his wife and the returning Gray and his wife. Their journey[7] had little of the romantic in it, as the newlyweds exchanged civilization for the rigors of a frontier. After appointments were made in early September at a meeting at Whitman's mission, Walker and his co-laborer Eells set out for Fort Colville to survey the Spokane country. On September 14, 1838, they reached the south bank of the Spokane River. The next morning a band of Spokane Indians turned out to hear them.

Unfortunately, we have no Indian appraisal of the two missionaries standing before them. The appearance of Walker—tall, rather spare, stoop shouldered, with a light complexion not matching his black hair and brown eyes—made the Indians fear him and call him "chief." He was no great speaker. As Gray would later recall, Walker was "always afraid to say *amen* at the end of his prayers." The Spokanes respected him for his kindness. Eells was short, slender, and brown of hair and eye. Gray wrote of him that "he was made to move in a small circle."[8]

Having found someone to interpret, Eells read to them from his New Testament. The Indians said Garry had read from the same book; but Garry's teaching effort had slackened off, presumably because of starvation conditions prevailing at his school.[9] The missionaries crossed the Spokane, pushing on toward Fort Colville. A service was held in the Colville Valley in the lands of the Chewelahs, a small band closely associated with the Spokanes through marriage. Big Head proudly made his presence felt at the services. He had spent a great deal of time at the mission stations in the lower country and was sufficiently aware of policies made there to know that the missionaries were coming his way. Eells

[7] Clifford Merrill Drury, *Elkanah and Mary Walker*, 67–95.
[8] W. H. Gray, *A History of Oregon, 1792–1849, Drawn From Personal Information and Authentic Observation*, 178. Hereafter cited as *A History of Oregon*.
[9] William S. Lewis, "Spokane History, Statement of Thomas Garry, Moses B. Phillips, Aleck Pierre, Charley Warren, John Stevens, David John, and William Three Mountains," 5.

would later remember the chief as "Big Heart." The missionaries found him capable, for he conveyed their signs and gestures to his peoples.

"Never did I so earnestly desire the gift of tongues as on this journey," wrote Walker, as he and Eells attempted to communicate to their hearers. Although Walker feared the natives would continue down the "broad road to destruction," he continued with his colleague up the trail to Fort Colville to a friendly reception from Chief Factor Archibald McDonald, a Presbyterian. McDonald recommended they establish their mission some fifty miles to the south in Tshimakain Valley. This location would be close enough for him to be helpful, yet far enough to protect his British establishment from proximity to an American institution in a time of tension when both powers held an uneasy joint occupation of Oregon, also far enough to safeguard its mercantilism and the Roman Catholic beliefs of the French Canadians who frequented it. With his shrewd understanding of the Indian mind, McDonald charged Big Head—should the missionaries go to Tshimakain—to help them build a house, provide them fish, behave himself, and not expect too much for his services, as they had come not to trade but to teach.

After a visit to receptive Indians on the shores of Lake Pend Oreille, a spot as near the Blackfeet-plagued Flathead country as they dared go, the missionaries left for the recommended mission site under the guidance of one of Big Head's men. They dubbed him "Solomon." He led them to a delightful pine-rimmed valley some twenty-five miles northwest of present-day Spokane, on the main trail between Forts Walla Walla and Colville, some fifteen miles west of the old trading post at the Spokane and Little Spokane rivers. The Indians called it "Tshimakain," meaning "the place of the springs." White men would call it "Walker's Prairie." The day after their arrival, September 25, 1838, Indians came down from Fort Colville with provisions and tools; the missionaries and Indians began felling and hauling pine timber to a spot below the hills on the southeast edge of the valley. Here they raised the walls of two houses. With winter approaching, the two missionaries left for Whitman's mission. Big Head followed with some of his family, and in one plaintive Sabbath-meeting speech, told of the death of his son, Spokane Berens, at the Red River school, a death which he said had not grieved him as much as had his son's inability to return to teach him about the way to heaven.[10]

As Walker and Eells wintered at the Whitman mission trying unsuccessfully to learn the Spokane language from Nez Percé Chief Lawyer, two French priests, Fathers Francis Norbert Blanchet and Modeste Demers, arrived at Kettle Falls to an enthusiastic welcome. The Indians now at long last saw with their own eyes the "chiefs" about whom the Canadians had told them, the Blackrobes, men of real cloth, not of leather, which the American Board missionaries often wore. During their four-day stay, the two priests conducted baptisms and celebrated mass many times in the presence of the Indian chiefs, "who attended with as great a respect as if they had been fervent Christians." In July, 1839, Father Demers returned to Fort Colville. He baptized children, heard a large number of confessions, and informed Canadians at the fort that, by "country marrying" Indian wives, they had not only broken the law of God, but of the company, which had stipulated in their contracts that they not marry during their term of service.

Big Head objected. He believed it was good to have a wife—and if one wife was good, more than one was better. Big Head had never had to respond to such a lecture from Walker and Eells, who had urged old Spokanes to keep their wives, but to take no new ones as long as one of their old ones was living; young Spokanes were to limit themselves to one wife.[11]

On February 26, 1839, Big Head—with eight Spokanes and a string of horses—arrived in the lower country to move the Walker and Eells families (five people now, with the addition of the

10 Information on the missionaries' Spokane journey is found in "Walker Letters," 60–69; Cushing Eells, "Reminiscences of Cushing Eells," No. 4, pp. 1–8 (hereafter cited as "Reminiscences"). See also, Drury, *Elkanah and Mary Walker,* 100–109; "Exploring Tour of Reverends Eells and Walker 1838," 1–12, Walker Papers.
11 "Walker Letters," 79.

Walkers' three-month-old baby boy). The Walkers and Eellses were glad to depart from the lower country, where the missionaries were beginning to step on each other's toes.

At Tshimakain, the Indians chinked the logs of the houses and built roofs out of poles, grass, and dirt. Walker found Tshimakain not big enough for both mission and mongrels—Indian dogs—which opened the first clash in a series of culture conflicts marking the missionaries' stay there. As was their custom, the Indians never killed the litters of pups left to pilfer around the camps. Walker put the Indians under an interdict of sorts until they promised to kill all the dogs and not just the eleven whose deaths they had thought sufficient to appease the missionaries.[12]

While the missionaries wished to have the Indians accept their teachings, the former knew they would have to adapt their own efforts to the latters' modes of gaining a living. Tshimakain was the center of a circle whose radius extended sixty miles and included some two thousand souls, many of whom seldom broke out of the circle. The Indians' migratory patterns made it difficult to hold services in the various camps. Lying as it did between the camass grounds and the fisheries, the site of the mission had been wisely chosen.

After observing Spokane industry during their fishing season, Walker believed the Indians to be less improvident than one might suppose. Keeping up with them was particularly difficult for Walker, who was plagued by poor health. In food-gathering season, during the first year of the mission, the congregation varied from thirty to a hundred souls, with not more than half of these remaining during the week. Usually natives came from distances up to thirty miles on Saturdays, departing on Mondays, although some came from greater distances for sojourns of one or two weeks to share with their friends the excitement and novelty of missionaries in their midst. The missionaries conducted morning and evening services on weekdays under the pines, singing,

---

12 "Walker Letters," 67–70; Eells, "Reminiscences," No. 4, pp. 1–8; Clifford Merrill Drury, *First White Women Over the Rockies*, II, 146–54 (hereafter cited as Drury, *First White Women*).

praying, and attempting to explain the Scriptures. On the Sabbath they held three services. As cold weather approached, a house was built to serve as church and schoolhouse; it opened in November.[13]

The missionaries realized more than ever their own weakness in mastering the Spokane language, which they characterized as having "crooked" and "hissing" sounds. They soon discovered the Spokane grammar had phrases compounded apparently according to no rules and contracted or changed evidently for the sake of euphony. There were plenty of prepositions; as for adjectives, there were no comparatives or superlatives. For example, when two horses were placed side by side, one was good, the other bad. When the better of the two was compared with one still better, it in turn became bad and the third horse good. There appeared to be no person, number, mood, or tense of verbs. Pronouns were often used in connection with verbs. The nouns, as might be expected, were key words for the missionaries. They soon must have discovered certain deceptions even in this part of speech, for in the twofold Spokane nomenclature, for example, people, depending on their own sex, used different terms for father and mother, son and daughter, grandson and granddaughter, and so on.[14] The amount of English the Spokanes learned in return for trying to help their teachers learn their language was perhaps very small. The introduction of the English language, Walker once observed, could open the way to the natives to "the works of Infidels & every abomination to be found in our own land & in fact the whole world."[15]

In the absence of an adequate grasp of the language, the missionaries often selected one of the more teachable Indians, to whom selected portions of the Scriptures were repeated again and

[13] Letter of Eells, February 25, 1840, *Missionary Herald*, Vol. XXXVI, No. 11 (November, 1840), 437–39.
[14] "Walker Letters," 25; Eells, "Reminiscences," No. 5, pp. 6–9; *Vocabulary of the Spokane Indian language and notes on Grammar (Containing George Gibbs' instructions for research relative to the ethnology and philology of America)*; Lewis H. Morgan, "Systems of Consanguinity and Affinity of the Human Family," 244–48.
[15] "Walker Letters," 61.

again. This "rehearser" improved on the words that stumbled from the lips of the missionaries and passed them on to his people. No wonder Mrs. Walker regarded November 25 as "An eventful day to the Flat Heads," for on that day an alphabet was completed and the first reading lesson given.[16] The lessons contained "phonetic orthography" based on an 1820 essay by John Pickering, America's leading authority on Indian languages, who had proposed a uniform orthography for Indian languages, prepared in part for missionary use among the Indians, "the degraded fellow-men of this continent."[17] The lessons were printed with pen on sheets suspended on the schoolhouse wall. The missionaries' writing was not as exciting as the pictures in Mrs. Walker's book, one of which was an animal the Indians had never seen, the elephant. At first, the pupils seemed eager to learn, probably, as Eells surmised, because of the "novelty." But the children tired of sitting still and became inattentive. Sometimes their elders fell asleep during lessons; many fell behind the children in attainment and eventually dropped out of school. There was not much sleeping, though, when the pupils sang songs.[18]

In school or out, Walker discovered the Spokanes to be "a very difficult race to manage." The mission soil had turned out to be more fruitful for gardens than for salvation. By Big Head's responses, he observed that the red man, like an unregenerate white, disliked being told he had a wicked heart.[19] Both missionaries feared he might defect to the Catholics, a stronger possibility now that one of the priests (possibly Father Demers) had returned to the Colville country and had dropped in at the mission in mid-July.[20] Big Head had taken his sick daughter back to a medicine man—one who made wounded people well, the salmon run, and the snow fall to catch game. His people were still gambling. Polygamy, which had produced relationships as tangled as "among

[16] Drury, First White Women, II, 179.
[17] John Pickering, "An Essay on a Uniform Orthography for the Indian Languages of North America," 3, 10.
[18] Letter of Cushing Eells, February 25, 1840, Missionary Herald, Vol. XXXVI, No. 11 (November, 1840), 40; Eells, "Reminiscences," No. 5, p. 9.
[19] "Walker Letters," 76.
[20] Drury, First White Women, II, 162.

a band of wild horses," was so rife that Walker feared to institute the rite of Christian marriage lest it desecrate the institution. "A most selfish set," wrote Walker, referring to their greater interest in material gifts than in those of the spirit.[21] The Reverend A. B. Smith in 1840 had set Spokane numbers at 500.[22] On the basis of estimates of a representative of the U.S. government traveling among them in June, 1841, their numbers, along with Colvilles, was set at 450. If reasonably accurate, this was about half their numbers fifteen years before.[23] On one of Eells's tours of twelve hundred miles, which, from March, 1840, to March, 1841, took him to the Spokane River just below Lake Coeur d'Alene, he was besieged by the sick and lame; they believed he had medicine to cure them of all their ills. About the only comfort he could give them was to tell them that even white people died and that no medicine on earth could cure the old and infirm.[24] Yet we find him in July, 1841, with Dr. Whitman dispensing medicines to Indians along the lower Spokane River.[25] As medicines became more readily available at the mission, we find its personnel trading them to Indians for berries, roots, and buffalo tongues.

Game animals dwindled. This may have been one reason Big Head spent the winter of 1840–41 in buffalo country, where increasing numbers of Spokanes would go in search of food and hides. Had he stayed home, he would have found the winter hunting good, as heavy snows had made the deer easier to kill.

With one important chief gone, another came. On January 5, 1841, Garry paid his first visit to the mission.[26] The missionaries were aware of his influence among the Middle and Upper Spokanes, among whom they had hoped to strengthen their ministry.

[21] "Walker Letters," 76–79.
[22] Clifford Merrill Drury, ed., *The Diaries and Letters of Henry H. Spalding and Asa Bowen Smith relating to the Nez Perce Mission 1838–1842*, 130.
[23] *Pacific Railroad Reports*, I, 417. The estimate is that of Wilkes. Also included are estimates of the succeeding twelve years by officials of British and American governments, allusions to which will be made further on in this text.
[24] Letter of Cushing Eells, March 1, 1841, *Missionary Herald*, Vol. XXIX, No. 2 (February, 1843), 82.
[25] Drury, *First White Women*, II, n. 217.
[26] *Ibid.*, II, 202.

Garry, however, shied away from them, possibly preferring the Anglican doctrines and ritual to the board's Calvinist doctrines and lack of ritual, or possibly confused by the differences between the two faiths. Walker and Eells must not have reprimanded Garry for having two wives. He would, for the next two years, from time to time, appear at the mission to give talks, interpret, and help translate portions of the Bible into Spokane. But his appearance there would become more infrequent because, as he put it, the Indians laughed at him. They "jawed him so much about it," was the way it was explained to George Simpson, who came on a return visit in 1841 to the country he had visited sixteen years before. Simpson did not hear these words from Garry's own lips, for the fur trader surprised Garry gambling at cards. This so embarrassed the chief that he did not come out of his tent.[27] Simpson might also have been shocked to learn that Garry had taken to wrapping himself in a buffalo robe and had drifted back into spirit medicine.[28] After three or four years the missionaries would no longer seek his help, although he remained friendly.

The gradual defection of Garry was just one of the many problems facing the missionaries as they entered their third year among the Spokanes. The year 1841 got off poorly with the burning of the Eellses' home. Indian children scampered through the Walker home. Mingled with the horde was the Walker lad (there would be several children born to the Walkers at Tshimakain), who his mother feared was turning aboriginal. Due to the lad's insistence, his father had even supplied him with a bow and arrows.

The missionaries not only felt the Indian children crowding in too closely, but on one occasion Eells requested Big Head and his family not to camp too near the Walker house.[29] And if the dogs were off the plains, it did not take long for others to return. The missionaries had no aversion to hiring Indian labor for potatoes and powder. They gave some of the Indians ridiculous names, like "Simpleton" and "Mufflehead." It was their practice to take In-

27 Simpson, *Narrative*, I, 144–45.
28 George T. Allan, "Journal of a voyage from Fort Vancouver Columbia to York Factory, Hudson's Bay, 1841."
29 Drury, *First White Women*, II, n. 221.

dian children into their households to help with the work. Shortly after arriving at Tshimakain, Mrs. Walker hired a girl, Swante-pester, and two or three years later would hire another, Shoshena-malt. The Walkers also had employed in their home in 1839–40 a bright Indian lad, Chettlesote ("William Three Mountains"). Some suggest that Big Head spirited him from the household because he feared that the lad, from his inside position, received more scriptural knowledge than he. William later confessed that he had understood Walker's teaching but had not regarded it highly.[30]

Occasionally, white visitors stopped by the mission. Members of the Charles Wilkes U.S. Naval Exploring Expedition arrived in 1841. Among the explorers was the physician-naturalist Dr. Charles Pickering, who seven years later would relate his travels in the Spokane country in a publication, *The Races of Man and Their Geographical Distribution*.[31] The expedition's reports on nearly every phase of Spokane life would soon be incorporated into Wilkes's *Narrative*. The explorers noted that the Hudson's Bay Company had reduced petty wars among the Spokanes and other tribes of the interior, one result being an increased number of marriages between them and the other tribes. They also noted that, in these marriages, the husband invariably joined the tribe to which his wife belonged and that she, far from being a drudge, held an exalted position because of her mastery over the lodge and the food stores. They observed that, as with Big Head, chiefs ruled more by persuasion than command, and that punishment inflicted by the tribes frequently resulted in the expulsion of the delinquent.

Two particular religious ceremonies caught their attention. One of them, the *huwash*, involved singing, dancing, and feasting. The Indians went from lodge to lodge until at last they entered one that was darkened save for a small opening at the top. Through this opening the spirit descended in the form of a small bone,

---

30 Eells, "Reminiscences," No. 8, p. 6.
31 J. Neilson Barry, "Pickering's Journey to Fort Colville in 1841," *Washington Historical Quarterly*, Vol. XX, No. 1 (January, 1929), 54–63.

which a shaman lay on the heart of his subject, from whom the spirit had departed and now returned to insure him against death. "The poor foolish Indians," wrote Mrs. Walker of this practice, "are playing their medicine to find their lost spirits. When will they care for their lost souls?"[32] The other ceremony, the *tohua*, involving dancing, walking barefoot, and "many other such pranks," was performed several days in the spring to insure an abundance of deer, fish, berries, and roots.

Dr. Pickering was surprised to see buffalo robes and conical skin lodges so far from the buffalo country, evidence to him that the interior Indians had been to the plains. He may not have known that the Middle and Upper Spokanes, among whom he was then journeying, traveled "to buffalo" more frequently than did their Lower Spokane neighbors. He was struck by the absence of game in the interior. Beaver, which Indians had formerly caught in baskets, had been all but exterminated by the introduction of white men's iron traps. He seemed not to have grasped the relationship between the shortage of game and the Indians' increased need of going "to buffalo."

In September, 1841, Horatio Hale, a philologist of the Wilkes expedition, arrived at Tshimakain to gather facts regarding the Indian language. It was a profitable visit, the missionaries believed, for he gave them important information on that subject.[33]

On February 9, 1842, a Coeur d'Alene chief arrived accompanied by Garry. He invited Eells to come to teach his people, half of whom favored the priests, and the other half, Walker and Eells.[34] Possibly the two chiefs were hoping to offset a renewed interest in the Catholic faith among the Indians, occasioned by the recent arrival (in September, 1841) among the Flatheads (who, with Iroquois, had made repeated trips to St. Louis for Blackrobes) of Pierre Jean De Smet, S.J. Even a member of the

---

[32] Drury, *First White Women*, II, 304.

[33] Wilkes, *Narrative*, IV, 437–64; Barry, "Pickering's Journey to Fort Colville in 1841," *Washington Historical Quarterly*, Vol. XX, No. 1 (January, 1929), 54–63.

[34] Drury, *First White Women*, II, 226.

aloof San Poils had visited De Smet that winter to learn the prayers the Blackrobe had taught the Flatheads.[35] Before spring, 1842, a band of Spokanes visited De Smet. They expressed happiness that the "right kind of Black-gown" intended to establish a mission in their country soon. He had already baptized one of their dying children, quite a contrast to the practice of Walker and Eells, who had performed the rite only on their own.[36]

De Smet appeared to have been at ease among the Spokanes, whom he regarded as children. He slept more soundly among them at night, and was more long-suffering with their dogs than the Walkers and Eellses were. These two missionaries were happy that he had apparently deferred to their occupancy in the field by not establishing a mission among the Spokanes. But in April, 1842, he laid the groundwork for a mission among the Coeur d'Alenes. The Mission of the Sacred Heart began operating in early November, when Nicolas Point, S.J., and Brother Huet built a log church on the St. Joe River. Finding the Coeur d'Alenes true to their reputation for "dissimulation, egotism, and cruelty," Point had his missionary work cut out for him. Some Spokanes joined a Flathead winter buffalo-hunting party in 1842; accompanying the plains-bound travelers was Father Point, to sustain them in the faith.[37]

With the conversion of many Coeur d'Alenes and some Spokanes at the hands of De Smet and Point, the Tshimakain missionaries found themselves now wedged between two missions of the Catholic faith, at Coeur d'Alene and Colville, where even the

[35] Pierre Jean De Smet, S.J., *Letters and Sketches, with a Narrative of a Year's Residence among the Indian Tribes of the Rocky Mountains*, 319. Hereafter cited as *Letters and Sketches*.

[36] De Smet could not understand the actions of the Reverend Samuel Parker, a "modern Iconoclast" who had smashed a cross over the grave of an Indian child.

[37] Reverend P[ierre] J[ean] De Smet, S.J., *New Indian Sketches*, 11; *Spokesman-Review*, August 27, 1939; reprint of article by Father James M. Brogan in *The Coeur d'Alene Tepee*, in Dubuar Scrapbook, No. 15. In 1846 the mission moved to the banks of the Coeur d'Alene River (De Smet, *Letters and Sketches*, 365 n.; Nicolas Point, *Wilderness Kingdom Indian Life in the Rocky Mountains, 1840–1847*, 59, 78, 81, 155). Josephy in *The Nez Perce Indians*, 86, and Jessett in *Chief Spokan Garry*, 30–31, state that Roman Catholic priests were the "Long Robes," whereas the Anglican missionaries were the "Black Robes."

pious McDonald had become a Catholic.[38] Between Colville and the Spokane, the St. Ignatius Mission would be established in 1844 among the Kalispels. From here, the following year, a resident priest would serve the San Poils, Okanogans, and certain Spokanes. That same year, 1845, at the request of Indians at Kettle Falls, Anthony Ravalli, S.J., visited them to build the first chapel in their midst, to be followed by other priests who ministered to them at a mission known as St. Paul's.[39]

The threat of a rival faith was not the only one the mission in the Tshimakain faced. There were haunting fears it would wither from within. The difficulty of converting the Spokanes continued as constant as ever. If faulty communication were the cause of missionary failures, something was being done about that. In December, 1842, Walker returned from Spalding's mission and its printing press with a sixteen-page publication, a "marvellous little book . . . the first ever printed in the Flathead [Salish]," Mrs. Walker described it. It was the result of a project Walker and Eells had begun in October, with Big Head's assistance.[40] Its title, freely translated, was *The First That Was Written. Thus Writes The Creator.* It introduced its readers to letters, with a key to their pronunciation, figures, lessons in spelling and numbers, lessons in simple sentences and short stories, and finally, more lessons in which Adam and Moses appeared prominently, as well as God and Christ.[41] At one time De Smet had suggested to Walker that, because of their common belief in the Trinity, they adopt a common phraseology, a suggestion to which Walker did not take kindly.[42]

Now that they had educational materials, the missionaries were concerned about a shortage of students. In January, 1843, Walker reported to the board that attendance at the mission school was small, and that a school established some five miles away was

[38] Drury, *First White Women,* II, 172.
[39] Jonathan Edwards, *An Illustrated History of Spokane County, Washington,* 138–41. Hereafter cited as *History.*
[40] Drury, *First White Women,* II, 239, 241.
[41] The Reverend Myron Eel[l]s, D.D., "The First Book Written in the State of Washington," *The Washington Historian,* Vol. I, No. 4, (July, 1900), 156–59.
[42] Drury, *First White Women,* n. 226.

better attended. Walker would later confess that he was happy when the Indians were out on their summer rounds, for then they could not crowd too closely on the mission.[43] "The reason," wrote Walker, "why so few have wintered here doubtless is they do not like the restraint our presence imposes upon them."[44] Some of the Indians practiced their medicine right under the eyes of the missionaries, to whom they made what must have been a shocking suggestion—that perhaps one of their medicine men might effect a cure on the sickly Mrs. Eells.[45] Particularly shocking to Walker was their belief in both God and an Evil Spirit, which they justified in the simple reply, "so [our] fathers believed."

In a November report to the board, Eells wrote that, with fewer salmon in the Columbia, the Indians would be forced to devote more time to farming, the means by which he hoped to make them like white men and accept his religion. Yet, in 1844, as Walker was building a schoolhouse for the Indians, they sat by, gaming. "Our ears," wrote Mrs. Walker, "are annoyed by night by the song of gamblers."[46] Early that year, Big Head had come a half-dozen cattle closer to being civilized.[47] By 1846, that chief was reported to have a herd of fifty cattle. But they were soon reduced to a mere two by the severe winter of 1846–47.[48] The dancers gyrating in the January Chinook (warm wind) ceremonies were more interested in saving their horses than Big Head's cattle; horses made the Indians less soil-bound than did cattle. The Indians returned to the mission (many on snowshoes) in greater numbers, thanks to heavy snows which not only had destroyed their horses but had increased their own diseases, driving them from the root grounds to the missionaries for medicines

[43] *Ibid.*, n. 278–79.
[44] "Walker Letters," 118.
[45] Drury, *First White Women*, II, 247.
[46] Letter of Eells, March 23, 1844, *Missionary Herald*, Vol. XL, No. 11 (November, 1844), 384–86; Myra F. Eells letter to Mrs. Aaron Rogers; Drury, *First White Women*, II, 274.
[47] In the summer of 1843, Walker had paid for a suit of clothes in part by trading cows to the Indians for horses which he exchanged for the clothes through Chief Factor McDonald at Fort Colville. "Walker Letters," 128–29.
[48] Loss of Indian livestock was heavy in the entire upper Columbia Valley that winter.

—cayenne pepper tea and light cathartics to induce skin eruptions, and salts of nitrous acid to relieve dryness and soreness of the throat.[49] By January, 1846, Walker had translated a portion of the Gospel of Matthew from the Greek into the Spokane language.

The artist Paul Kane, enjoying the hospitality of the mission for a week in September, 1847, noted that its occupants were "happily located," and that the Spokanes treated them with great affection and respect. "No influence, however," he wrote, "seems to be able to make agriculturists of them, as they still pursue their hunting and fishing, evincing the greatest dislike to anything like manual labor." The spectacular Kettle Falls and its natives caught his artist's eye, as it had every traveler in those parts. Kane wrote that, like salmon battering themselves to death against the falls, "suicide prevails more among the Indians of the Columbia River than in any other portion of the continent which I have visited." As he saw it, the deaths were largely the aftermath of gambling losses.[50]

Before leaving the falls, Kane dropped down to the nearby village of Kettle Falls (Chualpay) Indians to paint his now-famous "Scalp Dance by Spokane Indians" in oils on canvas. Its central figure, a woman who had lost her husband to the Blackfeet, whirled around a fire swashing and kicking in revenge a Blackfoot scalp on a stick. Behind her, eight painted women danced and chanted, as did the rest of the tribe to the beat of drums.[51]

Kane departed the mission to be followed by another artist, John Mix Stanley. He arrived in late October, 1847, to spend a month in the Tshimakain area painting portraits.

He painted more portraits of Spokanes than of any other Indians among the tribes of the interior. Unfortunately they were destroyed in the Smithsonian Institution fire in Washington, D.C. on January 24, 1865. Stanley intended to continue his por-

[49] "Walker Letters," 133–a.

[50] In *Traits of American Indian Life and Character*, by "a Fur Trader" [Peter Skene Ogden?], p. 49, the author, who had traveled in the Columbia River country, wrote that Indians killed themselves "under some momentary impulse of desperate exitement." He further wrote that suicides were most common among females, due possibly to the "cruel usage" to which they were subjected.

[51] Kane, *Wanderings*, 307–16.

A sketch of a photograph taken of three Spokanes by the British Boundary Commission between the United States and Canada in 1859. The gun held by the Indian in the center was borrowed from the chief trader at the Hudson's Bay Company at Fort Colville. From John K. Lord, *The Naturalist in Vancouver Island and British Columbia.*

The Spokane River in the general area of the Narrows, not far from Old Fort Spokane. This photograph dates from 1904.

A grave house on Peone Prairie, northeast of present-day Spokane, photographed at the turn of the century. Some Spokanes built this type of burial marker over the graves of their dead only after contact with whites.

Famed self-taught painter of the American West George Catlin portrayed two Indians he identified as Spokanes of the mid–1800's: Sims-tów-el, a chief (left) and Jim-jim-tén-ne, a warrior.

Courtesy of the National Gallery of Canada, Ottawa

Scalp Dance by Spokane Indians, a painting by the artist Paul Kane. It was done in 1847 in a village near Kettle Falls. The woman in the center had been widowed when the Blackfeet killed

Courtesy of the Oregon
Historical Society

Mrs. Mary Walker, one of the first two white women to live among the Spokanes, arriving in 1838.

Part of the Tshimakain mission, twenty-five miles northwest of present-day Spokane, from a sketch for the Pacific Railroad Reports. It was the first mission among the Spokanes, founded in 1838 by Walker and Eells. It lasted ten years.

The Reverend Elkanah Walker, one of the first two missionaries to the Spokanes. His appearance made the Indians fear him and call him "chief."

The Reverend Cushing Eells (left) hoped to make the Spokanes live like white men and accept his religion. Helen Clark (right), a Scottish Presbyterian, arrived on the Spokane Reservation in 1894 as a missionary-teacher to the Spokanes. When she arrived on the reservation there were only trails, no roads. She was the only white woman among the Spokanes, to whom she was devoted. She was innovative and taught them many practical methods for everyday life as well as spiritual concerns.

Courtesy of the Library of Congress

"Battle of Col. Steptoe on the In-gos-so-man Creek. W. J. fought 17th of May 1858," sketched by Gustavus Sohon.

A sketch of Spokane Garry (left) by Sohon, 1855. Colonel George Wright (right), who defeated the Spokanes in their war with the whites in 1858. Afterward, he told Garry: "I did not come into this country to ask you to make peace; I come here to fight. Now when you are tired of the war, and ask for peace, I will tell you what you must do."

"Battle on the Spokan Plain—Col. G. Wright in command and against combined forces of the Indians, 1858," drawn by Gustavus Sohon.

trait work at Whitman's mission, but from Fort Walla Walla on December 2 he wrote Walker and Eells that it was his "melancholy duty" to inform them of one of the most tragic massacres on record in Oregon. He was referring, of course, to the Whitman massacre of November 29, perpetrated by Cayuse Indians. Although shocked by the news, Walker and Eells must not have been completely surprised to hear it, as rumblings of Indian discontent in the lower country had grown louder each year. A historian of the American Board's Oregon mission has summarized the reasons for Indian restlessness around the Whitman mission as: (1) the large white immigration of 1843, which passed by it on the Oregon Trail, and was soon followed by others; (2) the death of one of the Indians, Elijah Hedding, killed on a trip to California[52]; (3) the Indians' belief that Whitman was more interested in ministering to whites than to them, particularly as regards physical needs resulting from the measles epidemic in the fall of 1847; (4) rivalries growing out of conflicting claims of Protestant and Roman Catholic missionaries; and finally, (5) lies spread by half bloods that Whitman was poisoning the Indians to get their lands and horses.[53]

The Spokanes immediately promised to protect their teachers. The Cayuse would have to kill them first, they said.[54] Three Spokane chiefs came with pledges of support, saying that Indians

[52] The Indians of the interior had often accompanied Hudson's Bay Company brigades to the area around the Sacramento in California in the 1820's and 1830's. Alice Bay Maloney (ed.), *Fur Brigade to the Bonaventura John Work's California Expedition 1832–1833*, iv–v. Thus, these Indians were no strangers to that area. According to the anonymous author of *Sketches of Mission Life Among the Indians of Oregon*, 199–207, Elijah Hedding, son of Walla Walla Chief Peupeumoxmox, had gone in the winter of 1844–45 with his father down to Captain Sutton's [Sutter's] fort to kill elk and deer and catch wild horses, which they were invited to bring to the fort to exchange for cattle. There, white men killed him because he had failed to bring branded horses and mules belonging to the fort, as agreed upon. Elijah's father had maintained that the animals had not been brought in because they had escaped. Certain white people were as grieved at his death as were the Indians. Particularly so were the Methodists who had taught Elijah in the Willamette Valley, after which, on his return home, he had "lost his piety," to have it restored at a Methodist camp meeting at their mission at the Dalles.

[53] Drury, *First White Women*, II, 305.

[54] *Ibid.*, II, 326; "Walker Letters," 133.

from below would not come north without first sounding out Big Head.[55] The missionaries also received assurances from Fort Colville that they could come to that place for sanctuary. Big Head, ailing badly, finally showed up at the mission on January 2, 1848, saying the Cayuses would not bother the missionaries so long as the Spokanes were camped near the mission; the crucial time, he said, would be when the Spokanes left for the root grounds. He sent messages to everyone to be calm and for the missionaries to darken their windows at night and not let Indians from outside the area enter their houses, whatever their reasons. Big Head knew that a rumor (soon found to be false) was spreading that whites in the Willamette Valley had killed sixty Indians who had gone there seeking winter employment, and that the Spokanes might retaliate against the two Spokane missionaries. Big Star conferred with missionaries in February, echoing what Big Head had said earlier—that if their teachers left, the Spokanes would be a laughing stock among the other tribes for not protecting them. Walker and his colleague chose to sit tight for the moment, deciding to regulate their actions by those of the Oregon Provisional Government.[56]

On March 6, 1848, word came that some three hundred Americans had defeated the Cayuses in a battle fought on February 24. The news had a subduing effect on the Spokanes. A week later the Walkers and Eellses, still uncertain of their own safety, decided to escape to the safer ground of Fort Colville. But after a three-day stay at the fort, the two men returned to Tshimakain.

On April 1, Eells left Tshimakain to hold council with Big Head and other important chiefs, one of whom was "Half-Sun" (Sulktalthscosum), the influential Columbia chief and father of the equally influential nineteenth-century chief, Moses.[57] After dark, the largest lodge in Big Head's camp was packed. The Indians said, "We are loyal to the Americans. We are ready to make

[55] Drury, First White Women, II, 326, n.
[56] Drury, Elkanah and Mary Walker, 209; Drury, First White Women, II, 336 n.
[57] Robert H. Ruby and John A. Brown, Half-Sun on the Columbia: A Biography of Chief Moses.

proof of what we say. We are scantily supplied with arms and am-munition. We wish you to write our words and send them to the White Chiefs—Those wise in heart, great in war, and powerful in speech." In a dramatic gesture, Eells took his New Testament from his pocket, extending it for Big Head and Half-Sun each to place his hand upon it and promise to live up to their commit-ments to remain at peace. Eells also wrote out a message that the Spokanes were peaceful and sent it to Fort Waters, a makeshift adobe post recently established on the site of the Whitman mis-sion. At the same time, a party of Yakimas was assuring the com-mandant at Fort Lee, a hastily built stockade at the Dalles, that neither they nor their neighbors, the Spokanes, wanted to fight the Americans.

Although the Palouses had assisted the fleeing Cayuse killers (of the Whitmans) in escaping across the Snake River and some Palouses had fought the Oregon Provisional Government forces in one battle, a Palouse chief, Hasilauiatsa, now sought to dis-associate his people from the hunted ones and throw in their lot with the Spokanes, who were on better terms with the whites. On May 5, two Spokane chiefs—Polatkin living near the site of old Fort Spokane, and Thlumanalakin, head of a small band some ten miles further up the Spokane River—rode into the mission with Hasilauiatsa to request Eells to intercede with the military on their behalf. Eells apparently did so. He helped effect an ar-rangement to send a friendly delegation to Fort Waters. Eells be-lieved that, through his intercessions, friendly relations had been established between the Spokanes and the military.[58]

On May 10, 1848, Eells received a letter from Colonel Jesse Waters, commanding First Company, Oregon Rifles, offering to aid him if he needed help.[59] About noon of May 22, an express reached Colonel Waters from Eells and Walker with news that a

[58] Eells to Greene, July 17, 1848, Eells Collection, Vol. 248, Letter 107.
[59] Although the boundary between Great Britain and the United States had been established two years earlier at parallel 49, the territory below it thus being American, the troops pursuing the Cayuse killers were from the Oregon Provisional Government. The Mexican War was greatly responsible for the absence of U.S. Army troops in Oregon and for the delay in its becoming a territory.

portion of the Spokanes had come down to join them should their services be needed. These Spokanes reported to Colonel Waters that there were in their country some thirty head of cattle belonging to Cayuse Chief Teloukoikt, and offered to drive them wherever the colonel ordered—which was straight to the army. Waters also accepted forty-three armed Spokanes as allies. The next day, the Spokanes brought him two Indians thought to be spies. They claimed to be Nez Percés and said that Teloukoikt and his party had fled to the mountains, leaving many horses and cattle behind guarded by a few Indians on the Snake River. Waters immediately dispatched a Major Joseph Magone to bring in the stock.[60]

On May 28, an Indian brought word to Eells from Magone that he expected to arrive at Tshimakain with a party to conduct the missionaries out of the country. Despite the feelings of their Indians, Eells and Walker accepted the offer from the troops. On May 29, the troops crossed the Spokane River. Arriving at Tshimakain, they planted their banners on one of the houses. When Eells and Walker returned from Fort Colville that same day, they said they did not fear the Indians but that they thought it best to withdraw for a while until matters assumed a more "pacific aspect." Several Spokanes came to bid them farewell, also to ask questions. Why had the soldiers come? Eells and Walker explained why, reinforced with words from Major Magone, that the conduct of the Spokanes had been gratifying to the Americans, but that if some mischief were to befall their teachers, the Indians would be blamed. Where were the soldiers going? To the lower country. How long would they be gone? A most difficult question to answer. It was not, they assured the Spokanes, their purpose to abandon the station for good, yet they could not be sure that such would not be the case. To his board (and not to the Spokanes), Eells wrote: "The future, to us is dark & uncertain."

As Mrs. Eells sat on a bale of goods awaiting departure, an old Indian in a dirty buckskin shirt and greasy buffalo skin sat beside

[60] *Oregon Spectator*, July 27, 1848, p. 4; Elwood Evans, *History of the Pacific Northwest: Oregon and Washington*, I, 284. Hereafter cited as *History of the Pacific Northwest*.

her to say his farewells: "Our hearts cry because you are going away. It will be dark when our teachers are gone. You do not need to go. No one will hurt you. Even if its best for Mr. Walker and his little children to go, you and Mr. Eells can stay. And, even if the Cayuses do come to kill you, I know where there is a hollow tree in the woods and I will take you and your little boys and cover you all with my buffalo skin so they can not see you."[61]

The party moved quickly from the mission that day. "Solemn thoughts crowd my mind," wrote Eells. "This is the termination of my labors for a time, perhaps forever." A decade earlier Spalding and Gray had looked north across the Spokane River in hope; now their successors looked across it in sorrow.

Equally solemn and baffling thoughts continued to crowd the minds of the Spokane flock at the removal of their teachers. The Spokanes knew that the killers were in retreat; the missionaries knew that, too. Yet they knew that as long as the killers were at large, they or other disgruntled Indians could do more damage. Not until two years later would the Cayuses, convinced that further war would be their ruin, deliver up five of their guilty tribesmen to the whites for hanging. The missionary party moved southward, past the Whitman mission, to the security of white civilization in the Willamette Valley.[62]

In 1851, a large party of Spokanes came there, to Oregon City, where they held morning and evening prayers in a tent and, at one time, sixty of them visited Anson Dart, Oregon superintendent of Indian affairs, to request him to send Eells and Walker, or other missionaries, to them.[63] An impressed Dart called them "the best and most honest tribe of Indians" in his vast superintendency. Eells was happy to hear that Spokanes in the 1850's had treated miners traveling to the interior courteously. One miner, Eells proudly reminisced, said that if he had dropped a twenty-dollar gold piece in a worshiping congregation of Spokane In-

---

[61] Dubuar Scrapbook, No. 95, p. 15.
[62] *Oregon Spectator*, July 13, 1848, p. 1.
[63] Drury, *First White Women*, II, 353; *Report of Anson Dart, Superintendent of Indian Affairs for Oregon Territory to Hon. L. Lea, Commissioner of Indian Affairs*, 478–89.

dians, he would more likely have got it back than had he dropped it in a congregation of whites.

Nearly a decade later, Eells spent the summers of 1860 and 1861 in the Walla Walla Valley, where delegations of Lower Spokanes came to confer with him. On a tour of Tshimakain with power of attorney from the American Board to mark out mission claims, Eells, in late August, 1862, was greeted by members of his old congregation hurrying horseback up the steep banks of the Spokane River, shouting, "Welcome, teacher!" William Three Mountains, more mature and pious now, told Eells that his homecoming had been in answer to their prayers to God. Big Star, now head chief with the death of Big Head, told him that no white man's blood had been shed on his peoples' lands. Yet between the time the missionary left Tshimakain and his return, certain Spokanes *had* spilled blood to bring dark days to all three bands.

CHAPTER FOUR

Gospel or Gunpowder?

Two events occurring in the 1840's at Sutter's Fort in the Sacramento Valley of California had a significant effect upon the Spokanes, although they lived a thousand miles from there. One of these was the death of Elijah Hedding. This was a contributing cause to the Whitman massacre, which embroiled the innocent Spokanes in all kinds of trouble. The other, the discovery of gold in 1848, brought miners in great numbers to the West in hopes of finding more. The Spokane country, lying open and tributary to the Columbia River valley, could not long escape their search.

George Gibbs, writing from Astoria on June 26, 1850, told a story he had heard of how miners had learned of gold in the Spokane country: an Indian chief took a bit of black sand he had found to his priest, telling him he had found the "Boston *Skookum pollalle*" ("American white man's big gunpowder"). The priest examined it carefully, then put it away, warning the chief he would curse him if he divulged the secret to anyone. If he did, the "Bostons" would soon overrun the country and exterminate his race. The Indian chief, still believing the black sand to be gunpowder, brought a powder horn full of it down to Portland and showed it to a trader, hoping to trade it for blankets or clothing. The trader recognized it as gold, and ascertained it to be "excessively rich." Hard times in the Willamette Valley gave it all the more glitter. The Indian, despite the offer of large bribes, refused to tell where he had gotten it.[1] An envoy of the French government, traveling in the Oregon country in 1851–52, confirmed stories of the close-mouthed attitude of the Spokanes regarding gold in their country. "These rascally Spokanes," he wrote, "stubbornly refuse to divulge its location. It is still a secret to be gotten from them."[2]

The secret, however, was soon out. The *Oregon Spectator* (Oregon City, O.T.) reported on May 2, 1850, that gold specimens from the Spokane country were on display at the Cascades townsite (below the Dalles).[3] On May 30, the *Spectator* reported that one of the richest mines on the Pacific Coast had been discovered in the Spokane country. This claim was based on the word of Captain N. Crosby, who had seen the Spokane sand and was convinced that it was, in the bulk, about a quarter gold.[4] On July 11, that same newspaper reported that, after some weeks of exploring the Yakima and Spokane countries for gold, several gentlemen had returned with but little of it. The editor hopefully opined that gold would be found in greater amounts when the streams in those parts receded.[5] But the next season or two along the Spokane proved disappointing, forcing the gold-seekers to try their fortunes deeper in the interior.[6]

In 1853 an exploring party under the command of Captain George McClellan, destined to be a national figure in the Civil War, made its way up the Columbia River. The party was on a

---

[1] Vernon Carstensen (ed.), *Pacific Northwest Letters of George Gibbs*, 12.

[2] M. de Saint-Amant, *Voyages en Californie et dans l'Orégon par M. De Saint-Amant envoyé du gouvernement Francais en 1851–1852*, 365.

[3] *Oregon Spectator*, May 2, 1850, p. 2.

[4] *Oregon Spectator*, May 30, 1850, p. 2.

[5] *Oregon Spectator*, July 11, 1850, p. 2.

[6] For an account of gold mining in the interior at that time, and in subsequent years, see William J. Trimble, *The Mining Advance into the Inland Empire*. Hereafter cited as *Mining Advance*.

mission of War Department railroad crews, who were surveying that country for possible routes to the north Pacific. They made their way to Fort Colville, staffed now only by its then chief factor, Angus McDonald, son of Archibald McDonald, and some twenty Canadian and Iroquois Indians. They, too, hunted gold along the way.

At Fort Colville they met Isaac I. Stevens, head of the northernmost Pacific railroad surveys. Stevens was governor of Washington Territory, which had been created by an act of March 2, 1853. Under this act, he was to be ex officio superintendent of its Indian affairs, representing federal control. Stevens had delivered many speeches to the Indians in surveying the country westward from St. Paul. He had held important councils on both sides of the Rocky Mountains, on the east with the Blackfeet, and on the west with the Flatheads. He sought to put an end to their ancient rivalry, which posed as great an obstacle to the building of a railroad as the Rocky Mountains themselves. He told the Flatheads that the Blackfeet desired to meet them, the Nez Percés, Spokanes, and Bannacks the following year at Fort Benton to end their numerous buffalo wars.

Young Blackfeet were for burying the hatchet—in the skulls of these intruders on their lands. Cooler Blackfeet heads were not averse to ending their wars with these western tribes, having found them to be tough fighters. Usually outnumbered, the Salishan tribes seldom picked fights. In pursuing buffalo herds, they left no brush bent or grass pressed to reveal their movements. When the sides were evenly matched, they won as many skirmishes as they lost. They were especially skilled in stealing Blackfeet horses, regarding the thefts not as athletic feats, as did Plains Indians, but enterprises to make their long journeys to the plains more profitable. After battles in which they lost no one to death or to the enemy, they celebrated victory dances for two or three nights, sometimes twirling Blackfeet scalps, a practice learned from the Blackfeet. The songs accompanying their dances must have seemed like dirges to occasional captive Blackfeet women and children. These human prizes, along with booty and buffalo hides, would be taken back across the Rocky Mountains, where the women would be adopted into the tribes and become wives of their captors.

It was customary for able-bodied Spokanes to go "to buffalo" in October and November and return in February and March. Often they carried parfleches of salmon, but they usually saved them to trade with the Blackfeet for buffalo hides. Stevens joined McClellan and three other men in a journey to the old Tshimakain mission. In the group was John Mix Stanley, the artist, who had come west with Stevens. For him it was a homecoming of sorts; he had been there six years earlier, but the mission presented a different appearance to him than before. The Walker house was standing, but the Eells house had burned down. Garry had permitted an American, Solomon Peltier, to settle near the mission. The party found at the old mission some two hundred Spokanes, and Garry, then in his forty-second year. "I have now seen a great deal of Garry," Stevens wrote, "and am much pleased with him. Beneath a quiet exterior he shows himself to be a man of judgment, forecast, and great reliability, and I could see in my interview with his band the ascendancy he possesses over them."[7]

Garry and his band had likewise warmed toward the party. They now knew that Stevens and McClellan were on a friendly mission. Less than three months before, another Pacific railroad group under a Lieutenant Rufus Saxton made its way toward the Spokane country. A rumor spread among the Indians that the party was coming to make war. North of the Palouse River, a Spokane Indian found four horses which had strayed from the party's camp; he returned them to the whites. Some of the party, thinking he had hidden the animals and was bringing them for a reward, were all for having him tied and whipped. "But the man had an honest-looking eye," Saxton wrote. "I believed him to be so, and paid him well for his trouble. Had we punished him unjustly, the whole Spokane tribe would have been our enemies, instead of being, as now, our fast friends."

Dr. J. G. Cooper of the McClellan party attributed consump-

[7] *Pacific Railroad Reports*, XII, 148.

tion among all Columbia River tribes to poor clothing and shelter combined with the weakness of constitution induced by poor nutrition. He further observed that all Columbia River tribes suffered chronic eye inflammations from accumulated smoke in badly ventilated lodges, teeth flattened not by decay but wear, leg muscles atrophied from lack of walking in their overdependence on canoes and horses for mobility. On the positive side he could report that, although they still relied on charms and incantations, their "severe hydropathic" practice of hot vapor baths followed by plunges into cold water was fast giving way to other remedies.[8]

The Spokanes were reduced in numbers from what they had been twenty years earlier. This was due not only to consumptive diseases, but also to the severe measles epidemic of 1847. The smallpox raging on the west side of the Columbia River, which was taking a heavy toll of life at the time of the survey party's visit, had not yet struck the east side of the upper Columbia, where Roman Catholic priests had vaccinated many of the principal tribes. But the smallpox moving along the banks of the Columbia soon caught up with the Spokanes. Adrian Hoecken, S.J., missionary to the Flatheads, wrote that the Spokanes and others near them feared the vaccine to be poison, and, as a consequence, "were swept away by hundreds." The Spokanes tried to avoid the contagion by scattering about the country in small bands.[9]

Garry conducted Stevens and McClellan from Tshimakain south across the Spokane River and east to his camp, about fifty yards from the site of the old Spokane House, now completely destroyed. The surveyors saw that the area would be a most likely stretch of land for any Pacific railroad. "All great difficulties of location upon the route . . . cease at the valley of the Spokane," wrote Lieutenant Saxton.[10] Although no wars had recently brok-

[8] *Ibid.*, I, 180.
[9] Adrian Hoe[c]ken, S.J. to Editor, *Précis Historiques*, April, 1856, in the Reverend P. J. De Smet, *Western Missions and Missionaries: A Series of Letters*, 302.
[10] *Pacific Railroad Reports*, I, 276.

en out over the jointly held Spokane–Coeur d'Alene land, an uneasy relationship existed between the two peoples, a coolness which had given Stevens considerable concern. McClellan learned, no doubt from Garry presenting the Protestant Spokane point of view, that the Catholic Coeur d'Alenes had taunted his people as heretic believers of a worthless faith. It was Garry who told Stevens of other Pacific railroad survey parties in the area, and Garry who supplied horses for the Stevens-McClellan group when they departed.

On his return to Olympia, capital of Washington Territory, Stevens wrote to the commissioner of Indian affairs about a matter destined to change the Spokane way of life more than any white man had been able to do before. Having been influenced by the thinking of Joel Palmer, his Oregon counterpart, Stevens recommended that the land title of Indians inhabiting the vast area between the Cascade and Rocky Mountains in his territory be extinguished and its aboriginal inhabitants placed on reservations. In Stevens' recommendations, the Spokanes, in the very heartland of this domain, would be placed in a central agency, with a subagency established somewhere in their lands. The commissioner must have welcomed Stevens' correspondence, for he himself had recently felt the need of a systematic policy for dealing with far western Indians to save them from extinction and also to save white settlers from the same fate at their hands. On February 9, 1854, he would urge that treaties be made with the Indians of Washington Territory to ward off trouble between the races, particularly those along the route of the railroad surveys.[11]

Stevens believed that events taking place in his territory necessitated the confinement of the red man. He knew that Indian dis-

[11] Stevens to Geo. W. Manypenny, commissioner of Indian affairs, December 29, 1853. "Communications From the Secretary of the Interior and the Commissioner of Indian Affairs to the Chairman of the Committee on Indian Affairs of the Senate, Recommending Certain Appropriations for the Indian Service," in Secretary of the Interior, *Annual Report, 1853–54* (*Sen. Exec. Doc. No. 34*), pp. 13–16. For an account of the emerging federal policies involving Indians of the Pacific Northwest, see C.F. Coan, "The Adoption of the Reservation Policy in the Pacific Northwest, 1853–1855," *Oregon Historical Quarterly*, Vol. XXIII, No. 1 (March, 1922), 1–38.

content had not been buried along with the Cayuse killers of Marcus Whitman. In the spring of 1852, the Reverend Charles Pandosy, O.M.I., missionary to the Yakimas, heard that all Indians on the left bank of the Columbia, from the Blackfeet at the top to the Chinooks at the bottom, were to assemble to make war on the whites for taking their lands. Pandosy thought the tribes too disunited for war.[12] At that time, the deft brush of artist George Catlin was painting Indian warriors along the Columbia River.

Stevens reported that the Spokanes were on friendly terms with certain settlers near them. The reason for this rapport may have been that most of them were half-bloods married to Indian women. Many of them lived in the Colville Valley, former Hudson's Bay Company servants engaged in raising grains and root crops. Antoine Plante, a French Canadian trapper, stockman, and guide for exploring parties, had settled in the Spokane Valley around 1848; near his home, he ran the first ferryboat service on the Spokane River. Joining Plante was a short, mustached half-blood, Camille, whom the Indians called "Wa-he." Another half-blood ex-fur man named Peone, like Jaco Finlay, had lived among the Spokanes for a long time. They called him "Sea-al" and gave him one of their women for a wife, by whom he had many children. Factor Angus McDonald placed one of Peone's sons, Baptiste, in charge of a company trading post northeast of the falls on a direct route between Lake Coeur d'Alene and the Colville Valley, a spot good for camping and horse racing. Baptiste, too, married an Indian woman, was head of the powerful Peone family, and became chief among the Upper Spokanes on a three thousand-acre fertile prairie (formerly Spokane Prairie) bearing the family name.[13]

Stevens informed the commissioner that Garry had permitted

---

[12] Po[a]ndoz[s]y [Rev. S.J.] to Rev. [Toussaint] Mesplié, April, 1853. Letters Received by the Office of Indian Affairs, 1824–81. Records of the Oregon Superintendency of Indian Affairs, 1842–1880, Roll 611. File Microcopies in Records of the National Archives. Hereafter cited as Oregon Superintendency.

[13] Lewis, "A Daughter of Angus MacDonald," 110–11; Lewis, "Indian Account of the Settlement of the Spokane Country," 4–5.

one white man to settle on Spokane lands. He did not identify him, but he may have been referring to Solomon Peltier at Tshimakain. In 1854 a James Sinclair would settle in the upper Spokane Valley. That same year Garry had a long talk with Colonel B. E. Bonneville at Vancouver on the lower Columbia. Garry had told the colonel that every family of his tribe had a farm and was so desirous of having a mill to grind their wheat that "each man [was willing] to put in a horse" toward the building of one. The relationship between Bonneville and Garry appeared to have been friendly enough. Not so, a year later. In 1855, Colonel Bonneville, evidently acting on reports that Garry had been stirring up trouble, planned to arrest him the first chance he got. James Doty, an Indian agent and secretary to Stevens, told Bonneville to leave Garry alone for fear of stirring up the Indians. This difference of opinion between Doty, representing the Office of Indian Affairs, and Bonneville, representing the military, was typical of the numerous conflicts to come between these two government services. Doty won this round.[14]

Doty urged the governor to arrange a treaty with the Cayuses, Nez Percés, Yakimas, Palouses, and Spokanes before a projected one with the Blackfeet. In May, 1855, Stevens went to deal with the interior tribes at the Walla Walla Council.[15] A delegation of Spokanes was there, joining a throng—some five thousand strong —of Nez Percés, Walla Wallas, Umatillas, Cayuses, Yakimas, and scattered Columbia River tribes. Garry led the Spokane delegation, having been designated by A. J. Bolon, subagent of the central district, as head chief of the Spokanes and interpreter for Indians on the east side of the Columbia River. No doubt, there were chiefs even among the Spokanes who believed Garry not qualified for either position, and that his influence with the whites

14 As late as the Indian outbreaks of the 1870's this conflict between the government agencies had not been resolved.

15 A.J. Bolon to Stevens, March 18, 1854, and A.J. Bolon's Annual Report for the Central District, Records of the Superintendency of Indian Affairs, 1853–74, No. 5, Roll 20 (hereafter cited as Washington Superintendency); Doty to Stevens, March 4, 1855, Washington Superintendency, No. 5, Roll 23.

stemmed only from his knowledge of English. At best, the government policy of designating certain chiefs as tribal heads over entire bands was unpopular among the Indians.

On June 4, Stevens sent up a trial balloon; he proposed a reservation in Nez Percé country, extending from the Blue Mountains to the spur of the Bitterroot and from the Palouse River to part way up the Grande Ronde and Salmon rivers. On this reservation would live Spokanes, Nez Percés, Walla Wallas, Umatillas, and Cayuses. To make the proposal more palatable, he promised these peoples farms and grazing animals, the surplus of which, he said, they could market on the coast to obtain much coveted white man's goods. He also assured them they would find on the reserve an abundant supply of their native foods, salmon, roots, and berries. The following day he clarified and defended his one-big-reservation proposal, explaining how it would protect Spokanes and other tribes much better than if they were placed on smaller reserves, where they would most likely be surrounded by whites. Then, too, there were the customary promises of aid in moving—blacksmiths, farmers, schools, houses, cooking utensils, milkpans, churns, blankets, clothing, and so on.

From the official record of the council we find no words from Garry. He did indeed have much to say—away from the official sessions and off the record—according to rumors passing around the Yakima camps. One which fell on the ear of Father Pandosy was that Garry, Yoctaowitz (Klickitat), the Nez Percé Looking Glass, and the Cayuse Five Crows were the first, in that order, to propose war at Walla Walla.[16] Garry's official silence certainly indicated a coolness, or better, an official detachment from Stevens' proposals. It was up to the governor to make the next move. With the council over, the governor tucked into his bag three treaties (instead of the hoped-for one) with the (1) Nez Percés, (2) Walla Wallas, Cayuses, and Umatillas, and (3) Yakimas, in which the five nations yielded to the United States over sixty thousand square miles of their land. From this "most satisfactory

[16] G[ranville]. O. Haller, "Diary 1856." Entry of July 1, 1856, Haller Papers.

council," Stevens confidently headed east to the land of the Flatheads to treat with them.[17]

By July 16, 1855, at Hell Gate (near present-day Missoula, Montana), Stevens wrung from the Flatheads (actually Flatheads, Kootenays, Pend Oreilles, and Kalispels) a treaty in which they yielded to the United States most of western Montana. Then he continued eastward over the Continental Divide. Near the mouth of the Judith River on the Missouri below Fort Benton (present-day Montana), he effected, on October 17, 1855, a tenuous peace between the Blackfeet and the Flathead confederates and Nez Percés relative to common hunting grounds east of the Rocky Mountains.[18] Stevens then turned westward to conclude treaties with the Spokanes and neighboring tribes, begun at Walla Walla. On October 28, a pony express reached his camp on the eastern side of the Divide with news of the outbreak of the Yakima War.

In this, as in most wars, underlying causes smoldered until sparks set it off. Major Granville O. Haller, one of its participants, later explained its underlying causes as "that aggressive, irritating policy[,] that ever present concomitant of American settlement in new or Indian country—not content with unauthorized and uncompensated seizure and appropriation of Indian lands, [which] finds its satisfaction only in the retirement of the aboriginal owner or occupant from his possessions, from his home, his country."[19] George Gibbs explained it in simpler words: "The *land* is the root of the war."[20]

The discovery of gold in the vicinity of Fort Colville furnished the spark to touch off the war. The same month in which Stevens was at Walla Walla treating with Indians for their lands in hopes

[17] For a good account of the council, see Josephy, *The Nez Perce Indians and the Opening of the Northwest*, 283–332.

[18] For a good account of this council, see Robert Ignatius Burns, S.J., *The Jesuits and the Indian Wars of the Northwest*, 96–123. Hereafter cited as *Jesuits and Indian Wars*.

[19] Granville O. Haller, "Autobiography Correspondence Notes," Folder H 142, Part I of Box I, Haller Papers.

[20] James G. Swan, *The Northwest Coast: or Three Years' Residence in Washington Territory*, 429.

of making the interior safe for whites, certain whites were trespassing on those lands. The intruders were gold prospectors in the
Spokane and Colville areas. There they discovered "fabulous
wealth," so affirmed one Dr. Wilson, a mineralogist sent by Port-
landers to the upper country to prove the wealth of its diggings.[21]
Portland, like cities along Puget Sound, stirred with excitement.
The editor of the *Weekly Oregonian* (Portland, O.T.) wrote
on June 30, 1855, that he had stopped the presses at the news of
gold discoveries at the mouth of the Pend Oreille River, some
thirty miles up the Columbia River from Fort Colville.[22]

In August came more proof of the discoveries—a gold display
at the Portland office of Wells Fargo. In that month Kaimishkon,
the Spokane chief, once a subject for the artistry of John Mix
Stanley, waited on the right bank of the Spokane River to welcome a party of miners with twenty-three horses on their way to
the Colville country. Kaimishkon and his men escorted them
across the stream, receiving for their good turn a shirt and a little
flour and tobacco. Then the chief led them up the trail to the old
Tshimakain mission, expressing along the way his wish of making
a treaty with the whites.[23] Fortunately for the miners, Kaimishkon
had been conditioned in contacts with white men, particularly the
missionaries, to be hospitable to strangers. The editor of the
Oregonian would also give credit to Chief Factor McDonald for
keeping the Spokanes and their neighbors from harassing the
miners. There were other testimonials of their friendliness. In a
letter to the editor of the *Oregonian*, J. J. Wolff wrote from the
Colville Valley that the Spokanes were so incensed at the killing
of a white man that they were all for hanging the guilty party
at once.[24]

Among the Indians of the lower country, particularly the
Yakimas and their Columbia River allies, there was little tolerance. The Yakima Chief Kamiakin, whose lands were more im-

---

[21] H.S. Lyman, "Indian War Recollections," *Oregon Native Son*, Vol. I, No
4 (August, 1899), 210–14.
[22] *Weekly Oregonian*, June 30, 1855, p. 2.
[23] *Weekly Oregonian*, September 1, 1855, p. 2.
[24] *Weekly Oregonian*, October 3, 1857, p. 2.

mediately threatened, sent runners to the Spokane and interior tribes to recruit warriors for his struggle against the whites, with promises of horses, cattle, and blankets to those joining his cause. Rumors had it that a deputation of hostiles had gone to the Walla Wallas, Cayuses, Columbias, and Palouses, authorized to pay them as high as 500 horses and 250 cattle to entice them into the war.[25] Kamiakin himself went to the Spokane country to secure its natives as allies. On more than one occasion, wearing a Hudson's Bay broadcloth coat with red trimmings and brass buttons, he appeared at Fort Colville to visit Angus McDonald; he received McDonald's warning that it was hopeless for Indians to fight the whites, that killing a white man was like killing an ant, eventually there would be hundreds more to overrun the Indian country.[26]

Acting-governor of Washington Territory C. H. Mason noted on September 23 that four Columbias had murdered a white man from Olympia.[27] Miners crossing the Yakima country had taken liberties with Indian women, which had only increased the war fever among the young braves.[28] Some miners on their way to the diggings had bought potatoes from the Indians; they were fortunate to return home with their scalps. One hotblood, Moses of the Columbias, would later confess that, at this time, his hands had been dipped in blood. So had those of his brother-in-law, Qualchan, son of an Upper Yakima chief. This brave had reportedly boasted to the Spokanes that he had killed plenty of whites and would kill all he could find.[29] It was his practice to relieve miners of their gold and take it to Portland to buy things for his people. In late September, 1855, Yakimas had killed

25 *Pioneer and Democrat*, September 12, 1856, p. 2.

26 Lewis, "The Daughter of Angus MacDonald," *Washington Historical Quarterly*, Vol. XIII, No. 2 (April, 1922), 108.

27 *Pioneer and Democrat*, July 18, 1856, p. 2; Hazard Stevens, *The Life of General Isaac Ingalls Stevens*, II, 114 (hereafter cited as *Life of General Stevens*); C. H. Mason, acting governor, to Major G. J. Rains, September 22, 1855; Virgil F. Field (ed.), *The Official History of the Washington National Guard*, II, 42.

28 Granville O. Haller, "Haller Indian War of 1855-6 in Washington and Oregon," in "Historical of the Early Immigration by American," Part II, p. 14, Haller Papers.

29 "Haller Diary 1855." Entry of September 29, 1856, Haller Papers.

Subagent Bolon, who had planned to take goods to a projected Stevens council with the Spokanes on the governor's return from the Blackfeet country, but had not taken that trip after Garry reportedly informed him that the Yakimas had killed eight white men on their way to the Pend Oreille mines and proposed a general war against the whites.[30]

Around October 1, 1855, Kamiakin was informed that Major Haller was advancing into the Yakima country with five hundred troops. At this news, the chief sent expresses to all the camps to rally their braves to check the major's advance. Haller's command reached Toppenish Creek in the lower Yakima country with a hundred troops and a howitzer to punish the hostiles, but was severely punished itself. Haller was chased back to the Dalles after a three-day seesaw battle with an Indian army estimated variously from eight to fifteen hundred warriors. Besides the Yakimas and Columbias, there had been the Wanapums (from Priest Rapids of the Columbia), Walla Wallas, Palouses, Wenatchees, Chelans and last, but no one knows how least, the Spokanes.[31] A pioneer of the Yakima Valley, A. J. Splawn, friend of many of its Indians and Kamiakin's biographer, claimed that Lot of the Spokanes had been among the hostiles. Which of the two Lots had been in battle, the elder (Big Star) or his tall, angular son, Splawn did not say. Most likely it had not been the elder Lot, friend of Walker and Eells, but his son. This young Lot, in typical brave fashion, may well have been with his close firebrand friends Moses, Quiltenenock, and Qualchan—all known to have been in the thick of the Toppenish fight.[32]

Lieutenant J. Withers, commanding Fort Vancouver, reported on November 12, 1855, to the adjutant general of the army that,

[30] H. H. Bancroft, *History of Washington, Idaho, and Montana 1845–1889*, p. 109; J. Cain, acting superintendent of Indian affairs, Washington Territory, to Manypenny, October 6, 1855, Secretary of War, *Annual Report*, 1855–56 (34 Cong., 1 sess., *House Exec. Doc. No. 93*), 53–54.

[31] Pandosy to Haller (n.d.), Haller, "Autobiography Correspondence Notes."

[32] A. J. Splawn, *Ka-Mi-akin The Last Hero of the Yakimas*, 50, 86. Like his friend Quetalican (Chief Moses), Lot later pursued a peaceful policy and even became an elder in the Presbyterian Church. This led many to believe he had never participated in the wars. Ruby and Brown, *Half-Sun on the Columbia*, 294.

although the Flatheads, Spokanes, Pend Oreilles, and some Nez Percés were not at war with the army, many of their young men were. This was certainly not a surprising development, since individual members of all interior bands were free in peace or war to act independently of their tribes.[33] The Toppenish victory was especially sweet to the young braves since Haller's command was well known to them as Indian killers.[34]

After learning of war to the west, Stevens formulated a plan to push via the Coeur d'Alene to Spokane and call a council of tribes in the vicinity. He would treat with them for their lands before pushing homeward via the Nez Percé country. By this plan he sought to kill several birds with one stone and to save his own scalp.[35] On November 24, 1855, with two of his men and four Nez Percé chiefs, he reached the Coeur d'Alene mission, to find that Yakima emissaries had left there only four or five days before. Had he found them there, it would be difficult to say whose surprise would have been greater, his or theirs. As it turned out, he was able to employ the element of surprise on the Coeur d'Alenes, throwing them off balance and forcing them to make gestures of peace. He learned that the men bringing goods for the originally proposed Spokane council were at Antoine Plante's, along with fifteen miners, under a virtual blockade. With typical dash, Stevens sought to rescue them, although some of his party thought him little short of mad, fearing he would walk into a trap set by hostile Spokanes. To further add to their apprehension, the Coeur d'Alene chief, Stellam, appropriated some of Stevens' supply wagons, which were later regained with Spokane help. Stevens set out for the Spokane country with Looking Glass, the Nez Percé chief, and "four other men of note," arriving at the Spokane

[33] Jno. Withers 1st Lieut. 4th Infantry, Com. Post to Colonel S. Cooper, Adjutant General U.S.A., Washington, D.C., November 12, 1855, Secretary of War, *Annual Report*, 1855–56, pp. 11–14. A letter from Father Joset to Father De Smet the same year told of the attempt of a Spokane chief to stir up war among the northwest tribes, Burns, *Jesuits and Indian Wars*, 147.

[34] Theodore N. Haller, "Life and Public Services of Colonel Granville O. Haller," *Washington Historian*, Vol. I, No. 3 (April, 1900), 103.

[35] Stevens, *Life of General Stevens*, II, 121.

village just below Antoine Plante's a little before sundown, November 28, 1855.

The Spokanes were as surprised as the Coeur d'Alenes at Stevens' sudden appearance, as they thought the Yakima War had forced him eastward down the Missouri River. Recognizing that time was of the essence, Stevens immediately dispatched an express to Colville. He requested the chiefs, the priest, and Angus McDonald to meet him in council. He sent another express to the Indians at the mouth of the Spokane River to come in. On December 1, he issued a proclamation mustering a volunteer company of gold miners at Antoine Plante's into the service of Washington Territory. The miners were among those who had gone into the interior on reading the glowing reports of gold discoveries written by news-hungry editors. War now made good copy for newspapers. Wrote the editor of the Olympia *Pioneer and Democrat* (Olympia, W.T.): "Suppose the Blackfeet, the Cayuse, the Flathead, the Nez Perces, and the Cour de Alines, the Spokanes, the Yakimas, Klikitats, and all the other hordes that infest the other side of the Cascade mountains, were to join in a concert of action against the settlements either of this or Oregon Territory, what have we to oppose them?"[36] Fortunately for coastal whites and miners among the Spokanes, the inland tribes were not acting in concert. Nevertheless, miners were pressed into the service as the "Spokane Invincibles," with a strength of fourteen officers and men, hardly invincible had the Indians been united. The Invincibles were under the captaincy of one Benjamin Franklin Yantis, known to Indians as "the American judge," a Kentuckian and first practicing lawyer in eastern Washington Territory. On December 3, 1855, the governor organized his party as a volunteer company and mustered them into the service as the "Stevens guards."[37]

---

[36] *Pioneer and Democrat*, November 16, 1855, p. 2.

[37] For a listing of personnel in these two companies, see William S. Lewis, " 'Spokane Invincibles' Organized Here in 1855," *Spokesman-Review*, September 5, 1920, Pt. 7, p. 20. Also, see William S. Lewis, "The First Militia Companies in Eastern Washington Territory," *Washington Historical Quarterly* Vol. XI, No. 4 (October, 1920), 243–49.

Stevens had termed the council at Walla Walla "most satisfactory." He would term the one at Spokane "most stormy." Sensing that the Yakima War had made the Indians quite restless, he feared some treachery would befall him, especially at the hands of the Nez Percé chief, Looking Glass. Consequently, he got a half-blood interpreter to eavesdrop. The informer told Stevens of a long conversation between the Nez Percé chief and Garry; Looking Glass had developed a plan to trap Stevens.[38]

By December 4, 1855, most of the chiefs had come in. The Colvilles came with their priest, the Reverend Joseph Joset, S.J. A group of miners of the Colville, who had joined the "Spokane Invincibles," also came. The Coeur d'Alenes attended with Father Ravalli. Some Spokanes and San Poils were there. The Lower Spokanes appeared, as did Garry. The day was snowy, as though nature were giving the governor a cold reception. Stevens called the council to order in Antoine Plante's cabin, hoping to break the ice with the same warm words he had spoken during the week in informal talks before the council opened: "I think it is best for you to sell a portion of your land and move on Reservations, as the Nez Perces and Yakimas agreed to." Sensing their coolness to his words, he said he would delay plans to treat with them for their lands: "My plans might not suit you. Your plans might not suit me. When you want to talk to me about your lands, by and by I shall be ready to talk . . . . I want your hearts. I want you to speak and tell me how you feel."

Chief Garry said: "When you first commenced to speak, you said the Walla Wallas, Cayuses, and Umatillas, were to move onto the Nez Perce Reservation, and that the Spokanes were to move there also. Then I thought you spoke bad. Then I thought when you said that, you would strike the Indian to the heart." Stevens replied that his had been a proposal, not a command.

The next day, a Lower Spokane chief told the governor that the Coeur d'Alenes were angry because he had stopped the traders from selling ammunition, and anyway, "since the word of God came into our country . . . we have arms only for hunting now."

[38] *Pacific Railroad Reports*, XII, 225.

After a Coeur d'Alene had spoken in the same vein, Sgalgalt (interpreted as "Daylight"), a Spokane chief, said that when the Cayuses killed Dr. Whitman, he had sworn never to fight the Americans, as had his fellow chiefs, Sulktalthscosum ("Half Sun") and Big Head, on the Reverend Mr. Eells's New Testament.[39] "I know," said Sgalgalt, "we cannot stop the River from running nor the wind from blowing, and I have heard that you Whites are the same, we could not stop you. For my children I am thinking. I wish they had thin hearts like mine." He meant that he wished they were not so prone to fight. The aging Lower Spokane chief, Big Star, said he had vainly warned Moses of the Columbias to stop killing the whites.

Quinquinmoeso, a subchief living by the old Walker-Eells mission, took his turn to blast the governor for his proposal of placing the Spokanes on Nez Percé lands. "When we received that news we all spoke—all my people, and I told them I could not move from my land. I would not travel the rough country that does not belong to me . . . . Why do you wish to know my heart? It is well arranged. It is you Governor who should take care of me, and I am good towards you. My heart is not hard if you treat me well."

Several other chiefs spoke. Koolkoolleelseh ("Red Blanket") flashed a paper he had got from Oregon Superintendent Anson Dart. Chuckcalloot ("The Bear upon His Back") said there should not be two writings, one good and the other bad, implying that the white man not only spoke with forked tongue but wrote with a pen with two points. Another Indian rose to say that, since the Indians below had been at war, his "heart had been crying"; also that his people had lost blood in the country where the war was, possibly a reference to the Haller engagement.

Garry and Stevens concluded the dialogue. Big Star's admission for the council record that he was deferring to Garry in matters of leadership served to give impetus to Garry's words: "When you look at those red men, you think you have more heart, more sense, than these poor Indians. I think the difference between us

[39] Sattillco or Sulktalthscosum, the Half-Sun, had recently been killed by Blackfeet on the plains.

and you Americans is in the clothing—the blood and body are the same. Do you think, because your mother was white and theirs black, that you are higher or better? We are black, yet if we cut ourselves the blood will be red, and so with the whites it is the same, though their skin is white. I do not think we are poor because we belong to another nation. If you take those Indians to make a peace, the Indians will do the same to you. You see now the Indians are proud. On account of one of your remarks,—some of your people have already fallen to the ground. The Indians are not satisfied with the land you gave them. What commenced the trouble was the murder of Pu-pu-mox-mox's son and Dr. Whitman, and *now* they find their reservations too small. If all those Indians had marked out their own reservations, the trouble would not have happened. If you could get their reservations made a little larger, they would be pleased. If I had the business to do, I could fix it by giving them a little more land. Talking about land, I am only speaking my mind. What I was saying yesterday about not crossing the soldiers to this side of the Columbia is my business. Those Indians have gone to war, and I don't know myself how to fix it up. That is your business. Since, governor, the beginning of the world, there had been war. Why cannot you manage to keep peace? Maybe there will be no peace ever. Even if you should hang all the bad people, war would begin again, and would never stop."

At the conclusion of Garry's exposition, the governor returned to his original theme: "I did not know where the Spokanes, Colville and Coeur d'Alenes would be moved to until I had consulted them, and they had given me their hearts about it." To which Garry responded "All these things we have been speaking of had better be tied together as they are, like a bundle of sticks, because you are in a hurry. There is not time to talk of them. But afterwards you can come back, when you find time and see us."

The governor packed his bags again, but this time there was no treaty in them. "I did not deem it expedient [considering their coldness, he might have added] to enter a treaty for the purchase of their lands, though I expressed to them my willingness to do so, if they were prepared for it; and accordingly agreed with them that a council should be held for that purpose as early in the spring as practicable."

As the council broke up, the chiefs offered men to Stevens to escort him through hostile country on his way to Lapwai in Nez Percé territory.[40] He declined their offer, saying he had not come among the Spokanes for their aid but to protect them as their father. On fresh mounts obtained from the Spokanes, Stevens and his party departed on a snowy, rainy trip made no more pleasant by rumors that Kamiakin had crossed the Columbia River, where he or his allies could have cut the governor's trip short. At Lapwai, Stevens found the Nez Percés "staunch and entirely reliable," but heard rumors that a portion of the Spokanes had already marched to Kamiakin's aid. To keep up with events in the Spokane country, he dropped a letter to Special Agent Colonel William Craig to communicate with settlers and Indians in the interior from time to time.[41] Before leaving Walla Walla, Stevens assigned the local special agent, B. F. Shaw, to "keep up a constant communication" with the friendly Indians.[42] Stevens also sent George Montour, a half-blood British subject, as special agent among the Spokanes. The governor returned to Olympia on January 19, 1856, to be greeted by a 38-gun salute, one for each state in the Union. He learned that less ceremonial shots were being fired on the coast, for the war had spread there from the interior.[43]

[40] A communication was sent from Anthony Ravalli, S.J., to the Honorable H. R. Crosbie to the effect that the Spokanes and other tribes meeting with Stevens had "promised never to help the Yakimas." Crosbie read this correspondence in the House of Representatives to oppose a bill introduced there, which would have prevented aliens acting as teachers or missionaries among the Indians of Washington Territory. Such legislation was aimed at Roman Catholic missionaries, whom some lawmakers believed to have encouraged the interior Indians in their resistance to whites.

[41] Stevens letter to Lieutenant Colonel Wm. Craig.

[42] Stevens letter to Manypenny, November 1, 1856, in Washington Superintendency, No. 5, Roll 2.

[43] Accounts of the Spokane Council are found in James Doty, "Journal of Operations of Governor Isaac Ingalls Stevens, Supt. of Indian Affairs and Commissioner, Treating With the Indian Tribes East of the Cascade Mountains, in Washington Territory," etc.; *Pacific Railroad Reports*, XII, 224–25; Stevens, *Life of General Stevens*, II, 130–42; *Pioneer and Democrat*, January 25, 1856, p. 2.

Immediately on his arrival at Antoine Plante's, Montour assembled the principal Spokane and Coeur d'Alene chiefs. Chief Sgalgalt promised he would do everything possible to stop his young men from joining the hostiles, vowing to chase the warriors until they surrendered their arms to him. Proof of his sincerity was evidenced only five days earlier when he had rebuffed Kamiakin, despite his "impassioned plea" for a general uprising throughout the area to expel whites from Indian land.[44] One of Garry's chiefs, the English-speaking Polatkin, said, "I love everyone now that I have grey hair." But he complained that, if the Spokanes were only better armed, they could chase their enemies from their lands.

Garry likewise warned Stevens that, in pursuing the hostiles, he should come no closer to Spokane lands than the Columbia Plateau by way of Rock Island on the mid-Columbia. As for the Spokane land cessions, he said, "If it is agreeable to you we will seal the bargain. If it is not, we won't do it and we will always be good friends. Something which one loves one does not sell and something we don't care much about we can give up." Garry rebuked Stevens for lingering too long in the Blackfeet country before coming to talk with the Spokanes, a delay which had kept Garry out of the lower country to care for his cattle. As a consequence, the hostiles had killed them.[45] Angus McDonald wrote Stevens that things were quiet in the Spokane country, that he had heard of no Spokane party joining Kamiakin.

The Scot could afford to take a lighter view of the situation; he was a factor of the Hudson's Bay Company, against whom the Indians would not have raised a hand. He personally disliked the governor's treaties and reservations as devices ruining both the Indians' primitive life and the fur trade. The Indians often came to the tall wiry factor with their grievances. He understood them,

---

[44] Stevens to Hon. Jefferson Davis, July 7, 1856, Secretary of War, *Annual Report*, 1856–57 (34 Cong., 3 sess., *House Exec. Doc. No. 894*), Vol. I, Pt. 2, p. 169.

[45] Letters from Spokane and Coeur d'Alene chiefs to Stevens, January 30, 1856. Translated from the French by Elizabeth Racy. Washington Superintendency, No. 5, Roll 23.

dressed like them, and even preferred living in a lodge to living in a house. One chief said to him, "'Tis many snows since I have lost my country. Two white chiefs split it in two with a line [the Canadian–American boundary], and they take both sides of it and say all belongs to them."[46] McDonald didn't like the boundary line any more than the Indians did.

Stevens advised General John E. Wool, commander of the Division of the Pacific, that a military force be placed on the Columbia Plateau between the Spokanes and the hostiles to prevent the latter from infecting young Spokanes with war fever. This was only one of many exchanges between Stevens and Wool regarding the conduct of the war in the interior, with Wool seeking to keep military operations there to a minimum.

In May, 1856, Stevens had intelligence from Craig in the Nez Percé country leading him to believe that the Spokanes were still friendly.[47] He received word the same month from Montour at the Dalles that the Spokanes wanted to see him very much, a wish confirmed in writing from Garry, Polatkin, and a Coeur d'Alene chief. Garry said he was keeping some Cayuses in his country advising them against war. Polatkin conveyed the message, by then almost a Spokane byword: "We have never shed the blood of the Americans." The next day, Stevens would write Polatkin saying he hoped they never would.[48] There were, however, in the chiefs' letters, strong overtones of impatience with the governor for his delay in treating with them. It made for a virtual quarantine of their people; they feared going into the lower country, where they could easily become entangled with the hostiles.[49]

These letters set poorly with Stevens, especially those relating to Garry's riding herd on the Cayuses. He believed these Cayuses

[46] McDonald to Stevens, January 27, 1856, and April 6, 1856, Washington Superintendency, No. 5, Roll 23; Albert J. Partoll, "Angus McDonald, Frontier Fur Trader," *Pacific Northwest Quarterly*, Vol. XLII, No. 2 (April, 1951), 141–42.

[47] *Pioneer and Democrat*, May 9, 1856, p. 2.

[48] Stevens to Pollotakan [Polatkin], June 5, 1856, Washington Superintendency, No. 5, Roll 2.

[49] H. Tilton to Stevens, May 27, 1856, Washington Superintendency, No. 5, Roll 23; Garry and chiefs to Stevens (received June 4, 1856), Washington Superintendency, No. 5, Roll 23.

and their leader, Five Crows, were up to no good. He authorized Colonel Craig to keep the peace by accepting their unconditional submission and the yielding up of offenders.[50] "The whole interior," wrote Stevens, "is ripe for war . . . [and] the Spokanes, Coeur d'Alenes, Colvills, and Okeakanes have accepted horses as the price of their service." Stevens wrote Garry, stating that he wished to treat with the Spokanes, but that it was not a good time to do so; he would put it off till the war was done.[51]

Father Ravalli wrote to Stevens on behalf of Polatkin, Sgalgalt, and Garry's brother Tlimikum. Polatkin asked the governor to stop the war. Sgalgalt said he was holding his people from war. "Please God," he wrote, "that we will make peace." Garry's brother said he had heard Stevens speak at Walla Walla the year before and that he "must not speak here that way." He also said, "When, after the peace, your children will come in our land for their business may they be very careful not to steal our women, nor even look at them."[52] Interestingly, the very day Father Ravalli recorded Tlimikum's words, General Wool issued an order keeping all settlers and whites, except Hudson's Bay Company personnel, out of the interior. It gave notice to gold miners in the Colville country that, "should they interfere with the Indians or their squaws, they [will] be punished and sent out of the country."[53]

August found Stevens at Walla Walla for a second council, a try at peace with the Indians. He sent a message to the Spokanes that he would advise miners not to enter their lands, but when they did, they should be well treated. The Spokanes, in return correspondence, acceded to the governor's obvious forked-tongue words.[54]

A Nez Percé, Captain John, warned the governor that the Spo-

[50] Stevens letter to Captain F.W.P. Goff.
[51] Stevens to Garry, June 5, 1856, Washington Superintendency, No. 5, Roll 2.
[52] Paoulotkin [Polatkin], Skalhalt [Sgalgalt], and Tlimikum to Stevens, August 2, 1856. Translated from the French by Elizabeth Racy. Washington Superintendency, No. 5, Roll 23.
[53] Secretary of War, *Annual Report*, 1856–57, p. 169.
[54] Stevens to Captain S. H. Robie, February 9, 1857, Washington Superintendency, No. 5, Roll 3.

kanes and their neighbors most likely would not come to the council. Father Ravalli tried, unsuccessfully, to see that they would; only two representatives from the Spokanes appeared— George Montour and Antoine Plante. Some of the military thought the council ill-timed.[55] It also came at the height of the late summer salmon runs. On September 12, 1856, the day after the council opened, Garry wrote to Stevens explaining the situation. It seems that the salmon runs had taken the Spokanes "off the hook."[56] Garry implied that Stevens should not look for his people when the runs were over, for then they planned to go, as was their custom, "to buffalo." He may have believed his peoples' absence would keep them out of the way of the hostiles.

After the breakup of his Walla Walla Council in September, Stevens and an army troop under Colonel E. J. Steptoe were attacked by hostile Nez Percés, Yakimas, Palouses, Columbias, Walla Wallas, and Umatillas. The hostiles forced Stevens back to the Dalles. The governor concluded that "the Indian must feel our strength before permanent relations of amity can be established with him." Stevens obviously questioned the sincerity of Father Ravalli's efforts to gather the Spokanes. Consequently, the father and his fellow priests did not escape the lash of the governor's pen, which wrote: "A hostile country is not the field for missionary labors."[57] Stevens' attitude toward the Spokanes was fairly well summarized in his words: "It will be time enough to consider them hostile when they commit hostile acts, which as yet they have not done."[58]

The year 1857 was quiet as far as the Indian war was concerned, with resistance in the Yakima country all but crushed. Kamiakin had fled that area to beat his war drums farther east. For the moment, at least, Kamiakin was the lesser of two evils facing the Spokanes, the second being an influx of miners taking advantage

[55] Secretary of War, *Annual Report,* 1856–57, pp. 197–98.
[56] Garry to Stevens, September 12, 1856, Washington Superintendency, No. 5, Roll 22.
[57] Stevens to Manypenny, November 1, 1856, Washington Superintendency, No. 5, Roll 3.
[58] Stevens to Robie, February 9, 1857, Washington Superintendency, No. 5, Roll 3.

of the lull in the war to travel over their lands en route to the diggings in the Pend Oreille country. Stevens sought to tranquilize the Indians by appointing "The American judge," Ben Yantis, as special agent to the Spokanes, Coeur d'Alenes, Colvilles, Okanogans, and Kalispels. The new agent believed his appointment had come none too soon, reporting the Spokanes as growing restless because of traffic in ardent spirits carried on by miners and traders in the Colville Valley.[59] The Indians, particularly the Spokanes, he wrote, were opposed to the traffic, and had warned that, if it were not stopped, they would be unable to restrain their young men from violence. Yantis also received complaints from Father Joset and even from some miners on the Pend Oreille River. In correspondence with Yantis about the problem, Colonel Steptoe wrote that he had recently told Garry, "I hoped he would stove in every barrel and keg of liquor he might see and either bring the man who owned it to this place or detain him till I could send a force after him."

Yantis opined that six or seven hundred Spokanes had retrograded since the departure of the Walker-Eells mission, the return of which they wished so strongly that they were willing to pay any number of horses to get it back. Garry, he wrote, was keeping the young braves in line. The Spokanes were surviving on wheat, potatoes, corn, and salmon from good late spring runs. Yantis requested more implements like the plow for the Spokanes, and an appropriation of $20,000 to buy them blankets, calicoes, and other goods. The Spokanes went along with this but wanted to know why the government dealt more kindly with its enemies than it did with them.[60]

On December 7, 1857, Yantis reported the Spokanes' plight as severe. High water had washed out the fall salmon runs; to avoid starvation, many Indians were preparing to go "to buffalo." Agent John Owen in the Bitterroot Valley was not happy to have the Spokanes come his way en route to the plains. In a letter to James

[59] Yantis' Letter, April 17, 1857, Washington Superintendency, No. 5, Roll 20.
[60] Yantis to Nesmith, May 17, 1857; Steptoe to Yantis, June 15, 1857; Joset to Yantis, May 21, 1857; Miners on Ponderray [Pend Oreille] River to Yantis, June 30, 1857, Washington Superintendency, No. 5, Roll 20.

Doty, he wrote that the Nez Percés had sent a general invitation to the Spokanes and the Pend Oreilles to come and kill him at his agency.[61] The Spokanes had no such designs on the major. Father Hoecken, now missionary to the Flatheads, likewise was unhappy the Spokanes were coming his way, for they "endeavor to spread a bad spirit among the Indians" in his "heaven in miniature" (in the Bitterroot Valley). The Spokanes of whom he was critical were not that small band living near his St. Ignatius Mission just below Flathead Lake but their Spokane brothers from the west.

To help the Indians settle down like white men, Yantis requested that the government send four young Americans to live among them, giving each family a hoe and a spade. He had already given them some hoes from those sent up by Stevens. So happy were they to replace the sharpened sticks they were using, wrote Yantis, that they "expressed more gratitude than if I had made them presents of horses."[62]

As far as the whites were concerned, the Indian war was over. J. Ross Browne, special government agent in the West, implied as much when he wrote that a war had taken place, albeit an expensive and disastrous one, the effects of which the territories would suffer for many years. "It was a war of destiny," wrote Browne, the primary cause of which was the "progress of civilization." Hostilities had ended for a while; hostility had not. Official white anger for the actions of the Indians in the war was expressed by Colonel J. W. Nesmith, the superintendent of Indian affairs for Washington and Oregon territories: "It is true that there had been considerable suffering among them, but inasmuch as they are responsible for the late war by their acts of commencing unprovoked hostilities, I have not been in a hurry, or over anxious to relieve them from the legitimate results of their own treachery and folly."[63]

[61] Owen to Nesmith, September 20, 1858, Washington Superintendency, No. 5, Roll 22.

[62] Yantis to Nesmith, December 7, 1857, Washington Superintendency, No. 5, Roll 20.

[63] During a five-week tour of the northwest, Browne found little to commend about the condition of Indian matters. See David Michael Goodman, *A Western Panorama 1849–1875: The Travels, Writings and Influence of J. Ross Browne on*

At the time Browne was writing his epitaph for a war and Nesmith his indictment of its warriors, Indians of the interior were growing increasingly restless. The Spokanes, themselves restless, were epicentral to disgruntled tribes—to the east, the Coeur d'Alenes; to the north, the Colvilles; to the south, the Palouses; and to the west, the Upper Yakimas and Columbias. Because of native demonstrations around Fort Colville, whites in that area petitioned Colonel Steptoe at Fort Walla Walla for a company of soldiers to be located in the valley to protect their lives and property.

Defeat in the war had only stimulated Kamiakin and other Yakimas to gather more Indians to join them in checking the white advance, which they believed to be inevitable with the Indian defeat. A projected government road between Walla Walla and Fort Benton only confirmed their fears. They believed the survey to be a prelude to the seizure of their lands, fears of which bound elements of the Spokanes, Coeur d'Alenes, and Flatheads in a pact to massacre any party making such a survey.[64]

Besides Kamiakin, who, in early spring, 1858, called another council with the Coeur d'Alenes, Palouses, Cayuses, Spokanes, and Nez Percés, another Yakima was keeping the war pot boiling —Qualchan. In the spring of 1858, he delivered an impassioned plea to an Indian assemblage to drive the palefaces into the sea. "Let the war cry be raised," Qualchan harangued, "and let your warriors chant the war song of our race; extermination of the paleface robber who comes to steal your inheritance from you and destroy your people."[65] The Spokanes listened more readily to Qualchan than to Kamiakin. A mild feud between Qualchan's Upper Yakimas and Kamiakin's Yakimas gave Qualchan little enthusiasm for beating Kamiakin's drum. The Spokanes, on their

---

the Pacific Coast, and in Texas, Nevada, Arizona and Baja California, as the First Mining Commissioner, and Minister to China, 121–37. Also, see Nesmith to Charles E. Mix, January 19, 1858, Oregon Superintendency, "Letters Received July 1853–August 1855, September 1856–September 1859."

[64] Steptoe to Major W. W. Mackall, May 23, 1858, Secretary of War, Annual Report, 1858–59 (35 Cong., 2 sess., Sen. Exec. Doc. No. 32), X, 76.

[65] M. M. Cowley, "Fate of Schon-shin," Spokesman-Review, January 1, 1892, p. 12.

part, had not forgotten that Kamiakin's father, Ci-iah (Kiyiyah), had killed some of their members in a feud which began when some Spokanes stole one of his wives.[66]

The older Spokane chiefs urged their people to be cautious in heeding the pleas of Qualchan, Kamiakin and other hotheads, including certain Coeur d'Alenes. The peacemaking of two Spokane chiefs was known in the lower country through the pages of the *Oregonian*, which editorialized that Garry and Big Star had done much to hold their young braves in check. Father Hoecken, it continued, had assumed a similar role among the Coeur d'Alenes.[67] Colonel Steptoe at Fort Walla Walla no doubt knew of these peacemaking attempts but believed them inadequate in the face of many reasons for the Indians to resume hostilities. For two years he had considered the Nez Percés and the Spokanes the key peoples of the interior around whom opposition to the whites would coalesce. "The necessity of controlling by a strong force the Nez Perce and Spokane tribes," he wrote the Secretary of War, "cannot be overestimated."[68]

On May 6, 1858, Steptoe left Fort Walla Walla with two companies of infantry and three of dragoons. His force included 152 men, 5 officers, and a few civilians. They had two mountain howitzers and were otherwise armed with antiquated musketoons, long Mississippi Yager rifles, muzzle-loading pistols—and insufficient ammunition. Their destination: Colville. Why? Probably for several reasons. First, to select a point for a fort on the 49th parallel to protect men then engaged in the international boundary survey. Second, to respond to a petition from miners in the Colville country. Third, to paw, but not maul, troublesome Indians there and along the way, particularly the Palouses. Fourth, to drain off the energies of his men, who were restless from winter confinement. Finally, there was his own restlessness. In a letter to his father, Steptoe had written: "It is a sad thing when one no longer finds excitement a pleasure . . . . Sometimes the greatest

[66] Tomio Kamiakin, "Chief Kamiakin."
[67] *Weekly Oregonian*, June 12, 1858, p. 2.
[68] Secretary of War, *Annual Report*, 1856–57, pp. 197–98.

misfortune of my life appears to have been my introduction to the military profession."[69] As his command moved northward from the Snake River, he did not know how true had been his words. News reached him that the Spokanes would dispute his passage.

Some twenty miles below the falls on a camass ground near present-day Spangle, Washington, in the middle of what the Spokanes called their "garden," the Spokanes were encamped between the Spokane and Snake rivers. When a hunting party brought them news of Steptoe's column moving north, the Indians rode south for a confrontation. It is believed that Big Star hurried his Lower Spokanes home rather than risk hostilities. Besides hostile factions of Spokanes, Coeur d'Alenes, Yakimas, and Palouses, the confrontation-bound Indians included elements of Columbias, Kettle Falls Indians, and disgruntled braves of other tribes. Some Indian sources claim Qualchan as their leader. He was popular among the young braves and married Polatkin's daughter. His brother, Lokout, who survived him, would marry her, too. This enhanced him among the Spokanes.[70] According to Major Owen, Lokout led his peacefully inclined father-in-law into the hostile cause. But we can imagine that Qualchan also played his part in winning over Polatkin.[71] Chief Garry appears not to have been among those wishing to stop Steptoe forcibly. Kamiakin, after an upbraiding by the Palouse chief, Tilcoax, joined the hostiles.

By May 16, they had taken advantageous positions on a ring of hills near Pine Creek, some thirty miles south of the falls. The Indians were several hundred strong; no one is quite sure of their number. Steptoe moved his command slowly forward until he was about to enter the ravine winding along the base of the hills that were crowned with "excited savages." Perceiving them about to attack, Steptoe turned to encamp.

From noon to dusk, the Indians remained a frightening, un-

[69] Steptoe to his father, April 5, 1858, Edward J. Steptoe, Correspondence, "Letters from Steptoe to Various Parties 1846–47, 1855–59."

[70] Cowley, "Fate of Schon-shin."

[71] Owen to Nesmith, September 20, 1858, Washington Superintendency, No. 5, Roll 20.

dulating mass of painted horses and painted men, taunting, war-whooping, yelling, shaking scalps, occasionally rushing the column as though it were a band of Blackfeet, from whom they had learned so much of the trappings and techniques of their warfare. As this preliminary to battle was going on, Spokane and Coeur d'Alene chiefs conversed with Steptoe. Chiefs Amtaken and Sgalgalt held their Spokane braves from attack. That evening a number of chiefs rode to Steptoe's camp to continue talks to ascertain his motives in coming their way. The colonel said his command was moving to Colville with no hostile designs on the Spokanes who, he said, had always been friends. What he did not say was that they had not always been *his* friends. He said the command hoped to effect good feelings between Indians and whites around Colville. Again, what he did not explain was why he needed 150 armed troops to do that. His lumbering howitzers were especially poor tokens of good will. His replies were obvious ad-lib remarks in an unplanned drama in which he was forced to change his lines. Before the council ended, the Spokanes refused his request for canoes. Without them, he could not cross their ancient Rubicon, the Spokane River.

Rebuffed, Steptoe concluded that it was best to desist; he prepared to head back to Walla Walla. The next morning, Father Joset visited him with some Coeur d'Alene chiefs. (Two of them, not seeing eye to eye as to what to do with Steptoe, engaged in a little war of their own, until the priest broke it up.) Steptoe told the father that the ill disposition of the Palouses had caused him to increase his escort on the trip and that, if he had known how the Indians felt about it, he would have conferred with the Spokanes and Coeur d'Alenes first. Joset came away from the parley almost as unconvinced as the Indians of Steptoe's sincerity. But he did manage to clear himself of accusations that he had supplied the Indians with arms and to convince Steptoe that he should get his command out of the country.

The command began to withdraw. They had not gone far when, near present-day Rosalia, Washington, someone fired a pistol. It may have been a Palouse. Regardless, the soldiers fired in a wild manner, from their already small supply of ammunition, all the while trying to protect their pack train. The Indians rushed the column, withdrew, and rushed it again. The Spokanes occupied a general northeasterly sector of the Indian line. Whereas the previous day's action had been dress rehearsal, this day's action was the real thing. The actors locked themselves in grim combat, sometimes at close range, moving across a stage of rolling hills and ravines, with powder flashes footlighting the drama.

On the right and left flanks, a Captain Taylor and a Lieutenant Gaston fell dead. Five others of the command soon lay dead, six badly wounded, seven less seriously so, and one missing; three of their Indian allies were dead. Indian losses were heavier; it was reported that at least nine were killed and forty or fifty wounded. One chief reportedly killed was Tecolekun of a Columbia River band. He was a relative of, and closely associated with, Qualchan and Polatkin, leaders of the Spokane resistance. They would not turn down an opportunity to avenge his death.

The command slipped away in the dark of night.[72]

Shock waves of Steptoe's defeat reached to the nation's capital, where Stevens was. He wrote: "Steptoe's defeat has made a great sensation here . . . . All the officers from Gen[eral] Scott down, the Secretary of War and the President expect a change, and that the present war will be crushed out with a strong hand."[73] In the

[72] For accounts of the engagement, see B. F. Manring, *The Conquest of the Coeur D'Alenes, Spokanes and Palouses, the Expeditions of Colonels E. J. Steptoe and George Wright against the "Northern Indians" in 1858*, 70–123; Burns, *The Jesuits and the Indian Wars of the Northwest*, 204–30; Secretary of War, *Annual Report*, 1858–59, pp. 59–82; Oregon Superintendency, "Letters Received January 1–December 30, 1858; C. S. Winder, "Captain C. S. Winder's Account of a Battle With the Indians," *Maryland Historical Magazine*, Vol. XXXV (1940), 56–59; J. Orin Oliphant (ed.), "The Story of Chief Louis Wildshoe," in *The Early History of Spokane, Washington, Told by Contemporaries*, 9–11; George F. Canis, "Steptoe's Indian Battle in 1858," *Washington Historian*, Vol. I, No. 4 (July, 1900), 162–70; Curtis, *North American Indian*, VII, 56–59; Thomas B. Beall, "Pioneer Reminiscences," *Washington Historical Quarterly*, Vol. VIII, No. 2 (April, 1917), 83–90; Edwards, *History*, 32–34; John F. Kelley, "The Steptoe Disaster," *The Pacific Northwesterner*, Vol. I, No. 1 (Winter, 1956–57), 9–16.
[73] Stevens to Nesmith, July 18, 1858, Ronald Todd, ed., "Notes and Documents Letters of Governor Isaac I. Stevens, 1857–1858," *Pacific Northwest Quarterly*, Vol. XXXI, No. 3 (October, 1940), 444.

Indian camps, the young braves danced, raced horses, and generally rested on their laurels, intoxicated with the joys of victory. Older, wiser men shook their heads. Above the din of victory, in the quiet of their own hearts, they spoke the words of an Indian agent, who wrote: "I am of the opinion we are to have a general war in the upper country."[74]

[74] Dennison to Nesmith, May 5, 1858, Oregon Superintendency, Vol. F.

CHAPTER FIVE

Fire on the Prairie

Colonel Steptoe estimated that about half the Spokanes, Coeur d'Alenes, and Flatheads could be numbered among the hostiles. He could have thanked his lucky stars all of them were not. He observed no such division among the Palouses; nearly all of them were hostile. The Yakimas, Nez Percés, and scattered families of smaller tribes were only partly so. Steptoe observed that tribes through whose lands the proposed Mullan Road would run, from Fort Walla Walla to Fort Benton, were resolved to prevent its construction. He must have known it was no coincidence that these tribes had the greatest numbers of hostiles. Captain John Mullan and his crew were surveying the route in the lower plateau when they were informed of Steptoe's defeat. They were probably aware that, had the Indians not taken their wrath out on the colonel, they might have taken it out on them. Stung by his defeat, Steptoe believed proper "chastisement" could remove any roadblock to progress. He further believed a force of three or four hundred infantry and two or three companies of cavalry could defeat or disperse the Indians, particularly were it sent against them before they had time to scatter from the root grounds.[1]

"War or peace is still in their hearts," reported Agent Owen, after he had sized up the Indians in council in the Colville Valley, where the Spokanes and their allies had come to revel in their victory. He had arrived there with a government brigade on July 4, 1858, after a war-whooping reception from Indians along the mouth of the Spokane River. Thanks to the intercession of Antoine Plante, they had called off their hostile reception, and the party continued on its way. War or peace, to the Indian way of thinking, wrote Owen, depended largely upon Colonel Steptoe; if he wanted war, they would accommodate him. The Indians on the mid-Columbia had just "accommodated" a party of miners gold-bound for Canada by driving them back from the Wenatchee River to Fort Simcoe in the Yakima Valley, despite the loss of Quiltenenock, son of Chief Sulktalthscosum.

Until Steptoe decided whether it would be peace or war, the Indians kept dancing. Wrote Owen: "Nothing but the War Cry day & Night from one End of the Valley to the other is heard," while Indians, "painted and looking more like demons than human beings are prowling about in squads armed to the teeth, revolvers under their blankets, Bows and iron pointed arrows in their hands." Charles W. Frush, in charge of the mess with Owen's expedition, wrote:

> I have seen many an Indian war-dance since, and have had a great deal of experience with the Indians, but I have never seen anything that equalled this affair. A great many of them were entirely nude, some painted half red and half black [from soot scraped from stoves at the post], and some daubed all over with white mud, a kind of pipe clay, and then spotted with red. All were armed with Hudson Bay guns, rifles, or with bows and arrows, and were drumming and singing, with an old hag in the center of a circle they had formed, who would recite the daring feat some brave had performed and, shaking in the faces of the warriors the swords and pistols and other trophies they had taken from the of-

[1] Secretary of War, *Annual Report*, 1858–59, p. 77.

ficers and men killed in the fight, tantalize them by telling them to go and do better.[2]

Dr. F. Perkins, at Fort Colville at the time, reported the Indians as saying that the white soldiers were women and could not fight, that the more sent into the country the better, for the Indians would kill them all. Dr. Perkins also reported the old chiefs as assuring whites at the fort they would fight to the death—that they had plenty of provisions, arms, and ammunition—and when the latter gave out, they would poison their arrows and fight with them. But guns were available, if not from the post, from the Canadian border.[3] The Indians were finding the border to have some advantages, despite one Spokane chief's angry words that parties of white men had come from "the cold side" and "the warm side" to establish this barrier in the land of the Indians without consulting them.

Owen and his brigade quietly departed the post early one morning and headed thirty miles up the Colville Valley to the home of Thomas Steiniger (Strenger, Stranger, or Stensgar). Three Indians harassed them along the way. Revolvers were drawn but no shots fired. The Indians made off with one of the major's mules. He and his party felt much safer at Steiniger's, as did several families taking refuge there. Steiniger, a Scot, had taken a Spokane wife, which gave him considerable influence among her people. The respite at Steiniger's let Owen catch his breath before continuing homeward to his Flathead Agency in the Bitterroot Valley—and to ponder the warnings of Chiefs Garry and Sgalgalt that he would face many dangers were he to return there via the Coeur d'Alene mission.

The following evening the brigade camped at the Little Spokane River for a comfortable night's rest. The next morning a

[2] Charles W. Frush, *A Trip From the Dalles of the Columbia, Oregon, To Fort Owen, Bitter Root Valley, Montana, in the Spring of 1858*, 339. Hereafter cited as *A Trip From the Dalles*.

[3] (Lieutenant) Lawrence Kip, *Army Life on the Pacific: A Journal of the Expedition Against the Northern Indians, the Tribes of the Coeur D'Alenes, Spokans, and Pelouzes, in the Summer of 1858*, 43. Hereafter cited as *Army Life on the Pacific*.

party of Spokanes and Kalispels entered their camp for a smoke and a long talk, the gist of which, thought Frush, was whether or not they should kill Owen. They concluded to let him go, despite his having written "bad things about them to the 'Great Father' at Washington." While still on the Little Spokane, Owen wrote details of his recent council with the Indians at Fort Colville: "I have just returned from one of the blackest councils, I think, that has ever been held on the Pacific slope. Five hundred fighting men were present elated with their recent success; the dragoon horses were prancing around all day; the scalp and war dance going on all night long." The Indians, he wrote, had said they had nothing against him as an individual, but looked on him as a spy for Colonel Steptoe and wanted to know why he wanted to go to the Flatheads. Was it to prevent them from making cause with the Indians of the west? If so, they said they would "have a dark Eye" on him. Of more practical value were the messages they said they had already sent to the Flatheads to join them in annihilating the whites. Owen revealed how they had threatened to hold him hostage, which he may have prevented by drawing on his own private account with the Hudson's Bay Company to purchase as many as eight hundred pounds of beef, flour, and tobacco for one chief, and tobacco and clothing for others "to secure for myself a safe exit out of the country." The trip had certainly been a loss for him; besides these presents he felt forced to give, the Indians had stolen ten of his horses and two of his mules. With the Indians so "cocked and primed for war," and in the mood, as Frush told it, "to shoot an arrow into a 'Boston' [white man] . . . for the sake of seeing him wiggle," Owen recommended to Superintendent Nesmith that a company of riflemen come and hold Fort Colville. He advised that this could not be done with the element of surprise, as the Indians had spies out on Steptoe's camp.

Before leaving the Spokane country he quietly dispatched the faithful George Montour, to whom he owed much for his safety from the Indians, to apprise Steptoe and Nesmith of the situation. Then he went to see Polatkin, whom he had known for eight years. Owen was disappointed with Polatkin because of the chief's prominence in the Steptoe attack. Polatkin made no effort to excuse himself; he seemed rather "sanguine of Exterminating the Soldiers." This policy, Owen told him, would get him nowhere. Polatkin promised Owen safe conduct out of the country, which he and Sgalgalt recommended should be north of the Coeur d'Alene country, as its people were still unsettled from the Steptoe affair. The brigade safely got under way, following a hazardous detour to Lake Pend Oreille, where trailing Colville Indians stole seven more Owen horses. The Pend Oreilles, eager to get Owen off their hands, helped him out of their country, where Spokanes and Coeur d'Alenes roamed freely. He arrived back at the Flathead Agency to a much warmer reception than he had received from Indians most of the way. The Flatheads were glad that he was alive, as they had heard his party had been scalped.[4]

Slowly the Spokanes began to temper the delirium of their victory with the realization that the white community would not take the recent Steptoe defeat lying down. Consequently, they contacted surrounding bands to gird themselves for war. Their first contacts were, quite naturally, with the Coeur d'Alenes. Just how formal the alliance was is not known, but word coming down the Columbia the latter part of June had it that hostile Indians had sworn among themselves to carry on a five-year war, for by then they believed they would have defeated the whites for the last time.[5]

Less successful were Spokane attempts to cement alliances with other tribes. The Kalispels, before whom the Spokanes most likely displayed Steptoe booty, were in no great hurry to rush into a war. Several of their chiefs denounced the idea. Among the Kalispels, as among all tribes, were hot bloods. One made a fiery speech, denouncing the pacifists. Some twenty-five braves, mostly related to the Spokanes, eventually rode off to join them. An even larger

[4] Frush, A *Trip From the Dalles*, 342; Seymour Dunbar (ed.), *The Journals and Letters of Major John Owen Pioneer of the Northwest 1850–1871*, II, 175–83; Nesmith to Owen, June 11, 1858, Washington Superintendency, No. 5, Roll 22.
[5] Kip, *Army Life on the Pacific*, 24.

number of peacefully inclined Kalispels would move north to the hunting and fishing grounds of Canada, some to remain as long as two years, keeping as far away from hostiles and whites as possible. Other Kalispels would isolate themselves east of the Rocky Mountains from developments to the west.[6] In their attempts to ally with the Pend Oreilles, the Spokanes were even less successful. The Pend Oreille chief, Alexander, declared that not only would he not join in any warlike action, but he would kill any man taking refuge among his people after having joined the war party against the Americans.[7]

Government response to the Steptoe defeat was swift, in an age not given to hurry. The estimate of a thousand troops was going the rounds. By June 18, 1858, three companies of the Third Artillery had arrived at Fort Vancouver, to the "rattle of the drum and the notes of the bugle" all around. One company was ordered from Fort Umpqua in Oregon, another from Fort Jones in California. General Newman S. Clarke, General Wool's vigorous replacement, arrived by steamer at Fort Vancouver on June 23 to an eleven-gun salute. He urgently requested Nesmith to see him at the fort regarding an expedition against the Spokane Indians.[8] Nesmith himself had not been idle; two weeks earlier he had written Agent Owen, requesting a report of the causes of the war, the tribes involved in it, and their numbers killed or wounded. Nesmith's exertions proved to be in vain, for at the moment he simply had no agent among the nontreaty Spokanes and Coeur d'Alenes, a situation for which he must bear some blame. Because there had been no influx of white settlers among these tribes, he had withheld agents from them, employing his help on the coast and other places which he thought had been more troubled. Also, because the interior tribes had recently commenced "unprovoked hostilities" in the Yakima War, he was not overanxious, as we have seen, to "relieve them [with aid and

[6] B. A. E. *45th Ann. Rep.*, 371.

[7] N. Congiato, S.J., to General Newman S. Clarke, August 3, 1858. Quoted in, Garrett B. Hunt, *Indian Wars of the Inland Empire*, 46–48.

[8] Lieutenant H. Walker to Nesmith, June 26, 1858, Oregon Superintendency "Letters Received January 1–December 30, 1858."

agents] from the legitimate results of their own treachery and folly." As far as he was concerned, they still merited no relief.

Owen had only remote responsibility for the Spokanes and Coeur d'Alenes. This agent gap removed one more restraint from these tribes as they moved toward a confrontation with the army. Partly because of this absence of Indian office personnel, the military would move into the interior without them. With typically weak liaison between War and Interior departments, the superintendent would experience a virtual blackout of information from the military in its moves, which were to affect the Indians so vitally.[9]

Even before General Clarke arrived at Fort Vancouver, Captain Erasmus D. Keyes, with Companies A and M of the Third Artillery, had left by Columbia River steamer. His destination: Fort Dalles. The first leg of their journey took them one day along conifer-flanked shores, broken by an occasional settler's clearing and Indian grave houses. Portaging, the troops embarked on another steamer, riding it to the Dalles by the ancient Wishram Village. Here, the travelers noticed (as had all others since Lewis and Clark), that Indians gathering there resembled those of the Great Plains—all mounted and looking like warriors.

From June 15 to July 6, 1858, Captain Keyes vigorously prepared his troops. The soldiers' effectiveness and efficiency matched that of their improved long-range rifles. Clarke would indeed have been more agitated than he was had the Indians obtained similar arms from the Hudson's Bay Company. On arriving at Fort Vancouver, he had sent a curt communication to James A. Graham, chief trader of the company at Vancouver, about his firm's sales of arms and ammunition to the Indians. Clarke was likewise con-

---

[9] Nesmith to the Honorable Charles Mix, commissioner of Indian affairs, September 30, 1858, Oregon Superintendency, "Letters Received July 1853–August 1855, September 1856–September 1859." In the midst of the forthcoming campaign, Captain John A. Mullan, on September 5, would write: "But I boldly, and fearlessly, and honestly say that *one* superintendent, with his headquarters at Salem, in Oregon, is not equal to the task of performing the responsible duties of superintendent for so many thousands of Indians." Secretary of War, *Annual Report*, 1858–59 (35 Cong., 2 sess., *Sen Exec. Doc. No. 32*) X, 32. Pages 1–79 of this report are hereafter cited as "Wright Memoir."

cerned about company purchases from the Indians of captured Steptoe horses and mules. Through Father Joset, he gave the Indians an ultimatum to prove their boast that "they had never dipped their hands in the blood of the whites" by coming down to Fort Vancouver to talk with him. "Coeur d'Alenes and Spokanes, you have committed a great crime," Clarke charged. He added that their deception at the hands of Kamiakin and certain Nez Percés had not relieved them from the need of atoning for the Steptoe deed by yielding up both government property taken from the command and their braves who had fired on it in disobedience of their tribal chiefs.

General Clarke did not wait for the Spokanes and Coeur d'Alenes to accept his ultimatum, so sure was he that they would not. On July 4, 1858, he ordered Colonel George Wright into the field to strike them from Fort Dalles like a right hand. At the same time, he ordered north from Fort Simcoe Major Robert Garnett, a Southern fire-eater with three hundred troops as a punishing left hand to deal with such hostiles as Qualchan. Following instructions, Wright ordered forces and supplies from Fort Dalles eastward to Fort Walla Walla, already garrisoned by four companies of the First Dragoons and two of the Ninth Infantry. It was a much better point from which to launch a northward attack against the Spokanes and their allies. The 177-mile journey from one fort to another, begun on July 7, 1858, was fatiguing for the little army, their progress over difficult terrain slowed by heat. Twelve-and-a-half days later they arrived at the fort in the pleasant Walla Walla Valley, almost on the same spot where the big council with Stevens had been held three years before. Only a few scattered Nez Percés in the vicinity were a reminder of the Indians who had attended the council. By friendly overtures, Wright, in a "treaty of friendship," won them to the army's side. This assured his command of guides and scouts. To other Indians opposing them, these Nez Percés would be called "the soldiers' slaves."[10]

As Commanders Wright and Garnett prepared to strike with

[10] Hunt, *Indian Wars of the Inland Empire*, 46–47.

their two-edged sword, their peacemaking counterparts, Father Joset and his superior, Nicholas Congiato, S.J., reached the Coeur d'Alene mission on July 16 to urge the Indians to come to terms with the soldiers. It took the two priests over three weeks to contact the Spokanes and Coeur d'Alenes, so scattered were they at the fish, root, and berry grounds. During this period, the fathers spoke to the Spokanes several times, but with no great success. For one thing, they could not use as a lever the threat of abandoning a mission station among them, for they had none.[11] Working against the fathers' efforts were the offers of horses from a hostile Palouse chief, Tilcoax, and certain Upper Yakimas to join them in war against the "Boston Men." And of course, Kamiakin, the Lower Yakima chief, was still around.

The fathers had brought two hard knots for the natives to untie —the yielding up of government property and of the perpetrators of the recent attack on the troops. Regarding the first, the Indians knew that the captured horses would be hard to reclaim, since they had been branded and handed from person to person to a point where they had become lost in a hopeless web of exchanges. Regarding the second proposal, the surrender of the perpetrators, the Indians were adamantly opposed. With their limited chieftain-type government, they knew that no Indian had the power to enforce such an ultimatum. Any who tried stood a good chance of losing his life. Since the Coeur d'Alenes and Spokanes had been unschooled in war making against whites, they were by the same token unschooled in peace making, too. To their sorrow, they discovered that the Americans would not settle disputes by mutual gift giving. Not only that, they punished wrongdoers by the very un-Indian method of slipping a big knot around a man's neck and hanging him from a tree until dead.[12] When the fathers finished explaining how many soldiers there were and what powers they wielded, some of the Indians temporarily cast off their war garments and stilled their songs of war.

[11] Burns, *Jesuits and Indian Wars*, 262.
[12] *Ibid.*, 260–61. Here Burns discusses Indian attitudes toward this kind of punishment.

On August 3, 1858, at a poorly attended meeting of Spokanes and Coeur d'Alenes, three of their chiefs replied through Father Congiato to General Clarke. The gist of Coeur d'Alene Chief Milkapsi's message was: "When I shall hear you, I shall tell you the truth and throw away my bow & gun." Garry sent his regrets for the recent "useless" fight which Steptoe had begun, and his people had finished, contrary to his advice. He said his ardor for a Steptoe peace had cooled on hearing of that officer's wish for revenge. He shrewdly sidestepped any mention of Clarke's demands, only regret for what had happened, with an expression of hope for future peace. Polatkin lectured the general on how Indians concluded their wars: "[We] bury the dead [including the exchanging of properties] and talk and live on good terms.... [We] don't speak of more blood." He may have known his words would have no more softening effect on Clarke than did his refusal to leave his country or deliver up his "neighbors" to the army, even if it killed him.

The words of Polatkin revealed that Indian and white concepts of war differed as widely as did other aspects of their cultures. Spokane warriors banded together into some semblance of military detachments, but the practice of forming themselves into battalions, companies, and lesser units was alien to them. Their Steptoe victory certainly had given them no inkling that, under right conditions, this type of military structure could be effective. Although they had been told of the superior rifle power of Wright's command, they would have had to see it to believe it. Even the howitzer held little terror for them, because of its ill use in the Steptoe campaign. The Spokanes employed an individualized style of fighting, with their warriors, like buffalo hunters, singling out and striking down their targets. Each one fought on his own responsibility. Even nature seemed to conspire against the Spokanes; the open plains of their country were like those of buffalo country where more than once, man for man, they had held their own, giving them an exaggerated sense of their fighting abilities. Their strategy of grass burning on their home plains, so effective in their hunts, might prove only moderately so against a human quarry who could intelligently respond to it.

Troop movements to Fort Simcoe and the Columbia River and to Fort Walla Walla and the Snake River, of which the Spokanes were apprised through their scouts, made them aware that General Clarke had spoken with no forked tongue when he said, "I am going to send troops into your country." Realization that, for a second time in a year, their homeland might be invaded, sent the war fever rising again. Council fires burned along the Spokane, and the same speeches were heard again as at the time of the Steptoe invasion—that the soldiers, an advance guard of thousands of palefaces, were coming to steal their lands and trample the graves of their forefathers.

The words of hostiles such as Polatkin had lost none of their incendiarism. Even Kamiakin appears to have had an audience, partly because Qualchan, with whom he had been feuding, was not present to challenge the old chief. Not until late August would Qualchan appear in the Spokane country, having spent most of the summer nursing a wound inflicted by miners. One argument used by the hotbloods to win over the wavering Indians was that, should they not join the war cause, the soldiers would kill them anyway. Not all the Indians believed this. One, Quil-quil-moses, and two brothers, kidnapped by Spokanes from their Yakima homeland five years before, rounded up some forty horses and took off for Snake River to defect to the army.[13]

It is possible that certain Spokanes urging peace and caution may have influenced the escapees in their decision. One chief trying to still the war talk was Sgalgalt. Another was Garry. Since several of Garry's relatives had joined the hostiles, some authorities have concluded that he did also. Evidence points in the other direction. His white man's education, his friendship for Stevens, albeit in trying circumstances, and his neutrality in the Steptoe attack, pulled him to the peaceful side. This exposed him, not only to the taunts of his warlike fellows, but to their threats on his life.

Father Joset was also taunted by war-minded members of his

13 Kip, *Army Life on the Pacific*, 45.

flock, who threatened to expel him once they had taken care of the Americans.[14] He persistently told them to lay their guns aside because, as he reasoned, their Steptoe victory was no measure of continued success, since enemy numbers were much greater now. But the dissident Coeur d'Alenes had less faith in the father than they had in their pact with the Spokanes to keep whites out of their country, at least until the government should establish reserves and pay for them. In the pact, they said they would not interfere with white encroachers on lands of other Indians, thus making the Spokane–Coeur d'Alene agreement a bilaterally defensive one.[15] Sometimes the father spoke wise words, the Indians believed. But to many of them, no words were wiser than the most elementary instinct to defend one's own land.[16]

Although Walker and Eells had been gone a decade from the Spokanes, their influence remained. Proof of this is seen in the fact that only a few Lower Spokanes joined the hostiles. William Three Mountains, now a young man among the Middle and Upper Spokanes, encouraged those peoples to follow the path of peace. Big Star (the elder Lot) did likewise.[17] Without minimizing the value of the Walker-Eells ministry, it should be said that, even before it began, the Lower Spokanes had shielded themselves more effectively from warlike traits than had their Upper and Middle Spokane brothers. It could be said that the missionaries had strengthened a peaceful tendency already there.

Below the Snake River, Wright ordered a detachment under Captain Keyes to the Snake to select a crossing, construct a field work to guard it, and keep communications open with Fort Walla Walla. About halfway in its second day's march, Keyes received

[14] Rowena Nichols, "The War of 1855–56."

[15] B.A.E. *45th Ann. Rep.*, 369.

[16] Coeur d'Alene Chief Stellam told of Joset's efforts to dissuade the people from entering the war. "The Story of Stellam," *Spokesman-Review*, October 4, 1891, p. 9.

[17] The role of William Three Mountains in this situation is found in an historical review written by H. T. Cowley, M. T. Hartson, and Colonel J. Kennedy Stout for the *Spokesman-Review*, May 30, 1897, p. 14. For the role of Big Star, see the Reverend Myron Eells, *History of Indian Missions on the Pacific Coast, Oregon, Washington and Idaho*, 236 (hereafter cited as *History of Indian Missions*).

an express from Wright stating that hostiles had driven off three dozen oxen from Fort Walla Walla. The pursuers had not caught the marauders. Keyes came upon black patches on the plateau, where the Indians had burned the grass to rob his command of forage for its animals, hoping to force it back to Walla Walla. These events gave an air of urgency to his instructions to build an outpost at the confluence of the Snake and Tucannon rivers. It was begun on August 11, 1858. There was a gunshot exchange that same day between hostiles across the Snake and sentries of the command. The very name of the fort, Taylor, in honor of the captain killed in the Steptoe attack, implied days of reprisal ahead. From Dr. Perkins at Fort Colville came word that he had seen the dead Lieutenant Gaston's saddle all covered with blood, and that an Indian had waved the scalp of Lieutenant Gaston in his face.[18] Members of these dead officers' dragoons were in the Wright command; they looked forward to avenging the deaths of their former comrades.

On August 13 a priest arrived, probably Father Ravalli of the Kettle Falls mission. He bore a warning from the Indians that, if any soldiers crossed the Snake River, none would return alive.[19] To the north, across that river, the troops saw the light of grass fires, proof that the Indians did not expect their warning to be heeded.

Wright reached the Snake River on August 18 to ready his command. His dragoons numbered 190, his artillery 400, his infantry 90, his attachés (packers and colorful Mexican muleteers), 200. He had, in addition, 30 Nez Percé scouts and guides, giving him a grand total of nearly 700 men with an equal number of horses and mules. At dawn on August 25, the artillery began crossing the swift wide stream. It was followed the same day by everything else, except the dragoons and part of the quartermaster corps, which crossed over the next day. On the twenty-seventh, the command set out, in heat and dust, to find and defeat its enemy in unfamiliar country.

[18] Kip, *Army Life on the Pacific*, 43.
[19] Burns, *Jesuits and Indian Wars*, 266.

John Mullan, topographical engineer with the command, knew more about the region between the Snake and Spokane rivers than any of the other officers. But he had obtained his information only through reports and maps of others.[20] Wright had little more than a month's provisions and small prospects of getting more. This shortage would permit him no time to play hide and seek with an invisible foe. In that strange country, circumstance would have to be his guide. Strange country it proved to be, killing two artillerymen who ate of its poison roots.

Wright must have known the enemy would reconnoiter the mile-long train. They attempted, through decoys, to deceive him about their real numbers and location, all the while hoping to provoke an attack. He must have known, too, that to have succumbed to such stratagems would have weakened his striking arm, which would be effective only if he fully arrayed his units against the enemy.

He advanced from the Palouse River to Cow Creek, which many Spokanes regarded as the southern boundary of their lands. No hostiles were seen, but there were fresh horse tracks. Despite the Nez Percé scouts, Wright appears not to have known the precise location of the Spokanes and their allies, as evidenced by his temporary indecision about which of two routes to take toward the Spokane River: a westerly route toward the old Walker-Eells mission on the old Colville Road or one farther east in the direction of the Spokane falls. He chose the latter. Wright had crossed his Rubicon, but was not sure which road led to Rome.

Fortunately for him, the Spokanes were encamped at the falls. An Indian courier rode into their camp to report the numbers of enemy, their horses and mules. Indian bands who had been apprised of Wright's movements even before he had crossed the Snake now gathered at the falls. As Wright had prepared his troops to cross the Snake, so the Indians had prepared for war in their own way, by dancing every night and practicing maneuvers on horseback.

---

[20] Captain John Mullan U.S.A., *Report on the Construction of a Military Road from Fort Walla-Walla to Fort Benton*, 9.

When word arrived that the soldiers were not far from the falls, a mass of Indians, including hesitant ones who came more as onlookers than combatants, moved down to the falls. Here they waited, Spokanes, Coeur d'Alenes, Palouses, Yakimas, Kalispels, Pend Oreilles, Colvilles, Columbias (and other tribes above the Columbia), Okanogans, and some Nez Percés who had not signed the alliance with Wright.[21] The women went out to dig roots as a few men on horseback rode to the top of the hills to see the soldiers approaching. These riders quickly turned back to report what they had seen. Soldiers began to appear on the ridge.[22]

When the soldiers first saw the Indians, it came as no surprise to them. The soldiers had been seeing Indians for two days. The Nez Percés had first exchanged shots with an advance party of hostiles two days before. The Indians had retreated as the dragoons approached. The attackers had accompanied the train the whole day, just as they had with Steptoe, yet this time keeping out of gunshot range. Before the command had encamped that day, the hostiles had ridden up near the column to burn the grass and fire upon the rear guard. An Indian attack under cover of smoke was foiled because the grass was too green; it burned poorly. The Indians had retreated.

Now the time of confrontation.

The Indians posted themselves in increasing numbers on the hills overlooking the soldiers. Shortly, Wright ordered the dragoons, four companies of artillery, the howitzer battery, and two companies of rifles to dislodge the scattered Indians from a hill. The units formed into two columns, one of about 100 dragoons, the other, 220 artillery and infantry. They left behind an artillery company, a detachment of dragoons, and a 50-man guard to defend the camp's four hundred mules and supplies.

Advancing about a mile and a half, the columns moved to dislodge the enemy from the hill. The dragoons marched to the left, a Nez Percé party wound to the right, and the main column advanced with Wright and a howitzer battery. The dragoons reached

21 *Ibid.*, 66.
22 Curtis, *North American Indian*, VII, 60–61.

the hilltop and dismounted, driving the Indians off with a volley exchange. On the way up, Wright received definite word that the Indians were gathered behind the hill at the foot in large numbers. They were estimated at five hundred Spokanes, Coeur d'Alenes, and Palouses—all ready to fight. Wright advanced.

Soldier accounts of what followed name no specific Indian chiefs in the engagement. One Indian account, narrated by white men many years later, had Qualchan rallying the Indians behind him, as he had in the Steptoe attack. He and his Yakima allies occupied the right center, Kamiakin and a mixture of Yakimas and Palouses the left center, Stellam and his Coeur d'Alenes the right wing. Garry and Sgalgalt (whom many believe were not there at all), with the Spokanes, were reportedly in the left wing and reserve.[23]

Lieutenant Lawrence Kip's pen recorded a classic account of the battle scene. A splendid panorama lay before him—Four Lakes. A large lake at the foot of the hill, and beyond, the smaller ones, with the plateau stretching away, ridge upon grassy ridge, merging into a dimly visible line of pine-covered mountains in the distance.

Every spot on the plain below was filled with warriors, in pines on the edge of the lakes, in ravines and gullies, on opposite hillsides, swarming over the plain on fleet horses. They formed a swaying mass, brandishing Hudson's Bay muskets, bows, arrows, lances, and hurling shouts of defiance made all the more frightening by wild trappings (one, rumored to have been the scalp of Lieutenant Gaston, waved by Coeur d'Alene Chief Stellam). Plumes, manes, and tails fluttered in the breeze. Horses and riders were painted and decked out in skins, trinkets, and fantastic embellishments. White paint was smeared, with crimson, in fantastic figures. Gaudy colored beads and fringes hung from their bridles.

Skirmishers advanced downhill to chase Indians from coverts onto the plain for the dragoons to attack. A howitzer battery, sup-

---

[23] Kip, *Army Life on the Pacific*, 55–58; "Wright Memoir," 19–22; (General) E. D. Keyes, *Fifty Years' Observation of Men and Events Civil and Military*, 268–70 (hereafter cited as *Fifty Years' Observation*).

ported by artillery and the rifles, sought to drive them out of the woods. Howitzer blasts drove the enemy to take refuge. Companies moved downhill, with parade-ground precision, firing at 600 yards (the most effective range was 200 to 250 yards). Indians advanced rapidly, counterfiring, then retreating, each man apparently fighting on his own. Now an Indian reeled from saddle to ground, and a half dozen others were dragged off by their comrades. This was their introduction to minié balls and long-range rifles.

Now the line of soldiers drew nearer. Heavy fire, and hostiles fled toward the plain. Major Grier's voice rang out, "Charge the rascals!" Gun and sabre flashes cutting Indians down—Lieutenant Gregg cleaving the skull of another. Yells and shrieks to no avail. Dragoons rode over the foe, some sprawled in death on the ground. Other Indians broke for clumps of woods or rising ground to escape. No further pursuit. Now the line on foot drove the Indians over hills for two miles. Indians in ravines and woods, beyond reach of the troops, with a single group left to watch the soldiers, were scattered by an overhead howitzer shellburst.[24]

Despite the chiefs' appeals to their braves to hold their ground, Indian "flesh and blood could not stand it." The "horse-soldiers with their reins in their teeth, their knives in their right hands and their revolvers in their left, galloped madly . . . and the bravest warriors . . . lost all sense of shame and fled from the field."[25]

Wright ordered recall sounded, returning his men to camp after an absence of four hours. Since the first attack, they had driven the foe back about 3½ miles, a rate of about a mile an hour. Returning, the soldiers passed over a litter of muskets, quivers, bows, arrows, and animal-hide robes left by the fleeing Indians. Since the Indians carried off their dead, there was no white estimate of their losses. Some seventeen were believed to have been killed, and possibly forty or fifty wounded.

No soldiers were wounded. It was a victory, wrote Keyes, all the sweeter for having been so bloodless for the soldiers. Return-

24 Cowley, "Fate of Schon-shin."
25 McCarty interview.

ing to camp after an eight- to ten-mile chase, Wright's Indian allies brought back loose horses and carried booty and scalps. It was a solid victory over foes which, wrote Kip, "were panic-struck by the effect of our fire at such great distances, and the steady advance of the troops, unchecked by the constant fire kept up by them." And a similar analysis from Wright: "Our long-range rifles can reach the enemy where he cannot reach us." Morale was high. The Nez Percés concluded the day in their own fashion, dancing about their camp far into the night.

There was no such dancing that night among the Spokanes and their allies. They spent it on the Spokane River, where they had fled. They nursed their wounded and danced for a victory. The victory messages they had prepared to send to all wavering tribes to join them could not now be sent. One Colville chief, an observer at Four Lakes, carried a message home to his people of soldiers who could march faster and farther in a day than horses, and who had guns whose bullets carried over a mile. He urged his people to stay friendly with them.[26]

There was no Indian Kip to record the battle. Indian history was handed down orally. If the Indians told stories of the battle, they did so around their own campfires, and painfully, too, saying little about it to white men. One account, written by a Spokane pioneer thirty-four years after the event, and based on conversations with a participant who "would rather be dead than to have to tell the story of our defeat," contains some improbabilities. Red men, in their stories, had no monopoly on improbabilities.

The command remained exhausted in camp for three days. On September 5, 1858, came an early bugle call. After a hasty breakfast, the soldiers marched about five miles to find the Indians riding along to their right, parallel to the command, in Indian fashion. Emerging from rough country onto a prairie, they saw more Indians in the woods to the right, apparently prepared to attack. According to one Indian account, Kamiakin, the most experienced warrior of the confederacy, occupied the right with

---

[26] Kip, *Army Life on the Pacific*, 86, 92–93.

Yakimas and Palouses. Spokanes and others occupied the left, and Coeur d'Alenes the center.[27]

When the soldiers advanced to the middle of the plain, the Indians set fire to the grass. By so doing, they sought to terrify the army horses and mules, explode the ammunition, and then charge the distracted command. The fire spread rapidly, windswept through tall dry grass. Under the smoke cover, the Indians formed an arc, pouring fire on the command, riding headlong down a steep hill, shrieking all the way. On the other side of the smoke-line, Mexican muleteers matched Indian cries with their shouts, just as spirited, herding their animals by a patch of rocks where they put out the fire to prevent a stampede. Wright ordered the advance skirmishers, howitzers, and a squadron of dragoons through a light spot in the wall of flames. As he had hoped, the many pounding hoofs scattered and beat down the fire, clearing the way for gunners and infantry to follow. In the face of this brave white advance, the chiefs rode up and down their line, urging their men to stand firm.[28]

A Pend Oreille chief, Spotted Coyote, one of the few of his tribe to join the hostiles, was believed to have been bulletproof. He twice rode the full length of the battle line, challenging the soldiers to kill him. The soldiers fired at him unsuccessfully, and for a while he appeared invulnerable, as he had boasted. At the same time, a good number of Indians spotted some soldiers trying to take howitzers up a hill. The Indians moved in. The soldiers turned the big guns around and fired into them, killing a number and scattering the rest. When Spotted Coyote saw this, his vaunted invincibility melted. He was supposed to have said: "There is no use of our fighting. We can do nothing against cannon. The whites are far superior to us in their arms. We must give up fighting and make peace, or leave the country." It was a conclusion in which most of the Indians, at the end of that day, concurred.[29]

---

27 "The Story of Stellam."
28 G. E. Dandy, "Reminiscences," 3–4.
29 Curtis, *North American Indian*, VII, 60–61.

Flight continued to the plain. Pursuing dragoons. Skirmish intervals. Straggling knots of Indians gathered in the woods. Artillery companies, after a sharp contest, dislodged them. The command continued to advance, skirmishing along the way. The howitzer scattered the enemy wherever they collected in large numbers in the woods. Kamiakin, on his horse, over a half-mile from the soldiers, was almost killed when a shellburst sent a tree limb crashing down on him. The foot soldiers chased the Indians toward the Spokane River. Kamiakin, never very popular with the Coeur d'Alenes or the Spokanes, was said to have made the best time of any in clearing out of the battlefield.

About 5 P.M., the Indians fired on the troops in the vicinity of Deep Creek Falls. But the command pushed north to the Spokane River, some three miles below Spokane falls, to encamp. Since the day began, the soldiers had covered twenty-five miles of hills, ravines, coulees, woods, rocks, bare ground. They had done this without drinking water. They were dropping from thirst and exhaustion, the excitement of the day having deceived them as to their true condition. The Indians camped a few miles from the soldiers, for that night the troops saw their campfires burning. Also, they saw what they thought to be an Indian village burning, no doubt a scorched-earth move directed against them.

The Battle of Spokane Plains was over. In many respects, it was the Battle of Four Lakes all over again. It had been a one-day engagement that had proved the efficiency of the new rifles and the discipline of the soldiers, only one of whom was slightly wounded. Again a battlefield was strewn with Indian litter. Again their human losses were not known, as dead and wounded had been removed before the troops could cross the ravines to get them. Somewhat in excess of five hundred hostiles were supposed to have been in the fight, more warriors than at Four Lakes.[30]

Wright remained in camp to rest and to reconnoiter the river. Small groups of Indians were seen on the other shore; a few crossed over to profess friendship. The next morning, Wright moved the command along the river, keeping an eye open for a good crossing.

[30] "Wright Memoir," 33.

He found none, which may have spared the village at the Spokane and Little Spokane rivers. Hearing of a concentration of Indians above the falls, Wright pushed upstream instead. At a narrow place in the river, more Indians were seen on the opposite bank. They shouted across the river their wish to talk. Garry was among them. He had just returned from Colville, after being informed that hostilities had broken out. Some reports placed Garry in the battle, anywhere from the rear to the front. Indians with Garry at the river, believing that his white man's speech and dress might set well with Wright, promoted him as their number one peace-maker.

Wright told them to meet him at the crossing some two miles above the falls. He then moved upstream, past the falls, and halted at the crossing; Garry came over. He told Wright that he had always opposed the fighting, but that his young men and many of the chiefs were against him and he could not control them. The military generally took this statement for truth, basing its opinion not so much on his words as an Indian as on those of Dr. Perkins, who testified to the chief's indecision in the face of possible war. At Fort Colville, during the big powwow, Perkins wrote that Garry had never said a word but merely looked on, "his heart . . . undecided."[31]

Wright delivered Garry a lecture: "I have met you in two bloody battles; you have been badly whipped; you have lost several chiefs and many warriors killed or wounded. I have not lost a man or animal; I have a large force, and you Spokanes, Coeur d'Alenes, Pelouses, and Pen d'Oreilles may unite, and I can defeat you as badly as before. I did not come into this country to ask you to make peace; I come here to fight. Now when you are tired of the war, and ask for peace, I will tell you what you must do: You must come to me with your arms, with your women and children, and everything you have, and lay them at my feet; you must put your faith in me and trust to my mercy. If you do this, I shall then dictate the terms upon which I will grant you peace. If you do not do this, war will be made on you this year and next,

[31] Kip, *Army Life on the Pacific*, 67.

and until your nation shall be exterminated."[32] Wright had chosen bluster to battle, a choice he could obviously afford.

Wright ordered Garry to convey his words to all the hostile Indians, telling them that, if they did as he demanded, their lives would be spared. He also directed Garry to send messages to the late Sulktalthscosum's son, Moses—who, despite a sojourn at the Reverend Mr. Spalding's mission school at Lapwai, had reverted from Christian teaching to making war—and to Big Star (the elder Lot) to bring in their respective people. This Garry promised to do. At noon Big Star's son, the younger Lot, came in on behalf of his father. Shortly after Wright encamped, nine warriors laid their rifles on the right bank of the Spokane and crossed over, expressing a wish to speak with him. Wright discovered the leader of this delegation to be Polatkin, who he knew had been in all the engagements. He told them to stay put while two of Polatkin's men were sent back over to fetch the rifles. On the other side, one of the Indians got cold feet and fled. The other brought back the guns. They were marked "London, 1847," evidence that the Indians had purchased them from the Hudson's Bay Company at Colville. Wright held Polatkin hostage and also one of the Indians with him who was suspected of killing two miners in the spring. The other Indians were told to go back and bring in their people.

During Wright's continued march across the plain where Spokane lands merged into those of the Coeur d'Alene, he burned Indian wheat stores and lodges. He ordered Indian cattle driven in, but the cattle being wild, they fled to the mountains. In the evening the case of the captive Indian implicated in the death of the miners was "investigated." The soldiers secured one end of a rope to a tree, its business end around the neck of the Indian, and he was dangled off Captain Mullan's instrument wagon.

Next morning two Indians on the opposite riverbank shouted over, demanding Polatkin's release. One of them was recognized as the old chief's son, who had been with him when Polatkin was captured; the other Indian was later recognized as another

[32] "Wright Memoir," 25–26.

son. In reply, Captain E. O. C. Ord and his men fired a sharp volley across the stream, wounding both Indians. They also wounded one horse and killed another.[33] The next day two of Big Star's men got a better welcome when they came in with friendly professions on behalf of their chief, proof to the military that its recent victories had produced a salutary effect on the Indians, the white men apparently being unaware that Big Star had not been in the engagement at all.

It was about this time and to this place that, according to Spokane stories handed down (but not in the military reports, because the event, if true, would have looked poor in the record), a neutral Spokane group sent one Amtoola, an interpreter with some knowledge of English, across the Spokane. He came swimming a horse and carrying a white flag. The soldiers shot him dead.[34] There were other such incidents.

The next two days, September 9 and 10, 1858, were black ones for animal-loving readers of history. On the eighth the command found many horses set loose by the Indians. They were the property of the Palouse chief, Tilcoax. Soon Major Grier and his dragoons wrangled in some eight or nine hundred horses.

Wright had a problem on his hands. He decided to kill the horses. Although killing horses on the frontier was a crime, this was war, and all was fair in it. Wright feared that to keep the animals would be to invite raids from the Indians. In retrieving the horses, the Indians might scatter those of the command as well. The horses were too wild to be herded, as the command moved east, and should they be permitted to fall back into Indian hands, their riders would have regained mobility to continue resistance and retaliation. Not to be overlooked as a motive for the horse slaughter was Wright's desire to punish the Indians for their resistance. A few simple words explained the thinking of the board convened by Wright to decide the animals' fate: "Without horses the Indians are powerless."

[33] This story appears in Kip, *Army Life on the Pacific*, 70, and is corroborated by John E. Smith in, "A Pioneer of the Spokane Country," *Washington Historical Quarterly*, Vol. VII, No. 4 (October, 1916), 270.

[34] McCarty interview.

About two hundred of them were selected by the officers, quartermaster, and friendly Nez Percés. Then the soldiers built a log corral. One by one, they took horses from the corral to a river bar. There the older ones were shot singly and the colts knocked in the head, causing the brood mares to neigh in the night. This process proving too slow, two companies lined up on the banks and fired volleys into the corral. Two more companies were later detailed to shoot the rest of the horses, until a gruesome total of about 690 horses had been killed. Wrote Keyes: "It was a cruel sight to see so many noble beasts shot down," fancying he had seen "in their beautiful faces an appeal for mercy." He described the soldiers' exaltation toward the end of their bloody task as evidence of the "ferocious character of men." The rotting flesh, in what Wright himself called the "Horse Slaughter Camp," became a bleaching skeletal pile known to folks around as "Wright's boneyard."[35]

During the horse massacre, an Indian runner came to Wright from the Coeur d'Alene mission with a letter from Father Joset. The Indians had requested his intercession with the colonel on their behalf for peace. The colonel received the courier and moved his command across the Spokane River. He continued easterly, raiding as he went, penetrating deeper into mountainous country bordering Lake Coeur d'Alene. Not until December would *Harper's New Monthly Magazine* carry for its readers the terse news item: "The soldiers are destroying the grain fields and provisions of the savages, who are reduced to great distress."[36]

As the soldiers noisily hacked their way through the dense woods, Donati's comet streaked silently by like a new broom which the Indians feared would sweep them from the earth before the vengeful Wright. The colonel, however, having penetrated into difficult terrain, was apprehensive that the Indians might frustrate

[35] "Wright Memoir," 26; Kip, *Army Life on the Pacific*, 69–71; Dandy, "Reminiscences," 5; Keyes, *Fifty Years' Observation*, 272–73; Smith, "A Pioneer of the Spokane Country," *Washington Historical Quarterly*, Vol. VII, No. 4 (October, 1916), 271.

[36] Anonymous, "Monthly Record of Current Events," *Harper's New Monthly Magazine*, Vol. XVIII, No. 103 (December, 1858), 113.

the expedition's objectives. He found it expedient to soften the punishment line advocated by his superior, General Clarke. Renouncing vengeance, Wright signed a treaty with the Coeur d'Alenes, demanding the surrender of their captured plunder, the passage of whites at all times through their lands, (which, for the moment, meant the Mullan Road builders), and the yielding up of hostages to be taken to Walla Walla as security for future Coeur d'Alene good behavior.[37] Polatkin, now unchained, made a short speech. He expressed satisfaction with the council and promised to round up the Spokanes for another council to be held within the week at Latah Creek. But Polatkin would be unable to assemble some Spokanes who, in fear, had taken off "to buffalo," preferring Blackfeet onslaughts to those of Wright. With Father Joset, Polatkin set about rounding up the Spokanes.

On September 22, Wright reached the prearranged place of council on Latah Creek, near present-day Waverly, Washington, some twenty-five miles southeast of the falls. On the grounds he found the Spokane chiefs and headmen who had come in with Father Joset, also leading Pend Oreilles, Kalispels, Colvilles, Palouses, Columbias, and San Poils. Kamiakin and Tilcoax had been in the evening before, but fearing the colonel's wrath, had fled. Garry was there, having helped Joset. On hearing of Polatkin's incarceration, Garry had feared to go out and bring in his people, as he had promised Wright he would. Joset calmed his fears and presented him to Wright.[38]

About 10 A.M. of the next day, Wright assembled the Indians. He enunciated the "crimes" they had committed and demanded a "treaty" on the order of one he had concluded with the Coeur d'Alenes. Actually, what Wright called treaties were merely surrender terms to be used as the basis for some future treaty. One Spokane chief said: "I am sorry for what has been done, and glad of the opportunity now offered to make peace with our Great Father. We promise to obey and fulfil these terms in every point."

[37] "Wright Memoir," 55. For further details of Wright's expedition to the Coeur d'Alene, see Burns, *Jesuits and Indian Wars*, 309–11.
[38] *Ibid*, 311.

Another said, "My heart is the same. I trust everybody is included
in the Colonel's mercy." Wright assured him they were, and that
those going with him to Walla Walla as hostages for their tribes'
good behavior would not be harmed.[39] The chiefs gave an aura of
sanctity to their words by promising, before the Great Spirit, to
remain true friends forever. During the council, Wright sent
Garry and Big Star after Kamiakin to tell him that, if he surrendered, he would not be harmed. But if he did not, the colonel
would hunt him down and hang him. Garry and Big Star returned
to report that they had hunted all night for Kamiakin until they
found him on the other side of the Spokane River, which they
could not induce him to cross, so fearful was he that Wright would
take him to Walla Walla.[40] The Kalispel chiefs claimed they had
not engaged in the war personally, but that some of their young
men had. Wright made no special treaty with them, but told them
they might consider themselves on the same footing as the Spokanes as long as they refrained from war and conformed to the
articles of the Spokane treaty.[41]

Polatkin and Garry signed the treaty first, the only ones writing
their names. Sgalgalt, Big Star, and thirty-one other Spokane
chiefs and headmen signed with an X, including one Louis
Weilsho (Peter Wyilsho), who would become a Coeur d'Alene
chief, and one Moisturm, who would become a Kalispel chief.

Things had been relatively smooth at the council through the
treaty signing. Then, that evening, came Owhi, the Upper Yakima
chief. Wright was angry with him for not having brought his
people in, as he had promised in the spring of 1856. Wright placed
the old chief in chains and sent a message to his son, Qualchan,
who was hiding at the mouth of the Spokane River, to come in or
he would hang his father. Qualchan's fellow depredator against
the whites, Moses, had been in Wright's camp, but escaped undetected, apparently unable to warn his friend to stay away. Qualchan came in the morning of September 25. Wright summarily

[39] Kip, *Army Life on the Pacific*, 93–94; *Weekly Oregonian*, October 9, 1858, p. 2.
[40] Kip, *Army Life on the Pacific*, 94.
[41] "Wright Memoir," 58.

hanged him, despite a desperate attempt by the young powerful brave, with an assist from his knife-wielding wife (Polatkin's daughter), to break free.[42] Having been tricked, Qualchan died, as did six Palouses hanged that evening.

The name of the creek, Latah, the scene of the tragedy, stemmed from a rhythmical Nez Percé word referring to "pine and pestle," objects used for hanging and grinding. Thanks to Wright, Latah thereafter bore a second name—Hangman Creek.

Wright moved south across the plateau in gloomy weather, hanging four Palouses along the way. One Palouse he hanged, there or somewhere else, was Epseal, who had taken no part in hostilities. With a terse, triumphant finality, on the last day of September, Wright could pen in his official report: "The war is closed."[43] The next day, Wright stood at Snake River, just five weeks after first crossing it. He now had thirty-three hostages from among Spokanes, Coeur d'Alenes, and Palouses.

For the Spokanes, too, the war was over. The "Big Fight" they would call it, using it as a time marker before and after which they would place events. From the soldiers they had learned bitter lessons, their own three R's: remorse, resignation, revenge. The captain's friend, Father De Smet, expressed a similar thought: "The drama of population reaches its last scene in the east and west bases of the Rocky Mountains. In a few years the curtain will fall over the Indian tribes and veil them forever."[44] Mullan, whose instruments had measured the path of conquest, measured its consequences. "Had the white man been to them more just, fate had proved less harsh." Mullan well knew, but no better than did the Spokanes themselves, that their fate had been white-determined, as it would continue to be in years to come. Awaiting the further workings of their fate, they may well have believed that by no means were all the hostages down at Walla Walla.

[42] Cowley, "Fate of Schon-shin."
[43] "Wright Memoir," 78.
[44] De Smet, *Western Missions and Missionaries: A Series of Letters*, 213.

CHAPTER SIX

Children of Two Fathers

The Spokanes had barely returned from the Wright council to their river, seeking respite from white men, when a trading expedition approached them in the latter part of September, 1858. It was led by William T. Hamilton and was on its way from Fort Walla Walla to the Blackfeet country. Hamilton was not certain what kind of reception he might receive from the Spokanes. He thought he was receiving a poor one when "about a hundred bucks came charging down on us, yelling like furies." Defeat in war had not changed their ancient custom of rushing upon strangers with "a sudden recontre," as an early fur trader described it, a maneuver that always scared the daylights out of white visitors. In trader fashion, Hamilton appeased the chiefs with plugs of tobacco, which did not prevent the young braves from casting covetous eyes on the expedition horses and mules. Hamilton thought they might have taken them had the animals not borne the government brand.

In reply to the chiefs' inquiry about the Spokane hostages, Hamilton said that their friends and relatives were welcome to come down to see how well they were treated, an invitation the Spokanes were not about to accept. When the Hamilton expedition returned to Fort Walla Walla in November, the Indian hostages, just as anxious about the welfare and behavior of their people on the Spokane, asked Alex McKay, a half-blood with Hamilton, how the Spokane people had acted. McKay said it had not been in a very friendly fashion. Again, Wright reminded the hostages of their responsibility for any hostile act of their people. He did, however, promise to release them to return home.[1]

Basing his remarks at least in part on words of the fathers, on November 5, General W. S. Harney, now commander of the Department of the Columbia, wrote: "From the different languages, interests, and jealousies existing among so many different tribes, a coalition of all of them in one common cause is impossible . . . . It is not too much to predict that the red men of America will gradually disappear about the same time from the different sections of the country." Until then, Harney would, the season permitting, establish a garrison of at least four companies of soldiers in the vicinity of Fort Colville.[2] Members of the American Indian Aid Association, writing from New York City to President James Buchanan, denounced the idea that it was the destiny of the Indian to perish before the white race. They advocated troops in Indian country not only to protect white settlers from Indians, but vice versa, "being as careful of . . . blows in the one direction as the other."[3]

When Father De Smet escorted the hostages from Walla Walla back to their homes in November, he became known to them as "Emancipator." What was perhaps not so apparent to them were his tireless diplomatic efforts on their behalf to make him also "Intercessor." He attempted to fulfill his charge, explained to him in a letter from Assistant Adjutant-General Captain A. Pleas-

[1] William T. Hamilton, A Trading Expedition Among the Indians in 1858 From Fort Walla Walla To Blackfoot Country and Return by William T. Hamilton, 33–123.

[2] Harney to General-in-Chief, Secretary of War, Annual Report, 1860, II, 93.

[3] J. Orton to [President] James Buchanan, October 26, 1858, Oregon Superintendency, Roll 611.

onton: "they can only expect to exist by implicitly obeying the commands they receive."[4] De Smet held frequent conversations with chiefs of the Coeur d'Alenes, Spokanes, Kettle Falls, and Kalispels, observing that, with the exception of a small band of Kettle Falls, all tribes were well disposed. The disillusionments of war had made them receptive to his words. Father Joset's stature was also improved, not only among his Coeur d'Alenes, but among the Spokanes. It was with no great difficulty, then, that the priests secured from their red children faithful adherence to conditions prescribed by Colonel Wright to any future requests, treaties, or proposals of the government, one of which was that they accompany Father De Smet to Fort Vancouver to pay homage to the government and the civilization for which it stood, or as Superintendent Nesmith put it, "to convince them of the madness and folly of war and secure peace with the United States as their permanent policy."[5]

On March 28, 1859, Garry wrote to General Harney of his people's desire for peace with the whites and of the willingness of the chiefs and Indians to treat with the government for the sale of their lands. The ensuing reservation would be located where the Spokanes would "not be interrupted by the whites, nor our people have a chance to interrupt the whites."[6] This friendly expression and similar ones from Spokane and neighboring chiefs seemed to have softened Harney's attitude toward them. In transmitting Garry's words to army headquarters in New York, we find him urging protection of the Indians to prevent extermination by "miserable warfare."[7]

Indian expressions of good will notwithstanding, Harney would still have Father De Smet bring the chiefs down to the lower coun-

---

[4] De Smet, *New Indian Sketches*, 89.

[5] Nesmith to Mix, June 6, 1859, Washington Superintendency, No. 5, Roll 4.

[6] Garry to Harney, March 28, 1859, Oregon Superintendency, Roll 611. In a letter to the commissioner, Stevens, on January 10, 1859, had recommended an agent for the Spokanes and their northern Salishan neighbors. Oregon Superintendency, Roll 611.

[7] Harney to assistant adjutant general, April 6, 1859, Oregon Superintendency, Roll 611.

try. Agent Owen came to the St. Ignatius Mission to say he had received orders from both the superintendent and the commissioner that the chiefs should accompany him to Fort Vancouver. It was another example of Interior–War Department conflict in Indian matters. The trip thus began awkwardly, although there was better feeling between De Smet and Owen than between the government services they represented. The Indian delegation consisted of Garry of the Spokanes, Bonaventure and Seltice of the Coeur d'Alenes, Alexander of the Pend Oreilles, Denis of the Kettle Falls, Adolph of the Iroquois, Francis of the Flatheads, and Victor of the Kalispels. They gravitated to De Smet, for the father, unlike the agent, had provisions to sustain them. Through the efforts of Garry and De Smet, Kamiakin, vowing never to "unbury" the hatchet, was induced to join the group at Spokane River. But at Fort Walla Walla, the source of so much misery to him, he once more slipped away.[8]

The last of May, 1859, the chiefs were at Fort Vancouver, talking with Harney to begin the process Owen once described as "pleasant subjugation." They assured the general they were on "no begging mission" (the Indian agent at the Dalles had just received two thousand dollars to help sustain destitute Indians visiting that place) and that "their hearts were good." They crossed the Columbia to Portland to see the sights. Here they had their pictures taken by the magic box. Garry was not present for the occasion; he may have been visiting friends at the time. Like many of his Spokanes, he had been to the settlements before. At the capital city, Salem, the chiefs were told that Oregon had just become a state and could wage a war of extermination against any who disturbed her citizens.[9] In Portland, they had seen prisoners in chains, and it made a profound impression on them, as their guides had hoped it would. They were also shown steam engines, forges, and printing presses—the handiworks of white civiliza-

---

[8] Owen to Nesmith, May 7, 1859, and Owen to E. R. Geary, superintendent of Indian affairs, Oregon and Washington Territory, May 31, 1859, Washington Superintendency, No. 5, Roll 22; Geary to Mix, June 1, 1859, Oregon Superintendency, Roll 611.

[9] Dubuar Scrapbook, No. 45, pp. 5–6.

tion[10]—big medicine, just like Wright's howitzers. They would
have much to tell their people, and something to show them, too
—"writings" from the general, official recognition of their chief-
taincies.

After three weeks they returned, duly impressed. Their sojourn
had produced good will between them and government officials.
Ironically, it had done nothing to produce good will among the
officials themselves, particularly between Owen and Harney. Officials of both army and Indian departments were satisfied the
chiefs were returning impressed and happy, but they were not so
certain their Indians back home felt the same way. Consequently,
Major Pinkney Lugenbeel was sent north toward Colville with a
battalion of the Ninth Infantry to establish a post. Reporting a
month later to E. R. Geary, new superintendent of Indian affairs
of Washington Territory and Oregon State (which had become a
state on February 14, 1859), Lugenbeel wrote of visits from well-
behaved Spokanes. They told him through George Montour that
they wanted missionaries and wanted their children to read and
write. He urgently requested Geary to send along blankets, a request to which Garry responded.[11] With blankets, Lugenbeel
hoped that diseases aggravated by exposure could be reduced. Dr.
James Mullan (Captain John Mullan's brother), passing through
the Walla Walla Valley during the summer, had met Spokanes,
Palouses, and Coeur d'Alenes at that place seeking relief from
consumption which, with scrofula, he thought to have been their
most prevalent disease.[12]

Writing again to Geary on September 24, 1859, Lugenbeel requested groundbreaking tools, such as hoes and plows, also seeds
to plant, especially since the wars had retarded Indian progress
in agrarian ways. He thought a twenty thousand-dollar supply
would help the Indians "settle down on farms and support themselves instead of living as they do now, on the precarious chances

---

[10] De Smet, *New Indian Sketches*, 92–93.
[11] Lugenbeel to Geary, July 16, 1859, Washington Superintendency, No. 5,
Roll 20; Secretary of War, *Annual Report*, 1859–60, II, 111–12.
[12] James Mullan, M.D., to Geary, August 20, 1859, Washington Superintendency, No. 5, Roll 20.

of catching fish and gathering berries."[13] Fishing the previous year had been poor. Hunting had its risks, too. The Blackfeet killed three Spokanes in the early fall in an engagement aggravated by a buffalo shortage that year.[14]

At this time Garry sought to relieve his people's food problem by building a grist mill closer to them to eliminate the long grain haul to the one at Fort Colville. Judge Yantis, with whom Garry made an agreement five years earlier for the project, hauled mill-stones muleback from Olympia to the site (Selheim Springs) on the Little Spokane. A millrace and waterwheel were built, but the stones ground only briefly, as some disagreement between the partners forced Yantis to move his millstones to the Colville Valley.[15]

To assist his Indians in hunting until they could find more stable means of sustenance, Lungenbeel authorized the sale of ammunition to them. He even gave them powder from his own stores. Their need of ammunition, thought Lieutenant Charles Wilson of the British boundary survey party, was the only thing keeping them peaceful. At the fort, awaiting their ammunition and other gifts, they appeared innocent enough, passing the time at the "odd and even" game, shooting arrows into a ring rolled along the ground, and playing cards "in a very eccentric manner," all the while betting sometimes two or three horses and skins they had worked so hard to get. Beneath the surface, Wilson detected an uneasiness about them, despite government benevolences. Even Garry, a "clever fellow," appeared to him to be as unsettled as the others. Wilson believed the Indians to be excited by news of recent Bannack attacks on an American expedition under Captain A. J. Smith just east of Harney Valley in Oregon.[16]

Undoubtedly the Indians were upset by the appearance that

[13] Lugenbeel to Geary, September 24, 1859, Washington Superintendency, No. 5, Roll 20.
[14] Henri M. Chase to Owen, October 18, 1859, Oregon Superintendency, Roll 611.
[15] Lewis, *The Case of Spokane Garry*, 21–22.
[16] Lieutenant Charles Wilson, "Diary Kept by Lt. Wilson of the British Boundary Survey Party June 1860–July 1862 Canada to Colville Country via the Dallas [Dalles]." Hereafter cited as Wilson, "Diary."

summer (1860) of Captain Mullan's Fort Walla Walla to Fort Benton road builders. They were nearly a hundred men, armed with a hundred-thousand-dollar Congressional appropriation for picks, shovels, whipsaws, wagons, packhorses. From Hangman Creek, a symbolic reminder of their authority, they swung boldly east to the Coeur d'Alene mission. They received a grudging reception from its Indians, who, thanks to Father Joset's influence, allowed them to continue east hacking a path out of woods and mountains to secure American civilization between two great rivers of the West, the Columbia and the Missouri.

In the winter of 1861, at the beginning of the Civil War, Companies C and D, Second Infantry, California Volunteers, replaced Lugenbeel's troops to maintain peace with the Indians. Presumably to shield themselves from illness, but in reality from cold weather and boredom, the soldiers dosed themselves with "Bourbon whiskey, 1812, at $17.60 a gallon." It was not a very good example to an Indian. The day Wilson left in 1862, he wrote that "whisky & civilization are doing their work quickly & surely amongst them, in twenty years time they will be a matter of history."[17] The Spokane chiefs were unable to keep their people on a dry trail; even Garry walked a crooked one.[18] Depressed and disillusioned by recent events, the chief sought to cushion with liquor his fall from what Wilson called "opulence for an Indian to perfect beggary."

Besides soldiers, there were what Lugenbeel called "miserable squatters" selling the Indians liquor.[19] Lugenbeel had pleaded with the Spokane county commissioners to close the whiskey shops along the Columbia River,[20] but the shops remained open, dispensing their wares to produce all kinds of troubles.[21] Aggravat-

---

[17] Aurora Hunt, *The Army of the Pacific*, 227; Wilson, "Diary," 88.

[18] Howard S. Brode (ed.), "Diary of Dr. A. J. Thibodo," *Pacific Northwest Quarterly*, Vol. XXXI, No. 3 (July, 1940), 339.

[19] Lugenbeel to Geary, January 5, 1861, and July 18, 1861, Washington Superintendency, No. 5, Roll 20.

[20] Lugenbeel to Spokane County Commissioners, July (n.d.), 1861. Winans Papers, Box 5, No. 38.

[21] Lugenbeel to Geary, March 31, 1861, Washington Superintendency, No. 5, Roll 20.

ing the problem still further was the constant shifting of supervisory personnel, not only at the fort, but in the office of the territorial superintendent of Indian affairs. With Lugenbeel's departure, there was no agent to look after the Indians' welfare. Taking advantage of the absence of an agent, an enterprising whiskey distiller began operating near the fort. Major James F. Curtis, Lugenbeel's replacement, found it necessary to destroy the stock and remove its works.

About all Superintendent of Indian Affairs of Washington Territory Calvin H. Hale could do from his office in far-off Olympia was to warn traders to stop peddling whiskey and to urge the commissioner to provide an agent to see that they did. Hale warned miners "SELLING, DISPOSING OF, BARTERING, OR GIVING LIQUOR to Indians, in the Territory, or *introducing or attempting to introduce* the same into the Indian country, is a grave offense, punishable by fine and imprisonment, by the laws of the United States."[22] Hale advised Commissioner of Indian Affairs William P. Dole of repeated applications from officers at Fort Colville for an agent for the three or four thousand Okanogans, Colvilles, Spokanes, Coeur d'Alenes, and some Kalispels and Kootenays, with whom some treaty should be made.[23]

The most important contact Fort Colville commanders had with the Indians was the interpreter. Only through him could they adequately protect their red charges from many new dangers. Unfortunately, the Interior Department often failed to realize the value of these men in its service, most often half-bloods.

The superintendent and other Indian department officials were under the impression that the Chinook jargon, so successfully used by the Hudson's Bay Company at Fort Colville, would continue to suffice at that place in communications with the Indian. One official said very few Indians outside the Colville Valley spoke the jargon, which had truly been a vehicle of the fur era. As need for treaties with these Indians became greater, so did the need for interpreters to convey terms involved in these arrangements—

[22] Notice by Hale, June 25, 1862, Washington Superintendency, No. 5, Roll 4.
[23] Hale to Dole, August 13, 1862, Washington Superintendency, No. 5, Roll 4.

lands, boundaries, markers, relocation—words foreign to the fur trade and its jargon.

During low water in the winter of 1864–65, the first bridge over the Spokane was built by two men, Joe Herring and Tim Lee.[24] The builders hoped to accommodate miners, at a profit to themselves. They were aware that many gold-seekers in the early 1860's passed that way from Lewiston, Idaho Territory, and Walla Walla to the booming Kootenay, British Columbia mines, a more practical route than any in Canada.

Numerous Indians crowded around the site (some seventeen miles east of the falls) to watch the building of the structure, called "Spokane Bridge."[25] Chief Garry was there demanding that Herring and Lee pay him a bonus for the right to build it.[26] In the fall of 1865, a man named Kellogg planned to build a bridge a mile below Spokane Bridge. He began selling liquor to the Indians and, according to a newspaper report, was indirectly responsible for the killing of a Negro by one of the Herring-Lee crew. Kellogg climaxed the troubles by running off with Herring's Indian woman.[27] The next year, 1866, despite declining activity in the Kootenay, there were gold discoveries and rumors of gold discoveries in the Coeur d'Alene, Big Blackfoot, Flathead, and Bitterroot areas east toward the Rockies.[28]

Focal points for the spread of social diseases were the parade grounds and streets of Pinckney City, where there were "as many prostitute Indian women and drunken Indians as there were soldiers and citizens."[29] Although there were some binding unions between Indian women and white men, the latter often took advantage of the difference between their marriage ceremonies and the Indians' simple voluntary-association marriages. The women thought they were married; the white men had other ideas, breaking the unions at will.

24 *Walla Walla Statesman*, April 13, 1866, p. 2.
25 *Ibid.*
26 Beall, "Pioneer Reminiscences," *Washington Historical Quarterly*, Vol. VIII, No. 2 (April, 1917), 86–87.
27 *Walla Walla Statesman*, April 13, 1866, p. 2.
28 Trimble, *Mining Advance*, 46–60.
29 Paige to C. A. Huntington, October 16, 1865, Washington Superintendency, No. 5, Roll 20.

Various army doctors were given the task of treating at the post diseases against which they made but little headway, not the least reason being the lack of funds, which meant lack of medicines. These diseases included scrofula, consumption, opthalmia, gonorrhea, syphilis, and rheumatism. On one occasion, the acting physician was forced to turn sufferers away for lack of funds for medicine.[30] Many Indians were too ill to come to Fort Colville for treatment.

The need of aid to promote the Indians' physical welfare was urgent because of increasing white pressures, poor salmon runs, poor hunting at home, and dangerous hunting on the Great Plains, where the elder Lot would be killed in 1868. His brother Chata would trek to the plains thereafter to avenge his death in company with other Salishans also seeking to settle old scores with the Blackfeet. By banding together, they were better able to retaliate against their old enemies than they had been for years.

Many Spokanes and other Indians sought to relieve their economic plight by making annual trips downriver to work in Portland and other settlements. The Oregon superintendent of Indian affairs wished these "wanderers and vagabonds" had stayed home. He claimed that their main support in the lower country was prostituting their squaws and running between white men who sold liquor and Indians who drank it.[31] Not all Indians going downriver followed this pattern. Some worked as domestics on river boats or in other odd jobs. One party of Spokanes canoed down to Portland three years in a row to clear brush in the fall. On another occasion, nearly a hundred Spokanes went down to the Portland area in seventeen canoes to spend the year sawing wood.[32]

Most Spokanes found it easier to get the things they needed at Colville. Goods were usually given out there through chiefs and

[30] *Ibid.*

[31] Secretary of the Interior, *Annual Report,* 1867–68 (40 Cong., 2 sess., *House Exec. Doc. No. 1*), Pt. II, p. 73. The editor of the *Oregonian,* January 27, 1865, complained of Indians he identified as "Spokanes" who had become involved in fights, mainly with other Indians in Portland.

[32] Curtis, *North American Indian,* VII, 57.

headmen, with presents thrown in for these leaders. In official reports, we read of Chiefs Sgalgalt, Polatkin, and Garry of the Upper and Middle Spokanes, and a Chief Senseta of the Lower Spokanes receiving gifts of seed potatoes, oats, wheat, flour, plows, hoes, axes, hatchets, blankets, tobacco, pants, and shirts. We find Garry in July, 1866, receiving, among other gifts, a bar of soap, presumably to cleanse himself of summer sweat and dirt like a white man.

It was customary for goods to be distributed at one time, usually before bad weather set in or after it was over. These goods distributions were called "potlatches," the old tribal designation for gift-giving ceremonies. That the gifts came from the Great Father and not from one who had recently died seems not to have mattered. In a potlatch in May, 1868, the Indians consumed a ton of beef.

The Indians feared that the distribution of goods was payment for their lands, to be followed by removal to a reservation. They had grounds for apprehension; settlers were invading much of their improved land. This of course focused attention on treaty making, around which many rumors circled.[33] Garry himself had contributed to Indian disquietude in these matters. Two years earlier, perhaps in exasperation, he had told Flathead Agent Guy H. Chapman that the Spokanes wished to settle on the Flathead Reservation. This suggestion sat poorly with other Spokane chiefs, who wished their reserve to be within, or convenient to, the country they had always occupied.[34] Garry constantly feared that, when away on one of his many trips "to buffalo," other chiefs would make a treaty without him. South of the falls, Kamiakin and about fifty of his band were living in heartbreaking exile, refusing government gifts.

Large reductions in Congressional appropriations soon threatened aid to the Indians. The problem became so grave that goods

33 McKenney to Paige, February 15, 1867, Washington Superintendency, No. 5, Roll 5.
34 Paige to Waterman, August 12, 1866, Washington Superintendency, No. 5, Roll 20; Chapman to D. W. Cooley, commissioner of Indian affairs, April 26, 1866. Records of the Colville Indian Agency, Federal Records Center, Seattle, Washington, Box 17. Hereafter cited as Colville Agency Records.

on hand like blankets and tobacco, the articles in heaviest demand, had to be sold for cash to pay for the deficits. The physician was discharged, presumably as an economy measure.[35] A shortage of aid funds—but no shortage of white pressures—increased the urgency of a reservation settlement with the nontreaty Indians.

An 1870 census reported the Spokanes as numbering 716 souls and possessing 949 horses, a mere 61 cattle, and 49 farms. They cultivated potatoes and corn, which, along with wheat, made up a third of their sustenance. They had to go to Colville to have their wheat ground, since Garry's grist-mill project had fallen through. Garry was listed as head chief, once trained by white men but now having a better "recollection" of their bad habits than "knowledge" of their books, probably because he had "so many living examples before him."[36]

President Ulysses S. Grant's peace policy, in which reservation agents were selected from religious denominations, focused official concern on the religious welfare of Indians. The Lower Spokanes were reported as having no religious instruction, but wanting Protestant missionaries. The Upper Spokanes, as Roman Catholics, were visited by the fathers once or twice a year. They had no school and were also desirous of religious instruction.

In 1865, Joseph Cataldo, S.J., came to the Spokane country from California. Pierre Quinchistilis and Baptiste Peone begged the father to remain through the winter to conduct his mission and to strengthen in the faith those previously baptized "in a great hurry." Cataldo replied that his mission was at most for two weeks, as he was under orders to return before snow fell on the "divide" between the Spokane and Coeur d'Alene countries. But he did promise to speak with his superior and, if permitted, would return for the winter. Back at the Coeur d'Alene mission, Cataldo was encouraged to return to the Spokanes. He did so in November. When the Blackrobe asked permission to build a church, Peone said to await Garry's return "from buffalo," where he had

35 McKenny to Lieutenant W. C. Manning, November 1, 1868, and McKenney to Parker, October 1, 1868, Washington Superintendency, No. 5, Roll 20.
36 Winans to Ross, August 1, 1879, Winans Papers, Box 4, No. 34.

gone for about three months. Aware of his responsibility to powers higher than Garry, Cataldo took his ax to the woods, made the sign of the cross, and began to chop a tree. When the Indians saw him chopping, they pitched in to cut down the trees. In a few days, the trees were hewn into length and hauled to the father's camping place, and the church was put up.

It was dedicated December 8, 1866, on Peone Prairie. It was a crude mud-covered log structure with extended roof, sheltering a dirt floor, altar, and fireplace—St. Michael's Mission, a Roman Catholic chapel among the Spokanes. News of the building spread. Indians who had avoided the church like poison now crowded in every morning for mass and catechetical instruction, and every evening for prayers and more instruction. After breakfasts and dinners, Cataldo called the children to a regular catechism school, at which many grown people also assisted. With the father leading, their voices filled the prairie with song. One evening after prayers and instruction, Baptiste Peone, Pierre Quinchistilis, and several old men said that, since they could not learn as quickly as the children, they wanted a chance to learn for themselves. Shortly, Cataldo held a catechism school at night for them, running sometimes until 11:30. At Christmas the little house was so crowded, it "looked like a barrel filled with indian humanity."

At Fort Colville, the winter of the new year, 1871, Garry was unhappy with what had happened when his back was turned. He complained that Catholic Spokanes would not visit Protestant Spokanes, and that if they did, they would go to hell together, a situation he feared would lead to bloodshed on earth.[37] Garry, like other Protestant chiefs, feared his hold over his people would be weakened by their conversion to the Roman Catholic faith. "As an Indian cannot be conservative," wrote Agent W. P. Winans, "and is from nature a fanatic, the feeling between the two factions is about as bitter, as between Orangemen and Hibernians." In the Colville Valley, to which the delegations came, the Catholics had established, in 1868, St. Francis Regis, an Indian mission some five miles east of Kettle Falls. A government appro-

[37] Winans to McKenny, March 13, 1871, Winans Papers, Box 4, No. 34.

priation that year of five thousand dollars to the mission for a school under the peace policy would cause the agent to complain that nothing had been done with his suggestion that a Protestant school be built on Walker's Prairie.[38]

Talk, which began in February, 1871, of the removal of Fort Colville had caused religious factions to temporarily lay aside their differences to weigh the disadvantages which would follow such a removal.[39] Winans thought the removal would jeopardize the lives and property of settlers. Wheat and seed had made the Middle and Upper Spokanes somewhat independent. The Lower Spokanes, accepting no favors, had eaten their traditional starvation food during the winter, black moss. They earned some money selling furs, as did other Spokanes.[40]

A decision not to abandon the post renewed the rift among the Spokanes. Ahmelmelchen (Amor Melican), a Middle Spokane, assumed leadership of a party friendly to whites. He urged his people to accept their presents, to cultivate the land and quit their roving ways. Garry, representing the majority, was all for appropriating white improvements made on the land. Both chiefs had come to the fort, Ahmelmelchen to express his friendship, and Garry to say but little. He returned, however, to warn settlers to make no more improvements, because he intended to appropriate them. In Garry's thinking, the Spokanes could build more than the eight log cabins they now had, but the whites should build no more.[41]

On May 6, 1872, Winans learned that the Colville Reservation, east of the Columbia River, had been set aside for the Spokanes and other nontreaty tribes in his care by Executive Order, April 8, 1872. This order was made possible by the Appropriation Act of March 3, 1871, whereby Indian reservations would no longer be

[38] Winans to McKenny, June 3, 1872, Winans Papers, Box 4, 34; Secretary of the Interior, *Annual Report*, 1873 (43 Cong., 1 sess., *House Exec. Doc. No. 1*), Vol. I, Pt. 5, p. 683.

[39] Winans, Annual Report (1871), Winans Papers, Box 4, No. 34.

[40] Winans to Rice, March 12, 1871, Winans Papers, Box 4, No. 34.

[41] Winans Diary. Entry of March 18, 1871. Winans Papers, Box 4, No. 34.

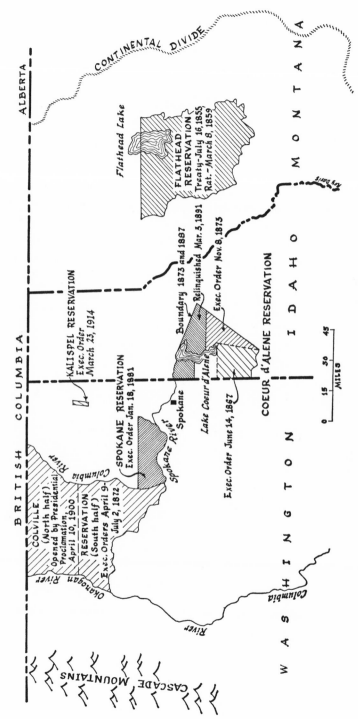

Major reservations to which the Spokane Indians removed.

established by treaty.[42] The new reservation began at a point on the Columbia where it received the Spokane; thence up the Columbia to where it crossed the Canadian border; thence east along the border to where the Pend Oreille or Clark Fork River crossed the same; thence up the Clark Fork to where it crossed the western boundary of Idaho Territory (meridian 117); thence southwesterly with the Little Spokane to its junction with the Spokane; thence down the Spokane to the place of beginning.[43]

Winans thought it would be easier to move the Indians from the new reservation than to move from it the tangible results of white civilization. On it, he pointed out, were over six hundred settlers, an obvious exaggeration to get his point across. They were mostly squatters cultivating large tracts of land. They had built homes and made other improvements. There were three flour mills and two sawmills, six stores and two small villages with shops, a courthouse, a jail, and other public improvements. Total improvements on the reservation cost not less than $200,000. It was too much to move.[44]

At Spokane Prairie, near Antoine Plante's, on June 21, 1872, Winans held council with the Spokanes, Coeur d'Alenes, Kalispels, Colvilles, and San Poils to inform them of the reservation set apart for them. Sgalgalt, whom Winans listed as a Lower Spokane, angrily denounced the white men for building roads and establishing reservations on Indian land without consulting its owners. Resigning himself to being removed to a confine, he proposed its southern bounds be moved to the Spokane River. Baptiste Peone and William Three Mountains of the Upper Spokanes, Ahmelmelchen of the Middle Spokanes, and Costeakan

[42] The Appropriation Act of March 3, 1871, provided not only for the termination of treaty making with Indian tribes (16 Stat. 544, 556, R.S. 2079, 25 U.S. C. 71), but also (sec. 3) for withdrawal from noncitizen Indians and from Indian tribes of power to make contracts involving the payment of money for services relative to Indian lands or claims against the United States, unless such contracts should be approved by the commissioner of Indian affairs and the Secretary of the Interior.

[43] Charles J. Kappler (ed.), *Indian Affairs: Laws and Treaties*, I, 915. Hereafter cited as *Indian Affairs*.

[44] Winans to McKenny, May 27, 1872, Winans Papers, Box 4, No. 34.

of the Lower Spokanes proposed the same thing, an indication that they had arrived at their decision before the council. The Coeur d'Alene chiefs said nothing. Winans continued on to the San Poils to receive from their spokesman this reply: "I want to know if you thought the President was God Almighty that he should make a Reservation for us?"

The following month Winans was approached by Ahmelmelchan. He had heard a rumor that the reserve would be moved west of the Columbia River. "We would rather live among the whites," he said, "than to be moved to a strange land. We will not go." The rumor proved to be true. Strong pressures had squeezed the President into signing, on July 2, 1872, an Executive Order restoring to the public domain the reservation occupied by Colvilles, Spokanes, and Kalispels. It established a new one for "said Indians and for such other Indians as the Department of the Interior may see fit to locate thereon." The proposed reservation, also to be called the Colville, contained only four settlers. It was bounded on the east and south by the Columbia River, on the west by the Okanogan River, and on the north by the Canadian border.[45]

It was easy to wipe out bounds of an old reserve and mark out bounds of a new one; it would not be so easy to move Indians from one to another. This would not be Winans' problem, for on September 14, he tendered his resignation to Washington Superintendent of Indian Affairs R. H. Milroy. He had just sent Milroy his annual report, in which he opined that it would be unfair to move the Indians, particularly those who had made improvements. They had been noteworthy for the Spokanes: three hundred acres producing sixteen hundred bushels of wheat, one thousand of potatoes, and four hundred of corn. The Indian land improvers, Winans believed, should be allowed to remain

---

[45] Strong pressures had been exerted on Selucius Garfielde, Washington Territorial delegate in Congress, who, in turn, blamed Winans for much of the old reservation dilemma. In defense, Winans replied that he had never recommended one east of the Columbia River, but one west of that river. Winans to Garfielde, July 15, 1872, Winans Papers, Box 4, No. 34.

where one plow would do them more good toward civilization than a hundred blankets.[46]

The new agent, John A. Simms, called the tribes together on November 6, 1872, to talk with them about moving to the new Colville Reservation, set apart by the new Executive Order. He explained the boundaries. They asked permission to mark off a reserve of their own choosing. Simms agreed to forward note of their wishes to Superintendent Milroy, along with their objections to the new reserve. When he told them the Northern Pacific Railroad would soon be built in their country, they naïvely replied it would benefit both whites and themselves. In reporting their ideas to Milroy, Simms added some of his own. One was that the east border of the Colville Reservation, running from the Canadian border to the mouth of the Spokane River, be enlarged to include a five-mile buffer east of the Columbia. This would help to control the liquor traffic of nearly five thousand gallons of whiskey and high wines shipped annually into the Colville Valley. The greater amount of it, he thought, must have been consumed by Indians, since the white population did not exceed 150 adults, exclusive of the military garrison of 40 men. The chiefs had complained much about it.

Simms had attempted to persuade the Indians to abandon their tribal relations and become citizens, acquiring property under the homestead and pre-emption laws of the United States. This suggestion set poorly with them. Garry, however, according to a story in the *Walla Walla Union* (Walla Walla, W.T.) asked Simms if he could take a homestead near his native Spokane River. Simms told him he could by severing his tribal ties. Garry thereupon picked a homestead site but failed to settle or file on it. When a white man took it, Garry got someone to write a general notice to vacate the land. As Garry lived some distance from the white man on his land, he gave the notice to a young Indian to serve on the settler. The Indian messenger proudly showed the written paper to all the settlers he met, permitting them to read it.

[46] Winans to Milroy, September 1, 1872, Winans Papers, Box 4, No. 34.

Each thought the notice was directed to him, when Garry had intended it only for one man.[47]

In concluding his report, Simms stated that 90 per cent of the Indians of the Colville Agency were Roman Catholic, "much attached to the Fathers who labour incessantly among them, and to whom they are mostly indebted for whatever advances they have made in Christianity and civilization."[48] Simms's appointment had been a vindication for the Catholics who, with the departure of the Walker-Eells mission, had the only sustaining mission among the tribes. Catholic officials had justly complained that, under President Grant's peace policy, Protestants had been given thirty agencies where Catholics had begun and sustained their missionary work.[49] This vindication brought little comfort to the majority of non-Catholic Spokanes. In answering a Baptiste Peone letter, which told of flaring rivalries between the faiths, Simms expressed satisfaction with the teachings of Paschal Tosi, S.J., and urged all Catholic Indians to listen to him.[50]

Simms believed he had, since his arrival, effected a marked improvement in the moral conditions of the Indians, a tremendous accomplishment for one on the job such a short time. Nature may have effected the improvement. On the night of December 14, 1872, an earthquake shook the natives in more ways than one. The quake left large cracks in the ground and massive landslides in an area fifty miles west of the falls. The Indians thought the world was coming to an end. They became very religious. Penitent Indians prepared to flee to Colville to have the priests baptize them.

The large number of Spokanes fleeing to the priests for baptism filled Garry with alarm. On January 29, 1873, with a sick son to care for along with his other problems, he had his second chief, William Three Mountains, write Simms complaining that Colville priests were baptizing women into the Catholic faith against

<hr />

47 *Walla Walla Union,* May 17, 1873, p. 2.
48 Simms to Milroy, November 20, 1872, Simms Papers, 3–B.
49 Charles Ewing (Catholic commissioner for Indian missions), *Circular of the Catholic Commissioner for Indian Missions, to the Catholics of the United States.*
50 Simms to Peone, December 11, 1872, Simms Papers, 3–A.

his wishes. He requested they baptize no more, as it was causing quarrels among the people.[51] Receiving no satisfaction from the agent, Garry called a meeting of interested Spokanes along the river a short distance above the falls to cope with the problem. Having heard of the Reverend Henry H. Spalding's successes among the Nez Percés, to whom he had returned after a long absence, Garry wrote to the missionary. Spalding was now in his seventieth year. Garry invited him to come north "to baptize his people and marry them according to the laws."[52] A short time later, Garry sent William Three Mountains, Nowitchitschemoqualte, Sha-amene, and Tschtsko, over a hundred miles to Spalding at Lapwai, urging him "to preach Jesus to the people." Responding quickly, Spalding left in late May for a three-week tour among the Spokanes. He met them at root grounds like those of Rock Creek south of the falls. On June 11 and 12 he baptized and received on examination into the church 122 adults and 43 children. Former Catholics said they "were not running from Jehovah but from man." One of these men from whom they were running was Father Tosi, who would be obliged to leave because his people were at the mercy of Protestant chiefs and ministers, who had succeeded in "perverting" a hundred of his people.[53]

General J. P. C. Shanks, chairman of the House Committee on Indian Affairs, was a member of a special commission to investigate and report upon Indian affairs in the territory of Idaho, and territories adjacent thereto. He came to investigate complaints of Indians against whites and vice versa, particularly those stemming from the switch in reservations. Shanks was joined by Superintendent Milroy, who had been directed by Commissioner E. P. Smith to investigate various complaints along the Spokane River.[54] Shanks held council on August 12, 1873, at the old Fort Colville with Colvilles, Lakes, San Poils, Okanogans, Upper and

[51] William Three Mountains (for Garry) to Simms, January 29, 1873, Simms Papers, 4–A.
[52] Clifford M. Drury, "The Spalding-Lowrie Correspondence," 46.
[53] L. van Ree, "The Spokane Indians, Sketch of the Work of Our Fathers," 357.
[54] Smith to Milroy, May 22, 1873, M–234, Roll 911 (Mfl. copy in Washington State Library).

Lower Spokanes, and Kalispels. His report afterward was highly critical of former agent Winans in procuring a change of reservation for "selfish motives" in removing Indians from their homelands, where their livelihood had been procured, in exchange for a barren land west of the Columbia. Shanks would recommend the Indians stay where they were and have a reservation there increased to include virtually both the new and old Colville Reservations as a home for the Coeur d'Alenes, Upper and Lower Spokanes, Lakes, Colvilles, San Poils, Methows, Okanogans, and nontreaty Kalispels, Pend Oreilles, and Kootenays.

Winans, quite naturally critical of Shanks, would later claim that the Protestant Spokanes, along with the San Poils and Methows, were not at the council.[55] Shanks did see the religious division of the tribes and that although Simms was Catholic, the Indians had more faith in him than in Winans, the Colville merchant whose partner in a trading post, Shanks claimed, sold liquor for furs, the principal trade in the locality. An old Colville chief's complaint that "liquor is coming up to our knees" did little to improve the Winans image, as Shanks saw it. Neither did his "permitting" another type of trade to be carried on at Colville, by "some bad Indian women" who kept "places of ill-fame."

Shanks claimed that when the first Colville Reservation was set aside east of the Columbia River, Winans had urged it be changed to useless lands west of the river. It was an "unjust assignment of reservation," wrote Shanks, where he hoped the Indians would never go. In all fairness to Winans, it should be remembered that in his last official report he had opposed moving to any new reservation Indians who had made improvements on their lands.

Shanks reported that the tribes wished for a reserve bounded as follows: beginning at a point in the center of the channel of the Columbia to a point opposite the mouth of the Spokane River; thence up the center of the channel of the Spokane to the mouth of Hangman (or Latah) Creek; thence up the center of that creek to the line dividing Washington and Idaho territories as recently

---

[55] Winans to the Reverend A. L. Lindsley, December 20, 1875, Winans Papers, Box 9, No. 67.

surveyed; thence south on said line to the top of the ridge between Hangman or Latah Creek and Pine Creek; thence easterly along the summit of said ridge to a point five miles in a direct line east of said territorial line; thence in a direct line north to the Canadian border; thence west along that line to the Okanogan River; thence down the center of that river channel to the place of beginning. In summary, Shanks said, it would be "expensive, troublesome, dishonorable and wicked" to drive the Indians from their homes where they had lived to give ground to "cunning men" who had supplanted them by government action.[56]

After the council, Shanks departed, leaving the Indians to pour out their complaints to Milroy. Milroy traveled over the new reserve. He reported that its inhabitants would starve there, as its only good land was in the Nespelem Valley, a fact Milroy well knew, having spent practically every day in the saddle traversing the reservation from August 20 to September. This was a considerably longer time than Shanks had spent with the Indians on his trip to Colville. In concluding his report, Shanks had written that it would "be both unjust and cruel to restrict these tribes to the reservation as now constituted, and I most certainly concur with them in asking the addition mentioned." Milroy likewise suggested some changes.

Spalding believed whatever action the government took on the Shanks report would affect his missionary program in the Spokane country. As far as he was concerned, that report was secondary to his own, such as one in August, 1873, in which he claimed to have baptized 334 souls into the church of Christ.

At that time there was a possibility that one of three churches might assume control of Protestant Spokane mission work—Presbyterian, Episcopalian, or Methodist. Any overall census of Spokanes that year would have indicated that a few Catholics who had defected to Spalding were returning to the faith of the fathers. However, at Easter time a large encampment of mostly Spokanes and Coeur d'Alenes gathered at Peone Prairie for services with

[56] The Shanks report is found in, Secretary of the Interior, *Annual Report*, 1873, pp. 527–32.

Joseph Giordi, S.J., Tosi, Joset, Cataldo, and Gregory Gazzoli, S.J. Snows kept many Pend Oreilles and Kalispels away. At Good Friday evening services boys with pitchwood torches carried "the sacred body of the Lord" on a bier to the sepulchre to the accompaniment of canticles rendered by their people. Communions were held on Easter Sunday, 180 men and women were confirmed, and a letter pledging loyalty, signed by the chiefs, was sent to the Pope.[57] Mindful of their failure to baptize no more than "a few infidels," and mindful of Protestant successes, Fathers Giordi and Tosi returned the following year to safeguard the Spokanes with a two-week mission. Each year thereafter one of the fathers would spend one, two, or three months every winter with the Spokanes "always with good results." Cataldo would erect a new chapel among them in 1878.

Gone was Spalding's hope of returning to the Spokanes with board authorization. He passed the Spokane mission mantle to the Reverend Henry T. Cowley. Cowley arrived on the Spokane in late June, 1874, with several Nez Percé helpers. Garry came to his tent to tell him that commissioners who had come to treat with the Indians were camped nearby. Cowley discovered the visiting group to be no commission but a party, under the leadership of General Jefferson C. Davis, on its way to inspect Fort Colville. At a meeting outside a store at the falls, Davis told Garry he had no interest in getting the Spokanes a reservation. He dismissed the chief curtly with a reminder of his knowledge of the chief's record in the Indian wars.[58] Hearing that more soldiers were being sent to the Colville, some half-dozen Spokanes, Kettle Falls, and Okanogan chiefs sent a letter to President Grant to send soldiers to Indians on the warpath, not to them.[59]

Cowley moved his family to the Spokane country in late October, 1874. In previous trips to the Spokane he had been most

[57] Harvey to Simms, April 30, 1874, Washington Superintendency, No. 5, Roll 20; *Catholic Sentinel*, April 24, 1874, p. 1.

[58] J. Orin Oliphant (ed.), "The Reminiscences of H. T. Cowley," in *The Early History of Spokane, Washington, Told by Contemporaries*, 44. Hereafter cited as Cowley, "Reminiscences."

[59] Burns, *Jesuits and Indian Wars*, 359.

favorably impressed with William Three Mountains, a man of "sterling principles, firm will, and indomitable energy," leader of an Indian band living west of Hangman Creek. Cowley proposed building his school in William's country. This plan caused friction among the various bands. Garry called a council of all Upper Spokanes to oppose it. Giving in, Cowley knew he had to be where he could get most support. By staying near Garry's people, he knew he could receive oats, furs, horses, and labor for his support. Yet he also knew that, by going with Garry, he would offend the Three Mountains people. So he chose to build on the lands of Enoch, a chief in the middle, where he could stay within reach of both Spokane groups.[60]

At Thanksgiving several families combined their tipis into one community lodge some eighty feet long. Reminiscent of another Thanksgiving, Indians and whites joined in an Indian-prepared meal of venison, fish, wheatcakes, flour, sugar, coffee, and dried camass roots. The longhouse was used three hours daily for school, equipped only with a blackboard on which simple words were printed. With moderating weather, in late February, 1875, a box house was built with lumber and long rough boards for seats. A stove and windows were brought from Walla Walla. By then, there were some government-printed primers for use in Indian schools. As it was too early for the Indians to gather roots and fish, attendance remained high. Some adult students had to sit on the floor.[61] Several times during the year, as many as 250 Indians came to the church and school. Cushing Eells, returning that summer for a nostalgic visit, was amazed at the results of the work. He attended church under the pines where 360 Spokanes congregated, the harvest of his own seed-sowing nearly four decades before.

By this time the Spokanes no longer called themselves "Children of the Sun." Missionaries had made them children of their Father in heaven. Government officials had made them children of their Father in Washington. They were now children of two Fathers. Yet white servants of the two Fathers believed there was

[60] Cowley, "Reminiscences," 48.
[61] *Ibid.*, 53–54.

no dichotomy in their respective Fathers' work; effort expended for one complemented that expended for the other. Cowley, for instance, encouraged "the children" to visit the Colville Agency for help from its agent, Simms, and himself asked the agent's help for a Spokane school. Simms said he had encouraged Spokanes to send their children to the agency school for food, clothing, and education. But they had declined, not so much "on the ground of religious preferences" as from the "interference of meddlesome white men." He said he was unable to provide aid to a Spokane school, but would help in any other way he could.[62] Simms and Cowley remained on friendly terms, and the agent would observe that Cowley labored zealously and successfully for the spiritual welfare of his Spokanes.

The separation of the Protestant Spokanes from the Colville Agency widened in January, 1875, when Cowley received an official commission from the Indian office to supervise Spokane education. At the same time he was instructed to encourage his Indians to enter their lands under the Indian Homestead Act, so as to maintain their holdings when the Northern Pacific Railroad would reach the region. The Indian Homestead Act of March 3, 1875, provided that Indians could homestead their tracts of land, improve on them, and sever tribal relations. Still waiting for the reserve Stevens had promised, Garry was as much opposed to the new act as he was to the Railroad Act of July 2, 1864, which called for the extinction, "as rapidly as may be consistent with public policy and the welfare of said Indians," of Indian titles to all lands falling under the act.

On July 4, 1876, at the falls, the centennial of the signing of the Declaration of Independence was observed. Reverend Cowley addressed an audience of between 50 and 75 people on the centennial theme, amazed that such an unexpectedly large number of settlers was present.[63] It had, in fact, been only a scant four years (1872) since the first white men, J. H. Downing and L. R. Scranton, had come to the falls. When they came, there was a

---

62 Simms to Cowley, December 11, 1874, Colville Agency Records, Box 17.
63 Cowley, "Reminiscences," 57; "Washington Dictations," P–B 81.

sprinkling of white settlers in the country—whites on the Spokane Plains by 1870 official census reports. In 1872 another Cowley, M. M. Cowley, established a trading post on the north side of the Spokane River at Spokane Bridge, now called Cowley's Bridge. He got a five- or six-year-old Indian lad to teach him the language, went into business with the Indians, and shunted white settlers down to the falls. In 1873, J. M. Glover saw the first spray of the falls, bought the Downing-Scranton mill, and opened a small store, hoping to do well when the Northern Pacific Railroad came. Soon learning that its financier, Jay Cooke, had gone by the economic boards, the disappointed frontier merchant turned to trading with Indians and stockmen for furs and stock, the principal media of exchange. Immigration for the next few years was small. Frederick Post and his family moved to the falls in 1876 to build and operate the first grist mill.

It was the Methodist minister, S. G. Havermale, a newcomer to the falls, who in 1877 brought word that the Nez Percés had gone on the warpath against the United States. The white community, a handful of houses surrounded by a much larger number of Indian tipis, was in peril. They sent a letter to General O. O. Howard, commanding the Department of the Columbia, praying for a military establishment somewhere in the Spokane country, as the one at Fort Colville was too far away. In late June, 1877, the Nez Percés sent a squad of warriors to stir up the Spokanes and Coeur d'Alenes. This sent the frightened whites scurrying to Havermale Island in the Spokane River for safety. Other whites south in the plateau fled to Colfax, Washington Territory, and Walla Walla, which at that time was larger than Seattle. The frightened residents hid in a makeshift fort on their small plot of earth, knowing full well that whether or not they returned to their homes depended on one thing, how responsive the Spokanes and their neighbors would be to the Nez Percé warriors dancing and drumming their invitation to join them in war.

CHAPTER SEVEN

No More Out

Most Spokanes and Coeur d'Alenes refused to heed Nez Percé appeals to join them in war. In fact, Garry, the Coeur d'Alene Seltice, and other chiefs of the two tribes told the Nez Percés to move on. Sgalgalt, now a Catholic, assured General O. O. Howard, in a long letter written for him by Father Giorda, that the church was "now his dearest possession," that he had no idea of fighting, and that he had restrained his Spokanes from stealing from the deserted homes of fleeing settlers, who, he said, could return any time. Garry was reported to have ridden around trying to put the whites at ease. Other peacemakers in the crisis were the clerics Cataldo and Cowley, who exercised a quieting effect on their Indians.[1]

[1] In the battle of Clearwater, July 11 and 12, 1877, "eight or ten" Spokanes and Coeur d'Alenes did join Chief Joseph. That chief later told Thomas Sutherland, a reporter with General O. O. Howard, that had he been successful in that engagement, the Indians from the Weiser Valley (in Idaho) to the Spokane country would have joined him and the soldiers would have been annihilated. Thomas A. Sutherland, *Howard's Campaign Against the Nez Perce Indians, 1877,* 8. Lewis, *The Case of Spokane Garry,* 42. For a detailed account of the prevention of Coeur d'Alene and Spokane involvement in the Nez Percé War, see Burns, *Jesuits and Indian Wars,* 356–409.

As the white citizenry gingerly returned home, praying that hostilities cease, the department felt a new urgency to remove the Indians to keep them from being destroyed by "fast-approaching waves of civilization." A proposed council between U.S. Indian Inspector Colonel E. C. Watkins, and the Indians was to have taken place on June 27, 1877, relative to their removal, but the outbreak of hostilities had postponed that meeting. With Chief Joseph and his Nez Percés on the run, Watkins was at the falls on August 9, backed by Colonel Frank Wheaton's left column of Howard's command, not so much to protect Watkins as to calm the shaky citizenry and impress the Indians with government strength.

The Indians began to drift in slowly. It was not until August 16 that the council got under way. In council, Garry said he wished to stay where he was. He expressed anger that Chief Moses had not been moved from the mid-Columbia to the Yakima Reservation. To make the Colville Reservation more palatable to the Indians, Watkins proposed an addition to it, to include the principal fisheries on the Spokane and Columbia rivers and sufficient arable lands for the tribes. Despite these concessions, and encouragement from their clerics Cataldo and Cowley to settle with the government, the Upper and Middle Spokanes were reluctant to leave their farms and improvements. Many of them said they did not wish to leave the area of the falls; this promised trouble, as citizens of that place, still unnerved from the recent scare, had told the inspector they wished the Indians to leave for a reservation. Watkins explained to the Indians how they could become citizens and get title to the lands they occupied. He gave Garry and his people around the falls until spring to take up lands or go to the Colville Reservation. The only tangible result of the council, as far as the Spokanes were concerned—besides receipt of substantial issues of beef, flour, and tobacco—was the signing of an agreement on August 18, 1877, with Lower Spokane chiefs to accept a reservation formed by, and east of, the confluence of the Columbia and Spokane rivers, an area which included part of their homeland. The Upper and Middle Spokanes, by postponing the day of reckoning, had slackened the reservation noose around their necks. Perhaps the wisest words at the council were spoken by Antoine, a Colville chief, who said, "I never saw a white man with a rope around his neck for killing an Indian."[2]

The Lower Spokanes roamed over the area that had been agreed upon for a reservation; they could afford to await the white man's council to approve their new home. But the recent meeting had engendered no good feeling between the Upper and Middle Spokanes and the government. Or, for that matter, between these Spokane bands themselves, particularly between two parties, one headed by Garry and the other by William Three Mountains. The "unusually intelligent and progressive" William, possibly tutored by the Reverend Mr. Cowley, was aware of advantages to be gained by accepting provisions of the 1875 Indian Homestead Act. Agent A. J. Cain, known as the Indians' friend, in a War Department report that year (1877), told of whites wishing to see no more land "roped off" for the Indian. Cain recommended that Indians be permitted to homestead without severing tribal ties (as they had to in the 1875 act), possibly to get more of them to file on their lands.[3]

Shortly after the Watkins council, William Three Mountains proposed that nineteen families remove to a location some six miles below Deep Creek Falls. Learning of the proposed move, Garry dissuaded—or perhaps frightened—all but five families from going there. More might have moved to that area, despite Garry's obstinance, but the land was unsurveyed. Without seed and implements, life there would have been most difficult. Five years later there would be only eight of William's families at Deep Creek, despite a recent five-hundred-dollar appropriation from the Lapwai agency for implements for Indian use at that place.

With the status of the Indians around the falls in doubt in the backwash of the Watkins council, many whites feared trouble.

2 Proceedings of the council are found in Secretary of War, *Annual Report,* 1877–78 (45 Cong., 2 sess., *House Exec. Doc. No. 1*), Vol. 1, Pt. 2, pp. 642–53.
3 Secretary of War, *Annual Report,* 1877–78, p. 639.

Consequently, James Glover prevailed on General Wheaton to send up two companies of troops for the winter.[4] Had the troops not been present, it is unlikely any trouble would have ensued. For the Indians, as yet, had felt no great white pressure. There were now only about fifty whites in the vicinity of the falls, and to the Indians, a white baby was still a curiosity. A white lady arriving there as late as 1878 wrote that people in Portland, the gateway to the interior, scarcely knew more about the Spokane country than they did about the interior of Africa.[5] At the time, a traveler on the Columbia River, from the Wenatchee to the mouth of the Spokane, would have thought he was in Asia, for working its bars and those of its tributaries were from five to seven hundred Chinese, a substantially greater number of Orientals than Occidentals. Leaving the Chinese to patiently work the streams for gold and to ward off hostile Indians as best they could, the whites began to discover their own treasure in the volcanic rich soils of the Columbia Plateau.

In June, 1878, General Howard and Washington Territorial Governor Elisha P. Ferry, bringing with them Chief Moses—who had just received from the Great Father a large reservation west of the Okanogan River—came to the falls for a council to resume the business Watkins had left the year before. The general and the governor, hoping to use Moses as a shining example of how an Indian who behaved himself could get a reservation, saw their plan backfire when some drunken Moses Indians appeared near the council grounds announcing that they would make slaves of the Spokanes.[6] Nevertheless, some young Spokanes agreed to go with Moses, provided the Colville Reservation be extended a little farther east, as promised by Inspector Watkins. Not having this extension in hand, Garry, for practical reasons, was not for going to the Moses Reservation. For one thing, it was distant from the Spokane River and already occupied by cattlemen, miners, and Indians. (Moses would not settle his people

4 "Washington Dictations," P–B 81:5.
5 *Spokane*, account of Mrs. J. J. Browne.
6 Eells, *History of Indian Missions*, 83.

there, but would collect rent from its cattlemen.)⁷ But the main reason Garry would not go with Moses was his personal animosity for the Columbia chief. "The growling Spokane Garry," as Howard described him, turned to Moses in council, declaiming, "If he is a good Indian, then is Garry a bad one, for Garry never killed a white man. Oh, no! There is no blood by these hands. I was born by these waters. The earth here is my mother [and not, he might well have said, just 160 acres of it, which the Great Father wanted him to homestead]. If the Great Father will not give me land at this place, I will not go to another reservation, but will stay here until the whites push me out, and out, and out, until there is no more out."⁸

The only positive result was the promise of Lower Spokane chiefs, Lot (Whistlepoosum, who took over the chieftaincy on the death of his brother), Quisemeon, Ahmelmelchen, Costeakan, and Cheaqua, to remain at peace with the government, to abide by its laws and to obey the orders of the Indian office. But most important, they promised to go to the reservation agreed upon in the Watkins council by November 1. Their new home would lie in an area beginning at Tshimakain Creek; thence down said creek to the Spokane River; thence down said river to the Columbia River; thence up said river to the mouth of Nomchim Creek; thence easterly to the place of beginning. The Reverend Mr. Cowley closed the council with a prayer.⁹ The Upper and Middle Spokanes would need one.

Because of their co-operative attitude, the Lower Spokanes proved to be the darlings of the officials, particularly of the one-armed general, Howard. During his current trip, Howard visited a frame house in which William Three Mountains was holding a Presbyterian service, a confessional-type meeting in which the Indians catalogued their sins. During the service, a sharp-voiced Indian girl rose in the back of the house, full of angry recrimina-

---

⁷ Ruby and Brown, *Half-Sun on the Columbia*, 167–90.
⁸ Secretary of War, *Annual Report*, 1879–80 (46 Cong., 2 sess., *Exec. Doc. No.* 1), Vol. II, p. 155: *Spokan Times*, June 19, 1879; *Wilbur Register*, August 24, 1894, p. 6.
⁹ Secretary of War, *Annual Report*, 1879–80, pp. 151–55.

tion and fault finding. Lot ordered her to sit down. The girl obeyed, and Lot said, "We can confess our sins; we have a right to do that, but we have no right to confess other people's sins." The religious Howard had never preached a better sermon than that! At any rate, he was impressed that the twins of American advancement, civilization and religion, had found their way to the Spokane frontier.[10]

The newspaper had also come to help civilize that frontier. The *Spokane Times* (Spokane Falls, W.T.) had gone into publication just the month before, on May 8, 1878, under its publisher, Francis H. Cook. He had brought his press with him up the plateau to the falls. The *Times* gave the region another voice to promote white immigration, as Cook assumed the role of regional spokesman to bring a railroad in to beat high transportation costs of its products.[11]

Through a booklet, *The Territory of Washington 1878*, Cook did much to make the region known to the world. That same year, there was published in San Francisco another booklet, *Settlement of the Great Northern Interior*, by Phillip Ritz. Its author told of the great Columbia Plateau, beneath whose deceptive barrenness lay the best soil in the world for producing wheat. Ritz would claim credit for furnishing the first reliable information of the region to officials of the Northern Pacific Railroad, stimulating them to build a line in that direction.[12] Ten years later the government would give official substantiation to Ritz's claims in a booklet, *Wheat Lands of Oregon and Washington*.[13]

Slowing immigration into the interior in 1878 was the Bannack-Paiute War in southern Idaho and eastern Oregon. Rumors spread of local tribes joining the hostiles and of hostiles moving across the Columbia into Washington Territory to ally with its Indians in an all-out attack on the whites. The Spokanes,

[10] General O. O. Howard, *My Life and Experiences Among Our Hostile Indians*, 434–42. Hereafter cited as *My Life and Experiences*.
[11] *Spokan Times*, May 8, 1879. In this issue Cook tells of the difficulty he encountered in moving the press from Colfax, Washington Territory, in the Palouse country of the lower plateau, to the falls.
[12] Phillip Ritz, *Settlement of the Great Northern Interior*, 7–18.
[13] *Wheat Lands of Oregon and Washington*.

with a traditional animosity to the Bannacks (unlike their ties with the Nez Percés), were in no danger of joining the hostiles. Thus, there was less fear among the white community at the falls than there had been the year before. The reverse was true in the rumor-riddled Yakima country, unnerved by all kinds of rumors of Bannack-Paiute aggressions. Instead of hostility to whites on the Spokane, its Indians fraternized with them and brought furs to Glover's store to exchange for goods they had taken a fancy to, thus saving themselves a trip to Cowley's Bridge or a longer one to Fort Colville. They sat by, watching construction of Frederick Post's grist mill, to which they would soon be bringing their wheat. This would save them the long trip to Colville. When the Reverend H. G. Stratton, a Presbyterian minister, preached on Sunday, September 6, 1878, at the falls, half his congregation were Indians, unlike that of the Reverend Cowley, of which all of them were.[14]

The Indians may have wished to keep things as they were that year. But white residents of the community, regarding themselves as bearers of American civilization on the frontier, had other plans. From his mill, Mr. Glover furnished lumber for the construction of Camp Coeur d'Alene, to be built on the lake of the same name the following spring. This would allow the military to keep one eye on the Coeur d'Alenes and another on the Spokanes, just in case they began to resist white progress. Aware of Northern Pacific Railroad stirrings from its depression slumbers, Glover platted a town, Spokane (Spokan) Falls. He sold out half interest to A. M. Cannon and J. J. Browne, reserving his improved lots to give many of them to folks as an inducement to come there. For Glover, the railroad could not come any too soon.

Increasing immigration to the Spokane country was already resulting in Indian-white conflict. The latter part of April, 1879, the Indians ordered a man named Grant off lands they claimed were theirs. Grant refused to leave. He swore out a warrant against the Indians, one of whom was arrested. As the prisoner was about to be locked up, twenty-five mounted Indians rode up. They demanded his release and threatened to take him by force should

14 Edwards, *History*, 297.

the sheriff not release him. Shortly, Chiefs Garry and Enoch came to the justice of the peace, saying they were sorry their men had caused trouble and that it would not happen again.[15]

Ritz's writings helped attract settlers, which eventually created more friction between them and the Indians. In 1879, Rush Hotchkiss brought a colony from Illinois to Deep Creek by way of California. Taking up homestead claims shortly before had been Daniel and Alfred Stroup. In 1880, John Bauman came from Portland to build a grist mill. Settlers began appearing in other parts of the northern plateau around new villages: Spangle, Medical Lake, Cheney, Sprague, and other places where Spokanes had once roamed freely. Newcomers and Indians quite naturally became intolerant of each other. The touring Carrie Strahorn (wife of railroad builder Robert E. Strahorn) thought the country not yet civilized when an Indian sought to purchase her in Spokane for five ponies. A Miss Maggie Windsor, who taught the first school in the Silver Lake district some five miles below Deep Creek, carried a loaded revolver in her lap. The Indians understood the authority of Miss Windsor's gun. They understood the authority of another weapon of the white man, smallpox, the mere mention of which sent them running from the settlements.

The white population increase in the Deep Creek area, where Cowley had encouraged the Protestant Spokanes to homestead and colonize, may have prompted the minister to write an urgent appeal to Commissioner E. A. Hayt:

> Their country is being rapidly settled by immigrants. Another year will see every tillable acre occupied. The Protestant Spokanes have thus far received less aid from the government than any other tribe of importance. They are strongly inclined to progress, but they are yet unable to cope with the whites who have now filled the country. They do not ask to be clothed and fed. They will be thankful for the implements of husbandry and instruction.[16]

Another white-invasion pressure point was Peone Prairie

---

[15] *Pacific Christian Advocate*, May 1, 1879, p. 8.
[16] Cowley to E. A. Hayt, January 23, 1880, *Colville Agency Records*, Box 28.

where, in the wake of Indian-white confrontation, the whites banded together for protection. They complained to Agent Simms that neighborhood Indians had the impression "they have a right to locate and settle upon any land they may want without regard to previous claims of white settlers."[17] Citing cases of intruding Indians, the settlers asked Simms to visit the Indians to instruct them differently in order to prevent trouble. Baptiste Peone also complained to Simms of the collision from the Indian viewpoint. Simms visited the prairie. He found the tension there very real. He assembled the Indians to explain to them the steps they needed to take to retain their homes.

These developments at Deep Creek and Peone Prairie gave all the more urgency to a meeting at the falls in June, 1880. Here, Colonel H. Clay Wood, assistant adjutant general of the Department of the Columbia and special agent of the Interior Department, met with the principal Spokane chiefs. General Wheaton was present to back Wood up, as he had Watkins. Coming quickly to the point, Wood said that the Secretary of the Interior had instructed him to announce to the Indians that they had to abandon their roving habits and choose between reservation life or citizenship. He stressed department preference that they go on one of three reservations as sanctuary from the worst kind of whites. He made no mention of government compensation for the termination of the title to their land.

Garry said he intended entering his place as a homestead. This prompted Wood, with "patient minuteness," to explain the kinds of lands subject to entry. He assured his listeners that he had promises from officials of the Northern Pacific Railroad that Indians on railroad land would not be dispossessed; the company and the Interior Department could arrange the matter between them. Sgalgalt, Paul, Friezie, Baptiste Peone, Ahmelmelchen, and Enoch stated their intent to stay where they were in order to continue adopting the white man's ways. Wood called upon those who had not decided on taking Indian homesteads to come for-

17 R. E. Towbridge, commissioner of Indian affairs, to Simms, May 22, 1880, Records of the Coeur d'Alene Indian Agency. Federal Records Center, Seattle, Box 17. Hereafter cited as Coeur d'Alene Agency Records.

ward and register their names. About a dozen of Baptiste Peone's band responded, principally those who had improved their lands. When pressed for a decision, the Catholic Sgalgalt said he would neither homestead nor go on a reservation. Despite Wood's careful explanation of what Indian homesteads were, Sgalgalt and other elderly Indians could not understand the white man's way of taking up lands that, in the first place, belonged to *all* Indians. The old chief also took the occasion to condemn Chief Moses, claiming that Moses had sought to represent the Spokanes in Washington, D.C., when he had been given his reservation the previous year. Expressing disappointment with the sentiments of the chiefs, Wood said that, in a few years, should the Spokanes find themselves "utterly homeless and destitute," they would have no one but themselves to blame for their wretchedness. Then he called Garry forward to sign a list of those willing to take homesteads. Garry and several others, including his son-in-law, responded. With this finished, the council ended.[18]

On October 23, 1880, Indian Inspector William J. Pollock arrived at the falls preparatory to effecting homesteads at the Deep Creek colony for homeless Indians. He met in council with representatives of the Upper and Middle Spokanes. Pollock told them either to homestead their lands or to go on the Colville and Coeur d'Alene reservations, as their lands were being titled by the coming of the Northern Pacific Railroad and the white settlers it would bring.

In January, 1881, Pollock submitted a list of Indian land claims on Peone Prairie to the land commissioner. Two of the claims had been "surreptitiously" entered by white men. Pollock recommended that these two entries be canceled and the lands withdrawn from sale and held for the Indians until they could raise the money to pay for them.[19] Since some of the Indians said they did not have the twenty-two dollars required for Indian homestead filing, Simms, in his annual report of 1882, requested

---

[18] *Spokan Times*, June 19, 1880, p. 3, and June 26, 1880, p. 3.
[19] E. M. Marble to Commissioner Land Office, January 25, 1881. Coeur d'Alene Agency Records, Box 17.

that the filing fees for Indians be remitted. It was not until the next June (1883), that government-appropriated money for Indian homesteading fees arrived, too late in the fiscal year for it to be expended. Simms recommended that it be spent for filing the following year. Congress took care of the matter in a new Indian Homestead Act of July 4, 1884. It not only provided for no payment of fees on the part of the Indian but required no tribal severance. It also extended the inalienation on Indian homesteaded land from five to twenty-five years.

Another reason Indians did not file with the land office for homestead entries was that the government held the land in trust, first for five years, then for twenty-five years, during which time the red men could not sell their individual tracts to enterprising settlers. Many Spokanes preferred not to file on homesteads but to claim squatters' rights, which they could sell for cash. As one white observed: "The average Indian would sell anything for a trifle of money in hand if his cupidity were tempted." Many Indians went to file claims, only to find that whites had already done so on their lands, and some had even gone so far as to make final proof on them.[20] In situations such as these, the Office of Indian Affairs advised the agent to encourage Spokanes to make applications to have final proofs set aside on their lands, from which they claimed to have been driven. The Secretary of the Interior would consider their applications. But most of the time, the Indians lost interest and failed to follow through in the maze of legal procedures. In these situations, the commissioner took the easy way out. He suggested that the agent encourage the Indians to select other parcels of land, particularly after the passage of the February 8, 1887, Dawes Act.[21] It was a high-water mark of Indian legislation, which permitted the allotting of Indians on reservations. Section 4 of the Dawes Act permitted non-reservation Indians to be allotted lands in severalty on the public domain. Such allotments were inalienable for twenty-five years,

---

[20] A case in point was that of one D. H. Dart, who had made entry and final proof on land belonging to an Indian, Abraham. Part of Abraham's claim was outside Dart's entry, but claimed by another white man, W. H. Stoneman.

[21] *Infra.*

and no entry, filing, waiting period, or fee was necessary. It is true that some Indians would make final proof, effortlessly and without disturbance.

On a trip to the northwest in 1883, General of the Army William Tecumseh Sherman—"Carrothead" to the Indians—explained the root of their problem simply: "They do not understand the mode of securing homesteads." Nor did they understand taxes, the cause of much strife, thought Sherman, who was impressed with the system used in Canada, whose government remitted them for Indians. The peppery Sherman had no hopes of improving the Spokanes or toleration for the time-consuming attention the Reverend Mr. Cowley was giving them.[22]

Even the Lower Spokanes, who had been sitting tight and rather happy on their promised, (but as yet unsurveyed) land, found that settlers had begun to encroach upon them, despite a measure of surveillance from Camps Coeur d'Alene and Chelan. In the fall of 1880, Camp Spokane (later, Fort Spokane) had been established on a high eminence overlooking the mouth of the Spokane River and the proposed reservation, from which point the military could oversee it in more ways than one. Despite the watchful eye of the military, the encroachments persisted. General Howard, who had been captivated by the Lower Spokanes, was particularly perturbed by the trespassing and brought the matter to the attention of General Sherman. Howard showed Sherman the order setting aside a portion of public land for the Lower Spokane Reservation. Sherman would approve the 154,898–acre reservation, the president would sign it, and Howard would have "the satisfaction of issuing it and seeing it executed."[23] From the Executive Mansion on January 18, 1881, came the following:

It is hereby ordered that the following tract of land, situated in Washington Territory, be, and the same is hereby, set aside and

[22] Sherman's trip in the Spokane country is found in Secretary of War, *Annual Report*, 1883–84 (48 Cong., 1 sess., *Exec. Doc. No. 1*), Vol. I, Pt. 2, pp. 226–33.
[23] General O. O. Howard, *Autobiography of Oliver Otis Howard*, II, 483–84. Hereafter cited as *Autobiography*.

reserved for the use and occupancy of the Spokane Indians, namely: Commencing at a point where Chemakane Creek crosses the forty-eight parallel of latitude; thence down the east bank of said creek to where it enters the Spokane River; thence across said Spokane River westwardly along the southern bank thereof to a point where it enters the Columbia River; thence across the Columbia River, northwardly along its western bank to a point where said river crosses the said forty-eight parallel of latitude; thence east along said parallel to the place of beginning.

R. B. Hayes.[24]

The settlement of the Lower Spokane Reservation would be one of Howard's last official acts in the Department of the Columbia. Hearing that the one-armed general was leaving, Lot rode horseback to Portland to board the general's ship as it was preparing to sail. He took the commander in his huge arms and, talking rapidly in broken English, said: "You no go, no leave! You leave, we have trouble; you stay, we have peace." Needless to say, Howard was touched by Lot's gesture—afforded him by only two other Indians in his service in the West—Moses of the Columbias (a close friend of Joseph, whom Howard had chased) and Cochise of the Apaches.[25] As the two parted, they may well have pondered the fate of Lot's reservation, for both knew that white men, gaining the ear of their Father which was in Washington, had a way of upsetting reservations once they were established, this despite the fact that, of all Spokane lands, those of the Lower Spokane Reservation were considered "the most worthless and barren."[26] Had lands of the Upper and Middle Spokanes been less desired by whites, perhaps a reservation might have been set aside for them where they lived. Maybe then, Garry and Lot would have ridden down together to bid Howard farewell.

The time would not be far off when travelers could exchange their present horses for iron ones to travel to Portland. The day —June 29, 1881—was a historic one for Spokane Falls, then a

[24] Kappler, *Indian Affairs*, I, 925.
[25] Howard, *My Life and Experiences*, 440–42; Howard, *Autobiography*, II, 483–84.
[26] *House Report No. 958* (70 Cong., 1 sess.,), II, 7.

city of nearly a thousand souls boasting just over fifty commercial and industrial establishments. On that day, the Northern Pacific Railroad came to town. Inhabitants of Spokane Falls had eagerly awaited reports of its progress while its rails were being laid across the plateau; the work progressed from Ainsworth on the lower Columbia in the Pend Oreille division. When these rails reached the falls, down to meet the first train came four hundred souls, a hundred more than the entire population of that place the year before. That a bigger celebration had been held in nearby Cheney to greet the railroad did not dampen the enthusiasm of Spokane Falls residents, like Glover, who climbed atop the car of the first train to wave a red bandanna and propose three cheers for the Northern Pacific. "Our fair young city [incorporated that year]," wrote one enthusiast, "had been united to the busy marts of commerce."[27] Perhaps, but not until a silver spike was driven in Montana on September 8, 1883, was the railroad completed.

As engines puffed across the plateau, some white men told the Indians that anyone within hearing distance of their whistles would be drawn to the iron monsters and killed. White men laughed when Indians held on to the bushes for dear life until the trains passed by.[28] But whistle screeching and steam-puffing engines magnetized white people more than they did Indians. This proved to be the biggest threat of the railroads to Indian lives, a fact best expressed by a Northern Pacific Railroad spokesman, who wrote: "The Northern Pacific Railroad has done what General Sherman predicted it would do—it has settled the Indian question in all the States and Territories it traverses. When the locomotive came the red man knew his fight against civilization was at an end."[29]

The Indian could never understand why a railroad had to have so much land (land grants)[30] when their engines ran on tracks

[27] *Spokan Times*, September 25, 1880, p. 1; May 19, 1881, p. 3; June 30, 1881, p. 1.

[28] Albert Sam interview.

[29] Eugene V. Smalley, A *History of the Northern Pacific Railroad*, 436.

[30] The Land Grant Act of July 2, 1864, gave the Northern Pacific Railroad all

no wider than a short man. That it was once all Indian land, and that some of it still was, did not matter to railroad promoters. The Indian, at least, would not have to share so directly in the white man's railroad freight rates. In 1881, Agent Simms was ordered by Commissioner Hal Price to prepare a list of names of Indians residing on odd sections of railroad-granted land who were desirous of entering their lands under the Homestead Act. Simms would further arrange with the Northern Pacific for the transfer of these lands.[31] Four years later, the presiding agent, Sidney Waters, would request the company to relinquish lands which Spokanes wished to enter under the Indian Homestead Act of March 3, 1875.[32]

In 1889, Indian Moses (not Chief Moses) would have to give up, near the mouth of the Little Spokane River, lands on which he had settled in 1868. His property fell in an odd section of railroad land which the company had sold to a Mr. Johnson. Other problems developed in 1889 and 1890, when the company selected lieu lands on which many Spokanes had lived.[33]

Perhaps the best-known case concerning the Northern Pacific Railroad and a Spokane Indian involved the Western Land Development Company, a subsidiary of the railroad, and Enoch, a Middle Spokane chief. (His Indian name has also been given, variously, as Silloqua, Sililoqua, Soliloquoioah, and Silaquois.) The Western Land Development Company presumably paid Enoch two thousand dollars for absolute title, and for any im-

odd sections of land in a forty-mile limit (the first indemnity belt) along the right-of-way of the railroad, excepting on Indian reservations. This gave land to the railroad to dispose of for $2.60 an acre to settlers who would produce a need for freighting service along the route of the line. The company filed its definite location, October 4, 1880, for which its rights to the land were patented May 17, 1894. (The Northern Pacific Railway was chartered as a corporation in 1896, three years after the Northern Pacific Railroad Company went into a receivership.)

[31] Hal Price to Simms, October 12, 1881, Coeur d'Alene Agency Records, Box 17.

[32] Paul Schulze, General Land Agent, Northern Pacific Railroad Company, Land Department Western District (Portland, Oregon), to Waters, April 11, 1885, Coeur d'Alene Agency Records, Box 28.

[33] For more information on railroad lieu land, see *Wilbur Register*, November 17, 1893, p. 1; January 26, 1894, p. 1; March 2, 1894, p. 1; March 30, 1894, p. 3. Lieu land was transferred to the Northern Pacific Railway Company, July 3, 1896.

provements he might have made, on 120 acres of land.[34] The area would be known as "Shantytown" in Spokane Falls, bounded west by Bernard Street, east by Division, north by Sprague, and south by Ninth.[35] Enoch gave the company a quit-claim deed to the property and moved to the mouth of the Little Spokane River. The company contracted to sell the land to the Reverend Mr. Cowley, but after ascertaining its value, which had appreciated in the boom of the 1880's, refused, as Cowley claimed, to execute a deed in compliance with the contract. Cowley would carry his suit all the way to the U.S. Supreme Court, which would rule in favor of the company.

In 1890 the Secretary of the Interior made a decision which was supposed to have ended the Enoch land controversy at that time. A Mr. Spicer and others claimed the right to enter the Shantytown tract by the fact that it was public land and opened to entry. They claimed that the area was exempted from the company's grant by reason of Enoch's occupancy and claim. On April 12, the secretary had directed a hearing on the property, then reportedly worth seven million dollars. His decision was that Enoch had not severed tribal relations (as required for an Indian to homestead land under the act of March 3, 1875) prior to the date of definite location of the railroad. Hence, he had no claim to the land in which the railroad title was confirmed.[36]

Most Spokane citizens, except Cowley, had been happy at the outcome, as the company had sold most of the land in lots to residents who had built homes on them. Had Enoch won his case, some citizens living in the area would have been involved in complicated litigation to secure titles to their homes. Enoch had also claimed that, when he left his Spokane property (in 1881), he had been told he could select 160 acres of other railroad land. He had chosen a spot in a fertile belt near the mouth of the Little Spokane River on which he would make improvements, only to have the railroad eventually sell the land to a white man. In his failure to reclaim his lands at the mouth of the Little Spo-

---

[34] That Enoch lived there was attested to by James Monoghan, who visited the Indian's ranch several times.

kane, Enoch had the company of other Indians, Paul, Solomon, and John Stevens, who had lost lands in the same area. Some of their people, shoved off the land, pitched their lodges on other grounds near the mouth of the Little Spokane, much to the disgust of white settlers there, and others went up to the falls to a similar reception.

Almost as strange to the Indians as setting aside lands for railroads was setting them aside for schools. Under the act of March 2, 1853, which created Washington Territory, that jurisdiction was given the thirty-sixth section in each township which, upon survey, was reserved for the common schools. By the act of February 2, 1889, creating the new state of Washington, sections 16 and 36 of each township were granted to the state, unless otherwise disposed of. Again Indians collided with the law. Jacob Quilamane, a Spokane Indian, had homesteaded a piece of land on which he had settled in 1882.[37] It would not be surveyed until the following year. The law required that entry be made within three months of filing the township plat. But it was not until 1884 that Jacob filed in the land office for his plat. The case was canceled when he failed to appeal in the allowed time.

Besides land squabbles, there were entanglements of other kinds. Citizens of Spokane Falls were again reminded that it was unwise to buy horses from Indians, for many of them had been stolen and sold at low figures. All of this meant trouble when the real owners found out about the sales. Falls citizens, however, discovered that Indians had no monopoly on wrongdoing.

Spokane Indians drunk with white man's liquor were in constant trouble with Spokane Falls police. Despairing from the loss of their lands, these Indians came to town to drink and to offer what possessions they had left—ponies, fish, and even their wom-

---

[35] Once streets are laid out, and tall buildings cover an area, there can be some question about the topography before improvements are made in a modern city. Cowley recalled years later that the boundaries of Enoch's land were at about Third on the north, Pine on the east, south at the Cliff, and west on Howard.

[36] *Spokane Falls Review* (Spokane Falls, Washington), July 17, 1890, p. 8.

[37] Jacob's land bore the description: sw¼ of ne¼, w½ of se¼, and Lot 1 of Sec. 36, T. 31 N., R. 40 E., W.M.

en, to opportunists and settlers. In these transactions, they bartered or accepted coin, but never paper money, which did not shine or ring. To work as white men in Horatio Alger fashion was not only an alien concept to them but, in their traditions, stigma. Bereft of traditional means of livelihood, the Indians drifted down the road of idleness, drunkenness, debauchery, and violence. Wrote the enraged editor of the *Spokan Times* for his community:

> Indians are becoming unbearable in this vicinity. They will not work, and are continually prowling about in search of something to steal, something to drink, or defenseless persons to molest. They have no shame. They let down fences, leave gates ajar, walk over gardens, and steal vegetables in their season.[38]

The community breathed more easily when the Indians were out digging camass. During the smallpox plague in late 1881, plans were discussed to keep them out of town.[39] But when the digging and the plague were over, they were back. As the community grew, "justice" became death for an unruly red man. One who got as far as the creek was known to have been wounded, for there was a "discolor [of] the water as he sank to rise no more."[40] Other Indians in town at the time of disturbances were ordered to leave or follow the same path.

It should be said that there were but few hardened criminal Spokanes drifting around the country, sometimes killing several whites and Indians before they were through. But white citizens did not distinguish between most Spokanes and the floaters. To them they were all red men, and most red men were bad.

Complicating the problem was the Indian concept of revenge. In the old tribal way, as we have seen, retribution was a matter between families, with wrongs settled by exchange of horses and other gifts. When Indians were wronged by white men, they tended quite naturally to seek personal revenge, not understanding that white men did things differently. One morning in 1880, an

[38] *Spokan Times*, April 28, 1881, p. 2.
[39] *Spokan Times*, November 8, 1881, p. 3.
[40] *Morning Review*, October 6, 1888, p. 3.

Indian helped himself to bread rolls (another Indian custom) at the California House, a Spokane Falls hostelry. The cook clubbed him. Garry told the authorities the wounded Indian demanded money for the injuries, just like the Indians did in the old days.

Indians disciplined their wrongdoers in various ways. Expulsion of tribal members had been resorted to in certain cases, and whippings had been administered. This precedent of whipping made it easier for factors and priests to do likewise. When that did not work they refused the wrongdoers skins and sacraments. A new form of revenge seems to have appeared on the Northwestern Indian scene in the latter half of the nineteenth century, that of inflicting injury to the head of an offender and, occasionally, to the abdomen. As early as 1853, there was a report of a Spokane beating his wife's head; other examples of this type of punishment were found as late as the twentieth century. In 1897, at the Indian camp three miles below Spokane, an Indian was disemboweled and his head laid on a rock and pounded with a stone. The judge taking the case under advisement was not certain whether jurisdiction lay with the federal or state governments, a dilemma plaguing Indian justice down to the present time.

By 1875, Spokane Indian social structure had degenerated to such an extent, as reported by Agent Simms, that tribal government had no effect on punishment of crimes of a serious nature. Simms had asked the government to enforce law and order among them and for the application of U.S. criminal laws against Indians in his charge.

Aggravating the problem was the matter of mixed tribal ancestry of some wrongdoers. For instance, Coeur d'Alene Chief Seltice hastened to point out, in June, 1885, that the Indian, Whilcome, who had killed a white man near Spokane Falls and, previously, his sister, a prostitute who went around with white men, was not a Coeur d'Alene, as the guilty man claimed he was, but a Spokane. Also, that the mother of the guilty man's grandfather was half Coeur d'Alene, and his ancestors, subsequently, either Colvilles or Kalispels. Thus the man was more Kalispel than anything else. Making this case additionally difficult was the mobility of the guilty party. Whilcome kept on the move, as had his ancestors.

Simms thought one way to alleviate the problem of roving Indians was to place the Upper Spokanes on the Coeur d'Alene Reservation, the Middle Spokanes on the Lower Spokane Reservation, and "refractory Indians" in a penal institution. He agreed with the commissioner that Indians should be allotted lands in severalty and issued patents for homesteads, for which no fees should be charged them.

The agents' problems became bigger with each passing year. By 1884, Agent Waters, in reporting events occurring since he had assumed office in October of the previous year, revealed that in his agency (which included the Spokanes and other tribes) there had been several murders. Most crimes among Indians continued to be punished by tribal justice in the form of revenge or a payoff.

William Three Mountains died by the hand of a half-blood, Bill Jackson, while rebuking him for wrongdoing. Son of a white settler, Jackson was reportedly the most notorious badman in those parts. For his crime, Jackson was sentenced to only a year in the territorial penitentiary, an indication that his victim, though beloved, was only an Indian. Something had to be done with, or perhaps better, *for* the Indian.

The problem of law and order had become critical. Acting under federal legislation, Indians on the Spokane Reservation had, by 1887, established a court and police force. Agent Rickard Gwydir said it did good work in suppressing drinking and gambling, a pair of evils that accounted for nine-tenths of the crimes on the reservation. The court was the only one in Gwydir's agency. Its judges—Lot, Sam, and Cornelius—tried to enforce the laws with "an integrity of purpose scarcely to be expected from a people so short a time on the pathway to civilization."[41] They began enforcing marriage laws on the reservation and, in 1891, we find Lot and the agent sending police to the Coeur d'Alene Reservation

41 Secretary of Interior, *Annual Report*, 1888 (50 Cong., 1 sess., *House Exec. Doc. No. 1*), Vol. II, Pt. 5, p. 223.

for a couple who had eloped in the old way, without benefit of marriage. (Hal Cole, agent in 1892, would report that year that adultery and bigamy among his Indians would be things of the past. But it would not be until 1899 that an agent could report that "the civilized form" of marriage prevailed over tribal custom.) This advance of law and order, Gwydir was careful to point out, prevailed mainly among the Lower Spokanes. The bands of Garry, Enoch, and Louis, having no such institutions to keep their people on the straight and narrow, loafed around Spokane Falls drinking and gambling. According to certain whites, they should have been forced to a reservation.

To offset troubles the Indians were getting into, the missionaries increased their efforts to advance the spiritual welfare of their parishioners. Hearing that Spokane Falls was on the line of the Northern Pacific Railroad, Father Cataldo had returned in 1881 to make final selections for churches in two places, one near Spokane Falls and another near Baptiste Peone's. After a visit to Agent Simms, Cataldo had purchased a spot along the banks of the Spokane River where Gonzaga College was opened in 1887. Garry's missionary zeal had cooled, as it had in his youth a few years after returning from the Red River school. Leaving others to carry on the work, Garry became a man caught in the middle between Catholics and Protestants (particularly the Deep Creek colonists).

With the death of William Three Mountains, natives of the Deep Creek colony would come under the ministrations of Chief Lot, who, according to one agent, took "more interest in churches and schools than almost anything else, or more pride in these institutions than any Indian I ever saw."[42] Lot came by his zeal for education honestly. He was in Washington, D.C., in the summer of 1883, where he heard Chief Moses request annuities for himself and concessions and gifts for his people. Lot told the same commissioners he wanted nothing but a church and a school for his. He subsequently sent heartbreaking appeals to U.S. authori-

---

[42] Secretary of the Interior, *Annual Report*, 1891 (52 Cong., 1 sess., *House Exec. Doc. No. 1*) Vol. II, Pt. 5, p. 441.

ties for a school close to his people. Making his effort all the more pathetic was the fact that his own daughter, with other children of his tribe whom he had sent to the Chemawa Indian School in Oregon, died there from tuberculosis in late 1881. There had been so many deaths at that place that the Spokanes said, "To go to Chemawa is to die."[43]

Lot was not alone in his ministrations. He had help of course, from the Reverend Mr. Cowley. In response to Cowley's request for help for the Spokane field, the Reverend George L. Deffenbaugh had established the Deep Creek Presbyterian Church in 1880. On July 23, 1880, a church had been organized among Indians at Lot's camp. Eventually a structure was built next to Lot's own place, about four miles from a racetrack and center of community life. Nez Percé preachers, in their own Shahaptian tongue, would name the community "Wellpinit" ("meadow stream which disappears"). It was more euphonious than the guttural Salish "Stchchwa," for the creek flowing there.

Deffenbaugh became all the more helpful to Lot in his christianizing efforts, since Cowley was beginning to bow out of the picture as a missionary and take a more active part in the business life of the Spokane community, primarily in the newspaper field. As he neared the close of his ministry, he could boast that in all his labors with the Indians he had never lost an item, except a bridle and a watermelon. The bridle was returned, and the melon thief repented. In 1883, after Cowley's resignation and William Three Mountains' death, Deffenbaugh reorganized the Deep Creek Church. The next year, Deffenbaugh received help from the Reverend James Hines, the first ordained Nez Percé pastor to the Deep Creek Church, and thereafter, from other ministers of that tribe, who pastored either or both of the Spokane Indian churches for varying lengths of time.[44]

Because of white encroachments, the Deep Creek colony was forced to move to the Spokane Reservation by 1888. In three

[43] Ruby and Brown, *Half-Sun on the Columbia*, 293.
[44] G. L. Deffenbaugh, "Report for the Quarter ending July 31, 1883, to the Board of Foreign Missions"; *The Spokane Indian Mission*.

years there was a neat little church, houses, and farms for a colony of about fifty souls near Detillion Bridge (eight miles upstream from the mouth of the Spokane River). The church became known as "the West End Church." William Three Mountains, son of the murdered Deep Creek leader, became head of the transplanted colony, conducting services along with Thomas Garry, as they assisted Silas H. Whitman and the Reverend A. B. Lawyer, Nez Percé ministers.

White settlers and government officials, particularly Indian agents, had persistently recommended that nontreaty Indians be placed on reservations. As a result of these appeals, Congress, on May 15, 1886, established a commission composed of John V. Wright, Henry W. Andrews, and Jared W. Daniels to treat with Indians of the state of Minnesota and the territories of Dakota, Montana, Idaho, and Washington to carry out these requests. The commission arrived at Spokane Falls by rail the night of February 23, 1887. They secured interviews with Garry and Louis Weilsho, endeavoring to arrange a time and place for a meeting. Religious differences between the two Indians produced a "want of harmony." Garry insisted the council be held at Spokane Falls; Louis, that it be held at the mission on Peone Prairie. The commissioners decided that more Spokanes would be accommodated by meeting at Spokane Falls.

The great body of citizens of that community wanted the red men removed. In all its travels the commission reported seeing no other Indians "so utterly degraded and helpless . . . bereft of every foot of land, which they and their ancestors once possessed . . . where they once proudly walked as masters . . . with all the vices and none of the capacities of the superior race . . . sad recollections of the past . . . no hope for the future, save the glimmering light of a far-off heaven."[45]

The council opened on March 7, 1887. Chief Louis, perhaps miffed at the location, was slow to arrive. When he did, he was unwilling to proceed without Father Cataldo, in whom the Spo-

[45] *Message from the President* (51 Cong., 1 sess., *House Exec. Doc. No. 14*), Vol. II, 45–46. Hereafter cited as *Message from the President* (1889).

kanes had great confidence. Their desire for the good offices of Cataldo and his fellow priests placed the fathers in a delicate position. Should they urge their neophytes to stand fast and not remove to a reservation, and should a massacre of whites ensue, the responsibility would rest on their shoulders. On the other hand, should they induce the Indians to yield to pressures to remove, there was danger of losing the confidence of their flock. After weighing the painful alternatives, the missionaries concluded that the lesser of the two evils was for their charges to remove from the contaminating influence of the whites. To implement their decision, they adopted a policy of gradually reducing religious services among the Spokanes.

So Father Cataldo was sent for, and the council officially began. Keynoting the affair, Wright told the assembled Spokanes that the commission had made treaties with twenty bands, encompassing some fifteen thousand Indians. He told them the government now wanted to protect them by removing them to the Coeur d'Alene and Flathead reservations, away from improper white influence. He made no mention of placing them on the Spokane Reservation, which the commission may have thought too small and too poor for them. He said that should they go to the Coeur d'Alene Reservation, they would be furnished implements and homes, to be theirs forever, and that they would not be going there as paupers.

Garry rose to speak, insisting that no white men be allowed in the meeting, as had been the custom whenever a government-Indian conference was held. The old chief bemoaned the fact, as he had in all the councils, that Stevens had not dealt with the Spokanes as he said he would, which would have eliminated much of the problem in the first place. The chief said he wanted his people to learn to read and write. He said he wanted to take 180 acres of surveyed land and didn't want to go off to a reservation in another country. "I don't like to be all the time an Indian," he said, stating that his people should work and practice the teachings of Jesus Christ. He asked the whites, through the commissioners, to take back their whiskey and cards, the only things they had given Indians.[46]

Wright explained how a law had been made to give the Indians land which would not be taxed, a reference, no doubt, to the allotment of reservation lands in severalty to Indians.[47] The commissioners did not explain that the allotting system would destroy existing tribal concepts by doing away with communal ownership of Indian lands, for it gave to each Indian up to 160 acres. With Wright's assurance that the system would prevent the corruption of their wives and daughters, the Indians did not divine that, after allotments were made, unclaimed reservation lands would be available to whites.[48]

The commissioners perhaps did not stress to these nonreservation Indians that section 4 of the Dawes Act provided for allotment on the public domain of Indians not residing on a reservation. Indians of nonreservation tribes could apply to local land offices for allotment of unappropriated land. Provisions called for no filing, entering, and waiting periods, as well as no fees.[49] Land patents for these allotments would be held by the government for twenty-five years.

With their traditional hesitancy, the Indians were opposed to being moved. Louis Weilsho, Garry, Sgalgalt, Elijah, Solomon, Enoch, and Ahmelmelchen wanted to secure lands, but in their home areas. They held little councils among themselves, then demanded of Wright a separate reserve on the Little Spokane River, with compensation for lands lost by going there. So urgent, stubborn, and unanimous were they in this demand that, at one time, it looked like the commissioners would lose all hope of successfully concluding the negotiations. They sent off a quick mes-

[46] The Reverend J. F. Kearney, S.J., tells of the pressures on the fathers in the *Catholic Sentinel* of August 4, 1921. "Proceedings of the Northwest Indian Commission Held at Spokane Falls Commencing March 7, 1887 and Ending March 17, 1887," 5. Hereafter cited as "Proceedings."

[47] *Ibid.*, 7; Kappler, *Indian Affairs: Laws and Treaties*, I, 33–36.

[48] The Dawes Allotment Act would make available by 1919 approximately three million acres of reservation land in Washington, Oregon, and Idaho.

[49] Kappler, *Indian Affairs*, I, 33.

sage over the "talking wires" to the Great Father, who wired back his refusal to go along with the Indian plan. The commissioners skilfully utilized Cataldo to help cushion the shock of the Great Father's refusal.

The commissioners soon found differing opinions among the Indians. A few subordinates began to assert themselves. Elijah of Garry's band said, "My chief is foolish; when he gets out of the way he will take a bottle of whisky and drink . . . . You came to do us good. You have given us plenty. You have made the sun to shine." One by one, other Indians made similar expressions. Seeing the direction in which their bands were heading, the chiefs signed the fateful agreement with the representatives of the Great Father.[50] Interestingly, the two government men who, more than any others, decided the fortunes of the Spokane Indians—one in war and one in peace—bore the same name, Wright. Maybe no one noticed this at the council.

By the agreement made and concluded at Spokane Falls, March 18, 1887, the bands of Spokane Indians in council deeded to the United States all right, title, and claim which they had, or ever would have, to any and all lands lying outside the reservation. They agreed to remove to and settle upon the Coeur d'Alene Reservation in the territory of Idaho. Indians who had settled on land and made improvements with the intent of retaining title to the same, under homestead, pre-emption, or other laws of the United States, would be protected. The United States agreed to expend for the Indians ninety-five thousand dollars for removal to the Coeur d'Alene Reservation. Also, for the erection of suitable homes, assistance in breaking ground, furnishing of cattle, seed, agricultural implements, saw and grist mills, threshing machines, mowers, clothing, etc. Also, to take care of the old, sick, and infirm. Also, to provide blacksmiths, farmers, educational facilities. For Chiefs Louis, Garry, Sgalgalt, Antarcham (Tarkan), and Enoch, a hundred dollars each per annum for ten years.

In the agreement, a provision was made for the Spokanes to go on the Colville or Flathead reservations, should they desire to do

50 "Proceedings," 14.

so, after the ratification of the agreement by Congress, with a pro rata share of all benefits provided in the agreement. Nearly ninety Indians signed the agreement on the spot. Baptiste Peone and seven subchiefs of his band, having already moved with their families earlier that year to the St. Ignatius Mission on the Flathead Reservation, subsequently signed the agreement.[51]

After effecting the agreement with the Spokanes to move to the Coeur d'Alene Reservation, Wright moved his commission there to ask the Coeur d'Alenes to accept the Spokanes. Seltice said he would welcome them to his reservation, for the Great Father would care for them all. He said they were interrelated, but when the Spokanes came, they should leave their whiskey at home.

Agreements were subsequently obtained from some Pend Oreille and Kootenay Indians to move onto the Flathead Reservation. After dealing with these peoples, Wright journeyed to meet with the Flatheads, getting them to agree to receive the various nonreservation Indians who had already agreed to go there.

Most Spokanes appeared to have wanted to go to the Coeur d'Alene Reservation, but they were equally welcomed on the Flathead Reservation. Most Spokanes wishing to remove to these places were Catholic, the predominant faith of the two reservations. In his speech, Seltice even welcomed half-bloods. In an aside, he expressed an interesting anthropological fact of life: "There is one thing which the whites do which we do not—they marry our women, but we never marry white women."[52] Most Spokanes would have preferred leaving at once for the reservations. But they had to await action from the White Man's Council (Congress). With their knowledge of how slowly that council moved, they knew that about all they could do was to sit and wait.

The Colville Agency had supervised three reservations, the Coeur d'Alene, Spokane, and Colville, in addition to free Indians: Spokanes, Kalispels, Kootenays, Chelans, Wenatchees, and others. Now it was moved from its peripheral location at Chewelah, where it had been since the late 1870's, to the southwest corner

[51] *Message from the President* (1889), 65.
[52] *Ibid.*, 77.

of the Spokane Reservation at the mouth of the Spokane River. It was located on a high bench opposite Fort Spokane, close to the military—one reason for the move. Another reason was to relocate the agency more central to the reservations to handle their escalating problems. Moving the agency was not easy. Transportation problems hampered the change. A bridge across the Spokane River to service the new agency collapsed in June, before all the lumber for the agency buildings was teamed over. The move was finally made before the buildings were completed, at an estimated cost of a little over four thousand dollars. Before the year 1887 was over, the new agency buildings were made usable, and water piped from a spring on the hill behind them. Among the buildings was a hewn-log jail, called by the Indians the "Skookum house." It was soon to be "filled to its utmost capacity with full-blood and half-breed whiskey-drunkers and handlers."

Moving down with the agency were the first-generation children of French and Scottish blood mixed Iroquois and Crees, who had come to the region in the fur era. They had first settled around Fort Okanogan and, with its decline, Fort Colville. They had married Colville, Lake, Spokane, Chewelah, and Kalispel women, following the agency in its move from Fort Colville to Chewelah. Some of the families of this background were the La Fleurs, Gengros, Fergusons, Desautels, and McCoys. Settling near the newly relocated agency, these families became recognized members of the Spokane tribe.

Once a diehard against moving to a reservation, Garry was beginning to think he should make the move. Schuyler D. Doak had purchased land for five hundred dollars from a German who, in 1873, had jumped a claim that was land Garry had lived on and farmed since 1864.[53] One day the German drove Garry's wife, Nellie, from the property with a club. He broke Garry's plow, tore down the barn Garry had built and paid for, and even carted off the lumber to build a house for himself.

For years Garry used every peaceful means to regain his land.

[53] Garry's farm was east of present-day Hillyard in Sec. 2, T. 25 N., R. 43 E., W.M.

But he was told to keep off it. In a conference with the German, Agent Waters had suggested he permit Garry to pay him off with a team of horses for his improvements, after which the German could leave. When Garry came with the team, the German announced he was leaving, but that he had sold the land to Doak. On January 25, 1889, Commissioner J. H. Oberly suggested that perhaps it would be better to induce Nellie, whose land it was, according to Garry, to take an allotment under section 4 of the Dawes Act. Garry was advised in May, 1889, and again in November of the same year, that Doak had filed on February 19, 1886, a pre-emption declaratory statement, and on August 3, 1888, had made a pre-emption cash entry for the land. Garry was also advised to assert to the land office his rights to regain his place. In January, 1890, Agent Cole visited Garry, who was then growing old and weary of the contest. Cole found that Garry had done little about the matter, as the old chief waited to see what Congress would do about the 1887 agreement. In the meantime, Doak kept demanding that his entry be approved. On March 25, 1891, Acting Commissioner R. V. Belt advised Cole that the general land office commissioner was unwilling to defer longer the necessary final action on Doak's entry, because the land was then valued at six thousand dollars. The land commissioner directed that, if Garry were going to enter a contest, he had ninety days in which to do so, or Doak's entry would be approved. Commissioner Belt (dedicated as was the department to protect the Indians) wrote that, in view of a department circular (May 31, 1884), registers and receivers of land offices were instructed to refuse entries and filings by non-Indians on land in possession of Indians who had made improvements. Another circular of October 27, 1887, enjoined local land officers not to permit entry upon Indian-possessed lands, that white entries upon lands in possession and occupation of Indians was "an act of inhumanity to a defenseless people and provocative of violence and disturbance."[54]

As such, Doak's filing had to be regarded as ineffectual. Added Belt, "Indians located upon the public lands are regarded as actual

[54] *Spokesman-Review*, May 28, 1895, p. 3.

settlers thereon and a settlement cannot be made upon any public land already occupied."[55] Agent Cole was directed to assist Garry in asserting his claims. Garry did not initiate a request for contest, so Belt recommended, on August 4, 1891, that Doak's entry for "the stolen land" not be approved until a special agent of the general land office could investigate the case. Doak had mortgaged the land and conveyed it, on February 27, 1891, to one F. L. Clark. Garry finally had a hearing on his land, and although he presented proof that he had lived earlier on the farm, which had appreciated in value to twenty-five thousand dollars, a decision was rendered against him.[56]

Garry did not relinquish his chieftaincy because of adverse circumstances. We find him writing to the agent on October 5, 1890, on behalf of an Indian whose land the whites had jumped at the mouth of the Little Spokane River. But he did tire of battling white men who fought in the courts with legal weapons as potent as the howitzers and improved rifles they had once used to defeat the Indians on the field of battle. Garry spoke for all nonreservation Indians, who, he said, were residing around town in destitute circumstances with nothing to eat and "ready and willing" to go on a reservation.[57]

Marking time for his own move to the confine, he went to Hangman Creek to join others of his same plight. By then his wife was blind, and white youngsters threw stones down on them. He visited Gavin C. Mouat, who in 1883 had settled above Hangman Creek west of the falls (present-day Indian Canyon), to ask him if they and other Indians living along the creek could make their camp next to his place. Mouat said they could.[58] Here would be the last holdout of the Spokanes until the early 1920's, a stopover for Indians traveling between reservations and a refuge for renegades.

[55] R. V. Belt to Cole, March 25, 1891, Coeur d'Alene Agency Records, Box 17.

[56] *Spokesman-Review*, November 25, 1917, Pt. 6, p. 7.

[57] T. J. Morgan, commissioner of Indian affairs, to Cole, November 22, 1889, Coeur d'Alene Agency Records, Box 17.

[58] William S. Lewis, "Reminiscences of Gavin C. Mouat as related to William S. Lewis Corresponding Secretary of the Spokane Historical Society," 3.

About the time the agency was being moved, Agent Gwydir had many reminders that he would be busier with Indian land contests in the new location than he had been in the old. The summer the agreement was signed, as he would later recall, one of Garry's band, named Masses, left his shack and garden on Northern Pacific land to go hunting. In his absence, the company destroyed the shack in a clearing project. Returning to find what had happened, Masses took the matter into his own hands by firing his Winchester at the head man, who was wearing a plug hat. As only three people in Spokane Falls boasted such headware, Masses assumed the man to be the big chief of the Northern Pacific. Luckily, the shot missed the man's skull but did destroy the hat. The man turned out to have no connection with the railroad. Masses was arrested and taken before the judge, to whom he confessed he had shot at the wrong man. His attorney advised him not to volunteer such information. But with an Indian's natural honesty and inability to understand white justice, he did so anyway. Agent Gwydir went before the court to tell the judge that it was simply a case of mistaken identity. They agreed to dismiss the case, after which the judge lectured the Indian on the impropriety of dealing out justice himself, advising him to seek justice in the white man's court another time. After court, Gwydir told the judge that, were they (he and the judge) of a similar cultural background as the Indian, they would have done the same thing.[59]

If some Spokanes were now willing to go on the reservations, members of the white community were even more eager to see them go. Yet no longer was the Indian an object of fear, hatred, and disgust, as he was before the agreement signing. Newspapers now carried quaint stories of papooses toddling around the streets or carried on their mothers' backs. The editor of the *Spokane Globe* (Spokane Falls, Wash.), in December, 1889, assured "Timid Eastern women and tenderfeet" they needed no longer fear coming to Spokane on account of "bad Indians."[60]

[59] Rickard D. Gwydir, "Statement of Major R. D. Gwydir as related to William S. Lewis."

[60] *Spokane Globe*, December 21, 1889, p. 4.

Spokane Falls was unique among American cities; around few others did the frontier pass so quickly. Indians were now beginning to look out of place in a city which boasted an opera house (opened on November 7, 1887) and other evidences of culture.[61] Indians racing horses at the Fair Grounds were disgusting to cultured members of the community, and to the betting crowd, too, because they often ran off with the prize money. Gambling in the city began to go underground, unlike Indian gambling, which was always carried on in the open. White men watched Spokane Falls take on new beauty in its factories, bridges, and electric-power installations. But as early as 1882 there were complaints that sawdust in the river was killing the fish.[62]

Perhaps no one caught the new spirit as did Eugene V. Smalley in the pages of the *Northwest Magazine* of October, 1887:

In all the broad northern belt of new country, which reaches from St. Paul to the Pacific Coast, I know of no scene of rapid development which equals that presented by Spokane Falls to-day; no such striking spectacle of the transformation of a frontier village into a large town, with extensive manufacturing, commercial and railroad activities; with solid business blocks and handsome dwellings, and with a bustling population recruited on the arrival of every train by a throng of energetic, quick-witted new-comers. The click of the trowel, the rasp of the saw and the resonant blows of the hammer make music over all the broad, forest-girdled plain through which the blue Spokane rushes and leaps on its swift way to the Columbia, and forms a sharp treble to the bass of the roar of the cataracts that furnish the incomparable water-power for the wheels of many mills and factories.

This is the music that the western man loves best—the rattle and hum of varied industry, laying the foundations and rearing the superstructure of a new civilization. And gazing in stolid wonder upon this wonderful transformation scene stands the sullen, blanketed Indians, who but a few years ago, looked upon the flowery Spokane plain as his choice and exclusive domain, and

61 Henry H. Hook and Francis J. McGuire, *Spokane Falls Illustrated*.
62 *Spokane Times*, March 4, 1882, p. 2.

upon the river as created by the Great Spirit to bring fish to his nets.[63]

The only time Spokane Indians would be called privileged characters around Spokane Falls (although some whites thought they were privileged to go to the reservations and get free land) was when they walked the streets with little emotion, inspecting the remains of the great fire of Sunday, August 4, 1889. Indian women poked around the ashes for washboilers with the tin burned off, cooking utensils, and other remnants from the hardware stores. Also for pieces of baked ham, bacon, and quantities of dirty sugar to take back to their "wigwam pantry."[64]

The last major Indian scare would prove to be as temporary as the fire. In January, 1891, there was some apprehension that local Indians were dancing the Messiah Dance. There were rumors of Sioux emissaries carrying the message of the dance to the west; some people believed it when they heard reports of dances in the vicinity of Fort Spokane and on the Colville Reservation. But these were not the Messiah Dances to overthrow the white men; they were simply the mid-winter Chinook dances to implore the Great Spirit to send a mild winter. There were other dances imploring Him to keep the smallpox away, for it had been severe the year before.[65]

Chief Seltice of the Coeur d'Alenes came to Spokane Falls in February, 1890, to repeat his offer to the Spokanes of a home on the Coeur d'Alene Reservation. There were rumors that Spokane Chief Louis would not listen to the proposition, although he had no reservation home for himself and his tribe. Rumor had it that, if he were to go to the Coeur d'Alene Reservation, he would have to take a back seat to Seltice as far as the chieftaincy was concerned, and he did not like that at all. In July, 1892, there was a big celebration on Hangman Creek at which the Coeur d'Alenes, after receiving some government money, invited their Spokane

---

[63] E. V. Smalley, "Spokane Falls, the Rapidly Growing Business and Manufacturing Metropolis of Eastern Washington," *Northwest Magazine*, Vol. V, No. 10 (October, 1887), 1.

[64] *Spokane Falls Review*, August 8, 1889, p. 1.

[65] *Spokane Falls Review*, January 14, 1891, p. 4.

friends and relatives to celebrate with them. Many Spokanes accepted this invitation. They all had a good time giving presents and cementing old alliances and ties of friendship.[66]

Absent from the festivities was Chief Garry. Confined to his couch for more than eleven weeks suffering congestion of the lungs, he awaited death. On January 14, 1892, death kindly spared him a journey to the reservation, which so many times he had vowed in councils never to take.[67] He left an estate of ten lean and "flea-bitten" cayuses—and a childlike faith that the white man would eventually do the right thing and compensate him and his people for the land they had taken.

[66] There was a distribution of $492,362.90 on a per capita basis to the Coeur d'Alenes as per act of March 3, 1891, in payment for cession of a portion of their reservation.

[67] Lewis, *The Case of Spokane Garry*, 52.

CHAPTER EIGHT

White Man's Image

On February 19, 1892, thirty of the late Chief Garry's followers met in the city by the falls to discuss with Agent Waters their agreement to remove to the Coeur d'Alene, Flathead, and Colville reservations. With their new chiefs, Joseph, Wilson, and John Stevens, they represented some 300 Upper Spokanes. The Indians, some of whom had fought Colonel Wright, sat on the floor of the police station in the Rookery Building, elbows against the wall, puffing a peace pipe passed from hand to hand with "calm dignity and scarcely a word of conversation," as elevators flew up and down like the shuttles of a loom.[1] The usual Indian laconism in the white man's environment may have been deepened by the recent death and burial of the chief, at whose funeral service at the First Presbyterian Church his blind widow, led to the open casket, had run her hands through her husband's gray hair as tears rolled down her cheeks.[2] Perhaps another reason for the Indians' taciturnity was what a reporter called their

[1] *Spokesman-Review*, February 20, 1892, p. 6.
[2] *Spokesman-Review*, January 17, 1892, p. 8.

"apathy . . . against the sharpest arrows of adversity" in whose "cruel destiny he comprehend[ed] nothing more than the fatalism of hard times, the pinching of poverty and the sharp tooth of hunger—to be taken as a matter of fact, just as one takes the hot winds of summer and cold blasts of winter."[3] Finally, to add to the contrast, the meeting was held in the city with a new name— Spokane. At an election the previous year, its citizens had dropped the "Falls" from the name of their city, as though it were a relic of the frontier they were trying to forget.

When smoke from the council cleared, the Indian delegation had signed a contract with Captain John Mullan, their acquaintance of thirty-seven years and builder of the road which, ironically, had helped break down their isolation and hasten their removal. The contract with Mullan would be approved by the Department of Interior that summer.

After the meeting, Spokane Indians visited the agency almost daily to inquire about the status of the agreement, made five years earlier between themselves and the "Tribe of the United States." Chief Enoch and an Indian named Love were so anxious over its fate that they talked of visiting Washington, D. C., to urge its approval. Commissioner Thomas J. Morgan informed Agent Cole that, despite two bills pending and strong urging from his office, a bill had not been passed ratifying the 1887 agreement.

Principal opposition in Congress to approval of the agreement came from Senator Fred T. Dubois of the newly established state of Idaho. He voiced disapproval of Spokane Indians coming into his state. His opposition was doubtless strengthened by other spokesmen who vigorously objected to quartering "hostile bands" coming to their states. His opposition may also have been calculated to hasten the subtraction from the Coeur d'Alene Reservation of a portion of land which had been erroneously included in it and on which lived many white settlers. They had undoubtedly written him of their plight. The senator would be successful in achieving the separation of this land.

Just a few miles west, in Washington State, the citizenry of

[3] *Spokesman-Review*, February 20, 1892, p. 6.

Spokane were beginning to take an almost charitable attitude toward the red man. Wrote the editor of the *Spokesman-Review* (Spokane, Wash.):

> These miserable remnants of a once powerful band are entirely harmless and laying aside all question of humanitarianism, the people of Spokane have no objection to their presence in this vicinity. They bother nobody. Menace neither life nor property, are possessed of a kindly disposition and rather add to the picturesqueness of the city and its surroundings. But that is not the consideration. The presence here of these harmless Ishmaelites— their struggle for subsistence in a country that was once entirely theirs—is a reproach to civilization. The people of Spokane desire that justice should be done to the Spokanes, and that they should be endowed with permanent homes and given an opportunity to educate their children. No person here would object to these Indians being placed upon the Colville Reservation in this State, but they have set their hearts upon the Coeur d'Alene Reservation and their desire ought to be respected.[4]

The foregoing represented a growing tolerance of the Indian, a faint glimmer of which was seen when the 1887 agreement was made. It became brighter each year as its fulfillment neared. With the approaching departure of its red neighbors, the city could afford to be charitable.

Some Spokanes had already gone to the Coeur d'Alene Reservation in anticipation of approval of the agreement. By so doing, they had been forced to lowly positions in that community, consequently lagging far behind their Coeur d'Alene neighbors in accomplishment. An employee on the Coeur d'Alene Reservation, J. J. Walsh, wrote Agent Cole on July 5, 1893: "I will say the Spokanes have done nothing here to speak of. They are mostly working for the Coeur d'Alenes."[5]

Five long years after it had been signed by the Spokanes and the commissioners, the Spokane agreement was ratified by Congress on July 13, 1892. In August of the next year, Special Indian Com-

---

[4] *Spokesman-Review*, April 1, 1892, p. 6.
[5] J. J. Walsh to Cole, July 5, 1893, Colville Agency Records, Box 22.

missioners T. P. Smith (of Washington, D. C.) and Montgomery Hardman, with Captain John W. Bubb, U.S. Army, were in Spokane to arrange for the Indians' removal. Bubb, Cole's replacement, had just been appointed agent in compliance with the act of Congress, July 13, 1892, by which the army, after a long history of friction with the Interior Department in Indian matters, was to have a hand at supervising peaceful Indians. All this displeased Republicans of the Benjamin Harrison administration, as army officers were replacing their agent appointees. The fact that Bubb was under orders from the Secretary of the Interior did not soothe matters.[6]

Many Spokanes expressed to the commissioners their opposition to monies appropriated by Congress[7] the previous year for them to build houses wherever they decided to locate, saying they wanted cash instead and that they were willing to build their own houses or go without any. This demand presented a dilemma to the commissioners; they had no authority to accede to the Indians' demands had they so wished. Out of four hundred Spokanes entitled to Congressional appropriations to fulfill the 1887 agreement, the majority said they wanted allotments in bulk to preserve their tribal ownership. Only a small number said they wished to sever tribal relations in order to own their own property and live like white men.

Shortly thereafter, Hardman and Bubb (without Smith, who had been called away), went to meet with the Coeur d'Alenes to get their reaction to the impending arrival of the Spokanes on their reservation. They found the Coeur d'Alenes in a sullen mood, aggravated by an unfortunate incident as they waited for the council to open. There was a horse race and much betting. At the finish line, two horses collided at full speed, tumbling one on top of its rider, a popular young man among the Coeur d'Alenes; he was crushed to death. Hardman said he wished the government

---

[6] For an account of army Indian policy on the frontier in later times, see Raymond L. Welty, "The Indian Policy of the Army 1860–1870," *The Cavalry Journal*, Vol. XXXVI, No. 148 (July, 1927), 367–81.

[7] The first appropriation of ten installments was approved by Congress, March 3, 1893.

to survey and set aside on the Coeur d'Alene Reservation ten thousand acres for the Spokane Indians. Chief Seltice vigorously protested this proposal, to be followed by warrior after warrior making long speeches in which they dug up old bones of wrongs done them in the past. From the heat of their talk, it became evident that the Coeur d'Alenes would permit Spokanes to take up separate farms on their reserve and mingle in the community. But for the Spokanes to settle among them as a tribe, as the Spokanes wished—that was something else.

Bubb began the difficult task of removing the Spokanes to the Coeur d'Alene Reservation, a project slowed by Coeur d'Alene insistence that Spokanes take lands indiscriminately. This was the manner in which the Spokanes would be settled. In January, 1894, thirty-two Spokane families aggregating ninety-one people were relocated on the Coeur d'Alene. Houses were built for them at a cost of $157.90 each, in the northeastern part, on a prairie strip in Rocky Creek Valley. Arrangements were made to supply them horses, harness, wagons, and farm implements. Because of department failure to provide Spokanes with the means of building fences, the new settlers suffered a partial loss of their first crop, certainly no way to start out in their new homes.[8] Disappointed at their peoples' inability to settle as a tribal bloc, Chiefs Enoch and Louis wavered as to which reserve they should go, the Coeur d'Alene or the Spokane. They were afraid of losing benefits by removing to the latter. By acts approved March 3, 1893, and August 14, 1894, Congress had appropriated their first and second hundred dollar installments to help implement the Spokanes' move to the Coeur d'Alene.

Nevertheless, nearly half the Upper and Middle Spokanes, numbering about 160 Indians, either awaiting arrangements for them on the Coeur d'Alene or unhappy once they had been made, went down to the Spokane Reservation. Here they joined the Lower Spokanes and 27 former Deep Creek colonists. Many went believing the Spokane Reservation to be part of the Col-

[8] Secretary of the Interior, *Annual Report*, 1894 (53 Cong., 3 sess., *House Exec. Doc. No. 1*) Vol. II, Pt. 5, p. 314.

ville Reservation, to which they were free to go, with full benefits, under the 1887 agreement. In this belief they were in error.
But Congress, by act of August 15, 1894, provided that "monies
heretofore or hereafter appropriated for the removal of said Spokane Indians to the Coeur d'Alene Reservation shall be extended
to or expanded for such members of the tribe who have removed
or shall remove to the Spokane, as well as to the Colville or Jocko
(Flathead) Reservations."

On March 10, 1894, George H. Newman replaced Hardman
to complete the work of removing the Indians who elected to go
on the Spokane Reservation. He had help from the U.S. District
Attorney to defend the rights of some Indians to their homes off
the reservation. In June, 1895, lumber was sawed for the construction of sixty houses on the Spokane Reservation, presumably
to accommodate those people recently arrived there. At the same
time, forty more houses were being built on the Coeur d'Alene
Reservation, under Newman's supervision, for Spokanes living
there.

In the confusion of seeking permanent homes, a remnant of
Spokanes did not move to the reservations at all, but clung to the
outskirts of Spokane, many of them down by Hangman Creek.
Whites who had been so charitable when thinking all of them
were about to be removed had second thoughts about these
hangers-on. One writer confessed there was just one feature of
"this Utopian city" she could never come to like or to scarcely
endure, namely, the Indian inhabitants dwelling nearby, even the
"fairest and most gaily bedecked" of her own sex.[9]

Nor were Indians who went down to the Spokane Reservation
free from white pressures. Early in 1894 the Union Grange No.
109 of Crescent, Washington—south of the reservation in the Big
Bend country—adopted resolutions asking the federal government
to throw open the Spokane Indian Reservation, which had land
"adapted for agricultural purposes." The Indians numbered only
"about one hundred and fifty souls, who make but very little use

---

[9] Beth Bell, "In and around Spokane," *Northwest Magazine*, Vol. XIII, No.
9 (September, 1895), 20–21.

of it in farming."[10] Grange Master C. A. Coulson sent the resolutions to Senator John L. Wilson, who passed them on to Commissioner D. M. Browning, who returned them to Bubb, asking him to "ascertain from the Indians whether it is their desire to take allotments of land in severalty and then to negotiate with the United States for the surrender of their surplus lands."[11]

Bubb held council with the Spokanes in April. Having seen their brothers removed to the Coeur d'Alene Reservation and required to take allotments, they wanted none of it for themselves. They held that their poverty and lack of education made it unwise for them to come into the inevitable contacts with whites, which would be certain to follow their taking lands in severalty. Agent Bubb thought this point a good one.

Maybe the Spokanes believed they could find support in their stand from Chief Enoch, who decided that year to move to the Spokane Reservation to join members of his band, 188 of them, according to a census report the following year (1897). He left a few of his people on the Coeur d'Alene. Interestingly, that same year Louis Weilsho decided to make a move in the opposite direction from Enoch. He went to the Coeur d'Alene Reservation to join members of his band, 145 of them, according to the same 1897 census report.[12] The Spokanes on the Flathead Reservation in an 1899 census would number ninety-one.[13]

Enoch's band found themselves living in close proximity to the Lower Spokanes for the first time. Cultural differences remained. The newcomers changed the religious picture on the reservation to such a degree that nearly half its estimated six hundred

[10] *Lincoln County Times*, February 2, 1894, p. 7. Crescent, Washington (not to be confused with Creston, Washington), a post office established in 1882 and discontinued in 1901, was located 6 miles northeast of Reardon, Washington, at Ne/Ne Sec. 11, T26N, R39E. (There was a Crescent, Washington, post office in Pend Oreille County 1906 to 1923.)

[11] D. M. Downing to Bubb, March 21, 1894, Coeur d'Alene Agency Records, Box 18.

[12] Secretary of the Interior, *Annual Report*, 1897 (55 Cong., 2 sess., *House Exec. Doc. No. 5*), XIII, 289.

[13] Secretary of the Interior, *Annual Report*, 1899 (56 Cong., 1 sess., *House Exec. Doc. No. 5*), Vol. XVIII, Pt. 1, p. 568.

inhabitants were Catholic. To keep things from getting too crowded, the Catholic Spokanes frequently took to the road to visit friends and relatives of the same faith, particularly on special occasions. Many of them traveled to Colville to celebrate the Feast of Corpus Christi, an occasion in the 1890's that attracted as many as four hundred Indians, as did Easter, Whitsunday, and even St. Patrick's Day. Sometimes the Indians journeyed to the agency at De Smet, Idaho, to celebrate similar occasions.

Perhaps foremost among the good times were the horse races, which always thrilled spectators. The *Spokesman-Review* described how the Indians raced at the Stevens County Fair:

> They are a picturesque sight, stripped to trousers and shirt, their coppered black heads bare, with mocassin feet clasped closely about the sides of their horses with the most graceful ease, despite the nervous tossing and plunging. At the word they shoot forward like an arrow from its bow, the rider lying not merely leaning forward on one side of his horse's neck, one hand grasping the reins, the other stretched straight back and grasping the pliable leather thong with which he lashes his horse's shinging [*sic*] flank. No one but an Indian could retain such a position, and at that speed, for an instant, horse and rider present one straight line, and all that shows the rider is there is the flash of a scarlet or orange-colored handkerchief, which he has girted about his waist. On they come, neck and neck, until at length a long limbed black forges slightly ahead, but a slender little gray clings to his flank, the excitement grows and shouts and yells fill the air. Bets on the black are yelled out and taken, the roar increases as the horses come head on toward us. There are shrieks and howls as they cross the line, hats are flung up by even the supposed stoical Indian onlookers, and it would take a pretty phlegmatic person who could refrain from adding their quota to the uproar. The riders, when they can restrain their excited horses, ride back with them prancing, while they are laughing and joking in a louder tone than you usually hear an Indian use, for that is all the excitement shows on them, and there is no bitterness in their rivalry.[14]

Indians would continue to be a source of entertainment for

14 *Spokesman-Review*, September 27, 1895, p. 8.

whites at special occasions, since the latter knew most of them would return to their reservations once the events were over. In the 1890's, Spokane began holding the Northwest Industrial Exposition. This gave Indians an excuse to leave their confines, which they always did at the drop of a high-crowned Stetson. In town they saw what progress white men had made in civilization. The women roamed, goods-hungry, through stores to purchase eye-catching calicoes and shawls, sometimes trading salmon for them. Their men ogled the white man's "medicine," like the telephone, whose wires talked much better than those of the telegraph. Friday, October 5, 1900, was Red Man's Day at the exposition. The Spokanes and Nez Percés were asked to perform in the city, which now boasted nearly forty thousand souls. With little concept of, or regard for, the white man's measure of time, they were late for a scheduled parade through the streets; the Royal Marine Band of Italy had to march without them. They were finally rounded up and, with faces daubed with paint, mounted a platform to dance for the crowd. As a reporter put it, "The performance was received with a good deal of interest."[15]

The Protestant Spokanes, although not particularly stay-at-homes, held many of their celebrations on the reservation. In 1883, Chief Lot had seen the biggest Fourth of July celebration of his life in Washington, D. C.; he returned home to sponsor similar celebrations. Emulating the whites, the Indians mixed patriotism and religion in the celebrations. Lot's Fourth of July celebrations also served a practical purpose. Agents found them the best time to take a count of the Spokanes, since it was the only time all of them were together in one place.

Lot had found it easier to bring home ways of celebrating the Fourth of July than of opening a school. His school request unfilled, he grew discouraged as he grew older. Commissioner Frank Armstrong, on June 8, 1894, wrote Agent Bubb that the Indian office wished to furnish Lot's people a teacher, books, and desks, for a school building, should one be located on the reservation. If not (a situation the office might have known, had they

---

[15] *Spokesman-Review*, October 6, 1900, p. 1.

remembered correspondence on the subject over the preceding ten years), Bubb could submit plans for one, not to exceed one thousand dollars. Bubb submitted the plans, but heard nothing from Washington.[16]

Through the offices of the Women's National Indian Association, a plan for a school was prepared. On October 2, 1894, the Secretary of the Interior permitted five acres to be set aside for the school, such land as was unclaimed by any Indian, for the temporary use and occupancy of the association, in which no right, title, or interest could rest.[17] The teacher selected was Miss Helen Clark, a Scottish Presbyterian born in Kensington, Quebec. She arrived on October 25, 1894, at the reservation at Wellpinit, twenty-five miles from a store or post office. "I drove the whole length of the reservation without finding a house which could shelter me," she would later write. While awaiting the return of Lot from a hunting expedition, she wrote: "God gives me peace and I dare not complain." In early November she occupied one of Lot's buildings and, looking forward to the building of the school, wrote: "If I can only get my children gathered and begin work I will willingly face the limitations which must come into my life."[18]

Of her interview with Chief Lot, she wrote: "He is a fine looking man, worthy of being Chief. His broad, high brow and thoughtful air give him a distinguished look; he has a keen sense of humor, and a smile often lights up his face." When the matter of the school was discussed, Lot listened in silence. Then Captain Bubb, through the interpreter, told him he could make his choice about having the school. Lot's answer was characteristic: "Does the Captain think I do not know enough to take a good thing when it is offered me?" Lot said he would agree to any terms, that his Indians would haul lumber, put up logs, and do anything they could. If the teacher wanted anything and he had it, she could have it. If he didn't have it, he would go to Bubb and get it.

16 Frank C. Armstrong to Bubb, June 8, 1894, and October 6, 1894, Coeur d'Alene Agency Records, Box 18.
17 *The Spokane Indian Mission.*
18 *Ibid.*

With Indian office approval, Lot offered the teacher five acres of meadow bottomland along Wellpinit Creek. He ordered his men to cut and hew logs and erect a school near the church. Shingles, nails, and some lumber were hauled in, and the area fenced. Miss Clark moved in on December 18, 1894.[19] School opened January 3, 1895, with thirty-five pupils in attendance. On the fifteenth, forty-one were enrolled; at the end of the month, fifty. Lot was proud. "My heart is big," he said. Every day he came to visit and observe the pupils' progress. Some of these were married people, so eager to learn from the teacher that they camped in tents near the schoolhouse in three feet of snow with the temperature below zero. Miss Clark was impressed with such zeal. Agent Bubb was enthusiastic, too. "I note more rapid progress in this school than in any other," he wrote, attributing its success to Miss Clark, an "indefatigable worker" in school and out, whose painstaking effort accomplished more than those who performed similar tasks in a "perfunctory manner."

An Office of Indian Affairs authorized school was built the same year as Lot's, but on the west end of the reservation, three miles from Detillion Bridge and ten miles from the agency. It mostly served the transplanted Deep Creek colonists. Opening day had been October 15, 1895, with ten pupils in attendance. John D. Russell, the teacher, said the first year was not what it should have been. The problem, as he saw it, was one of Indian indifference. The agent saw the problem as one of teacher inefficiency. After a year Russell got a transfer and left the school to John Butchart and his wife, who came on November 1 from the Colville Reservation's Nespelem School, which had closed down for poor attendance.[20]

Miss Clark found her duties similar to those of the government school teachers, namely to teach school, keep community peace, serve as subagent and, above all, break down the customs of generations. She believed she had one weapon in her arsenal, the Bible. "There is a road from every part of the Bible to Christ, and

[19] *Ibid.*
[20] Ruby and Brown, *Half-Sun on the Columbia*, 333.

I find it so," she wrote. The Butcharts had some advantages over Miss Clark, however. There were two of them to carry on the work. Mrs. Butchart worked with the girls in the sewing room on sewing machines, handled the commissary, and cooked the noon meal for the children. Her husband taught them from McGuffey *Readers*, supplemented by all the best materials white American children were reading in schools: Aesop's *Fables*, American history stories, *Cats and Dogs*, *Children's Kitchen Garden*, *Claws and Hoofs*, *Each and All*, *Feathers and Furs*, and *Gentle Manners*.

Before the needles on the 1897 Christmas tree were dry, it was Chinook dancing time again, and the children scattered to practice what Miss Clark called their "darling sin . . . the greatest barrier there is to civilization."[21] Truancy did not end with the winter dances. In the spring there was root digging, which took the children away. The boys, like boys anywhere, needed no special occasion to play hooky from school. Once Butchart cuffed a boy; he did not come back for some time. When Albert Garry was punished, he told the other children he would never come back. Eventually he continued his schooling at the Chemawa School. Ironically, some of the people came to school to escape work. Miss Clark complained of helpers who sat around all day in school instead of going out to the Big Bend towns for supplies and mail.

Knowing that good roads and good education went together, Miss Clark was anxious about road progress. The first wagon road on the Spokane Reservation was for agency use. Built in 1884–85, it ran north from the narrows of the Spokane River several miles up to the ferry crossing over the Columbia (above the mouth of the Spokane) and then to the Colville Reservation. An earlier footbridge suspended over the narrows and washed out in a spring freshet in 1883 was rebuilt by a young army engineer, George W. Goethals. Looking back over the years, Goethals would recall the building of this bridge of logs as his most difficult engineering job. Yet he was the engineer who built the Panama Canal.[22] Stevens and Lincoln counties (the latter just south of the reservation in

[21] Clark to Anderson (n.d.), Coeur d'Alene Agency Records, Box 30.
[22] *Spokane Times-Tribune*, March 1, 1923, p. 1.

the Big Bend) would, in 1901, open the Nee Bridge near the mouth of the Spokane.

For years the reservation road most used by whites had been the Detillion Bridge Road. It ran north out of Davenport and crossed the Spokane near the transplanted Deep Creek settlement. Stevens County commissioners, in 1895, had set aside funds for building a bridge at this natural location. They called it "Detillion" for a man by that name living there. The bridge would fall into the river in August, 1903. Stevens and Lincoln counties would then build a new span at a cost of five thousand dollars.

Until roads improved, the Spokanes jolted around their reservation as best they could. In early October, 1898, a band of them creaked across bumpy roads to the town of Wilbur in the Bend. Here they received a government consignment of furniture and other merchandise, including a large number of spring mattresses. It would be interesting to know how long the Indians slept on these "flowery beds of ease." In March, 1899, Miss Clark said they were selling their wagons to white men. This made her feel bad, particularly as the purchasers were getting them at only a fraction of their cost.

To Miss Clark the Indians appeared no more inspired in building shelters than in building roads. One New Year's Day, she gave them boards to build a shelter to protect horses when their riders were in church and school. The lumber still lay in midsummer. Only her threat to give it away prodded some Indians grudgingly to finish the structure.

Miss Clark was not only instructor but protector. She was appalled when a white man named King arrived at Wellpinit in the fall of 1898 with two loads of household goods, several cows, some horses, a "woman he calls his Wife," a bad reputation, and five children, whom he asked to be enrolled in the school. King thought Agent Major Albert M. Anderson "a lamb" who would not kick him off the reservation. "If he remains," wrote Miss Clark, "we will soon have many more, for white men all envy the indians [*sic*] their little garden spots."[23]

23 Clark to Agent? (n.d.), Coeur d'Alene Agency Records, Box 30.

Because of his common-law marriage to a "Cherokee" wife (so she claimed), King demanded the right to remain on the reservation. Some whites were to marry Indian women with the idea of getting no more than grazing privileges, most of them simply turning their herds loose on the reservation. Walker's Prairie residents were notorious for letting their stock eat nearby reservation grass. In 1901, agency farmer W. H. Kunse rounded up sixty-five head of cattle, all branded and belonging to several whites. Among the stock were those belonging to the Reverend Hiram White, a missionary soon to be assigned to the Wellpinit Presbyterian Church. Ben Frazier made a private deal with an Indian to pasture eighty head of cattle on the reservation in violation of regulations. Before the affair ended, it had come to the attention of First Assistant Secretary of the Interior Samuel Adams, who asked aid from the Justice Department to instruct the U.S. marshal to take possession of the cattle.[24]

"Every white man," wrote Miss Clark, "seems to think that it is his legitimate privilege to beat and trick an Indian in any kind of a trade or business transaction, and as a rule they have very little confidence in the white man's honesty. I tell them I am ashamed of my people."[25] The white man's lack of character only strengthened her own. All money she received went to the school. She put her own money into her little dwelling or into outside charities. She once hoped to keep on hand enough coffee and flour to sell the Indians at cost, since they had to go so far for supplies. But anyone under agency employ or control could not sell to Indians. Once she walked fifteen miles to get some fruit trees for the Indians. With seed (sometimes provided by the agency), she helped the youngsters plant gardens in small plots she marked out for them. After caring for them in summer, in the fall she would take each returning child to his own spot and, so they could enjoy their plantings, say, "This is your garden."[26]

[24] The agency inadvertantly erred in returning Frazier's check for assessment to him.

[25] *Lincoln County Times*, March 20, 1896, p. 7.

[26] Albert Sam interview.

In August, 1898, Butchart was transferred to a reservation school on the coast. Leonidas Swaim came that fall to accept the teaching position and the usual problems that went with it.

A month after arriving, he asked the agent if his predecessor had disinfected the house and bedding after the Butchart children had the measles, for he didn't want his own children "sick after inhaling the germs there in the house." When twenty-five pounds of dried fruit arrived it was so wormy Mrs. Swaim had to return it to the agent. Swaim had trouble with other school issues. He wrote Agent Anderson that the Fox boys returned with medicines all right excepting for the two pints of turpentine, which they said had leaked out. "The way it could have leaked out is rather mysterious to me," wrote Swaim.

To handle the poor attendance problem, in December Swaim offered any youngster a year's subscription to the *Youth Companion* if he did not miss school. But by mid-January, 1899, he wrote Anderson: "I have been offering prizes of different kinds for regular attendance in trying different ways to make school attractive, but the woods and ponds with the squirrels and ice seem to be more attractive to them."[27] What would it be like when spring came? On May 27, 1899, the agent advised him that, since attendance had been so poor, the acting commissioner had advised that the school be closed and the teacher transferred.

One reason for the closing of the west end government school was the department's plan, of which Miss Clark had heard rumors, of converting the Fort Spokane military installation into a boarding school for children from the Colville and Spokane reservations. With the coming of the fort school, the Women's National Indian Association prepared to move Miss Clark to a mission at Neah Bay on the coast. Her organization and the people she served would agree that she would leave the reservation a better place than she found it. Miss Clark did say that Lot and some of his subchiefs were as good Christians as any she ever saw. That summer she would leave her "beloved Spokanes." Attempts would be

27 Swaim to Anderson, February 13, 1899, Spokane Day School Records 1897–1899, Box 48.

made nine years later to have her return. Then she would say that "if I followed my heart instead of my head I would pack up and be off next week."[28] A staff member in the office of the National Board of Missions of the United Presbyterian Church in the United States of America wrote on Miss Clark's death that her Indian friends paid her a tribute she would never forget: "She came to us when we were in the depths of superstition, and everything bad but she stayed by us till we rose." Shortly before her death, in 1937, she left a message for her Indian friends: "When they tell you I am dead, do not believe it. My body will be laid away but my spirit will never die; and if it is possible I will return and walk among you, my friends, helping, comforting, and guiding."[29]

The opening of the Fort Spokane boarding school coincided with its abandonment by the army. Barracks that once housed soldiers who were keeping an eye on the Spokanes now sheltered the Spokane children. Drill grounds became playgrounds.

Indians got their chance to become soldiers when General John Gibbon, on March 27, 1891, issued an order recruiting them for four northwest forts, including Fort Spokane. Gibbon's action was in response to a War Department decision of experimental enlistment of young Indian men over eighteen. Many thought this would solve the "Indian problem," as military service would offer them congenial and remunerative employment. Being nearest the fort, the Spokanes had been the first to furnish recruits. In reply to Captain J. M. Lee's request for Fort Spokane recruits, Lot made a speech which was printed in eastern newspapers:

My Father was Chief of all the Indians and he used to tell them what it was right to do. After his death my brother became Chief and he was a good Chief too. I was bad ... When my brother died they wanted me to be Chief. But my heart was full of bad. I could not get good out of the bad. But Washington [Government] wanted me to be Chief. Then I studied to be good. I was anxious to learn to read and to use pen and ink. I like my family to go

28 Clark to Avery, May 18, 1908, Colville Agency Records, Box 22545–L. 9178.
29 "Helen W. Clark."

along side of me, and I was anxious to have my people learn to read and write. The minister tells us God is up there. I hear it but it goes in the ear and out. I lose it. I look up into the sky and see nothing. Where is the road to see God Almighty? I look through something that the white man uses to see a long distance and I see nothing but blue. I look down and see only the ground. The minister take the Bible and interpret what Jesus said, and that was to me a glass to see God. Then I worked harder than ever, and I wanted to see my people read and write before I died. That was my mind when General Howard saw me. He told me, "Washington wants you to send your children to a place towards where the sun goes down where they can go to school." God knows I love my children. God knows what I wanted. Captain Wilson [Wilkinson] came the next year and asked if I could send some. The people were afraid, but I sent mine. The next year he wanted some more. I gave him a lot of boys and girls. They sent the sick back; the rest died down there. (Of twenty-one pupils sent, sixteen died.) I made up mind that my people were right in being afraid to send the children away. Then I wanted a school house right by my house. I went to Washington and spoke only one thing: "I like a school house." Two men then told Moses, "Lot says he wants a school house; do you want a school house?" Moses answered, "No." Then they asked Tonaskit and again they used my name. "Lot says he wants a school house; do you want one?" "No, I sent my children to Catholic school." Then they turned to me: "Why do you not send your children to Catholic school?" "I want an **American and not an Italian to teach my children,**" [answered Lot.] They said, "**Lot you go home and in two months you will have a school house.**" (That was in 1883.) It was three years that I was very anxious. They built one for Moses, and one for Tonaskit, but none for me. I hear that they looked at a place on the hill ten miles from my house. My people do not want to send their children so far away. If I had had white people's children I would have put their bodies in a coffin and sent them home so that they could see them, I do not know who did it, but they treated my people as if they were dogs. My people are afraid; they won't allow any one belonging to them to be soldiers. But I want them to be soldiers. I shall never have a school house; but they can learn many things by being soldiers. I want my boy to be a soldier, and then if it is good for him it will be good for the rest . . . They should give me that school house. When they buried sixteen of our children they should pay by building a school.[30]

The speech moved Captain Lee. He was reported to have said in response: "Could that have been heard by an eastern audience how it would have opened hearts and pocket books." It was, and it did.

Concerning recruits at Fort Sherman (formerly Camp Coeur d'Alene), it was reported in the *Spokesman-Review* that: "Living in tents their facilities for cooking and messing are not as good as in the case of other troops. They may in time become soldiers but will always be a separate and distinct class of soldiers. They have no desire to affiliate with the white troops and the white troops have no use for the 'siwashes.' "[31] Another paper, the *Spokane Falls Review* (Spokane Falls, Wash.), editorialized that the Indian loved his "firewater," that the canteen and "gin mills" were open to him, permitting drunkenness, during which his "savage nature" asserted itself. Although Buffalo Bill's shows had a great success in Europe, the editorial continued, the attempt of the War Department to put a wild-West annex to the little regular army was not likely to succeed.[32]

These evaluations of Indian soldiering were not confined to the pages of newspapers. In his annual report for 1892, Cole reported the Indians as poor soldiers. Permitted too much freedom at the canteen, they squandered every dollar of their salaries, went into debt, and became addicted to a life of drunkenness, only to suffer punishment at the hands of the military authorities—a discipline the Indians were quick to point out was not administered equally to reds and whites. Wrote Cole: "I am of the opinion it would be a wise plan on the part of the Government to disband the Indian company, for they certainly will do no good for themselves, and much harm to the reservation Indians."[33]

[30] *The Spokane Indian Mission.* [31] *Spokesman-Review*, April 17, 1892, p. 6.
[32] *Spokane Falls Review*, April 21, 1891, p. 8.
[33] Secretary of the Interior, *Annual Report*, 1892 (52 Cong., 2 sess., *House Exec. Doc. No. 1*), Vol. II, Pt. 5, p. 488.

At Fort Spokane, Company I of the Fourth Infantry was composed essentially of Spokanes and a few Colvilles. Official records show that most all, in turn, were AWOL, causing them to forfeit portions of their pay. A number deserted. The experiment was such a failure that the company of seventeen, twelve of whom were Spokanes, was discharged by special order on August 2, 1893.[34] When other enlistees were discharged, the *Spokesman-Review* editorialized:

Now that the plan has failed, the problem of what to do with the Indian is as vexing as ever.

Six years ago the War Department ordered the enlisting of three companies of soldiers into the regular army. For a few weeks it looked as if the plan was to be a success, but then the trouble began. As soon as the novelty had worn off the Indian[s] began to complain. They found the uniforms too tight [so did white soldiers] and claimed they prevented circulation of air about their persons.

One company commander gave the men permission to remedy this defect as they saw best. The next morning they showed up on parade with the seat of . . . [their] trousers cut out. Every Indian soldier brought his squaw with him to the barracks, and refused to keep himself and his quarters in a state of soldierly neatness. The natural Indian disinclination to work asserted itself. There was no question as to bravery, for the Indians were as brave as any troops ever enlisted, but the fact remained that they could not be made soldiers of the modern type. Last week the last of the three Indian companies were mustered out of the service at Fort Omaha. The first company mustered out some years ago was, perhaps, the worst of the lot. It was attached to the second infantry, and was the one that made the alterations in trousers. Within three months of the discharge of the men from the service each had returned to the reservation and was wearing a blanket.

The experiment had demonstrated the truth of the statement made years ago by the late Major General Crook who declared that the Indian could never become a modern soldier; that as a soldier

[34] Regular Army Muster Rolls Company I, 4th United States Infantry December 1892–August 1893, "Records of the Adjutant General's Office," Record Group 94.

among tribesmen he has no superior; that his valor was unquestioned; but that reduced to accept modern conditions and modern arms he is a failure.

An Indian fighting as an Indian is an effective soldier; as a member of a civilized army he is useless. Until army tactics are changed to conform to the Indian style, it is folly for Uncle Sam to enlist his dusky wards.[35]

Uncle Sam did get that opportunity to enlist Indians, but before tactics were changed. During the Spanish-American War, the War Department sought to recruit Indians, thinking they would be good fighters in that war. A call went out from the agents. Eight Spokanes showed up, dressed as if going to a masquerade ball, agreeing to go if they could fight on their own terms and in their traditional way and without uniforms. Their offer was unacceptable.[36]

By 1902 the appearance of the old fort had begun to change. A community building was being remodeled for an assembly and auditorium, like those in public schools. Teachers and employees accepted officers' quarters, and half the guardhouse had been converted into a many-roomed bathhouse. The number of students from both Spokane and Colville reservations was on the increase, although at the beginning of school in September there were only a hundred present. But it was believed that after hop picking and other fall activities, enrollment would be increased to three hundred. The Colville Agency headquarters were moved across the river to occupy some of the buildings. The agency doctor was on hand, as was a lady doctor for the school and a dentist brought in from nearby Davenport to check teeth. Federal funds were requested to cover the cost of needed dental work. The uniformed children received shoes, some of which did not fit well, sending a couple of them to the hospital with sore feet.

There was an orchard; melons and tomatoes were planted. A pumping station down on the Spokane River, constructed by the

[35] *Spokesman-Review*, May 17, 1897, p. 4; Sadie Boyd interview, Wellpinit, Washington, July 2, 1965.
[36] Sadie Boyd interview.

military years before, was pressed into school use. The water was raised by a steam-pumping plant. Water for animals and domestic use came from a spring 350 feet higher to the south of the fort grounds. Buildings were lighted by kerosene lamps and heated by wood-burning stoves, since the structures were too scattered for a central heating plant. Support of the school operation was from the general appropriation.

Evaluating the school picture in September, 1902, the editor of the *Wilbur Register* (Wilbur, Wash.) wrote:

> One great advantage of this school, so workers among Indians say, is its proximity to homes of native parents. Instead of being taken away and placed among refined people to be educated and then brought back only to become disgusted with their surroundings, these children . . . are taught how to be civilized, without losing respect for parents and kindred, and will be able to go home and lend a helping hand, instead of treating their relations with disdain. They may not be so highly polished during the polishing process, but they will take on a finish that is bound to be more lasting.[37]

A sad month for the Spokanes and Coeur d'Alenes was April, 1902. Then their two great chiefs, Lot and Seltice, died. On Lot's passing, Red Hawk rode a fleet cayuse to Spokane to telephone the sad news to Indians of the Coeur d'Alene. Many of them came to the Spokane Reservation to the big Fourth of July potlatch held for Chief Lot. The world would remember the two chiefs, thanks to a writer and a sculptor. C. E. S. Wood, General Howard's former aide-de-camp, would present their stories in a *Century Magazine* article. It was illustrated by pictures of large medallions, on which the renowned artist, Olin Warner, had sculpted their likenesses.[38]

The month following Lot's death, Congress, on May 27, 1902, enacted legislation providing for subjection to entry of mineral lands only on the Spokane Reservation, not to take effect before

[37] *Wilbur Register,* September 26, 1902.
[38] C. E. S. Wood, "Famous Indians: Portraits of Some Indian Chiefs," *The Century Magazine,* n.s., Vol. XXIV, No. 3 (1893), 441–42.

December of that year. On June 19, Congress authorized the Secretary of the Interior to allot the Spokanes and, when alloting was over, to open unallotted and unreserved lands to purchase under the mining laws. Not until March, 1903, would Congress appropriate monies to survey the Spokane Reservation, and not until August of that year would a contract for the survey be awarded to H. H. Johnson, U.S. Deputy Surveyor. Davenport attorneys inquired as to whether they would meet opposition were they to enter the reservation where they claimed rights to do "our assessment work on our mineral claims."[39] From three to four hundred prospectors camped along the river in June, thinking they would be first onto the reservation. They were trigger happy (there were gunshots) over their prospects, as miners had been in 1896 when gold had been discovered on the north half of the Colville Reservation and, two years later, on the south half. One sooner secured a deputy sheriff's commission through misrepresentation, using it to take two prisoners, also sooners, away from the Spokane Reservation Indian police. Once out of sight, the presumed sheriff turned his two prisoners loose.

Critical days lay ahead for inhabitants of the Spokane Reservation. Never did they need more protection from the white man and, paradoxically, never a greater need to adjust to his inevitable presence surrounding their reservation. They could not face these times alone. Agent Anderson would be of no help; he was removed for irregularities, saying he would exonerate himself. As never before, they needed a protector, guide, and friend. That man was ready.

[39] M. F. Gibson, Davenport, Washington Citizens to Anderson, July 30, 1903, Coeur d'Alene Agency Records, Box 30.

CHAPTER NINE

Civilizing Agent

Captain John McA. Webster assumed leadership of the Colville Agency on August 1, 1904.[1] A product of the government's twelve-year-old policy of yielding supervision of Indian agencies to army personnel, Webster had spent twenty years of his military career on a frontier line from northern Montana to southern Texas. He began his term of service at a time of immense potential for the Spokanes. It was a time when his employer, the Office of Indian Affairs, began dealing with Indians en masse, rather than with chiefs and tribal representatives. On assuming his post, Webster was faced with the task of administering, in his Colville Agency, not one reservation, but three. The separation of the Coeur d'Alene Reservation on July 1, 1905, eased his burdens somewhat.[2] The sheer physical magnitude of his agency suggested

[1] "Webster, Address delivered to an 'Indian Institute' in Seattle on August 30–31, 1909," in (Captain John McA.) Webster Papers, W–8.
[2] As early as 1886, Agent Benjamin Moore had suggested that the Coeur d'Alene Reservation be established as a separate unit. With substantial per capita payments to the Coeur d'Alenes for the sale of a portion of their reservation Major Anderson had suggested on October 9, 1903, that it be administered separately. After separation from the Colville, the Coeur d'Alene would be administered separately until

problems of administration. A mountainous country of simmering heat and shivering cold, it stretched from Bonners Ferry in northwest Idaho, near the Canadian border where the Kootenays lived, south to the Spokane River and along that river to the Columbia, where that river, in turn, meets the Chelan, up to its lake, northward to the Canadian border and east to the point of beginning. In addition to protecting the numerous Indian bands of this area, Webster also administered a band of Wenatchee Indians residing outside the above confines.

In his annual report for 1906, Webster summarized his problem for the commissioner: "The introduction of new elements into existing conditions through the advance of the forces of a so-called civilization has caused a great increase in the business of the agency, the jurisdiction of which covers a large territory and now involves so many interests that it is physically impossible for the agent to give personal and needed attention to all."[3]

Webster inherited some of his troubles. His predecessor, Agent Anderson, refused to produce a list of Indian children for whom he claimed guardianship and for whom, Webster claimed, he had improperly made verbal leases of allotments. The captain began tracking down the properties in question. A year later, Webster would still seek the elusive list of children over whom the ex-agent claimed guardianship. "Failing to get any satisfaction from him," wrote Webster, "I finally applied to the superior court of Ferry County to which he had referred, and was not surprised to learn that he had never been guardian for *any* Indian children."[4] It shortly came to light that the Fort Spokane school physician, Mary H. McKee, and the additional farmer, John S. Meyers, had been induced to accept guardianships over the children. Webster suspected that Anderson had taken all the lease monies, for which he had given no accounting.[5]

July 1, 1933, when it would be attached to the Northern Idaho Agency at Lapwai, Idaho.

3 Webster to commissioner, August 27, 1906, Colville Agency Records, Letterbook 26, Box 32.

4 Webster to commissioner, June 2, 1906, Colville Agency Records, Letterbook 26, Box 32.

The school picture had improved but little. With the opening of school shortly after he took office, Webster fired a letter off to Farmer Kunse, advising him to "hustle" the children to the boarding school should their parents wish any favors from his hand. Incorrigibly truant runaways like George Hill, William Ubear, and Emma Hill were expelled to pursue their happy ways. At the school more problems arose. Both Indians and whites smuggled liquor into the school, where apparently some of the older students were developing a thirst for something besides knowledge. It was difficult to tag the offenders, because Indian testimony was not accepted by juries in the state.[6]

When it closed for the year on June 22, 1906, enrollment at the boarding school at the fort was 160 pupils, with an average attendance for the year of 141.4 pupils. The school would reopen in September for its last year, as it would soon be replaced by day schools. There was a growing governmental emphasis on Indian family group living and the teaching of children in gardening, farming, and the performance of household chores in their native environs. Webster was quite pleased with farming progress on the reservation. He saw in the Indians' noncash crops a means of helping to sustain the agency. It is significant that government officials, their thinking conditioned by nineteenth-century emphasis on farming, did not stress an education program oriented toward forestry and grazing for the Spokane Reservation, since the largest share of its lands were of these types.

In 1889, Commissioner Morgan had opined that Indians were far below whites in "general intelligence." He stated that responsibility for educating and converting the Indians into American citizens (to compete with whites to avoid hopeless degradation)

---

[5] Anderson had a hearing before the Federal Grand Jury in April, 1908. On the failure of the jury to return an indictment, Webster wrote the commissioner on May 2, 1908: "The District Attorney says that in all his experience as a lawyer he has never known a clearer case of guilt to be presented to a grand jury." Webster to commissioner, May 2, 1908, Colville Agency Records, Letterbook 28, Box 32.

[6] Webster to commissioner, April 20, 1906, Colville Agency Records, Letterbook 25, Box 32.

rested squarely with the government, which should operate in a nonpartisan and nonsectarian manner. Webster was not oblivious to the growing secularization of the day, which had prompted the commissioner to stress industrial training to equip Indians to earn an honest living on earth, speaking with English tongues rather than with those of angels. But where the commissioner had maintained that the "anachronistic" reservation system had no place in modern civilization, Webster believed the time had not yet come for the breakup of reservations. Nor did he share Morgan's enthusiasm for large boarding schools. He seems to have expressed no opinion on the "outing system," as practiced at Carlisle, of placing Indian children in white homes, which Morgan had believed a good way of impressing them with white civilization.[7]

In a Seattle speech Webster affirmed his support of day schools on the reservation. When it was learned that the Spokane Reservation was to have two day schools, the old day school, Number One, also called the "Three Mountains School," was proposed for rejuvenation. (The second school in preparation at Wellpinit was not yet completed.) The buildings of the Three Mountains School and four acres (which had been sold in 1902 to one John Desautel, who had added a barn on the place) were repurchased for four hundred dollars. Three young ladies, Misses Mary Fennell and Clara Degering, teachers, and a Miss Quillian, housekeeper, alighted at Davenport. They headed north twenty-eight miles to the Three Mountains School. The ladies set about to make their home livable in a land with no telephones and the nearest post office at Lott, just off the reservation near Detillion Bridge.

Another year and the two teachers had retreated to civilization, to be replaced by Abigail E. White, daughter of the minister. Abigail was even less tolerant of the children's horseplay than were her predecessors. She became embroiled in endless arguments with the children and had problems with one of her housekeepers. When the agency got wind of her troubles, they replaced her with Frederick W. C. Dew. Dew found Miss White unco-

[7] Thomas J. Morgan, commissioner, *The Education of American Indians* (n.d.).

operative in turning over to him needed papers and other materials. "She is lacking not only in 'balance,' " said Day School Inspector Frank Avery, who had recommended her appointment and also urged her removal, "but in many other important qualifications."[8]

Over at Wellpinit, construction was plagued by delays. Carpenters came over in June, 1906, only to find that officials had not decided on the exact location of the buildings. The mill which had agreed to furnish the lumber closed down. The Spokane River had dropped so low that no lumber could be barged down it, necessitating the hauling of materials by teams, which were busy at the time working in the fields. The Mission Road from Little Falls on the Spokane to Wellpinit, washed out by June rains, had to be repaired before materials could be hauled to the site. Despite these difficulties, teachers' quarters (built at a cost of $836.91) and the school (at a cost of $987.45) were ready by mid-September, 1906. They stood unoccupied until March, 1907.

Otto S. Hays of St. Louis was brought in as teacher, and his wife as housekeeper. An exacting person, Hays refused to sign his checks, questioning the amount of his pay. His problems were aggravated by his wife's illness, which necessitated his taking her to Seattle for hospitalization to end his brief career as Wellpinit school teacher. Replacements for the Hayses, Ross L. Spalsbury and his wife Gertrude, came in mid-September to open the school term. At the end of the first week, only eighteen pupils had enrolled. Before the year was over, the Spalsburys were gone, having tangled with Avery on leave policies, the last straw in a stack of troubles between the two. Avery charged that Spalsbury had not identified himself with the community and had done little or nothing to conserve the moral welfare of its children. Avery's headaches would have been greater had the Coeur d'Alene Reservation not been detached from the Spokane.

The Coeur d'Alene agent, Charles O. Worley, wrote Webster on December 24, 1907, of his troubles stemming from parents

[8] Avery to Webster, February 10, 1909, Colville Agency Records, Box 22545–L.9178.

sending, or wishing to send, their children to Chemawa; he claimed they were harassed and placed under an interdict of sorts by the fathers. In a reply to Worley, Webster wrote:

> I regret to say however that from what Coeur d'Alane and Spokane Indians have since told me I am convinced that there is altogether too much truth in the charges made and that there exists at De Smet Mission a most pronounced opposition to all forms of education under the laws of the United States except those under direct charge of the Catholic Church and its ministers.[9]

Avery's search for efficient personnel went so far as to include a letter to Helen Clark in May, 1908, requesting her to leave her position on the coast to return to Wellpinit. In vain. Avery also saw the need of a new school on the east end of the reservation for the Walker's Prairie children. In late summer, 1908, school construction began not far from the Walker-Eells first school among the Spokanes. Charles F. Morrison and his wife, Eleanor, arrived in December to teach.

With the old Fort Spokane definitely out as the site of the boarding school, plans were advanced for other uses of that facility. One suggestion was that it become an Indian reform school. Another was that it be used as a sanatorium for Indian children suffering from tuberculosis, scrofula, infectious diseases, eye disorders, and other illnesses. The sanatorium plan was adopted. To make ready for its projected opening on October, 1907, construction of the two day schools was rushed on both the Colville and Spokane reservations. The rush could have been avoided, since the sanatorium would remain closed for lack of a physician-superintendent, nurse, and teachers. The doors did not open until late winter; not until April did a nurse arrive, only to leave in three weeks due to a misunderstanding over her job assignment. Securing employees was a continuing problem. The physician-superintendent, a Dr. Slater, lacked energy and executive ability; while he did make three trips daily to attend to the children, he did no paper work. His lethargy spread like a contagion to the other em-

9 Webster to Worley, January 17, 1908, Webster Papers, 180–22.

ployees. Aware of the atmosphere he was creating, he resigned. Moreover, the sanatorium was poorly attended, with a maximum of only nineteen patients by August, 1908. In an attempt to attract a replacement for the physician-superintendent at the twelve-hundred-dollar salary offered, Webster held out to applicants the inducement of building up private practices in the surrounding countryside, which was beginning to fill with settlers.

The new physician-superintendent, Dr. Charles C. Van Kirk, took more interest than Slater in both the executive and health aspects of the sanatorium. Enrollment rose to 48, with an average attendance of 18.2 during the year 1907–1908, as more Spokane children known to be ill were brought in, like the Ferguson children, Adeline Desautel, Lena and Joe Brown. Some children in good health tried to gain admission to the sanatorium because of its more liberal allowance of clothing and incidental amusements than found in the day schools. Certain other youngsters oscillated between the two institutions, taking liberal self-imposed vacations from both. Requests came to place tubercular Cheyenne Indian children in the sanatorium as well as children from the Puyallup Consolidated Agency on the coast. With the resignation of Dr. Van Kirk, a Dr. Wimberly assumed leadership of the sanatorium until his resignation in 1912, at which time the institution closed.[10]

On the reservation, thanks to efforts of people like the agents and the Reverend White, polygamy had declined; but wife stealing had increased. The Indian could learn but little from white men in gambling. It was still rampant on the reservation. In midsummer, 1906, Reverend White refused his Indians permission to stay over Sunday at their churchside campground because they had gambled too much—"worse than for many years." Neither church nor courts had dented the liquor problem.

At first glance one would expect little relationship between social development on the reservation and the allotting of its lands. Webster saw the allotting program as a long overdue de-

---

[10] By Congressional act of March 3, 1911, lands of the old fort were to be disposed of by sale.

velopment in the preparation of his charges in self-support and citizenship. In an address in late August, 1909, he said:

> So long as there was plenty of land and game was abundant the Indian enjoyed comparative ease and freedom in the large vacant areas assigned to him in the little known West, but when the rising tide of cattlemen and settlers ran up against this reservation encroachments began, disputes arose, wars followed, and when thrashed into submission Mr. Indian was induced by fair means and foul, or by way of punishment for having the temerity to stand up for his rights, to trek to successive reservations until the supply of reservations ran short. Moved thus from pillar to post he had little opportunity and, with centuries of nomadic life behind him, less inclination to cultivate the soil or make the radical change in his manner of living, illogically expected of him. Common sense finally demanded that he be definitely settled for a permanent home making, and the individual allotment was wisely decided upon as the ultimate settlement of the Indian question.[11]

The allotment system, a reality for the Spokane Reservation by the act of June 19, 1902, would, in Webster's thinking, bring its people into contact with the law-abiding white community.[12]

The Spokanes had already made contacts with certain law-abiding members of the white community, men like John Hill, Henry Etu, and J. C. Wynecoop. Wynecoop and his half-blood Lake wife, Nancy—a woman blessed with intelligence, ambition, and physical strength—moved onto the reservation. Here they carved out a sizable domain, leaving descendants well endowed with more than average ambition.[13]

[11] "Webster, Address delivered to an 'Indian Institute' in Seattle on August 30–31, 1909."

[12] *Ibid.*

[13] There were a half-dozen whites of French extraction married to Coeur d'Alene women on their reservation, as they had likewise married Spokane women on theirs. On the Coeur d'Alene, the French and Irish bloods were generally regarded by many whites as scheming, lazy, and degraded. Webster Davis, Acting Secretary of the Interior, to commissioner, August 20, 1898, Coeur d'Alene Agency Records, Letterbox 18. They had lived on the Coeur d'Alene before the government dealt with the Coeur d'Alenes in 1887, making an agreement which provided that no white man could come upon that reservation to marry a woman of the tribe without first producing a certificate of good moral character.

Four years after legislation providing for allotting the Spokane Reservation, and three years after a contract was awarded to survey it, Clair Hunt was appointed to conduct the allotting on October 4, 1906.[14] When news of the allotting was made known, inquiries from Indians began to flood the agency, several coming from the closely related Chewelahs. Tribal approval was obtained from the reservation Indians before these Chewelahs were allotted. Some questions did arise when other Chewelahs began applying for reservation lands. Hunt pointed out that no attempt was being made to move to the reservation those Colville Valley Indians who had never been given to understand that, should they fail to make the move, they would lose their Indian rights. Wrote Hunt: "If there were regulations that provided that allotments on the Spokane Reservation should be made only to those who lived within its boundaries then many allotments that we have made to Indians living in the Colville Valley are unlawful, but we know that such is not the case." Hunt was charitable to those Indians who seldom visited the reservation, a fact accounted for "by their advancement in civilization," for which, he believed, they should not be punished by the exclusion of tribal benefits.[15]

Allotting even brought inquiries from reservation exiles, like Henry Fox in Knoxville, Illinois. He had fled the winter of 1908–1909 after being caught in the girls' dormitory at the Fort Spokane Sanatorium. Numerous inquiries came from Indians in California, Montana, Oregon, and Idaho, asking if they had allotment rights. One woman wrote from Spokane that she needed another application blank because her baby had partially burned the first one. Even whites inquired about unallotted lands.

All Spokanes requesting allotments were required to complete a four-page application asking the degree of their blood, pertinent personal information, and the listing of all relatives by name and relationship, places of residence, and tribal status. Allotments

14 Hunt would go on to allot the south half of the Colville Reservation, and then, to make his home at Colville, Washington, where he became county engineer and, in 1918, a candidate for county commissioner.

15 Hunt to Webster, January 7, 1910, Colville Agency Records, Box 22546–L. 9179.

were made not only to reservation residents, but also to nonreservation Spokanes and, eventually, to nontribal members. Requests from Indians for application for allotments were made even after the schedules were closed and excess land opened for settlement. Land, however, still remained to be allotted, and applications were considered for it.

On May 12, 1907, Hunt submitted a list of 149 receiving allotments (a few of which were suspended by the commissioner after review). Four days later, Webster sent the commissioner an application for the adoption into the tribe of John Hill, a white man who had married a Spokane woman in 1877. Hill had settled on land in 1877 before its inclusion in the reservation and afterward had continued to reside there, cultivating 160 acres. The tribal leaders approved Hill's adoption into the tribe in an unprecedented action, probably saving the Interior Department the problem of having to deal with him. His Indian children, however, were entitled to allotments and forthcoming benefits for the tribe.[16]

Another large council of the same nature was held on December 12, 1908, at which time the agency clerk, J. M. Johnson, met with Clair Hunt and 92 adult Indians.[17] Seventy-six applicants were considered, many with the blood of Crees who once lived along the Canadian border in Montana and worked for the Hudson's Bay Company. Scattered by the white-Indian wars, the Crees, not having negotiated with the government for a reservation, had been left to wander and fragment into small groups, taking up with various other tribes around the northwest. As a result of the two major councils, 104 half-bloods were approved for enrollment, and their names submitted to the commissioner.

By summer, 1909, 647 allotments had been made to Indians residing on the reservation. The department approved the schedule, with the exception of 99 persons who were suspended until adjudication of their right to allotment by enrollment. Other

16 "Proceedings of a Council of Spokane Indians held at Colville Agency June 7 and 8, 1907," typed copy in Colville Agency Records, Box 22546–L. 9179.

17 "Proceedings of the Council of Spokane Tribe called at Colville Agency, Washington, Dec. 12, 1908," typed copy in Colville Agency Records, Box 22546–L. 9179.

minor councils were called from time to time to consider one or more applicants. By August 19, 1909, with others added to the list, the department approved 104 persons for enrollment. Action even then was not final, for the department could contravene tribal wishes by excluding certain persons. With few half-bloods present in the councils, the full-blood Spokanes felt free to express their disdain of the former. Oliver Lot was particularly critical of the half-bloods. "When we did anything they did not help us," he said.[18]

In December, 1909, the department excepted a few from the list of 104 enrollments for various reasons, some for further investigation. Mrs. Rose Harris, adopted daughter of Bazil Brown, was eventually refused allotment. She was also denied an allotment on the Flathead Reservation for failure to make required reports.

Many Indians switched allotments, taking ones on one reservation, then canceling them for allotments on another. Some Spokanes who had removed to the Flathead and allotted there had since changed their favored residence, moving in with relatives on the Spokane Reservation to be allotted with the surrender of their former allotments. Others were to relinquish their allotments on the Spokane for ones on the Coeur d'Alene, and some families were divided, with some brothers and sisters allotting on the Spokane, some on the Flathead, and some on the Coeur d'Alene Reservation.

With allotments, a department had to be established at the agency to handle individual leases. F. B. Freeland was employed as clerk to establish the office for the Spokane and Colville reservations. Since the Spokanes had not yet turned to stock raising, considerable grazing land was opened for lease,[19] but only farm land of children and old and crippled Indians could be leased.[20]

[18] "Proceedings of a Council of Spokane Indians held at Colville Agency June 7 and 8, 1907," Colville Agency Records, Box 22546–L. 9179.
[19] Indians could pasture their own sheep, horses, and cattle on the tribal land at will.
[20] Collections for children and incompetents were placed in the individual's accounts at 3 per cent interest and could not be given to guardians, as per a 1907 U. S. Supreme Court ruling.

Leasing agricultural-land allotments of able-bodied men would have defeated the Department of Interior's plans of making Spokane Indians farmers.[21] There seems to have been some relaxation in leasing allotments of able-bodied men who had other visible means of support. Leases were contracted for five years, thus involving the agency in increased work, as did the responsibility of placing a particular individual's income into a bank account for him for his use at the discretion of the agent.[22]

Webster did not carry his unhappiness with Catholic educational policies into the realm of allotments. When those on the Spokane were being made, Aloisius Van Der Velden, S.J., of St. Francis Regis Mission, asked for 160 acres of land, as per the act of February 8, 1887, permitting such acreages for churches on reservations. Van Der Velden also kept up a rather brisk correspondence with the agency over the church's request for land. With the Colville Reservation being allotted, the father asked that Spokane land for churches be exchanged for land on the south half of the reservation, where the church was in better favor with the Indians. In the meantime, the mission sister superior told Van Der Velden he had "blundered" and should have asked for land on both reserves; he then did.[23] Webster wrote the commissioner that he was then "strongly" in favor of giving Catholics "one or more footholds" on the Spokane now that Father Van Der Velden had, by personal letter, assured him the church had abandoned educational aspects of its plan for Spokane children and would not interfere with the day schools. The selected Catholic land in the vicinity of Wellpinit was approved by the agency on November 1, 1907.

A controversy developed when it came to allotting land to the Presbyterian Church. Hunt set aside 16¼ acres for the church,

[21] The policy was the same for off-reservation allotments, leases for which also had to be made with Secretary of the Interior approval.

[22] Money from tribal lands and other tribal sources, and not the result of labor, was deposited with the Treasury Dept. for the benefit of the tribe by Act of Congress, March 3, 1883, and for some strange reason, became known as "Indian Moneys, Proceeds of Labor."

[23] Van Der Velden to Webster, February 1, 1907, Colville Agency Records, Box 22546–L. 9179.

Civilizing Agent

which included the church building, cemetery, residence, and church garden. He set aside for the government school 13¾ acres, which included the meadow in which lay the greater part of the original five acres the Women's National Indian Association had used. Hunt's reason for allotting the land to the school was so that it could be used, as Miss Clark had used it, for a garden and fruit tract. The Reverend White maintained, "with all the vigor that he is capable of," that the Presbyterian Church owned the area.[24] White began the new year, 1907, by writing the commissioner, trying to put his rival, Hunt, in a bad light. Hunt asked Webster to referee his contest with White. "I am a poor devil of a Western Surveyor," said Hunt, "with but few friends." Whereas White was a friend of the commissioner.[25] Unable to come to Wellpinit at that time, Webster called together Oliver Lot, Sam Andrews, Alex Pierre, George Jacobs, and William Three Mountains for an airing of the matter. What he learned confirmed Hunt's findings that the building and grounds White referred to were not church property "in any sense of the word," particularly since it was a cold fact that the Secretary of the Interior, on March 3, 1899, had given the Board of Home Missions of the Presbyterian Church only temporary use of the property. Despite this revelation, White continued to harass Hunt. The Spokanes, however, in appreciation of Hunt's fairness, rewarded him with a mock war dance.

Wishing to set the record clear in Washington by defending his capable allotting agent and exposing his antagonist, Webster wrote:

I have constantly opposed the exponents of graft and land thievery operation within the field of my jurisdiction, endeavoring as far as lay in my power to aid these easy going Indians in their unequal struggle for the lands promised them by the Government, and in doing so I make no distinction between the ordinary, every-

[24] Hunt to Webster, December 26, 1906, Colville Agency Records, Box 22546–L. 9179.
[25] Hunt to Webster, January 19, 1907, Colville Agency Records, Box 22546–L. 9179.

235

day land grabber who is not clothed in pious garb and one who draws the mantle of the church about him.

For the legitimate, unselfish and righteous desires of any church organization or association for the aid and advancement of dependent Indians I have the utmost respect, and will go as far as any man in furthering and pushing their work of humanity when their agents are worthy and honestly respresent them, but I am compelled to make the assertion that the man who represents the great Presbyterian church on the Spokane Reservation is a weakling utterly unfitted for the task, being an incompetent, inefficient, officous, gossiping, pessimistic, wet blanket theologian who would not be tolerated in any civilized Eastern community. His ministrations have been of no benefit to the red men. For individuals he has no consideration, regarding them as merely a mass for the maws of the church, and no tribal or personal interests must stand in the way of his desires.[26]

Not even talks with Miss Clark, who visited the reservation in October, 1905, could change White's mind. Hunt had the last word, however, and on February 9, 1909, chose land to be approved for allotting. Having lost the allotment battle, White resigned the winter of 1907. Miss Clark called him a failure.

Webster shed no tears over White's departure, but did write in his annual report in August, 1908, that the Spokanes would suffer from the absence of missionaries,[27] who had given them many things, least valuable of which were their baptismal names, which they could not pronounce. "Jeremiahs, Solomons, Isaacs, etc.," wrote Webster, "were thus absurdly planted among a people who deserved a better fate."[28]

The captain also believed that large expanses of Indian territory without towns would detract from the development of the country and its people. After consideration, Hunt found a suitable tract for urban development at the confluence of the Spokane and Columbia rivers next to a place called Lower Steamboat Landing

[26] Webster to commissioner, March 5, 1907, Webster Papers, 180–22.
[27] Webster to commissioner, August 24, 1908, Colville Agency Records, Letterbook 29, Box 32.
[28] Webster to Board of Indian Commissioners, November 18, 1905, Webster Papers, 18–46.

Chief Lot, the grand old man of the Spokanes. This picture was taken in 1901, a year before Lot died.

Captain John McA. Webster, agent to the Spokanes 1901–14, with a relatively short interruption. He always held the Indians foremost in his thoughts.

Spokane Garry in his declining years. This photograph was taken in 1889, when Garry was about seventy-nine.

A group photograph of Spokanes. First row, *left to right*: Alex Pierre, George Jacob, John Moon, Thomas Garry. Second row, *left to right*: John Stevens, William Three Mountains, Enoch, Charlie Bones (a Umatilla), Basil Peone. *Back row*: Unidentified, Pete Valley, John Solomon, Oliver Lot, Louie Peone. William Three Mountains was a chief of those Upper and Middle Spokanes who were Protestants. Enoch was a chief of those Upper Spokanes who were Catholics.

Another group of Spokanes photographed at Old Agency. Front row, *left to right*: Running Cow (Kwo-ness-ku), Chief Lot (Che-wis-tli), Jim Sam, Thomas George. Back row, *left to right*: Ke-whit, Socumticum, Quel-pesten, Quin-quin-moses, George Solomon, Titus Garry.

Indian children at the Indian school on the old Fort Spokane grounds. When the army abandoned the fort in 1899, the War Department turned it over to the Interior Department.

Indian beadwork displayed at the second all-Indian fair at Wellpinit in 1915. The fairs are still held to this day.

The Colville Agency, which administered to the Spokanes when it was located in the old Fort Spokane buildings, shown here. The old military fort is being restored by the National Parks Service.

The chapel building on the old Fort Spokane grounds. Indian children from the Indian school there attend chapel.

The dining hall for the Indian school at the old Fort Spokane grounds.

The laundry room for the Indian school at the old Fort Spokane grounds.

at the lower end of a nearly sixty-mile, all-year navigable Columbia River stretch. Part of the land at the site had been selected by Big Bend Transit for its terminus, and it was a potential crossroads of several railroads proposing to merge there to carry the trade of the upper Columbia. It was also a proposed site for development of electric energy. Given the name Klaxta, it was to be offered for sale to the highest bidder.

In September, 1908, Hunt completed his task, with the exception of allotting some late enrollees and newborn children. The passage of the Dawes Act in 1887, from which the allotment program sprang, was now seen in retrospect as the beginning of a new day for the Indian on his reservation. At the turn of the century, Congress passed many laws to hasten reservation development. On March 2, 1899, Congress enacted legislation enabling railroads to acquire rights-of-way for lines across Indian reservations. On February 15, 1901, it enacted legislation permitting rights-of-way through reservations for electric plants, poles, and lines for generation and distribution of electric power, telephone, and telegraph lines. Congressional legislation on March 3, 1901, authorized the Interior Department to grant permission to proper state and local authorities to establish reservation roadways. Directly pertaining to the Spokane area, Congress passed legislation on March 3, 1905, permitting citizens or companies the right to use waters of the Spokane River, where it formed the southern boundary of the reservation, for power production, no land to be granted unless the Secretary of the Interior was satisfied that persons or companies receiving such grants were acting in good faith, a restriction which saved the department considerable trouble.

David Wilson, a Davenport promoter with statewide interests,[29] owned land on the south side of the river at the falls; he applied for water rights there. His application was favorably reported June 7, 1905. Wilson's rights were contested by attorneys Martin and Mulligan, who had applied on May 27, 1905, for

[29] Wilson to Webster, May 27, 1906, Colville Agency Records, Box 22545– L.9178.

water rights at Little Falls. M. J. Gibson was yet another contestant who said he had located his claim on March 5, 1905, just two days after the act enabling the filing of claims for hydroelectric power. Webster was dubious of Gibson's intent, since his claim was not filed until May 1 and because the contents of the act could not have been known so far west so soon after its enactment. Gibson's rights were transferred to the Spokane and Big Bend Railway Company by September, 1905.

In a report to the commissioner in September, 1905, Webster wrote of a bitter contest waged by Gibson, who he said was in the employ of Martin and Mulligan. All were Davenport attorneys for whom Webster had little regard. Although Gibson was openly allied in business with Martin and Mulligan, Webster believed him to be constantly used by the two to do their bidding.[30] The captain, a man of decided likes and dislikes, showed little hesitation in expressing his feelings and opinions. To him it appeared that the three attorneys had insufficient financing for the undertaking. Martin and Mulligan contested claims at the narrows as well. All this wrangling led Webster to conclude that the potential power should be public property.

Two companies contended for water power rights at the narrows: the Spokane and Big Bend Railway Company and the Big Bend Transit Company. Webster believed reputable companies would help surround the natives with the beneficial cloak of civilization. "Any kind of rapid transportation," he wrote, "will be a God-send to the whites and Indians of this section." The Big Bend Transit Company, with exuberance similar to Webster's, began grading and laying track from the Lower Steamboat Landing on the Columbia River on the reservation near the mouth of the Spokane River, through its main terminus, the nearby townsite of Klaxta, to the Spokane River crossing site near the narrows. The Spokane and British Columbia Railway, known as well by its nickname, the "Hot Air" line, obtained its right-of-way along the San Poil in August, 1906. Damages to tribal and individual Indian lands on the Colville Reservation, and the corner of the

[30] Webster to commissioner, September 8, 1905, Webster Papers, 18–46.

Spokane Reservation it would transect, were assessed. Enterprising steamboat operators would not give up their plans of navigating the Columbia. In 1908 the Okanogan Steamboat Company hauled coke from the mouth of the San Poil River to Wenatchee.

The rich soil of the Colville, Webster warned, had "tempted the cupidity of numerous persons who had made *thousands* and *thousands* of entries of quartz and placer mining claims on splendid fruit, wheat and timberlands," a development in which many Indians had been "cheated, frightened, cajoled or bought out of their rightful possession." Making these transactions all the more bitter to him were the beliefs of "eminently respectable" people that such entries were justifiable on grounds that there was no other way in which the lands could be obtained within a reasonable time.[31]

Very few Indians of the Spokane Reservation had utilized water for irrigation. In 1903, Nancy Wynecoop and her husband had requested a water right for their ranch, at the same time seeking permission to cut timber to be sold for fluming. The Wynecoops were exceptions. Most requests for irrigation water were from whites for rights from the Spokane River, and Tshimakain and Stanley creeks on the reservation. Whites were often caught taking water illegally for irrigation from the various streams, and one, a local resident, by means of a water wheel. The contrast in what irrigation meant to whites and what it meant to Indians was seen at the Irrigation Congress held in Spokane in August, 1909. The whites came to hear prominent speakers discuss reclamation of arid lands; the Spokanes and other Indians came to parade for the amusement of the delegates.

White advances strengthened Webster's protective attitude toward the Indians in his care. He would have to be still more protective in the light of events just ahead. Three northwest reservations were ready to be marketed at about the same time—the Spokane, the Coeur d'Alene, and the Flathead. The Spokanes had already agreed to sell their surplus lands, having met with In-

[31] Webster to commissioner, August 27, 1906, Colville Agency Records, Letterbook 26, Box 32.

spector Edgar A. Allen in council in late January and early February, 1908. At the council, the Spokanes agreed to accept cash for their lands, sharing their benefits among themselves. To Webster, the Indians were as children contemplating the use of their money for extravagances and reckless living, with no regard for the future. Fortunately, there would be some limitations placed upon recipients of these funds. As part of their agreement, funds due children of incompetent and dissipated parents were to be retained by the United States (drawing interest), to be paid to the children on their coming of age. Others using their money wisely could continue to draw it, but those wasting allowances would be given subsequent payments in the form of merchandise, cattle, implements, furniture and the like, until the agent was convinced they could make good use of their funds.[32]

The farm land to be opened to white entry was near Tshimakain Creek, as well as along the Spokane River. Forest lands were not to be opened to entry, but Indians were to draw all the proceeds from the sale of timber from these lands. As a result of the council with Inspector Allen, an act was passed May 29, 1908, authorizing the sale of unallotted agricultural lands on the reservations. The President signed a proclamation May 22, 1909, to open them.

This act authorized sections 16 and 36 of each Spokane Reservation township to be set aside for public school purposes, the United States to pay the tribe for the school lands at the rate of $1.25 per acre.[33] The act also provided for the opening of surplus lands on the Flathead and Coeur d'Alene reservations. Just a decade after certain Spokanes had legally removed to the Flathead Reservation, the Flatheads had been approached about taking their lands in severalty and opening them for sale to whites. Several of the 135 Spokanes on the Flathead Reservation were inclined to regard the proposal favorably. But strong opposition to cession of any lands came from the half-bloods who, acquiring

[32] *House Report No. 394*, I, 2.

[33] "Memorandum of Wishes of Indians of Spokane Reservation relative to the disposal of their surplus unallotted lands and to the manner of disbursing the proceeds of the sale of such lands, or timber cut therefrom; as expressed in council January 30 and 31, and February 1, 1908," in Webster Papers, 270–336.

property on that reservation, were unwilling to give it up.[34] Many Spokanes on the Flathead were unhappy for reasons best explained by one of their chiefs to a commissioner a few years after removing to that place:

> When we were on our old reservation there came to us men from the government, who spoke as you have spoken. They told us that we would be treated right. They told us that they wanted to use us alright. They told us that, if we would move to this place, they would give us each a house, fence, seed, wagon and harness. They talked well and we believed them. We came to this place and gave up our old lands. We have no houses and we have no wagons. We gave up all that we had, and the government has given us nothing. If we do as you say, will we not be treated this way again?[35]

Lands of the three reservations would be disposed of by lottery. Sixteen sections of Spokane Reservation land, comprising 5,781 acres of agricultural land, would be opened. With 82,647 acres of timber land reserved for the tribe, one hundred homesteads would be permitted on the reservation, of which forty-five would be classed as desirable. Up to this time, 626 Indian allotments had been made on 64,794 acres; 1,247 acres had been set aside for church, school, township, and agency land.[36]

On the Flathead, 415,437 acres were opened for about 2,800 homesteads. On the Coeur d'Alene, lands were opened comprising about 1,250 homesteads. Forest land on the Flathead was to be sold at public auction and subject to entry under homestead laws. On the Coeur d'Alene, forest land was subject to entry under the same conditions as agricultural land.

Webster reported detecting some sophisticated and stimulating awareness on the part of many Spokanes to the sale of their lands, awakening them to a realization of change in conditions materially affecting them as individuals and as a tribe. They had, he optimis-

---

[34] A 1905 census placed the number of Spokanes on the Flathead Reservation at 135. The official 1910 census placed their number at 134.

[35] *Spokesman-Review*, October 31, 1897, p. 15.

[36] In June, 1918, fifty-seven thousand acres of forest and timber land would be opened for sale.

tically observed, been spurred "to a livelier interest in the lands on which their main reliance for future support must depend." No longer did he detect a "concerted and formidable" protest to the new order, believing that past habits of clinging to the old customs and hereditary behavior were beginning to give way to a spirit of personal independence and individual responsibility.[37]

Registration for each of the three reservations was held from July 15 to August 5, 1909, in the city of Spokane for the Spokane Reservation, in the city of Coeur d'Alene for the Coeur d'Alene Reservation, and in the cities of Kalispell and Missoula, Montana, for the Flathead Reservation. Each reservation area was well advertised in advance of the land drawings. The *Spokesman-Review*, in the summer of 1909, printed photos of Coeur d'Alene, Idaho, then a city of 10,000 souls; just nine years before, it had been a village of only 350. Four steam and twenty-six electric trains arrived daily from Spokane; a dozen steamers arrived from and departed daily to St. Joe River points and to Harrison, Idaho, where connections were made with the Oregon Railway and Navigation Company to Wallace, Idaho, and the Coeur d'Alene mining districts.

Anxious land-seekers flocked to the city like ants to spilled sugar. Applications by mail were permitted, those for the three reservations put in envelopes of different colors and deposited in three galvanized iron cans, one for each reservation. A Miss Helen Hamilton drew the first envelope for the Coeur d'Alene Reservation. Several days later, on August 12, Christina Dolan drew the first Flathead application. Miss Harriet Post drew the first for the Spokane Reservation on August 15, 1909.

Filing for the lands was to be on April 1, 1910, in the order the applications were drawn. Extra names had been drawn in case any of the originally drawn names were of applicants failing to appear to select land. Persons on the additional list had the opportunity of selecting land, since applicants not present lost their rights to do so. Persons who had won at the drawings could make quick inspection trips over the reservations or could use classification

[37] Webster to commissioner, July 19, 1907, Webster Papers, 180–22.

maps to select tracts of land. Actual residence had to be taken up on the lands selected. Spokane lands were appraised at five dollars per acre, on which payment could be made in full or at a minimum of one dollar per acre on filing and one dollar per acre per year thereafter. Yet one could obtain patent to his land after fourteen months of continuous residence and remittance of any unpaid balance of its appraised value (except on reservation-opened timber land, which required five years of actual residence). Claims were limited to 160 acres, except on the Flathead, where 80 acres was the limit of irrigable land which could be selected.

Entry on the lands was permitted on April 10, 1910.[38] Mable McNickle of Chicago held the first choice for filing on the Spokane Reservation. Her name had been the second one drawn. A man from Helena, Montana, whose name was drawn first, relinquished his right. Mable McNickle would soon be a defendant in a land suit involving the Northern Pacific Railway, which attempted to obtain all odd sections of land on the reservation. Those entering the Spokane Reservation went to work with hammer and nails to erect dwellings and work their soil. One of the lucky winners, Olive Lender Snell, remembers putting the coffee pot on for her red neighbors, who stopped by frequently. One day, Lawyer Sam inspected her house from top to bottom and, after eying the bric-a-brac in it, announced that she would go to hell; she was "too high toned."

[38] Plans had been made in February, 1910, before white entry, for leasing Indian allotted land before the farming season began that year.

CHAPTER TEN

Between Two Streams

Captain Webster had tried to pull the Spokanes from the stream of Indian life to the stream of white civilization pulsing about them with early twentieth-century buoyancy. But as the captain approached the midpoint in his years among the Spokanes, they, like their reservation—which lay between the Spokane and Columbia rivers—were a people between two streams.

Near where Walker and Eells had established the first school for the Spokanes and their neighbors, almost three-quarters of a century later, Charles Morrison sought to bring the technical benefits of civilization to those under his care from his post at Day School Number Eight.

He succeeded in bringing the telephone to the school. Morrison was attempting to fulfill his position, not only as teacher, but subagent of sorts, looking after the welfare of his community. At his urging, a kitchen was built at the school in May, 1909. The contractor, a Mr. Sullivan, had picked a good time to build it; scarcely a child was underfoot at the school, for it was the time of the death and burial of Chief Oliver Lot who, while drunk, had drowned in Sheep Creek. By summer, a stable was completed to shelter the cayuses, each one of which often carried as many as three children to school.

Occasionally Morrison faced setbacks in his civilizing efforts. The morning of February 19, 1910, he arrived at school to find the organ pushed over, a rather surprising bit of vandalism, since Indian children were fascinated by its stops and pedals. Although the organ tipping was a prank, Webster was deeply concerned about "energetic youngsters who through unfortunate combination of circumstances" got a wrong start, stumbling into evil ways and, in the absence of friendly counsel, were "apt to go to the devil." "Viciousness," he wrote, "is a rare attribute of the Indian of pure blood, most of that now existing having been acquired or developed from an environment of unscrupulous whites, principally saloon keepers and their hangers-on, moral lepers who eke out a precarious existence by inducing and pandering to the worst instincts of the red men and women."[1]

During most of his tenure, Morrison clashed with School Inspector Avery. After the school year was over in 1910, Morrison left. He was replaced in the fall by Otis Mellon. Mellon, like Morrison, also had his critics. More to Avery's liking was Harry C. Norman, a native of South Dakota, who came in August, 1908, to teach in the Wellpinit school. Performing all the tasks of an ideal Indian agency teacher, Norman served as welfare caseworker, civil leader, midwife, truant officer, sheriff, agency custodian, health officer, sanatarian, extension agent, real estate agent, and communications center operator.

Norman's primary task was, of course, teaching school. He seems to have had as good rapport with the children as he had in the community. On the basis of his reports, and of those teachers in the other schools, a satisfied Webster wrote the commissioner a lengthy description of the play habits of the children. He said the boys took naturally to baseball. In the spring, marbles and mumble-peg had a brief run of popularity with smaller boys. To

[1] Webster to commissioner, July 19, 1907, Colville Agency Records, Letterbook 27, Box 32.

get the larger girls to do something outdoors, they were introduced to the game of shinny, an informal sort of hockey. Boys and
girls of all sizes enjoyed roaming to gather wildflowers. Swings
were popular, and the boys enjoyed climbing on horizontal bars.
Indoors during wintertime the little children played with scraps
of wood from the shop. While the boys batted one another around
with boxing gloves, the little girls played house (and tipi), having
a familiarity with two types of homes. They played "hide the but-
ton," a game familiar to them from both cultures, like houses and
tipis. As Walker and Eells had discovered years before, all the
children enjoyed singing; many took lessons on the mandolin,
violin, and organ. Webster thought it "worthy of remark that a
few talking machines, with records of good music, have surpris-
ingly increased their appreciation of such music." The children,
like American frontiersmen, took to square dancing, little caring
that its steps and music bore small resemblance to those of their
own people.[2]

Of more concern to agency officials than to its children was the
problem of water for the Wellpinit school. The 13¾ acres which
Hunt had set aside for the school had no spring on it. When Spalsbury was there, he had carried water, as they had at the other two
schools, in a bucket, from which the children drank with a common dipper, as they also had at the other two schools. Spalsbury
had written Avery on October 21, 1907, of the unfitness of the
school's water supply, since Joseph Levi, on whose place the spring
had its source, washed his pans and kettles and watered his cattle
in it. Hunt, Avery, and Webster had been aware of the problem,
intending to trade land to Joseph for his land on which the spring
ran. Refusing to trade, Joseph had agreed in some measure to
protect the purity of the water. A watershed was built over the
spring, but the sanitation did not improve, for Joseph's stock still
trampled around in it.

Once, Spalsbury had found a dead dog in the spring. Avery had
taken to upbraiding Joseph about the situation. Knowing that

[2] Webster to commissioner, February 2, 1909, Colville Agency Records, Letterbook 27, Box 32.

well diggers were on Walker's Prairie, Avery had sought Webster's permission to obtain a bid for digging a well, but had discovered that funds to do so had run dry. At one time in the water hassle, Webster had told Avery that, unless Joseph gave his land to the school in exchange for other land, the spring would be taken from him. Hunt had thought the captain's words "an expression of momentary irritation rather than of settled judgment." In Webster's dealings with the Spokanes, it was probably the only time he had made a threat unsupported by law or regulation to coerce an Indian into action against his will. The conflict between social action and rugged individualism had found its way to the Spokane Reservation, where Webster, in utilitarian fashion, had sought to achieve the greatest good for the greatest number.

The final push for settlement of the water problem was made in the fall of 1909. Avery asked Hunt if he thought an arbitrary amendment of Joseph's allotment before its final approval would be feasible, just, or expedient. It actually would have been none of these, lacking Joseph's approval and consent. Avery believed Hunt favored taking the spring from Joseph, but Hunt, also having the Indian point of view, would not have supported such a move, aware of the bitter feeling such arbitrary action would have engendered in the community. Avery wrote that the question should "be disposed of promptly and finally, and that, without wasting any more time, patience, good-nature, dignity, [and] self-respect."[3] But this did not solve the problem. Neither would the cistern Norman was constructing.

Norman alternated his cistern construction with other chores. When Dan Scott deserted his family, which became destitute, Norman reported it to the agency. By that time most roaming Indians had returned to the reservation, but Willie Boyd and his wife were off again. With seven days' work needed to clear a fine Willie owed, Norman suggested he pay it off by telephone line work. Norman also had the problem of seeking out tubercular children and getting them into the sanatorium. Ordering all teachers in the day schools to "consider health as a primary im-

[3] Avery to Hunt, October 5, 1909, Colville Agency Records, Box 22546–L. 9179.

portance,"[4] Avery told them to pay close attention to the physical condition of their pupils, excluding any from attendance who seemed tubercular. After inspecting the Wellpinit school, Office Supervisor of Indian Schools H. B. Peairs ordered the children to have annual physical examinations. Peairs commended Norman's work in trying to improve community health, reporting his school as more nearly approaching what a day school should be than any of the other schools he had visited. Norman had to take holidays and special occasions into his planning. At Christmas, he was authorized to buy "appropriate supplies" for the big dinner, but expenditures were not to exceed ten dollars, or twenty-five cents per pupil.

While the agency attempted to press the Indians into its mold, whites continued to press the reservation and its environs into a mold of their own. In 1911, Captain Fred McDermott, a riverboat pilot, revived the plan of opening a Columbia River route from Bridgeport to Kettle Falls. But a Washington State appropriation of fifty thousand dollars to open the river was but a drop in the bucket for what was needed. On October 10, 1911, the steamer *Yakima*, with three large government barges and about fifty workmen, began moving from Peach at the mouth of Hawk Creek to clear a channel at the rapids to open the river route to Kettle Falls.

With all the talk of railroads in and around the Spokane Reservation, not one had yet been built there. The only roads developed were wagon roads. In his annual report for 1908, Webster noted that, although Indians had done commendable work on building and repairing their roads, more needed to be done than that performed by Indian labor.[5] Appropriations in general were easy to ask for but hard to get. In December, 1911, Webster urged reimbursement out of the proceeds of the sale of surplus lands for financing roads on the reservation. That same month, he requested an appropriation, so that roads used only by Indians could be

[4] Avery to Webster, January 20, 1911, Colville Agency Records, Box 22546–L. 9179.
[5] Webster to commissioner, August 20, 1908, Colville Agency Records, Letterbook 29, Box 32.

built on the reservation. He specifically urged that a road be built between the agency and Wellpinit, the "largest center of population" on the reservation. The only road between the two places traversed sand hills, which required an outlay of one thousand dollars. Webster also proposed a water grade road along the Spokane River.[6]

Webster's constant requests for road funds were justified in light of the fact that, in the previous two years, the government had spent only nine hundred dollars, scarcely enough to build adequate roads. None of the new roads were better than their river crossings. The bridge built by Reardon citizens over the Spokane River near Chamokane (a townsite, spelled differently than the site of the Walker-Eells mission) washed out in April, 1910. A ferry was established at the crossing but was moved to the foot of Little Falls in September, 1913. Lincoln and Stevens County officials met to discuss building a bridge at the foot of Little Falls; they were saved the trouble when the Washington Water Power Company built a steel bridge over the river at that point.

The coming of the automobile brought a renewed interest by Reardon businessmen in bringing reservation business to their town. Led by H. G. Burns, president of the Reardon National Bank, townsfolk wanted to donate money to improve the Reardon-Wellpinit Road. Hopefully they sought five hundred dollars, but the most they raised was two hundred dollars. Nor did they get much help from the government, for the agency informed the citizens that federal funds had been expended on the reservation portion of the road the previous year with little prospect for more. In order for Reardon money to be used, road work would have to be under agency supervision.

Back on the reservation, the teachers were attempting to raise children to a civilizational level on which they could one day produce the goods to ship over the roads then being built. Education had as many frustrations as road building. Ever since Indian Office Supervisor Fred A. Baker's report that Mellon needed better dis-

---

[6] This road did not materialize. It would be proposed again in 1956, when there was extensive mining activity in the area.

cipline at the Walker's Prairie school, that teacher had tried to deal more firmly with problems as they arose. In January, 1911, he punished Ben Wilson for pushing a smaller boy who was carrying wood, causing him to hit his face against a stick. Mellon slapped Wilson "hard enough to let him know I meant to punish him for fighting."[7] Fireworks started when Cole Moses, the boy's uncle, wrote Mellon a note which said in part: "Mr Millon [sic] I want you to stop slapping the children iF [sic] I heard you slapping the children I will tell the chief or I will go and see if you can slapping me from Cole Moses."[8]

Avery took the teacher's side in the affair, admitting he knew little about Mellon as yet, but that he did not seem abusive or severe with the pupils. Avery was probably more aware of Moses' reputation as a bully, with "recklessly vicious tendencies, of which he seems to be rather proud."[9] After the criticism from Supervisor Baker, Mellon submitted detailed work plans. His busy schedule included music, open reading, spelling and pronunciation, arithmetic, industrial work, language and history, geography, hygiene, and English for the various grades. His textbooks for the five grades were the Brooks Readers, Wooster's *Natural Builder*, Milne's *Primary Arithmetic*, *Primer of Sanitation*, *Cause, Prevention and Treatment of Tuberculosis*, Dodges' *Elementary Geography*, *Pioneer Stories of the Mississippi Valley and the Rocky Mountains and the West*, *The Three Bugs in a Basket*, *Sweet and Low*, *Three Companions*, *Morning Son*, *Red Riding Hood*, *Little Boy Blue*, and Sprague's *North American Indians*. Mellon resigned June 23, 1911. With the new school year, a new teacher, Mr. Fay J. Snoddy took over.

Webster continued to safeguard those in his care in matters other than their physical health. On October 30, 1911, he resubmitted an application for Isabella McCoy for a fee patent for her entire allotment. Although uneducated, she was intelligent and

---

[7] Mellon to Avery, January 17, 1911, Colville Agency Records, Box 22545–L. 9178.

[8] Moses to Mellon (n.d.), Colville Agency Records, Box 22545–L. 9178.

[9] Avery to Webster (n.d.), Colville Agency Records, Box 22545–L. 9178.

lived after the manner of whites. She was "competent,"[10] a word
to denote that an Indian handled his money and affairs wisely, in
the manner of whites, before receiving a fee patent for his lands.[11]

Of the McCoys (and many Spokanes in general), Webster
wrote: "They feel that they are not really secure in their possessions while the land is held in trust."[12] In October, 1911, lands
listed for sale were mostly west end allotments of half-bloods. In
1915 the superintendent would recommend fee patents, largely
for mixed-blood west enders. By these means, thought Webster,
possibly enough lands would get on the county rolls to obtain
sufficient tax monies to establish a state school district, whereby
a public school could be established.

Various counties levied taxes on Indian fee-patent land, and
some, as Chelan, levied taxes on trust land for those Chelan Indians allotted around Lake Chelan. The Washington State Tax
Commission threatened to change the taxing laws, should the
State Supreme Court rule the counties could not tax trust land.

The first transfer of Spokane land was a sale in September,
1911, of Millie (Mrs. Albert) Morrell McCoy's land to Archie D.
Gabbert of Peach. Webster noted that, since each Colville Indian
was getting a five-hundred-dollar installment for ceding the north
half of their reservation, and since fine tracts of land were being
allotted on the Spokane Reservation, each unmarried maiden on
these reserves was "an heiress of some importance." Of the Spokane women, most of whom were half- and full-bloods, Webster
thought the full-bloods the most beautiful. Most Spokane wom-
en, he believed, had fair educations and made good wives. They
were sought after and married by young men, particularly when
the men knew their Spokane spouses would soon have lands. One

[10] The Secretary of the Interior on June 7, 1929, would order that the word
"incompetent" no longer be applied to Indians unless the Indian was *non compos
mentis*.

[11] The Land Office was issuing fee-simple patents "to ignorant and incompetent
Indians" in lieu of trust patents on off-reservation homesteads, sometimes aided
by Congressional legislation authorizing the fee-simple patents, and as such the
Indians were fast losing their lands.

[12] Webster to commissioner, October 30, 1911, Colville Agency Records, Letterbook 40, Box 32.

interested gentleman, a Mr. Newmann, of Harrison, Idaho, wrote
Webster in December, 1911:

> Captain John McWebster
>   soead [*sic*] Indian Agency
> Washington
> Sir:
>   I am in the mercantile business here in Harrison and most every
> one knows me and know that I am OK. Now I have mad [*sic*] up
> my mind to go too [*sic*] the reservation and find me a real good
> Indian maid and no half way goes with me. I want a full blood and
> coars [*sic*] one with a good homestead and one that is tall in fact
> a heavy weight is the kind I want if I knowed [*sic*] all the maids
> could read I could have sent this to the Spokesman Review. I
> could have found the address of all the Indian girls.
>   Yours truly[13]

Other events on the reservations suggested that whites, witness-
ing the Colvilles reveling in their recent land-cession payments,
wanted Spokane lands and money. On December 4, 1911, the Indian office wired the agency: "How much money to credit of
Spokane Indians? Reported here that some who have money are
in great need." J. M. Johnson, clerk in charge of the Colville
Agency, answered the next day: "Seven Spokane Indians have
$6,000.00 in all. Can learn of no Spokanes in need. General con-
ditions better than at any time in last three years. More grain,
hay, and stock sold this year and more money earned in outside
fall work than for several years past. Rations issued to 18 old and
destitute. No other applications."[14] The office wanted more information on these "18 old and destitute." Before long, Johnson
learned the source of the complaints sent to the office of the plight
of the "old and destitute." Spokane County Commissioner W.
H. Collins had written that his board was being importuned by
an Indian woman, Susan Smawtah, living on the outskirts of Spokane at the Indian camp opposite Hangman Creek. "We cannot,

13 Newmann to Webster, December 29, 1911, Colville Agency Records, Box
22545–L. 9178.
    14 Johnson to Webster, December 14, 1911, Colville Agency Records, Box
22545–L. 9178.

of course," wrote Collins, "do this [give her aid] for many reasons as you know these Spokanes would come here in droves to live off our charity."[15] Susan Smawtah had an allotment on the Spokane Reservation next to that of her husband's. Unlike him, she chose to live off the reservation at the Indian camp as one of its last five residents. Of the five, another woman, Rose Long, was allotted on the Spokane, two women were allotted on the Coeur d'Alene, and the fifth resident, Curly Jim, a colorful character, was also allotted on the Coeur d'Alene, although he chose to "allot" on the streets of Spokane. William Three Mountains, perhaps remembering his father's death, hoped the camp could be broken up, since it harbored Indian criminals escaping justice and loafers who hung around Spokane depending on handouts from their friends. The Colville Agency clerk suggested that, should the allotments of Rose Long and Susan Smawtah not provide them sufficient support, the agency could issue them rations, just as the Coeur d'Alenes at the Indian camp could receive aid from that tribe's over half-million-dollar fund. But the clerk thought that, for the Indians' own good, they should be removed from "this rendezvous" in the neighborhood of Spokane.

Webster answered an Office of Indian Affairs telegram of December 11, 1911, which had requested additional information on the destitute. Attempting to minimize the cause of the complaints, he opined that the Indians were not bad off at all. Merchants, he said, had informed him that they paid their debts more readily than whites. They were well dressed, he assured the office, showing no evidence of being ill fed. "In fact," he asserted, "the Indians this year are in almost opulent circumstances as compared with some of the white farmers in the Big Bend Country who are at present finding it difficult to make both ends meet."

Meanwhile the captain went on caring for the indigent, issuing them beef, bacon, baking powder, beans, rice, coffee, corn, flour, salt, and sugar. This brought no comfort to several Spokanes, who signed affidavits prepared by a Spokane notary public, stating they were without food, clothing, and money, and in need of govern-

---

15 *Ibid.*

ment assistance. On January 10, 1912, approximately forty Spokanes, three of them women, met at Garden City (a post-office town off the east end of the reservation, not far from Springdale) with Engle, a merchant, and Haines, an interpreter. Chief Jim Sam opened the meeting by saying that, in the early days, the government furnished rations, farm machinery, and wagons to Indians, expecting them to cultivate the land. But the machinery was worthless, the plows broken, and the wagons fallen to pieces. Also, the Indians had no rations.[16] Sam said he had talked with Webster, who had been unable to get them some money. Consequently, being worse off than ever, continued Sam, they had hoped the notary, Mr. Stephens, would be successful in getting them some money.

Webster asked Norman to investigate the Garden City Council. The teacher did and suggested that storekeeper Engle had organized it, probably with the help of Chief Sam. Sam ordered all the Indians, including children over ten years of age, to attend a second Garden City council called for February 7, 1912. Of the 110 who attended, all but four signed a "power of attorney" for Stephens to secure money from the government, in what Norman described as an attempt to get "something for nothing."[17]

The Garden City insurrection was only a tempest in a small teapot, but it did tend to put agency officials on the defensive about their care of the Indians. As to their condition, Norman reported more gardens planted than the previous year, more acreage in grain and grain hay, more wild and timothy hay harvested than in the previous three years. In November, twenty-two head of cattle were sold for six hundred dollars; in December, four head for one hundred dollars; and in January, eighteen head for five hundred dollars—all exclusive of cattle butchered for home use and private sales. Norman reported that several families had done day labor digging potatoes, picking fruit, and husking corn; some had even made money dancing at the Spokane Fair. Certainly, Norman believed, they were not in dire need.

[16] Issues promised as per the 1887 agreement had been fulfilled.
[17] Norman to Webster, February 8, 1912, Webster Papers, 10–391.

Norman knew they still needed new houses and barns. Their houses were unpainted shacks, government-built at a cost of $250 each. Most of them had tipis outside, used for living quarters in summer and storerooms in winter. Many of their occupants ate and slept on the floor, "as the old time Indians," not so much from inability to purchase or make furniture as from custom. A producing sawmill was a necessity for turning out lumber for the needed homes. A steam mill, purchased from the Hallidie Company of Spokane, was installed at Wellpinit. A second mill was built on the west end near McCoy Lake, with special funds authorized personally June 26, 1911, by President William H. Taft. The Wellpinit mill was slowly put to more and more use. The Spokanes cut and hauled their own logs to the mill, then helped each other saw them for lumber for a few new homes and outbuildings. The west end mill lay unused.

The Department of the Interior never slackened its efforts to make farmers of the Spokanes so they could sustain themselves without having to depend on day labor alone. Their desire to purchase bright-colored calicoes, sweets, and other white men's goods stimulated them to produce for sale grain, watermelons, and other produce. But to get a little extra money, they hired out to others who owned allotments or to white farmers in the surrounding country, just as their parents had done for years. William Three Mountains maintained a fine ranch. When his own harvests were over, he worked for whites picking fruit and potatoes, setting an example of industry for his people in tasks which chiefs in earlier days would never have performed. Three Mountains, whom Webster termed one of the most progressive Spokane leaders, sat on the bench of the tribal court representing the Middle and Upper Spokanes, with Jim Sam representing the Lower Spokanes. William kept a sharp eye on his people. In 1913 he disapproved an agency-favored social-athletic club organized by west end young people, doing so on the grounds that it would lead to "lewdness, lawlessness and drunkenness" among the young braves.

Despite William's opposition to the club, agency officials were pleased that he was setting an example in farming, the highest vocational goal to which government officials believed an Indian could aspire. Webster had planned to enlarge school garden tracts, where pupils could raise vegetables, so they could supply the school for noon lunches. This would be an object lesson to them on how to run a model farm and home. Blacksmithing and carpentry for the boys and training in the domestic arts for the girls were calculated to prepare them for life on their future farms.

While exchanges of allotments were being effected to solve certain school problems, which gave the school 48¾ acres,[18] John Hill, who had an allotment not far north of Klaxta, planned to plat his own place into a townsite to be called "Rapid City," named for the Columbia River rapids nearby. Hill had no doubt been motivated in his plans by Great Northern grading for a spur line from the Big Bend down Hawk Creek to within two miles of Klaxta. At the same time, there were plans afoot to divide the Colville Agency into two agencies, one for the Colvilles and one for the Spokanes. If the agency for the Spokanes were moved to the city of Spokane, a subagency should be set up on the reservation, thought Webster.

The Great Northern Railway Company received by transfer the questionable right of the Inland Empire Electric Railroad to the sand bar near Klaxta. This brought the Great Northern into conflict with Big Bend Transit, which had a grip on most rights-of-way at the mouth of the Spokane River. This contest barred Great Northern from any progress in grading north toward Kettle Falls.

In 1914, Big Bend Transit and Electric, formerly Big Bend Transit, acquired the entire flat at Spokane Steamboat Landing on the Columbia. It proposed to establish a townsite on the bench below old Fort Spokane across the river from Klaxta, which appeared to be a doomed townsite. Big Bend Transit and Electric also proposed a bridge at the narrows to compensate for Detillion Bridge, which would be submerged by backwaters of a proposed

---

[18] Later, Nancy Wynecoop would relinquish for lieu land the forty acres which had once been her daughter's. This land would go to the agency when it was moved to the area and in need of land.

eighty-foot dam at the narrows. For several years Big Bend Transit and Electric proceeded with its plans, attempting several times in court to condemn Indian land on the Spokane Reservation. It also fought the Spokane and British Columbia, which had surveyed a line through the Fort Spokane Military Reservation, only to be compelled to raise its surveys there to avoid holdings and rights held by Big Bend Transit and Electric. This latter company had enjoyed easements, road, and hydrodevelopment rights at the narrows for sixteen years, during which time it had expended one hundred thousand dollars, with little to show for it. It appeared to upper Columbia and lower Spokane Valley citizens that the company was merely trying to hold its franchise while "playing the dog in the manger game." Thus, these citizens petitioned the Washington Water Power Company to extend power lines to these areas.[19]

No railroads would ever reach the Spokane Reservation. Supplies for Wellpinit, Webster's choice for the agency, would have to come from the Great Northern (formerly Spokane Falls and Northern Railroad) at Springdale twenty-two miles away, and from Reardon, also twenty-two miles away, on the Northern Pacific. For the time being, supplies were freighted via the Creston-Peach wagon road from Creston.

Until a move was made to Wellpinit, Webster would have to handle his continuing problems from the agency at the old fort. With allotment of land to individual Indians, and with death, there were heirs to be determined. With families divided among reservations, there was considerable correspondence with officials of the Flathead and Coeur d'Alene reservations concerning relatives on those tracts. Another delicate problem concerned the determination of heirs of Indian-style marriages, which, in the late nineteenth century, the government had insisted be replaced by legal marriages by procurement of licenses and performance of ceremonies, clerical or civil. Such unions were recognized as legal

---

[19] Davenport and Spokane people who owned the Big Bend Transit and Electric Co. apparently withdrew their efforts to build a dam at the narrows, for the government, in February, 1924, was surveying for the establishment of monuments for overflow from the Crystal Power Dam to be built at the narrows.

marriages for tribal members living on reservations and not dissolving tribal relations. Indian Office supervisor at the Nez Percé Indian Agency, Lapwai, Idaho, O. H. Lipps, wrote June 18, 1912, that the U. S. Circuit Court of Appeals for the Ninth Circuit had ruled that an Indian allotted and living in tribal relations on the Umatilla Reservation was not compelled to comply with the laws of the state of Oregon regarding marriage. Lipps believed that, from this case, it was clear that the government still had to recognize Indian custom marriages, "from which it would also naturally follow that we must recognize the Indian custom divorce."[20]

In determining heirs of husbands after their deaths, there was no consideration of plural spouses of polygamous unions. It was not unusual for a man to have a number of wives, in the old manner; however, in looking for Indian heirs in the Inland Empire, agency personnel found "squaws" with plural husbands. Wife stealing prevailed. Apprehended offenders were jailed—that is unless the Skookum house was filled—like it was the time Thomas Sherwood turned himself in, only to find no room in the jail. Although a widower with children, he had eloped with Agatha Felix (who had not been divorced from a man who had come to her with a marriage license taken out in their names) without benefit of ceremony.

With such frequency of spouse abandonment and wife stealing, many offenders skipped from reservation to reservation, particularly to the Coeur d'Alene and Flathead, hoping to be undetected. These mobile arrangements caused the canceling of allotments in some cases and the taking of other allotments on other reservations for a time after the original allotting process.

Travel among the reservations filled an age-old Indian need to congregate and revel. After 1900, with white supremacy assured, Indians were invited to off-reservation gatherings, particularly fairs, to amuse spectators by displaying remnants of their culture. At first the Indians were unpaid for their efforts. Later, fair officials contracted with reservation Indians, like Obid Williams, to

20 Lipps to Webster, June 18, 1912, Colville Agency Records, Box 22546–L.9179.

hire their people to perform, a practice prevailing to the present time. Whites also paid them for setting up their villages and dancing. With such remuneration, Indian attendance at these affairs increased. At the 1911 Spokane Interstate Fair, an event in which the Spokanes had participated for many years, its manager promised a dollar a day plus board for 100 Indians. When word of the offer got around, 697 Indians representing twenty-one tribes showed up. Instead of the anticipated eight tipis, a total of thirty-two were pitched. The Spokanes were among the first to arrive, toting tipi poles and canvas lashed to the sides of buckboards. The wagons were full of passengers—old ones, middle-aged ones, young men beginning to "feather out," maidens turning into womanhood, and children.

The fair that year was especially important for fifty-nine-year-old Blind Alec, sightless since the age of six from one of the eye diseases common among the Spokanes. One of Alec's youngsters at the fair recognized a horse stolen from his father. Despite his handicap, Alec had made a home for his wife and children on the reservation. But his winter's wood had not been gathered, because the whites had stolen his horse. The next month he walked all the way to Spokane to claim his horse. He felt the animal over. He identified a raise on the right ear. He smiled; it was his horse. It was discovered that the horse was owned by the Union Transfer Company, who had purchased it from a horse trader.

In September, 1913, Spokanes would attend the National Indian Congress, held in conjunction with the Interstate Fair. They heard recorded messages from President Taft, Interior Secretary Franklin K. Lane, and Acting Commissioner F. H. Abbott. At the big Fourth of July celebration on the reservation in 1912, a squabble broke out between two Indian factions. Obid Williams sought to oust Chief Jim Sam, because Williams opposed a ten-day celebration, believing four days time enough to celebrate.

The agency to which Williams and his petitioners came with their grievances was then located in the city of Spokane. For a long time, Webster had urged that the Colville Agency be divided. Agency headquarters had been neither on the Colville nor the

Spokane reservations; nor were they in easy reach of all Indians under agency jurisdiction. Increasing problems arising with allotting, sale, and leasing of Indian lands, with supervising the day schools and a dozen other operations that ranged from building telephone lines to maintaining forests, was too much work for a single agent. At one time he could treat with one chief speaking for his entire tribe; now he had to treat with Indians individually. Consequently, he needed to be an educator, banker, lawyer, merchant, real estate broker, and agriculturist. On leave the spring of 1910, Webster had personally asked Commissioner R. G. Valentine for a divided agency. His request was granted in an act of March 3, 1911, which provided for the establishment of the two agencies and the sale of lands and buildings on the old Fort Spokane Military Reservation. In September, 1911, Chief Clerk of the Office of Indian Affairs J. A. Hall arrived to arrange for the removal of the Spokane Agency to the city of Spokane.

Rooms in the Federal Building in that city had been assigned to the Spokane Agency as early as July, 1911. Webster moved there on October 4 of that year to become, under his new assignment, Superintendent of Spokane Indian Schools, and Special Disbursing Agent.[21] Official separation of the two agencies occurred on January 26, 1912. The old fort location was used for the Colville Agency until October, 1913, when the buildings of the new agency at Nespelem would be completed.[22] In November would be effected the final shipment of goods and materials from old Fort Spokane down the Columbia River on the *Enterprise* to the mouth of the Nespelem River and freighted from there to Nespelem. In terminating his official duties on the Colville, Webster regretted severing his relationship with Etienne Stephen De-Rougé, S.J., of St. Mary's Mission, whom he saw as a valuable ally in the attempt to rid the reservation of many evils. Webster

21 Routine matters at the agency office at the fort were handled by J. M. Johnson, who, on January 2, 1912, was appointed superintendent and disbursing agent for the Colville Agency.

22 Building of that agency was begun in March, 1913, under supervision of Roy R. Bradley, superintendent of construction for the Office of Indian Affairs, with twenty-five carpenters hired from Wilbur, Creston, and Davenport.

found the city of Spokane location more central to Indians under his jurisdiction—Spokanes, Kalispels, and Kootenays. The agency's few Wenatchees living at Cashmere, Washington, near Wenatchee, would take but little of Webster's time and travel as compared with the others.[23]

The superintendent shuttled back and forth between Spokane and Fort Spokane in two hours in his Great Western five-passenger touring car to supervise the 629 residents of the Spokane Reservation. The agency physician, Dr. Lane, had a buggy horse which was so lame the doctor would not drive him to Spokane for fear the humane society would take the animal away. On February 13, 1912, James Hall, white husband of an Indian woman, developed smallpox from contacts in Creston, where there were several cases of the disease. Lane quarantined the west end, closed Day School Number One, and vaccinated 105 Indians. He then planned to vaccinate those near Wellpinit and Walker's Prairie, but poor transportation delayed him. Already the newspapers were alarming the countryside with word of the epidemic.

Dr. Lane snail-paced around some 140 miles, vaccinating for five days; he reached the east end of the reservation, only to find more trouble. Charlie Polenstulem, Henry Etu (Senior), Mrs. Moses, and the Wilson girls (Lucy and Esabella), refused to be vaccinated, possibly because Mrs. Moses, a medicine woman, strongly opposed the practice. Webster wrote Lane to have another hearing with her and, if she were still "insulting and rebellious," to threaten her with the Skookum house at the fort. Lane also encountered cases of trachoma, judging that as many as thirty per cent of the Spokanes suffered from it. In treating the disease, the doctor used the old "blue-stone" irritant treatment. He re-

---

[23] The records do not make clear why the Wenatchees at Cashmere were included in the Spokane Agency, being far from its other areas, unless it was to place all nonreservation Indians under the Spokane Agency, since there were to be no such Indians under the jurisdiction of the Colville. The Wenatchees were related more by blood and custom to tribes on the Colville Reservation. Webster suggested that the Lake Indians be included under the Spokane Agency—a suggestion vetoed by Assistant Commissioner C. F. Hauke, who opined that the Lakes were historically more often allied with tribes on the Colville, a point of view open to question.

quested permission to establish a surgery room to treat eye cases in general, but the request was denied. He also treated tubercular cases.

Webster went along with the plan for the subagency at Old Agency on the southwest corner of the reservation, despite the dilapidated condition of its buildings, although he would just as soon have seen it transferred to Wellpinit. He still hoped a railroad would come into the Old Agency area and suggested that, of the 153 acres reserved there, eight be made into a garden on an experimental farm for the benefit of the already agrarian-minded mixed-bloods of the west end. The following year, Robert McCoy, a quarter-blood who had, in 1911, received a fee patent to land, formed a partnership with James Hill to purchase a threshing machine to harvest their own and their neighbors' crops.

No sooner had things settled into working order in his headquarters in Spokane than Webster announced his resignation to become effective April 30, 1912. With a career spent among Indians, the captain planned to write romantic novels about these people. Avery hoped to obtain Webster's position, but it went instead, on a temporary basis, to Dr. Charles E. McChesney, commissioner of Indian schools. He would remain with the agency until August, when E. A. Peffley was to succeed him as superintendent.

The Spokane location for the agency was beginning to pose problems, and a location closer to the reservation was deemed more suitable. In early April an office supervisor of Indian schools was sent to visit the old agency site along with Avery. The office, favorably considering the reports of Avery and the office supervisor, ordered the removal of the Spokane Agency from the Federal Building to the old agency. Removal began on November 13, 1912.

In a surprise move, Webster returned to the old agency as superintendent on February 10, 1913. He picked up the swing of agency business where he had left it to wrestle with the same problems as before. He set about to have a number of Indians receive fee patents. In September he began probating lands of deceased reservation Indians, hoping to market about eight estates in time for the buyers to plant their crops in the spring. In December, those hoping to acquire fee patents anxiously awaited action by the Department of the Interior. There were hazards in receiving fee-simple patents. Webster reported that a Miles merchant, A. E. Lewis, had taken a deed on twenty acres of McCoy's land and on other Indian fee-patented land for indebtedness, hoping his debtors would cancel their obligations by deeding him land, "at a tithe of its value," as it appeared to Webster. Other outsiders, the captain noted, were anxious for "competents" to get fee-simple patents so they might purchase the land.

Government officials were desirous that the outside world learn of reservation educational activities. Avery had seen to it that the *Spokesman-Review* (Nov. 14, 1909) carried a picture showing the fine vegetables raised by children on the Spokane Reservation. Word of Robert E. Weaver's big 1913 Christmas party at Day School Number One was sent to the *Lincoln County Times* (Davenport, Wash.)[24] and to the *Spokesman-Review.*[25] Webster voiced his praise of Norman's farming instruction, believing it had made the Indians much better off than when they depended upon fish and game for their living. All of that notwithstanding, the captain was surprised to discover that not one of his seven hundred Indians on the Spokane Reservation had incomes large enough to be taxed, although he admitted it to be "a well-known fact that the Spokane Indians are poorer than many of their race in other parts of the country."[26]

By 1914 there was a fresh surge of road building. There had to be, as the roads, being unsurfaced, washed out constantly in spring freshets. The Wellpinit-Springdale Road washed so badly that supplies could not be hauled from the railroad station at Springdale for long periods of time. Webster pointed out that poor roads had reduced the Indians' incentive to raise produce, because of inadequate surfaces over which to haul their produce to market.

[24] January 2, 1914.
[25] December 28, 1913, p. 10.
[26] *Spokesman-Review,* March 11, 1914.

The stipulation[27] that they could be required to do no more than five days' road work a year may have helped explain the poor condition of the roads, as did the absence of a grader, which had never arrived, despite Webster's three-year pleas for one.

Webster wanted a new agency at Wellpinit, or at least to move across the river to the Fort Spokane buildings housing the Colville Agency. Aware that the latter agency would move that fall to Nespelem on the Colville Reservation, he believed a move to the old fort would help protect its buildings from vandals, as well as provide more sanitary quarters for agency employees.

In a report to the commissioner, the captain leveled both barrels at the "worm eaten, decayed and tinder dry" Old Agency located on a "bleak and blunt peninsula . . . where terraced sand dunes have been formed by the prevailing southwest winds blowing up the valley of the Columbia . . . [producing] sand storms adding to our other miseries." Not only was it the "hottest place in northeastern Washington," but it was "farther from the mass of Indians than any other point on the reservation," and infested "with millions of bugs and insects of every description *except bed bugs*," surrounded by "myriads of flys and mosquitoes . . . wood rats and mice . . . among the pests sojourning," including a "flourishing colony of rattle snakes," and the ruined buildings serving as a camping place for "travelers, hunters, prospectors, tramps, bootleggers and horse thieves" with no fire protection, or sanitation, and threatened from "ancient water closets" on the side hill under the spring oozing poison throughout the agency grounds.[28] Webster didn't like the place.

He suggested to the commissioner that, were no other funds available, those of the tribe be used to build new agency head-

[27] The commissioner wrote O. C. Upchurch, "Section 652 of the Indian Office Regulations provide, 'All able-bodied male Indians belonging on the Reservation, between the ages of 21 and 45 years, ... will be required to perform without compensation therefore, such a number of days of labor in each year, not less than two nor more than five, as may be required for opening and repairing the roads.' " E. B. Merritt to Upchurch, November 20, 1914, Colville Agency Records, Box 22545–L. 9788.

[28] Webster to commissioner, August 29, 1913, Colville Agency Records, Box 22545–L. 9178.

quarters. There was $38,482.05 in the treasury to the tribe's credit, some from sale of a portion of surplus unallotted agricultural lands and $5,000 appropriated by the government to pay for school land sections. In addition, $1,488 had recently been received from the Great Northern Railway for right-of-way damages. Webster was not unaware that the Spokanes "would seriously protest the use of a portion of these funds" for agency building purposes, as they had hopes of receiving a per capita payment in cash. No one but Webster could fully realize the wrath of Indians (prodded by whites) wanting to receive federal monies.

Webster's wish to occupy the fort buildings when the Colville Agency pulled out was granted September 8, 1913, only to be revoked September 19, since the Fort Spokane grounds were to be put up for sale. He then requested, on September 27, to remove the agency once again to the Federal Building in Spokane. He was now an old man, totally deaf in his left ear and depressed at the thought of spending a winter at the old agency on the "edge of nowhere." Commissioner Cato Sells advised him, on October 3, that he could move into Spokane until a plant was ready for occupancy at Wellpinit, where it was decided (as Webster had wished), the agency should be permanently placed. An official notice, dated October 17, ordered the agency to move on November 1, 1913, into Spokane.

Fed by scheming whites, the Spokanes for years had been led to believe that Webster was withholding appropriated funds from them. Led by Wellpinit full-bloods Obid Williams and John Alexander (who resigned from the police force before Webster fired him for being drunk), the Spokanes sought to petition President Woodrow Wilson to relieve Webster of his job, so that they could get larger allowances from the government.[29] They asked to have their former agent, Rickard Gwydir, returned. It was ironic that

[29] The one-thousand-dollar 1913–14 appropriation for "Support of Spokanes" (as per agreement of March 18, 1887, approved July 13, 1892) was unused by March, 1914. [There was no appropriation for the Spokanes (as per Section 6 of the articles of Agreement per March 18, 1887), money for a carpenter which position was abolished in 1902, and for a blacksmith which position was abolished in 1906.]

much of the money appropriated for Indians had a way of getting into the hands of white men who swindled Indians by preying upon their excesses and other weaknesses. It was equally ironic that complaints (many more than just those of Williams and Alexander) were lodged against Webster, who had always held the Indians in the forefront of his concern.

In his own defense, Webster said that he covered the reservation well, reaching all of its districts by phone from the agency to each day school. He explained that, although there was no farmer for the Spokanes, they were producing from the land, and their children were learning gardening techniques in the schools. There were, he assured, no old and destitute Indians. No one had died from cold or hunger since he had been at the agency. He said that rations for such eventualities were held on both ends of the reservation, ready to be issued if investigation showed need. There was plenty of firewood; every Indian was housed. If one of them died from cold, it was because of his own stupidity. Webster did admit that, from Spokane, he had insufficient time to care for all the Spokanes' personal needs, as his duties called him to Indians in the north and to places like Cheney and Lind in the Big Bend. With long evenings filled with paper work, he was obviously a bit angry at the "envious enemies and needy pothouse politicians."[30]

Not all of these politicians were whites. Webster was blamed for "getting Sam elected chief" when, in reality, while the captain was on leave, a Spokane council had elected Sam chief after Oliver Lot had drowned. Williams and Alexander resumed their complaints that the Spokanes, becoming lawless, were stealing wives and horses. This was certainly a case of the pot calling the kettle black, as Williams, suspected of horse stealing, had been arrested and jailed, only to escape two or three years before Webster came to Spokane. The wrongdoer had been rearrested in the Pend Oreille country to escape again and was not seen until he appeared on the Spokane Reservation when allotments were being made.

On March 19, 1914, Williams, Alexander, and Moses Lot went to Spokane to purchase provisions and see their friends. They got

[30] Webster to commissioner, March 23, 1914, Webster Papers, 12–145 B.

to drinking and returned to their camp a mile northwest of the city. During the night, in a drunken brawl, Williams stabbed Alexander through the heart; he died instantly. Thus, Webster had no difficulty establishing for the commissioner the true character of his Indian critics.

On top of everything else, Webster received a letter from Commissioner Sells, asking him to prepare to move back to the old agency. This was too much for the captain. Ill with grippe and "advancing age and enough accident and surgical operations to kill a Government mule," which had disabled him to the extent that he was no longer physically able to do any rough work in the field,[31] he wired his resignation to the Office of Indian Affairs on March 25, 1914. Three days later he wrote Sells: "I firmly believe you are up against the hardest task committed to any official of this Government below the rank of President and his Cabinet, and that you are also aware of the petty annoyances, complaints and serious charges to which Indian Agents are constantly subjected, nearly all of which are absolutely without foundation."[32]

And then this epitaph, self-written on the monument of the captain's decade of service to the agency, to his country, to humanity: "I have given the best that was in me to serve these red men, and feel that those years were better spent and have been of more general benefit to me than all the remainder of my sixty-five years."[33]

[31] Webster to Cato Sells, March 28, 1914, Webster Papers, 12–145 B, 463–505.
[32] *Ibid.*
[33] Webster to Sells, March 24, 1914, Webster Papers, 12–145 B, 463–505.

CHAPTER ELEVEN

Civilization–Fruits and Frustrations

The new agency superintendent was O. C. Upchurch. A farm expert from the Winnebago Indian Agency in Nebraska, Upchurch arrived May 21, 1914, eager to begin work. Housing the agency was not the only matter he inherited from his predecessor. A story in the Seattle *Post Intelligencer* (May 17, 1914) carried the headline: WEALTHY INDIAN MAIDS WANT WHITE HUSBANDS, SQUAW WITH GOOD LAND ALLOTMENTS WILLING TO CONSIDER HONORABLE PROPOSALS, ONE WRITES. The article went on to say that Webster had received a letter from Miss Jane Tugleshelt, an Indian girl of the Flathead tribe at Kalispell, Montana. She wrote that, since young Indian women with allotments were anxious to regard serious honorable marriages with white boys, would he not refer some of them. It is not known if Webster filled her request; the newspaper article was referral enough.

Webster did not stay long enough to answer mail resulting from the article. An A. B. Burr of Seattle wrote:

Noticing an article in the Seattle P. I. paper in regards to Indian girls of good land allotments wanting white husbans [*sic*] If such is the case I would be pleased to have you forward my address and discription [*sic*] to some deserving squaw. I am a young man of about 26 years age light brown hair dark blue eyes 6 [the six crossed out and five written down] and a half in hight [*sic*] weight about 190 of temperate clean habits fair edicutation [*sic*] and am not lazy, willing to keep up my end with anyone.

The kind of girl I would wish is one who can talk and understand English readly must have a general knowledge of English ways of house keeping, and of good disposetion [*sic*]

Trusting an early reply I beg to remain.

Yours and oblige[1]

Established at the old agency, Upchurch promised action in leasing, selling, and patenting Indian lands. Just before Christmas, 1917, 46 Spokanes received fee patents making them full-fledged citizens, taxpayers, and voters, to add to the hundred-odd fees granted until then. The superintendent noted that most of the Indians lived on their allotments, farming from two to forty acres, despite yields below the comfortable subsistence level. He also noted that competent mixed-bloods were anxious to get fee patents in order to break from tribal relations and government supervision. At this time there were approximately 200 mixed-bloods on the reservation. There were 410 full-bloods.[2] Five years later, according to official records, mixed-bloods would outnumber full-bloods.[3] Upchurch also prepared for sale of lands of about 100 allottees who had died since being allotted and called meetings at Day School Numbers One and Eight to determine heirs to certain lands, a tangled legacy from the allotment system.[4]

Despite their growing numbers, many west end mixed-bloods had no say in the proposed agency move to Wellpinit. This was

---

[1] A. B. Burr to Webster, May 19, 1914, Webster Papers, 145 B, 463–505.

[2] *Reports of the Department of the Interior For the Fiscal Year Ended June 30, 1915*, II, 69.

[3] *Reports of the Commissioner of Indian Affairs to the Secretary of the Interior For the Fiscal Year Ended June 30, 1920*, 72.

[4] *Spokesman-Review*, July 24, 1914, p. 8.

another source of friction between themselves and the full-bloods, who were concentrated more in the Wellpinit area.

Construction would begin at Wellpinit in April, 1915, on five cottages with facilities more modern in plumbing than in lighting (three additional houses were needed for a laborer, blacksmith, and carpenter). Also, a guard house and miscellaneous other buildings, sheds and shops, would be built from lumber milled on the reservation. There was at this time a cottage, occupied by the forest guard, the school building, and sawmill. Needed also was a garage to shelter the automobile, covered by a tent.

That fall the agency had encouraged an all-Indian fair to be held at Wellpinit to further assist the Spokanes in becoming agrarians. The event, "the only all Indian supervised event of its kind in the country," with printed premium lists like those of white men's fairs, was held on Labor Day weekend. The idea caught on. A fair was held the following year, and annually thereafter to the present time. Fairs, of course, had attracted Spokanes for some time. In November, 1914, the Seventh National Apple Show had been held in Spokane, at which Obid Williams contracted to bring thirty Spokanes to ride in the parade to advertise the Redskin brand of apples. At the big Interstate Fair in Spokane in September, 1917, the Spokanes would join other Indians in tipi-erecting contests.

When west enders visited the second Wellpinit Fair, they took a long look at the new agency buildings and returned to their end of the reservation without the spirit of togetherness the officials may have hoped the celebration would engender. They met at Detillion Bridge on February 23, 1916, to take action on Congressman C. C. Dill's failure to direct word to them of the "waste" of twenty-five thousand dollars of tribal funds to build the agency buildings at Wellpinit, funds which they believed could have been better spent in caring for their own immediate needs.

From its new buildings, much agency purchasing was channeled from large Indian warehouses, whose superintendents took sealed bids on supplies for the Office of Indian Affairs. Supplies purchased from outlets for all Indian agencies made the purchases less expensive. In 1915, one bidder, F. M. Martin, in nearby Cheney in the wheat belt, contracted to supply flour for the agency. In Chicago was a large warehouse from which, in 1917, lye, toilet soap, and flour were purchased. From the St. Louis warehouse came such supplies as hard bread, lard, and laundry soap for the reservation police, and kerosene, cook stoves, and garden hose for the school. Other supplies such as matches, beeswax, and laundry starch came from the San Francisco warehouse. Purchases from these outlets indicated changing Spokane tastes, or perhaps, more correctly, changes government officials were making in their tastes. Indians were provided with such items as shoes, which some old timers would not put to their feet, and toothbrushes, which they would not put to their teeth. There were also issues of mutton, beef, and pork, which all Indians ate. But the old ones would have settled for salmon.

With agency headquarters at Wellpinit, the Indian office decided to establish a hospital on the grounds of the Fort Spokane Military Reservation. The agency needed a sanatorium. Four Spokanes had died in 1915 with tuberculosis, and nearly fifty were suspected of having it. Forty were suspected of having trachoma. In February, 1916, Dr. J. R. Collard took charge of the institution.

At Day School Number One, teacher Frank B. Allison and his wife Phoebe taught the three Rs and a few other subjects, waging the ever present battle against truancy. Emphasis continued to be on gardening and farming, with new stress placed on health and education. Allison was ordered to give careful instruction in preparation of the soil, seeding, and care of farm and garden crops.[5] The Spokane Reservation now had 217 houses (no tipis). They were small, poorly ventilated, ill lighted, overcrowded in winter, unclean. Several of them were "very, very dirty." Housekeepers were to lead the crusade against dirt, frequently visiting homes, instructing in housekeeping, cooking, and care of the sick "to impress upon the minds of the mothers the baneful effect of allowing

---

[5] Acreages at the school for 1915 were: 2½ alfalfa, ¼ corn and beans, ¼ beets, ½ potatoes, ⅛ cabbages and tomatoes, ¼ other smaller vegetables, 1/16 strawberries, raspberries, and gooseberries, 3 wheat, 2 oats, and ½ orchard.

their homes to become breeding places of disease."[6] Housekeepers were expected to have prepared the groundwork for their visits by preparing noonday meals at the schools.

Schooling had become quite secularized since the days of Grant's peace policy. Presbyterian Reverend Mr. G. E. Van Parnis was given permission to use the day schools for one hour of religious services in May, 1916, provided they not be held during school hours. During the period 1915–20, thanks to the constant hammering of agency officials and teachers, the Indians had come to see the need of education for their children, although they often failed to lend it their full support. When Malcom McDowell of the Board of Indian Commissioners visited the sanatorium and schools in 1920, he paused near McCoy Lake Day School, where a full-blood, speaking his native tongue through an interpreter, told the commissioner he wanted an order forbidding the use of the Indian language on the school premises.[7] All Indians on the reservation spoke English, except himself and 150 of his fellows.[8]

About the same time, certain whites, believing the Spokanes to be a vanishing race, sought to preserve their language. A. E. Lewis sent the editor of the *Lincoln County Times* in Davenport a list of much-used Spokane words, which he believed should be saved for posterity. Among them was the word *o-lo-lim*, meaning any kind of metal; it was applied to money, especially dollars. Lewis wrote that "the burden of talk" of a stranded Spokane Indian in Spokane when telephoning was "send *o-lo-lim*," much like their white cousins in similar situations.[9]

Statistics showed that the Spokane Indians, unlike Lewis' prediction, were not a vanishing race. But if they were not vanishing, neither were they burgeoning. Each year following Webster's departure there was an excess of some seven births over deaths.

[6] E. B. Merritt, assistant commissioner, to Upchurch, January 30, 1915, Colville Agency Records, Box 48.

[7] *Fifty-Second Annual Report of the Board of Indian Commissioners to the Secretary of the Interior for the Fiscal Year Ended June 30, 1921*, p. 73. Hereafter cited as B.I.C. *52nd Ann. Rep.*

[8] French was still the tongue of several mixed-blood families.

[9] *Lincoln County Times*, August 3, 1917, p. 5.

To some Spokanes, their growth in civilization seemed to be at no greater pace than their growth in population.

Congress had, on October 6, 1914, set up an appropriation, "Industry among Indians Reimbursable," to provide an agreement whereby Spokanes could borrow money from the government to purchase teams of horses, wheat, oats, potato seed, barbed wire, etc. Such loans were to be repaid without interest in a specified time, usually after harvest. These loans were not only to encourage Indians in farming and fencing, but to teach them care in making legal agreements.[10]

March 18, 1916, Commissioner E. B. Merritt asked Upchurch which Indians were behind on payments and owned property attachable, in case judgments were rendered against them. Also, he asked whether it would do to reclaim property sold to these persons and to sell it to other Indians who would value it and make payments on it as they fell due. Upchurch advised the commissioner that none with delinquent payments had property which could be attached through suits, but that all save one or two were trying to make payments by cutting wood "or otherwise." There were established for the Spokanes individual accounts deposited to their credit, but the Indians could withdraw the monies only with the superintendent's approval. They could not withdraw money for personal use without giving specific reasons for its use, which had to be beneficial. They were permitted withdrawals for care of the decrepit and blind,[11] for paying funeral expenses of relatives, medical bills, clothing, for purchasing horses, saddles, seed, farm equipment, and household items. The withdrawn money was paid to the Indian if he were "competent," which at that time

[10] When Edward Whalawhitsa failed to meet his payment, his debt was paid in time by an "Interunit Transfer Voucher," which transferred funds from his individual account coming from the appropriation "Indian Moneys, Proceeds of Labor, Spokane Indian Support 1921," which appropriation was made up from leasing, timber sales, and other monies. Whalawhitsa was finally relieved of his embarrassment when the money was again transferred to the original account from "Industry Among Indians" when it was learned his debt had been for galvanized wire he had never picked up, and after a long time the agency had used the wire for erecting a pasture fence for its livestock.

[11] Fifty dollars was withdrawn from the account of John Kuya, born in 1856, to pay Annie Moses for his care, since he fitted this category.

meant that he placed some value on money, realizing its worth, spending it accordingly on worthwhile things rather than on liquor and gambling.

Several plans of stimulating Indian farming on the reservation were not successful. Webster's plan of setting a good example by permitting as much white farming as possible under existing policies had not worked. The Spokanes, who had been free to roam before allotments, had tilled the soil; now allotments had reversed the land-usage pattern on the reservation. They were using their lands primarily for grazing. The big wild-horse roundup of 1914 had improved reservation grazing possibilities somewhat. By 1920, only about a dozen sections of grazing land were leased to white cattlemen. By then, all Indian families owned from two to fifty head of cattle, which grazed on forest lands. But possibilities of livestock raising could have been better had more land been cleared for pasture and raising hay. And, of course, winter feeding was affected by the lessened production.

Perhaps under stimulus of World War I, Congress enacted legislation (which President Wilson signed May 18, 1916) directing the Secretary of the Interior to lease for mining purposes unallotted mineral land for twenty-five years, with the privilege of renewal. The proceeds were to go into the Spokane tribal fund. Shortly thereafter, there was a rush to the reservation for filing mining claims. Applicants were stacked up at Detillion Bridge to the south, and in the Deer Trail and Germania mining country to the north. By June, two hundred applications were filed with the superintendent, sometimes as many as ten for the same piece of ground where prospects looked good. In trying to control these mineral seekers from tromping too hard on the reservation, the Indian police earned their pay traveling in two's and four's for protection.

More directly involved in the war were Spokane men from their reservation who joined other Spokanes from the Coeur d'Alene in the service as volunteers, because they were not as yet citizens of the United States.[12] The Spokanes, however, had officially

[12] Pertinent records of the Office of Indian Affairs, in the National Archives,

sealed their loyalty to the American government and its flag in a dramatic ceremony in September, 1913, after which their chiefs and those of over a dozen neighboring tribes sent greetings from the banks of the Spokane to the Great White Father on the banks of the Potomac. During the war, proceeds from a Fourth of July celebration war dance, stick games, horse races, and baseball games between Spokanes and Colvilles were donated to the Red Cross.[13] Less than sixty years earlier, these Indians had war danced and fought American soldiers.

On his postwar visit to the reservation, Commissioner McDowell noted that, of some fifty mining leases made four years earlier to prospectors for copper, lead, silver, and tungsten, only one small copper mine had developed. He also noted that a timber unit of a quarter million board feet had been sold and its logs taken off the reservation, not to one of three mills working there under permits. Discovering only a half-dozen allotments had been sold, McDowell wrote: "I found the Spokane Indians pretty well advanced along the road to progress."[14]

An act of June 2, 1924, declared all Indians born within the limits of the United States citizens. The First National Indian Congress, representing all northwest tribes, was held in Spokane in October, 1925. Although Spokane Indians were present, they were usually not as politically active as other northwest tribes. In fact, whites played the predominant role in the 1925 congress, stressing Indian cultural and social development. They laid plans to raise $150,000 to build a structure to house northwest Indian relics and other items of their culture. Two features from white fairs were included in the program—(1) the selection of a prin-

reveal no information as to the exact number of Spokane Indians who served in the war. Records do show that in 1921, Joseph Kossuth Dixon, in preparing a book concerning the American Indians' participation in the war, sent questionnaires to various Indian agencies to obtain information on the men who served in the military. Five questionnaires were sent to the Spokane Agency, which would make it appear that at least five men from that agency served in the war. Jane F. Smith, director, Social and Economic Records Division, National Archives and Record Service, Washington, D.C., to authors, August 18, 1967.

[13] *Spokesman-Review,* July 3, 1918, p. 2.

[14] B.I.C. *52nd Ann. Rep.,* 73.

cess, an Indian beauty, Alice Garry, great-granddaughter of Chief Garry and (2) the selection of a perfect baby, the seven-month-old boy of the Sam Friedlanders. The next year, Indians figured prominently in the program, discussing social and economic matters, with the elders generally wanting the government to help them remain Indians, and youth talking of freedom and emancipation.[15]

At a time when the Spokanes were beginning to exhibit the first glimmer of independence, the market crash of 1929 occurred. It forced them, like their white brothers, to greater dependence on the government, specifically to an increased need of relief supplies. It should be noted that relief to the Indian did not bring with it the stigma that it did to whites; the government had been giving Spokanes aid for seventy years. In 1931 they were participating in an Office of Indian Affairs loan of forty-five million dollars from an emergency appropriation for farming, but were notified by the superintendent that the Secretary of Agriculture had stipulated that a chattel mortgage would be taken upon their crops and a first lien on the 1931 crop.[16] These restrictions notwithstanding, the government felt it had to make a special effort to encourage the Spokanes to plow their lands, purchase seed and livestock, plant gardens, and extend their farming activities. To further encourage them in farming and render assistance to insure proper care of crops and animals, farm agents in 1932 were employed to work over and above agency farmers in providing extension service. Under the Federal Emergency Administration, Indians—ward and nonward—were entitled to share in the distribution of surplus food commodities. The first distribution was pork products. Aside from the distribution of surplus commodities, the Spokanes came in for two issues of mutton, shipped from Navaho country of New Mexico in an effort to cut down the size of range flocks there. Declining salmon runs had made it difficult for Spokanes to supplement their diet with fish.

[15] *Omak Chronicle*, July 29, 1926, and August 5, 1926.
[16] Commissioner C. J. Rhoads to all superintendents, February 19, 1931, Colville Agency Records, Box 42.

The New Deal had something for the Indians, as it did for the whites. In 1933, under the Recovery and Relief program, the Indian Emergency Conservation Work Fund was established. It was similar to the Civilian Conservation Corps. Camps of Indians maintained by managers were moved about the Colville and Spokane reservations. A camp at Wellpinit Creek employed Spokanes at $1.50 a day, with an additional allowance of 60 cents if the family worker furnished his own food and lodging. No one could earn over $30.00 a month.

Probably the most important legislation of the New Deal as far as Indians were concerned was the Wheeler-Howard Act, or the Indian Reorganization Act of June 18, 1934. It sought to reverse governmental repressive policies, which over the years had banned the Indian languages, tribal organizations, religions, and family life, and had also caused the destruction of the Indian land estate through the system of forced land allotments. The Reorganization Act sought to save both the "Vanishing American" and his vanishing land through the instrumentality of tribal government, that is, to return to the dictum of Justice John Marshall that "A weak state, in order to provide for its safety, may place itself under the protection of one more powerful, without stripping itself of the right of government and ceasing to be a state."[17]

After 1900, legislation was designed to deal more and more with peoples as a whole on the reservations. Thus, the government was just as eager to minimize the role of chiefs now, so that they would not oppose government-encouraged changes, as it had been before to recognize them, so that they could exert their influence to simplify agreements with the Indians. But the government found it difficult to upset the traditions of centuries. The word "chief" died hard. With the passing of Lot in 1902, it may be said that the Spokanes lost their last chief. His son Oliver bore the title until his death, to be followed by Jim Sam and, after him, Sam Boyd, the last recognized chief of the Lower Spokanes. William Three Mountains became chief of the Upper Spokanes on the

[17] Secretary of the Interior, *Annual Report for the Fiscal Year Ending June 30, 1940*, p. 363.

death of Enoch. With the change in attitude of the government in 1934 for dealing with Indians, there would be no more chiefs. The government would then seek to deal with Indian tribes through councils and elected officers.

The Reorganization Act prohibited the further individual allotment of lands owned by tribes or to be acquired by them. It returned to tribal use lands withdrawn for homestead purposes but not settled. It authorized annual appropriations of funds for such purchases. Besides making mandatory the practice of conservation in the administration of Indian lands, it established revolving productive farming and industrial operations. It did this through the organization and incorporation of the tribes for self-management of economic resources, while providing funds out of which loans could be made to Indian students seeking higher or vocational education. The act gave Indians preference, under Civil Service rules, for employment in the Indian Service. (It had been the policy of the office, even before the passage of the act, to hire Indians wherever possible.)

In the democratic spirit in which it was enacted, the legislation provided for a referendum of tribes wishing to take advantage of its provisions. Preparatory to its passage, Superintendent Harvey K. Meyer met with the Spokanes in mid-February, 1934. He urged them to organize so they could participate at one "to as large an extent as possible in self-government and the management of matters of purely local policy and interest."[18] Without the benefit of legal counsel, and after several days of discussion, the politically cautious Spokanes voted not to adopt a constitution and bylaws or to reorganize under provisions of the Reorganization Act. Although the Spokane Indians chose not to act within the provisions of the act, the office nonetheless dealt with them, as with all Indian tribes, in a more representative manner. The Spokanes were touched by the more liberal hand of the government as it extended its new Indian policy to them.

In 1949 the Spokanes refused again to adopt a constitution and bylaws. Not until May 12, 1951, by a vote of ninety-five to thirty-

18 *Wilbur Register*, February 15, 1934.

four, would they approve formal organization, with the adoption of a constitution and bylaws. Interestingly, on November 17, 1951, the United American Indians was organized. This was an intertribal group who sought to advance Indian political and social welfare, a group in which Spokanes and neighboring tribes played the dominant role. On June 27, 1951, Commissioner D. S. Meyer for the Bureau of Indian Affairs (no longer the Office of Indian Affairs by legislation of June 19, 1947) would approve the Spokane constitution and bylaws.

Just as it had sought to reorganize Indians, the New Deal also sought to reorganize nature, providing the Spokane tribal council with one of its greatest concerns. Following the August 30, 1935, authorization for the building of Grand Coulee Dam, at a site downstream forty-four river miles from the reservation, there was granted to the United States by Congressional action on June 29, 1940, subject to the provisions of the act:

(a) all the right, title, and interest of the Indians in and to the tribal and allotted lands within the Spokane and Colville Reservations, including sites of agency and school buildings and related structures and unsold lands in Klaxta town site, as may be designated therefor by the Secretary of the Interior from time to time: PROVIDED, That no lands shall be taken for reservoir purposes above the elevation of one thousand three hundred and ten feet above sea level as shown by General Land Office surveys, except in Klaxta town site; and (b) such other interests in or to any of such lands and property within these reservations as may be required and as may be designated by the Secretary of the Interior from time to time for the construction of pipe lines, highways, railroads, telegraph, telephone and electric-transmission lines in connection with the project, or for the relocation or reconstruction of such facilities made necessary by the construction of the project.[19]

By further provision of the act, the Secretary of the Interior was to set aside approximately one-quarter of the entire reservoir area for the paramount use of the Indians of the Spokane and

[19] Act of 76 Cong., 3 sess., June, 1940 (*54 Stat.* 703).

Colville reservations for hunting, fishing, and boating purposes. This would be subject only to such "reasonable regulations" as the secretary might prescribe for the protection and conservation of fish and wildlife, provided that the exercise of the Indians' rights over the area set aside for them should not interfere with project operations. The secretary would also grant to the Indians, where necessary, reasonable rights of access across any project lands. Provision was also made for compensating the tribe and individuals for land lost and for removal of the dead to relocated cemeteries, which would be held nontaxable in trust by the United States.

The Spokane Tribal Council passed a resolution March 17, 1949, asking the Secretary of the Interior to compensate them for damage to lands below the 1,310-foot contour. As elevation of waters of Lake Roosevelt behind Grand Coulee Dam had taken 2,898 acres of reservation land, reducing its area from 154,898 to 152,000 acres, the Spokanes sought compensation for this loss. They received it. But they had not taken into account areas at the water's edge, plagued by slides from high above the 1,310-foot level.[20] Yet there were some compensations to the formation of the reservoir. Writing in 1961, the chairman of the Spokane Business Council (the elective tribal governing body under the 1951 constitution and bylaws) would term the development of the thirty-five-mile lake-front land, "the greatest single potential on the reservation."[21]

The building of Grand Coulee Dam, with corresponding losses in fish runs and wildlife, prompted the Spokanes to write up, in 1944, a Fish and Wildlife Code. They appointed three members to the wildlife committee to investigate the status of wildlife on the reservation, to protect endangered species, and to propose sites for development and improvement in wildlife habitats. This was a far cry from the days of their ancestors, who had given little thought to wildlife preservation. Indian police were to act as game

[20] Alex Sherwood interview, Wellpinit, Washington, September 2, 1967. Spokane fears about this are well founded. In March, 1969, for example, a landslide from the reservation temporarily blocked the Spokane River.
[21] Glenn F. Galbraith, "The Spokane Indians Redevelopment Area, 1961," 4.

protectors, patrolling streams, forests, and fields. They would enforce federal, state, and reservation laws. While Spokanes could hunt and fish at all times, nonenrolled Indians could not do so without written permission of the tribal council. Limits were placed on all game animals taken. In 1945, when a large number of coyotes were killing calves, the council passed a resolution asking for assistance from the Fish and Wildlife Service to control this predator. In order to build up their herds, the Spokanes began seeking reimbursable monies appropriated by the government under a new economic program for purchases of cattle by tribal members. At the same time, the tribal council passed many resolutions to the Office of Indian Affairs for the tightening of leasing practices on reservation lands.

Not even the building of Grand Coulee Dam created such a stir among the Spokanes as another development, which began in 1954. Many times when whites shoved Indians off to reservations, there lay beneath the land surfaces minerals of great wealth. In Oklahoma, it was oil; on the Spokane Reservation, it was uranium oxide.

In the spring of 1954, two brothers, James and John LeBret, made preliminary studies in company with Leo Bruce, a Chippewa, of where uranium might be found. They went one midnight, with Geiger counter and mineral light, to a spur on Lookout Mountain[22] about twelve miles from the agency. Here they discovered radioactivity.[23] Assays of the LeBret prospect showed they had discovered rich quantities of autunite, a secondary uranium-bearing mineral. The LeBrets appropriately named their find the "Midnite Mine." Taking three uncles and a son (the Wynecoops) into their project, they got a prospector's permit, then a lease on 570 acres of tribal land for ten years, with an option to renew it. They then wrote their congressman, Walt Horan, on September 3, 1954, asking him to urge the Secretary of the Interior, Douglas McKay, to hurry the signing of the lease. As Horan

[22] Sec. 12, T. 28 N., R. 37 E., W.M.

[23] In late 1955 three promising uranium discoveries were made in the vicinity of the Le Bret discovery—one, a good deposit of autunite. A second lease was signed by the tribe, March, 1956, with the Big Smoke Uranium Corporation for ten years.

put it, "some very excited Indians" had a "purported Uranium discovery" and should have speedy clearance.[24]

The partners filed with Stevens County and the state articles of incorporation of the Midnite Mines Incorporated, listing capitalization of sixty-five thousand dollars divided into 5,000 shares of Class A (voting) stock and 150 shares of Class B stock.[25] Immediately interested, the Atomic Energy Commission put down test holes and guaranteed the six-member corporation a purchase contract through 1956. The LeBrets moved in equipment. By early December, they had shipped fifty-four tons of ore to Murray, Utah, to be milled by the Atomic Energy Commission. The first ore body, surface mined, appeared to be five feet deep. Actually, it extended from fifteen to twenty feet, improving with depth. By December, 1955, a year after the initial shipment, the strike was found to extend several hundred feet deep, with a final average of .285 per cent uranium oxide, a good average. Nine ore bodies found at Midnite were estimated to be worth fourteen million dollars.

In the meantime, requests had been made to the Spokane Business Council to prospect seventy-five thousand acres of tribal land. The council ruled to grant prospecting permits only to members, whom they required to show work completed. The council would cancel permits of those wishing to speculate, or of those influenced by outside mining interests which had already attempted to lease areas under permit, or which had participated in an act violating the "peace and dignity" of the Spokane tribe. The tribe knew they had a "gold mine," yet one which had to be developed within the code of federal regulations. Fear of fast operators had kept the Business Council members opposed to leasing directly to the public. The council wanted permittees to negotiate with outside mining interests for prospecting and subleasing without advertising, provided the superintendent approved. The Secretary of the Interior amended the code of federal

[24] Horan to Secretary of the Interior Douglas McKay, September 4, 1954, (Walt) Horan Papers, 356.

[25] In July, 1955, the shares of Class B stock had been re-evaluated into 150,000 shares.

regulations, so that leases could be negotiated with Bureau of Indian Affairs approval, but without advertising.[26]

Where allotted land was concerned, the code of federal regulations provided for mineral leasing with the Indian allottee, after permission had been obtained from the superintendent through the Secretary of the Interior, not through the Business Council, which wanted to approve the leases as well. On February 19, 1955, the council sent a letter to Congressman Horan asking him to seek Department of Interior approval of its resolution of February 2, which sought to secure the uranium business as solely a Spokane tribal enterprise. But the department was fearful that, if the Spokanes were permitted to negotiate leases, they would be swindled. Tribal members disagreed, claiming support for their views from the Washington State Department of Conservation and Economic Development, Washington State College, and the National Congress of American Indians.

Midnite's success brought requests for prospecting permits. It also brought a suit by Leo Bruce against the owners for a third interest in the mine, since he and the LeBrets had prospected together until the time the LeBrets had made their find. At this time, Midnite was negotiating with Newmont Mining Corporation of New York to purchase an interest in its operations. When the suit was filed in Superior Court, a restraining order was placed against the owners by the court for Bruce. The defendants asked that Bruce be made to post a million-dollar bond for their protection against damage by reason of the restrainer's interference with negotiations. This ban was lifted in April, 1955; an agreement was then made with Newmont, wherein that company acquired a 51 per cent interest in Midnite. The new organization, in which Midnite owned 49 per cent, was called "Dawn Mining Company."[27] Finally, "for the primary purpose of terminating

---

[26] Horan to Glenn F. Galbraith, Spokane Agency credit clerk, February 19, 1955, Horan Papers, 357.

[27] In April, 1956, all outstanding A voting and B nonvoting stock in Midnite was made one class of voting nonassessable common stock. Midnite owned 3,900,000 shares of stock in Dawn Mining Co. In December of that year, 223,980 shares of Midnite stock were offered to the public.

expensive litigation," an out-of-court settlement was reached in early July, whereby Mrs. (Betty) Bruce, a Spokane niece of the LeBrets, received ninety-eight shares of Class A voting stock.

Adjacent to the tribal uranium land, property belonging to descendants of Edward Boyd contained an even higher percentage of primary ore. Before the code of federal regulations was changed, the Boyd land had been put up for bid. Sadie Boyd, mother of the deceased Edward, arranged for nine persons to share in the distribution of the monies in what she thought to be a prospecting permit, but which was actually a mining lease with a man from Spokane. She claimed he gave her no money, but a turkey for Christmas. He claimed to have paid the Boyds nine thousand dollars for a lease, and even threatened to force Secretary McKay to prove leases on the tracts he obtained from the Boyd family when the Boyd units first went up for bid in 1955. Mrs. Boyd wrote Congressman Horan on March 26, 1955, asking him if he could not get the contract and prevent it "from going through." "Maybe," she wrote hopefully, "you can send me the paper if it is there . . . ."[28]

Colville Agency Superintendent Floyd Phillips advised Mrs. Boyd to put her land up for bid. In mid-July, the bids were opened. Mrs. Boyd, who managed the family affairs, did not like the high bidder; consequently, the land remained idle nearly a year before the Dawn Mining Company, in 1956, presented a higher bid of $317,000 for the property. The company would finally pay $340,-000 for a lease on the property, which bordered the Midnite Mine.[29] The bloc of land now under control of Dawn was essential to its production, and the additional holdings gave strength for the plan to erect a uranium mill. Consequently, the company made the high bid on the Boyd property to gain the advantage of having a large enough production to start the local mill.[30] The Dawn payment to the Boyds was divided mainly between two members of

[28] Sadie Boyd to Horan, March 26, 1955, Horan Papers, 357.

[29] *Spokane Daily Chronicle*, June 20, 1956, p. 1.

[30] Spokane Tribal Council to Horan, August 3, 1956, Horan Papers, 357.

the family, Richard and Lucille Boyd Gallegos (Gilham), son and daughter of the deceased Edward Boyd and his wife.[31]

Interviewed in a Spokane jail about her good fortune, Mrs. Gallegos, then thirty years of age, said, "It's got me running around in circles. I am so excited I have been drinking too much. That's why I am here." She added, "I don't know what to do with so much money. I guess I will build a home on land which my brother and I own on the reservation."[32] She also said she wanted to pay medical bills for a broken arm, then in a cast. Her brother Richard, according to newspaper accounts, also became entangled with the law.[33] Mrs. Gallegos was married in New Mexico in 1946 and separated two weeks later from her husband, with divorce proceedings to follow in 1956. Under new bureau regulations, her money could not be held in trust for her, but plans were made to counsel her about it. Regardless of these plans, Mrs. Gallegos became a fairly regular inhabitant of the Spokane jail, to which she presented a television set for the women's ward. Six years later, in 1961, she was killed in an automobile accident. Her brother Richard died on January 19, 1969, at the age of thirty, having choked to death on a piece of meat in a restaurant near the Idaho-Washington border. The *Spokesman-Review* of January 31 noted that Richard Boyd had left an estate estimated at more than $700,000, with bequests totaling $1.3 million.

The government contended that, since it had entered the Boyd affair, the resulting high bid by Dawn for the Boyd property necessitated Department of Interior control and bid advertising. The tribe opposed this contention, maintaining that it had been the tribal program which allowed for development of the Midnite Mine, thus clearing the way for the big Boyd-property bid. There was merit in the tribe's argument, since bidding without excavation or drilling amounted to blind bidding. Should other areas of the reservation be advertised, only token bids would be received

[31] Two cousins, Willie and Albie Boyd, shared small amounts, as did two uncles, Roy and Raymond Boyd; an aunt, Lizzie Boyd Ford; a grandmother, Mattie Boyd; and Sadie Boyd.

[32] *Spokane Daily Chronicle*, June 20, 1956, p. 1.

[33] *Spokesman-Review*, May 3, 1957.

on unopened land. In July, 1955, a three-man Spokane delegation had gone to Washington, D. C., instructed to stand behind the tribe's original resolution, which limited the prospecting permits and leasing to tribal members only but allowed them to negotiate with reputable mining firms for assistance in prospecting and development. The tribe was holding out for yearly permits on 160 acres, with option to renew. The tribe and the department arrived at a plan whereby, in the main, permits to prospect uranium would be issued only to qualified members of the Spokanes for a period ending September 30, 1956 (later extended), to give permittees (1) exclusive right to prospect uranium and associated minerals in limited areas and (2) the right to negotiate with legitimate companies for financial help in prospecting and then to lease their land on discovery of ore. Assignments of leases to outside companies moved slowly because the bureau hesitated to approve them.

When the Walkers and Eellses taught the Spokanes at their mission, they could not have dreamed that the descendants of their pupils would be involved in the largest uranium-producing mine in the northwest. Newmont constructed the plant in 1957 and began milling in August, processing ore for other mines on the reservation and from areas as far away as Canada. The mill had a daily volume of from 440 to 500 tons and a payroll of forty-five men; half of them were Spokanes. They worked a five-day week until October, 1963, when a seven-day week was begun. Thirty-five men were employed at the mine on a two-shift basis, five days a week, ten months a year, when Isbell Construction Company of Reno, Nevada, contracted to mine the ore. With $500,000 worth of earth-moving equipment, Isbell removed approximately 3.2 million tons of rock, hauling it twenty miles to the mill, where 1.1 million tons of ore were extracted. With the closure of the mine in October, 1963, Dawn had sold 2.85 million pounds of uranium oxide to the Atomic Energy Commission at $8 per pound, totaling $22.8 million.[34]

[34] The spring of 1957, the Dawn Mining Co. discovered two more ore bodies, making a total of 11 bodies of ore in all, a reserve of over 700,000 tons. While

The Atomic Energy Commission stopped its purchases in 1958. In October, 1963, Dawn closed its mine, the last of its type operating in Washington, Oregon, Idaho, and Montana. Enough ore was stockpiled at the mill to process through July, 1965. At that time, sufficient ore would be obtained to complete Dawn's contract with the Atomic Energy Commission, which called for regular deliveries until December 31, 1966. The buildings at Ford were sold to the tribe. Things would be quiet on the uranium front until the late 1960's, when increased peacetime uses of atomic power and diminished stockpiles would stimulate new mineral probes. These later explorations were conducted by the Western Nuclear Company of Denver and others.

Tribal royalties from ore mined on tribal land averaged 10 per cent of the "mine value per ton," which varied from $3.74 per ton for .11 per cent uranium oxide ore to $9.86 per ton for .17 per cent ore. Royalties were on a sliding scale of from 10 to 20 per cent, depending on the grade of ore. Other mining firms paid royalties to other Spokanes. Payments to the tribe from Dawn ran about $6,500 a month during maximum processing. In addition, the tribe received royalties from other mines. By 1961, tribal payments had totaled more than $275,000.

Arthur C. Flett, a tribal member living at Fruitland, just off the reservation to the northwest, was concerned that the Spokanes were not receiving all uranium royalties due them. He feared that those the tribe received were not reflected in the per capita payments to members. Questioning leases made, Flett wondered why some lease land was not being developed. He hoped to focus attention, as some Spokanes believed, on his failure to get a permit.[35] He organized a group, composed largely of Spokanes living off the reservation who called themselves the SIA (Spokane Indian Association). It was patterned after the CIA (Colville Indian Association), which had been formed in the early 1930's and

primary ore (uraninite and coffinite) was present in the bodies, they were heavy in secondary mineral, metaautunite, uranophane, and sootyuraninite.

[35] Roger Ernest, Assistant Secretary of the Interior, to Horan, August 26, 1960, Horan Papers, 360.

had received a charter from the state of Washington, its primary aim being the termination of Bureau of Indian Affairs control over the Colville Reservation.

Flett first became interested in royalties paid the Spokanes in 1957. In a letter to the *Spokesman-Review*, he noted that the Spokanes were to be the richest Indians in the nation because of the uranium discovery. "Now that hole they are digging on our land," he complained, "is getting deeper and rich getting richer and poor getting poorer." He deplored the "low per ton income" of the ore, all because "our leaders cannot or will not stand up and fight for what belongs to us." He implored the Spokanes to vote in an upcoming election to change faces on the Business Council.[36] But his words were not heeded at that election.

The SIA petitioned Congress to investigate mining on the reservation. Flett was informed that the Spokane Business Council was the duly elected representative of the Spokanes. Assistant Secretary of Interior Roger Ernst informed Congressman Horan that the producing mines were regularly inspected by engineers of the U.S. Geological Surveys; their reports had shown no improper operations. Flett charged that accounts of the royalties from mining operations were incomplete. Other attempts of the SIA to dislodge the members of the Business Council failed. In 1961 tribal royalties fell off, because most production had shifted from tribal land to that of the privately owned Boyd land. Flett continued his charges that Indians were not getting their royalties.

In 1962 the SIA would join the CIA in calling for emergency action by the Washington State governor and legislature to extend law and order to Indian lands in the state. They asked for laws making Indians amenable to all state criminal and civil laws, with the exception of hunting and fishing. This SIA request would follow the case of Paul Seymour, a Colville Indian arrested for a crime on his reservation in East Omak, Washington, and sent by the state to its penitentiary. Federal authorities said they lacked manpower to provide proper law enforcement in East Omak, because the previous state legislature had refused to extend

36 *Spokesman-Review*, June 18, 1957, p. 4.

state jurisdiction over the reservation. Flett and the chairman of the CIA, Frank W. Moore, said the state's refusal to extend its jurisdiction was not in accord with the wish of most Indians. They also maintained that, in the absence of federal law concerning juvenile lawbreakers on Indian land, the state, under Public Law 280 (passed August, 1953), had the full and unqualified right to legislate with regard to Indians in Indian country, but the state of Washington had not legislated. In 1965 the state did establish a Commission on Indian Affairs, but some Spokane tribal leaders criticized it, believing it had been given powers too broad in the fields of taxation and housing. They also believed increased state jurisdiction in criminal and civil matters would harm tribal sovereignty, amounting to a breach of federal government treaties and proclamations. This would be a first step toward a development they did not want, termination of federal control over them.

Although the matter of termination of federal supervision of the reservation was somewhat peripheral to the aims of the SIA, Flett sounded out the Spokane mixed-bloods who had sold their reservation lands. He sought to elicit their support in the termination move, but stirred little interest among them. A group composed of many Northwest tribes had prepared to meet in Yakima, Washington, in 1947 to push for termination. The Spokanes, at their council held June 20, 1947, had decided to send a delegate from their tribe to Yakima with instructions to do "anything he could to keep things as they are now."[37] A meeting on the Colville Reservation, November 18 and 19, 1947, resulted in formation of the Affiliated Tribes of Northwest Indians. At the meeting opposition was again voiced to termination. Daniel Scott, a Spokane from Spalding, Idaho, said that because of racial discrimination, an Indian would have difficulty in attaining his place in any community, so consequently he would be better off on the reservation. Scott said he did not blame older Indians for requesting continued federal help in retaining old traditions and heritages.

At the beginning of the Eisenhower administration (remembered popularly by Indians as the one that permitted Indian

[37] Minutes Spokane Council, June 20, 1947, Colville Agency Records, Box 45.

purchases of liquor),[38] the bureau advanced a termination plan for all reservations in December, 1954. When the Spokanes learned of this plan, on January 4, 1955, they immediately rose to challenge it. For three days the tribe met to prepare a statement for the then new commissioner, Glenn L. Emmons, who was coming to the Northwest on a tour. In their meeting with Emmons, elderly Spokane tribal members cited agreements of the past wherein their reservation had been promised them forever. The recent uranium developments no doubt helped influence Spokane hesitancy to move on termination. The Indians suggested that no thought be given to termination, unless it had tribal endorsement. One member said no individual in the tribe was "openly working for it." The general consensus was that, before any thought be given to termination, attention be given to several other pressing Spokane matters—heirship (a legacy from the allotment system which the Reorganization Act had not solved), housing, roads, mineral leases, and the operation of four hundred acres at Fort Spokane, above the flood level of Lake Roosevelt as a recreation and tourist center. Reclamation possibilities of the Grand Coulee project had also stimulated tribal interest in irrigation on the reservation, which, as late as 1920, had no irrigation ditches.

The nearby Colvilles showed increasing interest in termination. They elected proterminationists to their council, people with CIA backgrounds who were vocal in their objectives, backed by a Stanford University study in 1961 showing that 87 per cent of their tribe favored some form of termination. They were all primed for hearings held in August and November, 1965, on federal legislation to terminate their reservation. The Spokanes came to the hearings with a prepared statement opposing termi-

---

[38] There are no federal prohibitions on the sale of liquor outside of Indian reservations, such laws being substantially repealed by Congress in 1953. Tribes do have the power of local option to allow sale of intoxicants on reservations, subject to state laws and tribal requirements. The Spokanes along with forty or more tribes, have exercised this option, and stores located on the reservation now regularly sell beer. Elmo Miller, superintendent, Colville Indian Agency to authors, July 20, 1967.

nation; they believed it would affect them badly in many ways. Many Colvilles had inherited lands on the Spokane Reservation through marriages with Spokanes. Should the Colvilles terminate, heirship lands and Indian blood of the Colvilles would become terminated to add to the already chaotic heirship problems, making it impossible to determine correct blood quantum in the neighboring tribes.[39] The Spokanes suggested that, if termination came about for the Colvilles, only the Colville blood of persons on the Colville tribal rolls be affected. The Spokanes believed that, in mixed families on other reservations, the Colville blood should continue to be Indian blood.

At the hearings, it also came out that the Kalispels did not want to terminate. Neither did the Flatheads, whose Chief Paul Charlo led a delegation to Washington, D.C., to ask that no such bill be passed. Ironically, Charlo's grandfather, Chief Victor, had gone to Washington nearly a century before to try unsuccessfully to keep his people off a reservation. The Coeur d'Alenes did not wish to terminate. Joseph R. Garry, chairman of the Coeur d'Alene Council and nationally recognized Indian leader, was much against the plan. He stated that, at one time, the government had used guns and bullets to dispossess the Indian of his land, but now used words and contrived laws to do the same thing. Reverend Michael Shannon of the Sacred Heart Mission on the Coeur d'Alene said, "Take away the money incentive and the termination problem would disappear."[40] A spokesman for those terminationists on the Colville Reservation regarded the bureau as holding a "degrading lordship status" over the Indian in the belief that Indians should be set aside for jurisdictional purposes, because of their general incompetency to compete with more experienced and enterprising non-Indians. These sentiments came from a memory of times when only those Indians considered competent

[39] House of Representatives, *Hearings Before the Subcommittee on Indian Affairs of the Committee on Interior in Insular Affairs.* Hearings held in Washington, D.C., June 18 and August 13, 1965; Spokane, Washington, November 3, 1965; and Nespelem, Washington, November 4 and 5, 1965, pp. 319–21.

[40] Rowland Bond, "Agency After is Target," *Spokane Daily Chronicle*, August 14, 1965.

could conduct business or spend money. Competency, as noticed before, was an ill-defined word.[41]

The chairman of the Spokane Business Council, Alex Sherwood, said that, while the bureau had its faults, it was still essential to tribal welfare. He pointed out how that agency was established under military rules to guard the Indians and keep them on reservations. The Indians, said Sherwood, were not encouraged at first to improve; they were given horses and plows but no good land to farm. Had the government really intended them to become farmers, he said, they would have given the Indian better ground. Once he got good land, the whites came and took it away. The Indian, he continued, was taught to take his problems to the bureau and, with sharp and constant supervision, fell further and further behind. Instead of becoming free and independent, he became a child dependent on the "man at the agency." Sherwood concluded that, since World War I, the Spokanes, aware of the American society about them, were trying to catch up with it, but still needed the bureau even for that.[42]

In an interview with newspaperman Rowland Bond, Wellpinit merchant and tribal judge Glenn Galbraith, who foresaw nothing better with termination, noted that, where once the Spokanes used to go to the agency to make telephone calls and get help in filling out mail orders, they now handled such things for themselves.[43] Galbraith indicated that the Indian was a supercitizen:

They talk about "freeing" the Indian. What are they going to free him from? The privilege of not paying taxes? He now has more rights than any other American citizen.

He even has the privilege of owning land like any other citizen and of paying taxes on it, too, if he's enterprising enough to go

[41] An order, Number 360, from the Secretary of the Interior, dated June 7, 1929, instructed agents that in all official correspondence, memoranda, etc., the word "incompetent" as applied to Indians, should be avoided wherever practicable, as "incompetent" carried with it the stigma of mental incompetence and should be used only in such context and not applied indiscriminately to all Indians either as a class or as individuals.

[42] Bond, "Agency After is Target."

[43] *Ibid.*

out and work and buy it on his own initiative. Many of our people have done just that.

He can even have his land allotment on the reservation deeded if he wants to have it patented and put on the tax rolls. Many have done it because they didn't want to be under the Bureau of Indian Affairs supervision.[44]

Having made clear their position on termination, the Spokanes turned to another matter which understandably was an important topic of their conversation—to secure claims to their lands lost to the government. As the previous course of Spokane development had been tempered by the loss of these lands, so also was its recent development by prospects of compensation for that loss. Unlike the Father to whom they committed their dead to enter the courts of heaven, the White Father in Washington had not given, but had taken away. Through courts on earth the Spokanes sought from him a recompense.

[44] Rowland Bond, "Area's Indians Wage Hot War of Words Over Status," *Spokane Daily Chronicle*, August 9, 1965.

CHAPTER TWELVE

Whither the Children?

Twenty-two years after the ratification of the 1887 agreement for removal of the Upper and Middle Spokanes to the Coeur d'Alene and Flathead reservations, Chief Jim Sam of the Lower Spokanes walked into the Federal Building in Spokane to ask Superintendent Webster why his people should not receive compensation for the land on which the teeming city of Spokane was built. If the superintendent thought a reiteration of the benefits of the 1887 agreement would satisfy the tribal leader, he was mistaken. That very year, 1914, the Spokanes entered a claim not only for land on which the city of Spokane was built, but for all their lands lost. In 1928, Congressman Sam B. Hill introduced a bill, H. R. 5574, with the combined claims of the Lower Spokanes and Kalispels for $9,125,000 for compensation for lands as well as for loss of hunting and fishing rights. It was presented to the U.S. Court of Claims.[1] Besides amounting to $1.25 an acre

[1] The U. S. Court of Claims was established by act of Congress February 25, 1855, to hear and determine all claims founded upon any law of Congress, or upon any regulation of an executive department, or upon a contract, express or implied, with the government of the United States, which may be submitted to it by a

for 6,500,000 acres, there was also $1 million for loss of fishing rights on the Columbia River and its tributaries and of hunting rights and privileges held with other Indians in the "common hunting grounds" east of the Rocky Mountains as reserved by, and described in, the treaty with the Blackfoot Indians on October 17, 1855. The Senate approved the bill, S. 1480, authorizing these tribes to present their claims to the Court of Claims. But President Calvin Coolidge vetoed it on May 18, 1928, stating that the claims were not based on "treaty or agreement." Also, that the date was too late for seeking the claims, and that no adjudication could be made of them without unmistakable evidence of their merit.[2]

The House Committee on Indian Affairs had favored the bill, but the Interior Department had opposed it, believing the Blackfoot treaty had not included the Spokanes. There was no doubt, however, that the Spokanes had traveled to the buffalo hunting grounds. It was put forth in the bill that the Lower Spokanes had

petition filed therein, and also claims which may be referred to the court by either house of Congress. After 1862 (by act of Congress, March 3, 1863) only Indian tribes who obtained special jurisdictional acts of Congress could have their claims heard by the Court of Claims.

2 The land involved in the Lower Spokane claim was as follows:

Commencing in the State of Washington the east and west Government survey township line between townships 24 and 25 north at a point whose longitude is one hundred and nineteen degrees ten minutes west; thence east along said township line to the first draw leading and draining into Hawk Creek in Lincoln County, Washington; thence down the center of said draw to said Hawk Creek and down the center of said Hawk Creek to its conflux with the Columbia River; thence up and along the south and east bank of the Columbia River to the north bank of the Spokane River at its conflux with the Columbia River, which said boundary lines separate the lands of said Lower Spokane Tribe or Band of Indians from these, the several so-called Colville and Okanogan Tribes or Bands of Indians; thence easterly up and along the north bank of the said Spokane River to a north and south line whose longitude is one hundred and eighteen degrees west; thence south along said line to its intersection with the forty-seventh parallel of latitude; thence west along said forty-seventh parallel to a line whose longitude is one hundred and nineteen degrees and ten minutes west; thence north on said line to the point of beginning, which two latter lines of boundary separate the lands of the said Lower Spokane Tribe or Band of Indians from the lands of the confederate Yakima Indians as defined by the treaty between the United States and said Yakima Indians concluded at Camp Stevens, Walla Walla Valley, Washington Territory, June 9, 1855, *Message from the President of the United States*, (1928), II, 2.

not ceded the area they claimed, as the Upper and Middle Spokanes had already ceded the Spokane areas in the 1887 agreement.

Despite these reversals, the Spokanes on their reservation did not abandon pursuit of their claims; they even gained support in their effort from the Bureau of Indian Affairs. Again in 1931, 750 expectant Spokanes from the reservation pressed the office with claims for three million dollars for loss of their old lands south of the Spokane River, as well as loss of their hunting grounds east of the Rocky Mountains. In pressing their claims, the Spokanes were joined by Colvilles, Kalispels, and San Poils.

Congress passed an act on August 13, 1946, establishing an Indian Claims Commission. Here, the various tribes could present claims, obviating the need of securing Congressional approval to bring suits against the government in the Court of Claims. Decisions on claims reviewed by the new commission could be appealed to the Court of Claims, and then, if necessary, to the U. S. Supreme Court. At a meeting on October 21, 1941, the Spokane Tribal Council had chosen John Raftis of Colville as their attorney to pursue their claims,[3] but after the Indian Claims Commission Act, through another lawyer, Glenn A. Wilkinson of Washington, D.C., they filed claims on August 10, 1951,[4] for land taken and for any amount found due them from a general accounting of trust funds and other assets of the tribe.[5]

At this time the Spokanes sought compensation at 1892 prices for land lost between the Columbia River and the Idaho state line north of Steptoe Butte to Hunters in Washington State, a total of three million acres. For several years after these 1951 negotiations, hearings bogged down in a determination of exact boundaries of Spokane land. As a showdown neared, the outcome hinged on two essential points: (1) could the Lower Spokanes

---

[3] Minutes Spokane Council, October 21, 1941, Colville Agency Records, Box 45-L. 13997.

[4] *Petitioner's Proposed Findings of Fact and Brief, Before the Indian Claims Commission Docket No. 331*. Prepared by Ernest L. Wilkinson, attorney, Washington, D.C., 2. Hereafter cited as *Petitioner's Proposed Findings*.

[5] Erma Walz, Chief, Branch of Tribal Operations, United States Department of the Interior, Bureau of Indian Affairs, Washington, D.C., to authors, August 2, 1967.

sue the government as an entity apart from the Upper and Middle Spokanes, and (2) could they show ownership of a definable area of land, which they claimed by proof of use and occupancy in the accustomed Indian manner, land which the Upper and Middle Spokanes had already ceded? Lawyer Wilkinson presented a picture of Lower Spokanes integrated with those of the Upper and Middle Spokanes to show Spokane tribal unity to assure his clients' claim to the land ceded by these latter two groups. He prepared a brief using the testimony of Verne Ray, experienced anthropologist and acknowledged authority on plateau tribes. Ray testified there truly had been a form of tribal unity, a single form superior to both village unity and the three subdivisions of the Spokane nations. Wilkinson pointed out that Dr. Ray had done his work as early as 1928 without any thought of its possible use in litigation.[6]

Expert defense witness for the United States was Stuart Chalfant, of whom the petitioners stated: "It is difficult to imagine upon what basis defendant fathoms its contention that Chalfant 'is now the best qualified expert' on the use and occupancy of area by Plateau tribes." Representatives from the tribe claimed that his subsequent interviews with the Spokanes were with only two Indians, one elderly and the other not very well versed in Spokane history.[7]

In their endeavor to weaken the government argument that Spokanes, with solely a village autonomy, lacked tribal unity and ethnic cohesion, the petitioners maintained there had been an all-Spokane chief. His name was Chief Raven, and he resided at Little Falls in the territory of the Lower Spokanes where the majority of the Spokanes resided—where, too, an all-Spokane council met once or twice yearly to consider important issues. Whereas, the petitioners continued, the tribe once consisted of separate

---

[6] *Reply to Defendant's Objections to Petitioner's Proposed Findings of Fact, Objections to Defendant's Proposed Findings of Fact, and Reply Brief, Before the Indian Claims Commission Docket No. 331.* Prepared by Ernest L. Wilkinson, Attorney, Washington, D.C., 23. Hereafter cited as *Reply to Defendant's Objections.*

[7] Dave Wynecoop interview, Wellpinit, Washington, August 13, 1966.

bands, as the Indian Claims Commission acknowledged, it had by the mid-nineteenth century become a single entity, remaining so ever since.[8] Anthropologist Ray testified, and the petitioning Spokanes claimed, that the tribe had no decisive words indicating "east," "west," "north," "south," "high," or "low." The indecisive terms "Upper," "Middle," and "Lower," said Ray, could have originated only with non-Indians. A Dr. Anastasio, also an expert witness for the petitioners, testified that the Spokanes had organizational and political unity, both evidence of the existence of a single tribe. Spokane unity, he maintained, followed a typical plateau pattern in which Flatheads, Kalispels, and other tribes were organized to facilitate action at several levels from the village unit to a loose confederation of larger groups. Spokane political organization manifested itself at levels necessary to accomplish particular tasks and to deal with traders, missionaries, government officials, and others.[9]

The Spokanes sought consideration from the Claims Court which agreed with the Spokanes' contention that they had an overall form of government, thus disallowing any division of the land area claimed or limiting of the Lower Spokanes to a smaller area which the commission had hitherto considered to be theirs alone. The Court recognized the Spokanes as a tribal entity on the basis of a common language. It also recognized that, although frequenting fisheries of other tribes, the Spokanes had used a vast area for hunting game and gathering roots and berries. The Court further recognized the Spokanes' right to bring action because they had, since 1951, been formed into a tribal organization with constitution and bylaws.

The Indian Claims Commission would not give in on its determination that the Spokane tribe was "entitled only to sue 'in a representative capacity on behalf of all such survivors or descendants of the membership of the Spokane Tribe as it existed on July 13, 1892.'" The persistent Spokanes also took this issue

[8] *Appellant's Reply Brief, In the United States Court of Claims Appeals Docket No. 5–62*. Prepared by Ernest A. Wilkinson, Attorney, Washington, D.C., 3. Hereafter cited as *Appellant's Reply Brief.*
[9] *Petitioner's Proposed Findings*, 11.

in their arguments to the Court of Claims. The Court agreed that the commission had erred in its findings, which were written in language that required the Secretary of the Interior to determine the membership of the tribe as it was in 1892, identify the descendants, and utilize the judgment for each, even though they were not members of the present Spokane tribe. It conceded that these findings concerning membership were beyond the jurisdiction of the commission. The Spokanes contended that, "Membership is the keystone to the right to share in tribal property."[10] The Court agreed that the Lower Spokanes were entitled to institute action for their claim, thereby eliminating any uncertainty arising from the words "representative capacity." The Court believed that withdrawal from membership in the Spokane tribe was accompanied by loss of all tribal rights. Loss of membership in the tribe by former Spokanes living elsewhere prevented the necessity of determining certain tribal descendants, long since members of the Coeur d'Alene and Flathead tribes, and of their offspring, from intermarriage with Indians of other tribes.

The Spokanes went back to the commission for a compromise settlement. Since not only tribal membership, but also landownership had to be established when presenting a claim, the commission acknowledged the Spokane tribe's title to its land on the basis of occupation.[11]

[10] *Appellant's Reply Brief*, 1–4.

[11] That exclusive occupation of ancestral home land by aboriginals gives them title was ruled on by the U. S. Supreme Court. *United States* v. *Santa Fe Pacific R. Co.*, 314 *U.S.* 339, 345 (1941). Mastery of a tribe over the soil to the exclusion of others and joint possession of two or more tribes such as to give to each a fixed habitation establishes title, the U. S. Court of Claims had ruled previously. *The Choctaw and Chickasaw Nations* v. *United States*, 34 *Cls.*, 17, 51. Use and occupancy is determined with reference to the standards, habits, and culture of the Indians. This may be proven by such evidence as given in the decision of the Court of Claims in *The Snake or Piute Indians* v. *United States*, 125 *C.Cls.* 241, 254 (1953) as follows:

At best, the ultimate fact of beneficial ownership by exclusive possession and occupancy can only be *inferred* and found from any separate events and a variety of documentary material such as reports of early explorations, maps of explorers or Government engineers, reports of military expeditions, letters and contemporaneous reports of Government representatives writing from the areas in question, annual reports of the Secretaries of War prior to 1849, and of the Secretaries of the Interior after that date, Senate and House

The Spokanes maintained that the 1887 land agreement had been obtained for an "unconscionable consideration" under duress through unfair and dishonorable means; namely, they ceded 3,140,000 acres (approximately 2,985,102 acres plus the 154,898 acres of the Spokane Reservation), and the government paid them only $95,000 (which included the cost of their removal to the reserves). This came to about .032 cents per acre. There seems little doubt that the compensation had not been a fair market price. The commission dealing with the Spokanes in 1887 had been governed by stipulations of treaties made with neighboring tribes by Governor Stevens in 1855,[12] when property in the Spokane area was worth considerably less than it would be in 1887. Nearly three-quarters of the money they received for ceding their land had been spent the first three years (1892–95) after ratification of the 1887 agreement in building about a hundred small (two-room) houses for Spokanes on the Spokane and Coeur d'Alene reservations, with some also put up on the Flathead. Wagons and harness, about all the equipment the removed Indians had received, were issued to all Indians on the Spokane Reservation, to Spokanes on the Flathead Reservation, and to about half those locating on the Coeur d'Alene. Also, by the 1887 agreement, under article 5 and 6, the Spokanes had been promised cattle, seed, saw and grist mills, clothing, provisions, blacksmiths, carpenters, care of the old, sick, and infirm, and educational facilities—none of which they received in adequate amounts, they claimed.

The area claimed by the Spokanes was marked by boundaries with definite geographic features, recognized by them and their neighbors as Spokane Territory. As determined by Ray, their original territory began

Executive documents, contemporary newspaper articles, evidence of an expert type from anthropologists and historians, correspondence in the records of various Government departments and officials with reference to or having a bearing on the tribes or the area in question, and, in fact, anything having any relevance which can be unearthed . . .

Petitioner's Proposed Findings, 85–87. The petitioner (the Spokanes) presented the commission with some evidence in each category of evidence enumerated in the Snake case.

[12] *Petitioner's Proposed Findings,* 74.

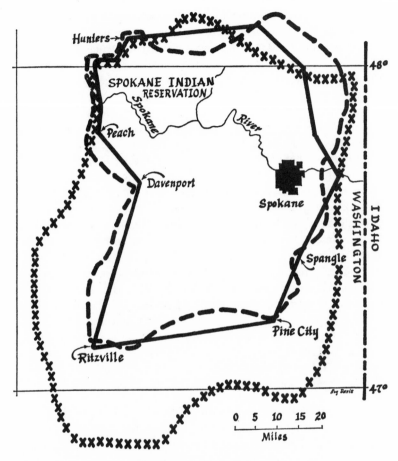

Spokane Tribal Claims

Solid line: Original Indian title Spokane Tribe (Finding 31, 9 Indian
Claims Commission, 236, 252).

Broken line: "Spokane Area of Exclusive Use and Occupancy," map
of Stuart Chalfant (1955). Defendant's Exhibit No. 71.

"X"-marked line: Territory of the Spokane Indian tribe according to
Dr. Verne F. Ray, "Map of Aboriginal Habitat and Permanent Village Location" (1955), Petitioner's Exhibit No. 160.

at the town of Peach on the Big Bend of the Columbia River northerly along the Columbia to another bend north of the mouth of Hunters Creek; thence almost straight easterly to join Hunters Creek for a short distance, leaving it at the confluence of the two main tributaries of Hunters Creek; thence along the ridge forming the divide between the drainage of the Columbia and Colville Rivers, crossing the Colville River in the Colville River Valley and then picking up the ridge on the opposite side which forms the drainage for the tributary streams of the Colville to the north and Loon Lake and its drainages to the south; thence generally southeasterly along that ridge to the headwaters of the tributary streams of the Little Spokane River easterly to Mount Spokane; thence south to include Shadow Mountain and Antoine Plant's Ferry (Opportunity) following the drainage ridge southerly to Rock Creek, around the headwaters of Thorn and Cottonwood Creeks to the present town of Steptoe; thence in a westerly direction along the escarpment of the Palouse River until the line crosses Rock Creek, and from that point southwesterly following sharp peaks in the plains skirting Rattlesnake Flat; thence northerly from the western perimeter of Rattlesnake Flat, including the headwaters of Rocky, Farrier and Bowers Coulees, passing between Sylvan and Pacific Lakes near the town of Odessa, including Coffee Pot Lake at the head of Crab Creek; thence northeasterly along the ridge that forms the watershed for Welsh and Hawk Creeks; thence along the watershed to the place of beginning.[13]

Their area as defined by Chalfant for the United States was considerably less along all boundaries except at the northeast corner.

The Indian Claims Commission, in a decision April 17, 1961, described the area taken from the Spokane tribe as much less than that which Ray maintained belonged to them (especially along the western boundary). The disagreement over size of this area was one reason the Spokanes appeared in the Court of Claims, on which appearance the Court ruled October 11, 1963, that the Indian Claims Commission had been too restrictive in drawing the northeast and southeast boundaries of the area taken from the Spokane tribe. The Court thus remanded the case to the

[13] *Ibid*, 33–34.

commission for further proceedings on the fixing of these boundaries. The Spokanes remained very vocal about the western boundary cutoff, which, as designated by the commission, ran southeast from Peach to Davenport, thence southwest to Ritzville, insisting that the boundary line run more or less straight south from Peach to Ritzville.[14]

In December, 1966, members of the Spokane Indian tribe voted 155 to 3 to accept a compromise offer by the Indian Claims Commission for an award of $6.7 million in settlement of their claims. The Indian Claims Commission approved the proposed compromise settlement on February 21, 1967, and issued a final judgment the same day, awarding $6.7 million to the Spokane tribe. With this compromise settlement, the boundaries were never fixed by the Indian Claims Commission.

Elderly Spokanes tell how government representatives lured their people to the reservation by promising them so much gold it would have to be hauled in on muleback.[15] If these same representatives had been told that one day the tribe would receive over six million dollars, they would not have believed it. The per capita payment for each of the more than fifteen hundred tribal members, however, would not have made a very big load.

The final commission ruling was that the award was to go to the tribe as then constituted, rather than to descendants of original Spokanes, such as those Spokanes now enrolled on other reservations and mixed-bloods. Descendants of Spokanes long since intermarried with Flatheads and Coeur d'Alenes were considered members of the respective tribes on their reservations, where they were enrolled and, consequently, became eligible for compensation already awarded or to be awarded these tribes.[16]

The Coeur d'Alenes filed November 15, 1950, with the Indian Claims Commission for the loss of their lands. On May 6, 1958, they were awarded $4,342,778.03, appropriated by Congress on August 27, 1958. The Kootenays, on April 25, 1960, were awarded

[14] Dave Wynecoop interview, Wellpinit, Washington, July 2, 1965.
[15] Ignace Pascal, "Statement of Ignace Pascal."
[16] Alex Sherwood interview, Wellpinit, Washington, July 3, 1965.

$425,000 for the loss of 1.6 million acres of land in northern Idaho and northern Montana; the money was appropriated on September 8, 1960. The Kalispels, on March 21, 1963, were awarded $3,000,000, which was appropriated May 17, 1963. The August 1, 1966, award to the confederated Salish–Kootenay tribes on the Flathead Reservation was for $4,443,162, for which the money was appropriated and the first per capita payment made in June, 1967.[17]

Before the Spokanes received their land-claim money, they were required to present an acceptable plan to Congress for use of the money after which necessary authorizing legislation was enacted to pay them.[18] Once paid, they took the money out of the U. S. Treasury, which paid a 4 per cent interest rate, and invested a large share of it at a higher rate in a commercial bank in Spokane.

As a portion of tribal claims money had to go into development projects, the Spokanes began laying plans for such improvements even before a dollar amount had been placed on their lost lands. Through their Business Council, they investigated enterprises to produce annual incomes to be distributed among the members. A committee was appointed to study the possibility of making soil and water tests for setting out three hundred acres of dwarf apple trees, to be irrigated by water pumped from the Spokane River— a seven-hundred-thousand-dollar project.[19] (At present, virtually all reservation agricultural lands are watered by precipitation.) The tribe has contracted with a counseling firm to advise it in

[17] Richard M. Balsiger, Assistant Area Director, Bureau of Indian Affairs, Portland Area Office, to authors, September 22, 1967; Harold D. Roberson, Superintendent of Flathead Indian Agency, to authors, July 19, 1967.

[18] When some Spokanes were assessing their losses for a news story, they included horses killed in the Wright campaign. Glenn F. Galbraith interview, Wellpinit, Washington, September 2, 1967. A Spokane newspaper reporter, much interested in the Wright campaign, picked up the story and sent it over wires of the Associated Press on December 8, 1966, telling of the Indian Claims Commission's recognition of the Spokane tribe's claim to compensation for the loss of more than a thousand head killed during the 1858 Wright campaign. However, records of the Washington, D.C., office of the bureau show that no claim was filed on behalf of the tribe for the loss of these horses. Erma Walz, Chief, Branch of Tribal Operations, to authors, August 2, 1967.

[19] Rowland Bond, "Loss of 'Rights' Angers Spokanes," *Spokane Daily Chronicle*, August 18, 1965.

establishing the project and in use of acreages adjacent to it.[20] It could be assumed that no plan would have met with full approval of all tribal members. Oldsters, expectantly awaiting per capita payments of claims money, were opposed to the orchard project. Not only was it foreign to them, but they feared money expended on it would in one way or another "get back into white man's hands."

More unanimity was expressed in the council's approval on February 24, 1965, of a bureau report, which advanced several recommendations for timber development. This included increased sales of reservation timber to approach an allowable annual cut of eighteen million board feet, recognition of the multiple-use concept of management, and the exploration of possibilities for a modern woodworking industry on the reservation.[21] Two years after this proposal was made, two mills were built there. One is owned and operated by Indians; the other, by interests outside the reservation, which employs Indian help.

One of the recommendations in the bureau report was conservation education. Many tribal leaders have said that education has been the greatest need of their people. An act of May 15, 1936, authorized the expenditure of seventy-five thousand dollars for a public school at Wellpinit, to replace the old public school begun shortly after the agency was established there. Also, on June 24, 1946, a thousand dollars of tribal money was budgeted for orphans and other children from broken homes to attend mission schools.

A big stride in Spokane education was taken on September 1, 1945, when the council had passed an ordinance to enforce school attendance, to have the policemen act as truant officers to keep children in school, and to enforce compulsory attendance for youngsters seven through sixteen and for youth sixteen through eighteen not gainfully employed. Twenty-five-dollar fines or thirty-day jail sentences were imposed on families of violators. Incor-

[20] Alex Sherwood interview, Wellpinit, Washington, September 2, 1967.
[21] The recommendations were included in a booklet, *Potential for Intensive Timber Management on the Spokane Indian Reservation*, published by the U. S. Department of Interior, Stewart L. Udall, Secretary, Philleo Nash, Commissioner of Indian Affairs, Spokane Tribal Council, Alex Sherwood, Chairman.

rigibles were to be bound over to the Superior Court or placed in a reform school if necessary.[22] In the early 1960's, the council allotted three thousand dollars from its annual budget for qualified tribal members for scholarships above the high school level. (Today this amount has been doubled.) Mechanization in the Yakima hop fields, whose harvests absented children from school as late as the post–World War II era, helped tribal leaders in their crusade against truancy. For the first time in over a century of exposure to formal education, the Spokanes were beginning to take it seriously. By 1960, school attendance had improved and by the mid–1960's, results were apparent. Spokane school attendance was above the national averages, even for public schools: 92 per cent graduated from high schools, whereas the national average was 70 per cent. Among the Coeur d'Alenes, once considered the most progressive tribe in the northwest, only 50 per cent of the grade school students from the mission school and public schools have gone on to high school. Of those going on to high school, only half (or 25 per cent of all Coeur d'Alene children of high school age) graduate.[23] Also by comparison, of Kalispels attending public schools near their reservation in 1960, some finished the eighth grade and few finished high school.[24] In the press for formal education, courses in the domestic arts, which dominated early reservation schooling, have today taken a secondary place in the curriculum in the Wellpinit public school.

Beside the home and school, that other bulwark of civilization on the reservation, as in white American society, the church, has continued down to the present time. Rising waters of Lake Roosevelt in 1940 forced the West End Presbyterian Church to move to higher ground, not long after which it was abandoned. At the Wellpinit Presbyterian Church, high and dry except during spring thaws, ministers in recent years have been the Reverend Robert

[22] Minutes Spokane Council, September 1, 1945, Colville Agency Records, Box 45–L. 13997.

[23] Rowland Bond, "Coeur D'Alene Reservation Paradox Cited," *Spokane Daily Chronicle*, August 20, 1965.

[24] E. L. Wight, *et al.* (eds.), *Indian Reservations of Idaho, Oregon, and Washington*, 84.

Hall, who later served in Alaska; the Reverend Sam Lee, a Korean, who later served in Hawaii; the Reverend Robert L. Wasson, who used to drive into the country to gather the children for church functions (and was so well liked he was returned from Oregon the spring of 1965 to preach the funeral sermon of Mrs. Albert Sam, a Catholic). The Reverend Walter Moffat, latest in a succession of Nez Percé ministers, came next, to be followed by David L. Heyser, who preached on alternate Sundays. To fill the void, the Harold Bryants, against the wishes of the presbytery, gave up a comfortable home in Spokane to live in the abandoned manse at Wellpinit and serve as lay workers.

Government reports in 1915 listed a missionary for the 250 professing Roman Catholics and one for the 185 professing Protestants on the reservation.[25] The Catholic growth is a testimony in part to the efforts of Hermann Schuler, S.J., who in 1911 built the first Catholic church on the reservation at the east end and dedicated it to Saint Joseph.[26] The church has been renamed Saint Philip. Five years later, government reports would place the number of Catholics at 250 and Protestants at 275, a difference possibly due to efforts of an additional Protestant missionary.[27] Most other reservation inhabitants followed their native religions.

In September, 1938, Patrick Savage, S.J., dedicated the second Catholic church on the reservation, Our Lady of Lourdes, at the west end.[28] With a church on both ends, but none in the middle, the priest came over to Wellpinit to hold mass in the Presbyterian Church for mixed-bloods who had come down from Chewelah to live in that area. Sometimes, especially in the Wellpinit area, one spouse attended Catholic services, and the other Presbyterian. Having no cemetery at Wellpinit, Catholics buried their dead in Presbyterian lots behind the church. In 1943 the Church of the

---

[25] *Reports of the Department of the Interior For the Fiscal Year Ended June 30, 1915 (1916),* II, 78.
[26] Wilfred P. Schoenberg, A *Chronicle of Catholic History of the Pacific Northwest 1743–1960,* Item 1528, p. 292.
[27] *Reports of the Commissioner of Indian Affairs to the Secretary of the Interior For the Fiscal Year Ended June 30, 1920,* 81.
[28] Schoenberg, A *Chronicle of Catholic History,* Item 2169, p. 408.

Sacred Heart was built at Wellpinit[29] and a cemetery set aside nearby. Priests recently serving the reservation have been Louis Taelman, S.J., Eugene Glatt, S.J., and Bernard Osterman, S.J.

An Assemblies of God Church was established near Wellpinit in April, 1961, by Sister Ella Evans and her husband, Frank, who were succeeded in 1967 by the Robert Kenneys. Those who have not given up membership in either Catholic or Presbyterian churches often attend evening services in the Assemblies of God Church. The bell calling them to worship is the same one moved long ago from the Presbyterian Deep Creek Church to the one on the west end.

Just as the bell has an ecumenical ring, so are there other faint signs of religious unity on the reservation today. In February, 1965, when a Catholic lady died, Protestant family members sought to hold funeral services for her in the Presbyterian church. The priest agreed to this and said the rosary in the Presbyterian church, but he insisted on conducting a funeral service in the Catholic church immediately prior to burial. As part of the Protestant services, Mrs. Evans cooked the traditional death feast. On April 24, 1964, members of Protestant, Catholic, and native faiths met at a root festival, an ancient ceremony bearing today but a shadow of its former self, to thank the Great Spirit, today called "God," for His bounties. Mrs. Evans blessed the food.

The Spokane Root Festival, in which the Christian ceremony overlay the Indian, in a sense epitomized a most important chapter in a long history of the Spokanes: their confrontation with the white man. It was first marked by faltering acceptance of his ways, then war to hasten that acceptance, then grudging acceptance, as seen in the removal to reservations, and finally, a struggle to survive in a world not of their own choosing. In passing from one way of life to another, it is understandable that the Indian would, like man everywhere, keep one foot in the past. In the modern stick game, for instance, contestants no longer play to win markers, but money. That the stakes increase each year reflects an inflation in the white man's economy rather than on Indian mores. Fears

29 *Ibid.*, Item 2236, p. 420.

that professional gamblers have moved into the games, as at the Wellpinit Fair, are not new. A. Diomedi, S.J., nearly a hundred years ago, complained of their infiltration into the games.[30] There lives in Spokane, a city of nearly two hundred thousand people, a Spokane Indian woman who comes to the reservation to conduct the traditional winter dance of the Salish people; there are signs of rejuvenation of the old ways among other Indians. It was much easier for tribal leaders to adopt a wildlife code than it was to enforce codes against wild living; today, missionaries, like their predecessors, are still concerned about cohabitation among the people.

Yet tradition has had a harder time surviving on the Spokane Reservation than on most others. Possibly this is because the Spokanes quite early took to white men's ways, and possibly because many of their half-bloods have not shared a common body of tradition with other Spokanes. During World War II, Isaac Camille was the last on the Spokane to cut his braids. At the Wellpinit Fair will be seen the only tipis on the reservation. Yet on the more traditionally minded Colville Reservation, the Fourth of July celebrations at the tipi-studded campground were not held in 1967 because of lack of interest. The fair, a proposed cultural center at Wellpinit, Indian heritage programs in the schools of Spokane, and participation in the American Indian Community Center in that city all indicate that the Spokanes, while trying to hold on to the past, are in reality moving from it. Forty years ago they came to a funeral at the West End Presbyterian Church in sedans, touring cars, trucks, but mostly on horseback and buckboard. Today, not the least concern of tribal leaders is traffic safety on the reservation's twisting roads, where a rider on horseback or in a horse-drawn hack would scarcely venture. Certainly gasoline and whiskey mix no better there than elsewhere, and the automobile—while replacing the horse in carrying Spokanes to other reservations and to towns and cities of the Inland Empire—has also permitted them to become embroiled with the law. One study of racial conditions in Spokane in the immediate post–

[30] Diomedi, *Sketches of Indian Life,* 8.

World War II period indicates that Indian residents of that city did not become embroiled with the law, as did their visiting reservation cousins, whose violations most frequently involved liquor and sex.[31] Some white friends of those so involved assert that justice is more difficult for the Indians to obtain in the city than for their offending white counterparts.

First Lieutenant John Wells of the Third Platoon, Company E, 28th Marines, once said, "Give me fifty men who aren't afraid to die, and I can take *any* position!" In the first squad of that platoon a full-blood Spokane Indian, Louie Adrian, accepted this challenge to die just a few feet from the top of Mount Surabachi, so that the American flag could be raised there. Less than a century before, that flag had been carried into battle against his ancestors.[32]

Tribal leaders expressed a wish to do something for the boys returning from the war, to make the reservation a place "fit for heroes." But Indians began moving from the reservation in the 1930's, during the white man's Depression. The war and postwar periods saw no lessening of this trend. By 1961, over half the total Spokane tribal membership of 1,380 (such increased numbers being an indication, among other things, of the improved health of the tribe)[33] lived off the reservation. The bureau's Relocation Program, established during the Eisenhower administration, has sent additional members away. Sometimes whole families have gone to cities for training and for jobs, both of which could not be found on the Spokane Reservation. Besides the pull of employment on the outside, the rather limited economic opportunities on the reservation, aggravated by fragmented heirships to its land, have tended to deter Spokanes from returning.

With increasing numbers living off the reservation, the Spo-

---

[31] T. H. Kennedy, "Survey of Racial Conditions in Spokane, Washington 1945," Appendix A.

[32] Richard Wheeler, "The First Flag-Raising on Iwo Jima," *American Heritage* Vol. XV, No. 4 (June, 1964), 54–58, 102–105.

[33] The U.S. Public Health Service accepted the responsibility of Indian health in 1955, but major medical care on the reservation is handled by contract with hospitals and private practitioners. The last resident doctor at Wellpinit was Dr. John M. Ryder in 1958–59. At the present time a doctor is at the Wellpinit Clinic on Mondays and Thursdays, and a dentist is there all day Thursdays.

kanes are once again a house divided. Those off the reservation are surrendering their culture to that of the white man; not so much, their brothers back home. A recent study of assimilation patterns of Spokanes on their reservation led researchers to the conclusion that the Indians were occupationally and socioeconomically better assimilated into white culture in the latter years of the nineteenth century than they are today.[34]

Termination for the Spokanes would hasten and force their assimilation into the dominant white culture. Yet termination talk has become less audible in the past few years among Spokanes, both on and off the reservation. Tribal leaders became frightened at talk in Congress of incorporating termination in the settlement of claims. There are also fears that termination would jeopardize plans of the Business Council, which, working harder than old-time chiefs, is striving in a new aura of freedom to retain the identity of the reservation, despite continuing bureau control in such matters as buying, selling, and exchanging reservation lands. From this springboard, the council wishes to project its people into the modern world. A major deterrent to this plan has been the traditionalist who seeks bureau control to protect the status quo, or even to return to the socioeconomic patterns of the past. It would appear that goals of tribal leaders can be achieved only when cemented by just enough bureau supervision to hold it together. As a step in this direction, a Spokane agency was established November 30, 1970, separate from the Colville. Perhaps the ideal form and setting of this enterprise would be that of an independent corporation within a land unit conforming to the reservation and utilizing the resources of the land for the good of all. But such independence could jeopardize reservation and tribal

[34] Prodipto Roy and Della M. Walker, *Assimilation of the Spokane Indians,* 49–51. Specific conclusions from the study indicate the Spokanes have about 43 per cent white blood, with a correlation between age and per cent of Indian blood, indicating their amalgamation has been continuing during this past generation with about 30 per cent of marriages taking place between full-bloods and involving no amalgamation. Indians with a high quantum of Indian blood were found tending to marry full-bloods or people with high quantum of Indian blood and vice versa. Years of schooling completed and per cent of Indian blood were inversely correlated, as were social participation and socioeconomic variables.

entity and, perhaps, the entire program as well.

"In 1981, a century after the establishment of their reservation, the Spokanes were steering a cautious path, eschewing those who would have them cut their ties with the federal government. In 1973, when the American Indian Movement was most active, its militant representatives made little headway on the Spokane Reservation. Through their cautious policy the Spokanes were able to secure programs to bolster their economy and also their social well-being. Aware that their future lay with their youth, they developed an active work-experience program for this age group. Serving to give the youth and their elders a greater sense of cohesion and tribal spirit was the Alex Sherwood Memorial Center, dedicated June 7, 1975. In its museum they could see reminders of their past, while, as they entered the last two decades of the twentieth century, they had cast off much of their traditionalism. They did not have to strive as hard as formerly to find their place in the modern world, into which they had emerged through the shadows cast by the white men standing between them and the sun, under which they once lived in harmony and balance, calling themselves its children. Perhaps no proof of their emergence into the modern world was more evident than their plan to establish a nuclear power plant. Although in 1981 the project was only in the dream-planning stage, it appeared that, like the sun itself, the Spokanes were beginning to swing full circle.

Bibliography

MANUSCRIPT MATERIALS

Allan, George T. "Journal of a voyage from Fort Vancouver Columbia to York Factory, Hudson's Bay, 1841." Manuscript, Washington State Library, Olympia, Washington.

Joseph M. Caruana, S.J., Papers. Biographical and autobiographical notes, Crosby Library, Gonzaga University, Spokane.

Joseph Cataldo, S.J., Papers. Letters and biographical and autobiographical notes, Crosby Library, Gonzaga University, Spokane.

Deffenbaugh, G. L. "Report for the Quarter ending July 31, 1883, to the Board of Foreign Missions." From the Collections of the Presbyterian Historical Society, Philadelphia.

Dandy, G. E. "Reminiscences." Typescript copy in the William C. Brown Papers, Holland Library, Washington State University, Pullman, Washington.

Doty, James. "Journal of Operations of Governor Isaac Ingalls Stevens, Superintendent of Indian Affairs and Commissioner, treating with the Indian Tribes East of the Cascade Mountains, in Washington Territory, and the Blackfeet and neighboring Tribes, near Great Falls of the Missourie, in the year 1855; including therein details of the celebrated Indian Council at Walla Walla, and of the Blackfoot Council at Fort Benton, and the commemcement of the Indian Wars 1855–8." Typescript copy in Eastern Washington Historical Society, Spokane.

Durheim, Roger. "History of Peone." Typescript copy in possession of authors.

Cushing Eells Collection. Letters and "Reminiscences of Cushing Eells." Holland Library, Washington State University, Pullman, Washington.

Eells, Myra F. Letter to Mrs. Aaron Rogers, January 4, 1844, in Jefferson, Harriet A. (comp. and indexer), "Family Records of Washington Pioneers (Prior to 1891) Volume VIII 1938 Collected by the Daughters of the American Revolution of the State of Washington." Typescript copy in Eastern Washington Historical Society, Spokane.

Eells, Myron. "A Trip from Walla Walla to Tshimakain Near the Spokane River and Return." Mimeograph copy in University of Washington Library, Seattle.

Gwydir, Rickard D. "Statement of Major R. D. Gwydir as related to William S. Lewis." Typescript copy in Eastern Washington Historical Society, Spokane.

Granville O. Haller Papers. Correspondence, notes, diary entries, records, articles, and reports, University of Washington Library, Seattle.

Hegler, Rodger. "A Racial Analysis of Indian Skeletal Material From the Columbia River Valley," 1957. Typescript Thesis No. 813020 in University of Washington Library, Seattle.

"Helen W. Clark." Staff memo written on the death of Miss Clark, Library of Board of National Missions of the United Presbyterian Church in the United States of America, New York.

Walt Horan Papers. Records, documents, papers, and correspondence, Holland Library, Washington State University, Pullman, Washington.

Joseph Joset Manuscript. Crosby Library, Gonzaga University, Spokane.

Kamiakin, Tomio. "Chief Kamiakin," in the L. V. McWhorter Papers in the Holland Library, Washington State University, Pullman, Washington.

Kennedy, Alexander, Chief Factor. Spokane House Report 1822–23,

H.B.C. Arch. B. 208/e/1–3, fos. 1 and 3–3d, Hudson's Bay Company Archives, London.

Kennedy, T. H. "Survey of Racial Conditions in Spokane, Washington, 1945," Appendix A. Typescript thesis in Holland Library, Washington State University, Pullman, Washington.

"Letters of D'n Finlayson, March 1832," in "Journals and Correspondence of John McLeod, Senior Chief Trader Hudson's Bay Company . . . ." Copied from the originals in the Dominion Government Archives by R. E. Gosnell, microfilm in Library of Congress.

Lewis, William S. "Indian Account of the Settlement of the Spokane Country." Eastern Washington Historical Society, Spokane.

———. "Reminiscences of Gavin C. Mouat as related to William S. Lewis Corresponding Secretary of the Spokane Historical Society." Typescript copy in Eastern Washington Historical Society, Spokane.

———. "Spokane History, Statement of Thomas Garry, Moses B. Phillips, Aleck Pierre, Charley Warren, John Stevens, David John, and William Three Mountains." Typescript copy in Eastern Washington Historical Society, Spokane.

———. "Spokane House, the History of an Old Trading Post." Manuscript in Eastern Washington Historical Society, Spokane.

———. "Statements of Nellie Garry, Susan Michel, Curley Jim." Typescript copy in Eastern Washington Historical Society, Spokane, May 28, 1916.

William Cameron McKay Papers. "Early History of the Dalles." Microfilm in University of Oregon Library, Eugene, Oregon.

Nichols, Rowena. "Items Collected at the Mission," in "Notes on Indian Affairs in Oregon." Microfilm No. 41 in Bancroft Library, University of California, Berkeley.

———. "The War of 1855–6," in "Notes on Indian Affairs in Oregon." Microfilm No. 41 in Bancroft Library, University of California, Berkeley.

Pascal, Ignace. "Spokane Root Festival," April, 1964. Typescript copy in possession of authors.

———. "Statement of Ignace Pascal," 1967. Handwritten copy at Assemblies of God Church, Wellpinit, Washington.

John A. Simms Papers. Correspondence, reports, records, and documents, Holland Library, Washington State University, Pullman, Washington.

Edward J. Steptoe Papers. Correspondence, University of Washington Library, Seattle.

Stevens, I. I. Letter to Captain F. W. P. Goff, June 4, 1856, Washington State Library, Olympia, Washington.

———. Letter to Lieutenant Colonel Wm. Craig, Special Agent Nez Percés, December 21, 1855. Copy in Washington State Library, Olympia, Washington.

"Vocabulary of the Spokan Indian language and notes on Grammar [containing George Gibbs's instructions for research relative to the ethnology and philology of America]." Typescript copy in Bancroft Library, University of California, Berkeley.

Elkanah Walker Papers. Correspondence, records, articles, reports, and "Letters Concerning Elkanah and Mary Walker." Holland Library, Washington State University, Pullman, Washington.

"Washington Dictations," P–B 81. Typescript copy in Bancroft Library, University of California, Berkeley.

John McA. Webster Papers. Correspondence, reports, records, addresses, and articles, Holland Library, Washington State University, Pullman, Washington.

Wilson, Lieutenant Charles. "Diary Kept by Lt. Wilson of the British Boundary Survey Party June 1860–July 1862 Canada to Colville Country via the Dallas [Dalles]." Verifax copy in Holland Library, Washington State University, Pullman, Washington.

W. P. Winans Papers. Correspondence, reports, records, and documents, Holland Library, Washington State University, Pullman, Washington.

Work, J. "Some Information relative to Colville District by J. Work Ap[ri]l 1830." H.B.C. Arch. B. 45/6/3, fos. 2, 3d., and 7–7d., Hudson's Bay Company Archives, London. Published by permission of the Governor and Committee of the Hudson's Bay Company, R. A. Reynolds, Secretary.

INTERVIEWS

Boyd, Sadie. Wellpinit, Washington, July 2, 1965.

Cornelius, Tom. Wellpinit, Washington, July 3, 1965.

Galbraith, Glenn F. Wellpinit, Washington, September 2, 1967.

McCarty, Ella. Spokane, Washington, September 21, 1966.

Moore, Clara. Belvedere, Washington, March 4, 1961.

Sam, Albert. Wellpinit, Washington, July 2, 1965.

Bibliography

Sherwood, Alex. Wellpinit, Washington, July 3, 1965; July 4, 1965; September 2, 1967.

Wynecoop, Dave. Wellpinit, Washington, July 2, 1965; August 13, 1966.

LETTERS TO THE AUTHORS

Balsiger, Richard M. Assistant Area Director, Bureau of Indian Affairs, Portland Area Office, Portland, Oregon, September 22, 1967.

Miller, Elmo. Superintendent, Colville Indian Agency, Grand Coulee, Washington, July 20, 1967.

Roberson, Harold D. Superintendent, Flathead Indian Agency, Ronan, Montana, July 19, 1967.

Smith, Jane F. Director, Social and Economic Records Division, National Archives and Record Service, Washington, D.C., August 18, 1967.

Welander, Arthur D. Professor of Fisheries, University of Washington, Seattle, Washington, October 17, 1967.

Walz, Erma. Chief, Branch of Tribal Operations, United States Department of the Interior, Bureau of Indian Affairs, Washington, D.C., August 2, 1967.

FEDERAL DOCUMENTS

Annual Report of the Board of Indian Commissioners, 1921.

Annual Reports of the Secretary of the Interior, 1853–54, 1860–61, 1867–71, 1873, 1888, 1891–92, 1894, 1897, 1899, 1940.

Annual Report of the Secretary of War, 1845–60, 1877–80, 1883–84.

Bushnell, David I., Jr. "John Mix Stanley, Artist-Explorer," in Annual Report of the Board of Regents of the Smithsonian Institution, Washington, 1924.

Caywood, Louis R. Archeological Excavations at Fort Spokane 1951, 1952, and 1953, U. S. Department of the Interior National Parks Service, San Francisco, 1954.

Department of the Interior. Circular No. 597, January 6, 1912.

Dill, Hon. C. C. Speech in House of Representatives, January 21, 1916.

Galbraith, Glenn F. "The Spokane Indians Redevelopment Area, 1961." Xerofax copy in possession of authors.

Gibbs, George. "Tribes of Western Washington and Northeastern Oregon," in United States Geographical and Geological Survey of the Rocky Mountain Region, Washington, 1877.

317

Haeberlin, H. K., *et al.* "Coiled Basketry in British Columbia and Surrounding Region," in *Forty-first Annual Report of the Bureau of American Ethnology, 1919–24,* Washington, 1928.

House of Representatives. *Hearings Before the Subcommittee on Indian Affairs of the Committee on Interior and Insular Affairs,* June 18, August 13, November 3, 4, and 5, 1965.

Kappler, Charles J., ed. *Indian Affairs: Laws and Treaties,* 58 Cong., 2 sess., *Sen. Exec. Doc. No. 310.* 2 vols.

McClellan, Captain George B. "Papers—Engineering Notebook and Memoranda 1853 et al., Journal May 20–Dec. 16 [1853]." McClellan Papers. Microcopy from Library of Congress.

Message from the President, 51 Cong., 1 sess., *House Exec. Doc. No. 14,* Vol. II.

Message from the President of the United States, 70 Cong., 1 sess., *Sen. Doc. No. 110.* Vol. II.

Mooney, James. *The Aboriginal Population of America North of Mexico, Smithsonian Miscellaneous Collections,* Vol. LXXX, No. 7 (Publication 2955), Washington, 1928.

———. "The Ghost-Dance Religion and the Sioux Outbreak of 1890," in *Fourteenth Annual Report of the Bureau of American Ethnology, 1892–93.* Washington, 1896.

Morgan, Lewis H. "Systems of Consanguinity and Affinity of the Human Family," in *Smithsonian Contributions to Knowledge,* XVII, Washington, 1871.

Mullan, Captain John, U.S.A. *Report on the Construction of a Military Road from Fort Walla-Walla to Fort Benton,* 37 Cong., 3 sess., *Sen. Exec. Doc. No. 43.*

Peale, Titian R. "On the Uses of the Brain and Marrow of Animals Among the Indians of North America," in *Annual Report of the Board of Regents of the Smithsonian Institution, showing the Operations, Expenditures, and Condition of the Institution for the Year 1870,* 42 Cong., 1 sess., *House Exec. Doc. No. 20.*

Potential for Intensive Timber Management on the Spokane Indian Reservation, Washington, 1965.

"Proceedings of the Northwest Indian Commission Held at Spokane Falls Commencing March 7, 1887, and Ending March 17, 1887." Typescript copy in the Eastern Washington Historical Society, Spokane.

Bibliography

Records of the Coeur d'Alene Indian Agency, Federal Records Center, Seattle.

Records of the Colville Indian Agency, Federal Records Center, Seattle.

Records of the Oregon Superintendency of Indian Affairs, 1842–80. File microcopies of records in the National Archives.

Records of the Superintendency of Indian Affairs, 1853–74. File microcopies in records in the National Archives.

Regular Army Muster Rolls Company I, 4th United States Infantry, December 1892–August 1893. Records of the Adjutant General's Office, Record Group 94. Microfilm in the National Archives and Records Service, Washington.

Report of Anson Dart, Superintendent of Indian Affairs for Oregon Territory to Hon. L. Lea, Commissioner of Indian Affairs, 32 Cong., 1 sess., *Sen. Exec. Doc. No. 1.*

Reports of the Commissioner of Indian Affairs to the Secretary of the Interior for the Fiscal Year Ended June 30, 1920. Washington, 1920.

Reports of the Department of the Interior for the Fiscal Year Ended June 30, 1915. Washington, 1916.

Reports of Explorations and Surveys, to Ascertain the Most Practicable and Economical Route for a Railroad from the Mississippi River to the Pacific Ocean 1853–55. 12 vols. Washington, 1855–60.

Schaeffer, Claude E. *Le Blanc and La Gasse Predecessors of David Thompson in the Columbia Plateau. Studies in Plains Anthropology and History, Number 3,* U. S. Department of the Interior, Indian Arts and Crafts Board, Browning, Montana, 1966.

70 Cong., 1 sess., *House Report No. 958,* Vol. II.

63 Cong., 2 sess., *House Report No. 394,* Vol. I.

Smith, E. P. Letter to R. H. Milroy, May 22, 1873. M–234, Roll 91. Microcopy in Washington State Library, Olympia, Washington.

Spokane (Indian Reservation) Day School Records, 1897–99, Federal Records Center, Seattle.

Stanley, John Mix. "Catalogue of Portraits of North American Indians, With Sketches of Scenery, etc." in *Smithsonian Miscellaneous Collections,* II, Washington, 1862.

Swanton, John R. "The Indian Tribes of North America," in Smithsonian Institution Bureau of American Ethnology, *Bulletin 145,* Washington, 1952.

Symons, Thomas W. *Report of an Examination of the Upper Colum-*

bia River and the Territory in Its Vicinity in September and October, 1881, to Determine Its Navigability and Adaptability to Steamboat Transportation, 47 Cong., 1 sess., *Sen. Exec. Doc. No. 186.*

Teit, James A. "The Salishan Tribes of the Western Plateaus," in *Forty-fifth Annual Report of the Bureau of American Ethnology, 1927–28,* Washington, 1930.

Wheat Lands of Oregon and Washington, 1880, 50 Cong., 1 sess., *Sen. Exec. Doc. No. 229.*

Wight, E. L., *et al.,* eds. *Indian Reservations of Idaho, Oregon, and Washington,* U. S. Department of the Interior, Bureau of Indian Affairs, Portland, Oregon, 1960.

NEWSPAPERS

Colville Examiner. Colville, Washington, 1913.

Lincoln County Times. Davenport, Washington, 1894, 1896, 1914, and 1917.

Morning Review. Spokane Falls, Washington Territory, 1887–88.

Omak Chronicle. Omak, Washington, 1926.

Oregonian. Portland, Oregon, 1865, 1935.

Oregon Spectator. Oregon City, Oregon Territory, 1848, 1850.

Pacific Christian Advocate. Portland, Oregon, 1879.

Pioneer and Democrat. Olympia, Washington Territory, 1855–57 and 1867.

Spokane Daily Chronicle. Spokane, Washington, 1956 and 1965.

Spokane Falls Review. Spokane Falls, Washington, 1889–91.

Spokane Globe. Spokane Falls, Washington, 1889.

Spokane Times-Tribune. Spokane, Washington, 1923.

Spokan Times. Spokane Falls, Washington Territory, 1879–82.

Spokesman-Review. Spokane, Washington, 1891–92, 1895–97, 1900, 1905–1906, 1911, 1913–14, 1916–18, 1920, 1939, and 1957.

Stevens County Standard. Colville, Washington, 1893.

Walla Walla Statesman. Walla Walla, Washington Territory, 1866 and 1868.

Walla Walla Union. Walla Walla, Washington Territory, 1873.

Washington Statesman. Walla Walla, Washington Territory, 1863.

Weekly Oregonian. Portland, Oregon Territory, 1855, 1857–58.

Wenatchee Daily World. Wenatchee, Washington, 1943.

Wilbur Register. Wilbur, Washington, 1893–94, 1896, 1901–1902, 1907–1909, and 1934.

Bibliography

Yakima Republic. Yakima, Washington, 1966.

Books and Pamphlets

Anonymous. *Sketches of Mission Life Among the Indians of Oregon.* New York, 1854.

——. [Peter Skene Ogden?]. *Traits of American Indian Life and Character.* New York, 1954.

Armstrong, A. N. *Oregon: Comprising a Brief History and Full Description of the Territories of Oregon and Washington.* Chicago, 1857.

Ballantyne, Robert M. *Hudson's Bay; or Every-Day Life in the Wilds of North America.* Edinburgh and London, 1848.

Bancroft, Hubert Howe. *History of Washington, Idaho, and Montana 1845–1889.* Vol. XXXI in *The Works of Hubert Howe Bancroft.* San Francisco, 1890.

Blanchet, F. N., and others. *Notices and Voyages of the Famed Quebec Mission to the Pacific Northwest, Being the Correspondence, Notices, etc., of Fathers Blanchet and Demers . . . .* Portland, Oregon, 1956.

Burns, Robert Ignatius, S.J. *The Jesuits and the Indian Wars of the Northwest.* New Haven, Connecticut, 1966.

Butler, Robert. *Contributions to the Prehistory of the Columbia Plateau: A Report on Excavations in the Palouse and Craig Mountain Sections.* Pocatello, Idaho, 1962.

Carstensen, Vernon, ed. *Pacific Northwest Letters of George Gibbs.* Portland, Oregon, 1954.

Catlin, George. *George Catlin: Episodes from "Life Among the Indians" and "Last Rambles."* Ed. by Marvin C. Ross. Norman, 1959.

Chittenden, Hiram Martin. *The American Fur Trade of the Far West.* 2 vols. Stanford, California, 1954.

Clark, Ella E. *Indian Legends of the Pacific Northwest.* Berkeley and Los Angeles, 1963.

Clark, W. P. *Indian Sign Language.* San Jose, California, 1959.

Cline, Walter, *et al. The Sinkaietk or Southern Okanogan of Washington. General Series in Anthropology No. 6, Contributions from the Laboratory of Anthropology.* Ed. by Leslie Spier. Menasha, Wisconsin, 1938.

Collier, Donald, *et al. Archaeology of the Upper Columbia Region.*

University of Washington Publications in Anthropology, IX. Seattle, September, 1942.

Coues, Elliott, ed. *History of the Expedition Under the Command of Lewis and Clark.* 4 vols. New York, 1893.

———. *The Manuscript Journals of Alexander Henry Fur Trader of the Northwest Company and of David Thompson Official Geographer and Explorer of the same Company 1799–1814.* 3 vols. New York, 1897.

Cox, Ross. *Adventures on the Columbia River.* 2 vols. London, 1831.

Curtis, Edward S. *The North American Indian, Being a Series of Volumes Picturing and Describing the Indians of the United States and Alaska.* 20 vols. Norwood, Massachusetts, 1907–30.

Daugherty, Richard. *Early Man in Washington.* Olympia, Washington, 1959.

Davidson, Gordon Charles. *The Northwest Company. University of California Publications in History,* VII. Berkeley, 1918.

De Saint-Amant, M. *Voyages en Californie et dans l'Orégon par M. De Saint-Amant envoyé du gouvernement Francais en 1851–1852.* Paris, 1854.

De Smet, Pierre Jean, S.J. *Letters and Sketches, with a Narrative of a Year's Residence among the Indian Tribes of the Rocky Mountains.* In Vol. XXVII, Reuben Gold Thwaites, ed., *Early Western Travels.* Cleveland, 1906.

———. *New Indian Sketches.* New York [n.d.].

———. *Western Missions and Missionaries: A Series of Letters.* New York, 1859.

Diomedi, A[lexander]. *Sketches of Modern Indian Life.* [N.p., n.d.].

Douglas, David. *Journal Kept by David Douglas During His Travels in North America 1823–1827.* New York, 1959.

Drumheller, "Uncle Dan." *Uncle Dan Drumheller Tells Thrills of Western Trails in 1854.* Spokane, 1925.

Drury, Clifford Merrill. *First White Women Over the Rockies.* 2 vols. Glendale, California, 1963.

———. *Elkanah and Mary Walker.* Caldwell, Idaho, 1940.

———. "The Spalding-Lowrie Correspondence," in *Journal of the Department of History of the Presbyterian Church in the U.S.A.* Vol. XX, Nos. 1, 2, 3. March, June, September, 1942.

———. *The Diaries and Letters of Henry H. Spalding and Asa Bowen*

Smith Relating to the Nez Perce Mission 1838–1842. Glendale, California, 1958.

——. *A Tepee in His Front Yard: A Biography of H. T. Cowley One of the Four Founders of the City of Spokane, Washington.* Portland, Oregon, 1949.

Dunbar, Seymour, ed. *The Journals and Letters of Major John Owen Pioneer of the Northwest 1850–1871.* Transcribed and edited from the original manuscripts in the Montana Historical Society and the Collection of W. R. Coe., Esq. 2 vols. New York, 1927.

Edwards, Jonathan. *An Illustrated History of Spokane County, State of Washington.* Spokane, 1900.

Eells, Myron. *History of Indian Missions on the Pacific Coast, Oregon, Washington and Idaho.* Philadelphia, 1882.

Elliott, T. C. *David Thompson, Pathfinder and the Columbia River.* Kettle Falls, Washington, 1911.

Ewing, Charles. *Circular of the Catholic Commissioner for Indian Missions, to the Catholics of the United States.* Baltimore, 1874.

Evans, Elwood. *History of the Pacific Northwest: Oregon and Washington.* 2 vols. Portland, Oregon, 1889.

Glover, Richard, ed. *David Thompson's Narrative 1784–1812.* Toronto, 1962.

Goodman, David Michael. *A Western Panorama 1849–1875: The Travels, Writings and Influence of J. Ross Browne on the Pacific Coast, and in Texas, Nevada, Arizona and Baja California, as the First Mining Commissioner, and Minister to China.* Glendale, California, 1966.

Gray, W. H. *A History of Oregon, 1792–1849, Drawn from Personal Observation and Authentic Information.* Portland, Oregon, 1870.

Fargo, Lucile Foster. *Spokane Story.* New York, 1950.

Field, Virgil F., ed. *The Official History of the Washington National Guard.* 7 vols. Tacoma, 1961–1965.

Franchère, Gabriel. *Narrative of a Voyage to the Northwest Coast of America in the Years 1811, 1812, 1813, and 1814 or the First American Settlement on the Pacific.* New York, 1854.

Frush, Charles W. *A Trip from the Dalles of the Columbia, Oregon, to Fort Owen, Bitter Root Valley, Montana, in the Spring of 1858. Contributions To The Historical Society of Montana, II.* Helena, Montana, 1896.

Fryxell, Roald. "Through a Mirror, Darkly," in *The Record*. Washington State University, Pullman, Washington, 1963.

Hamilton, William T. *A Trading Expedition Among the Indians in 1858 from Fort Walla Walla to Blackfoot Country and Return by William T. Hamilton. Contributions To The Historical Society of Montana, III.* Helena, Montana, 1900.

Hansen, Henry P. *Postglacial Frost Succession, Climate and Chronology in the Pacific Northwest. Transactions of the American Philosophical Society*, Vol. XXXVII, No. 1, Philadelphia, 1947.

Hawthorne, Julian, ed. *History of Washington the Evergreen State From Early Dawn to Daylight.* 2 vols. New York, 1893.

Hines, Gustavus. *Wild Life in Oregon.* New York, 1887.

Hook, Henry H., and Francis J. McGuire. *Spokane Falls Illustrated.* Minneapolis, 1889.

Hosmer, James K., ed. *The Expedition of Lewis and Clark.* 2 vols. Chicago, 1917.

Howard, O. O. *Autobiography of Oliver Otis Howard.* 2 vols. New York, 1907.

———. *My Life and Experiences Among Our Hostile Indians.* Hartford, Connecticut, 1907.

Hunt, Aurora. *The Army of the Pacific.* Glendale, California, 1951.

Hunt, Garrett B. *Indian Wars of the Inland Empire.* Spokane [n.d.]

Hutton, May Arkwright. *The Coeur D'Alenes or a Tale of the Modern Inquisition in Idaho.* [N.p.], 1900.

Irving, Washington. *Astoria.* Portland, Oregon, 1950.

Jessett, Thomas E. *Chief Spokan Garry, 1811–1892, Christian Statesman and Friend of the White Man.* Minneapolis, 1960.

Johansen, Dorothy O., and Charles M. Gates. *Empire of the Columbia.* New York, 1957.

Josephy, Alvin M., Jr. *The Nez Percé Indians and the Opening of the North West.* New Haven, Connecticut, 1965.

Kane, Paul. *Wanderings of an Artist Among the Indians of North America.* London, 1859.

Keyes, E. D. *Fifty Years' Observation of Men and Events Civil and Military.* New York, 1884.

Kip, Lawrence. *Army Life on the Pacific: A Journal of the Expedition Against the Northern Indians, the Tribes of the Coeur D'Alenes, Spokans, and Pelouzes, in the Summer of 1858.* New York, 1859.

Lee, D., and J. H. Frost. *Ten Years in Oregon.* New York, 1844.

Lewis, Albert Buell. *Tribes of the Columbia Valley and the Coast of Washington and Oregon. Memoirs of the American Anthropological Association.* Vol. I, Pt. 2. Lancaster, Pennsylvania, 1906.

Lewis, William S. *The Case of Spokane Garry. Bulletin of the Spokane Historical Society,* Vol. I, No. I, Spokane, January, 1917.

Lockley, Fred. *History of the Columbia River Valley.* Chicago, 1928.

Maloney, Alice Bay, ed. *Fur Brigade to the Bonaventura John Work's California Expedition 1832–1833.* San Francisco, 1945.

Manring, B. F. *The Conquest of the Coeur D'Alenes, Spokanes and Palouses, the Expedition of Colonels E. J. Steptoe and George Wright against the "Northern Indians" in 1858.* Spokane, 1912.

Merk, Frederick, ed. *Fur Trade and Empire George Simpson's Journal.* Cambridge, Massachusetts, 1931.

Morgan, Thomas J. *The Education of American Indians.* [Washington?, n.d.].

Morton, Arthur S. *Sir George Simpson Overseas Governor of the Hudson's Bay Company a Pen Picture of a Man of Action.* Portland, Oregon, 1944.

Mullan, John. *Miners and Travelers' Guide to Oregon, Washington, Idaho, Montana, Wyoming, and Colorado Via the Missouri and Columbia Rivers . . . .* New York, 1865.

Oliphant, J. Orin, ed. "The Story of Chief Louis Wildshoe," in *The Early History of Spokane, Washington, Told by Contemporaries.* Cheney, Washington, 1927.

Palladino, Lawrence B., S.J. *Indian and White in the Northwest.* Lancaster, Pennsylvania, 1922.

Park, Wilard Z. *Shamanism in Western North America: A Study in Cultural Relationships.* Evanston and Chicago, 1938.

Parker, Samuel. *Journal of an Exploring Tour Beyond the Rocky Mountains.* Ithaca, New York, 1844.

Payette, B. C. *The Oregon Country Under the Union Jack.* Montreal, 1962.

Pickering, John. "An Essay on a Uniform Orthography for the Indian Languages of North America," in *Memoirs of the American Academy of Arts and Sciences.* Cambridge, Massachusetts, 1820.

Point, Nicolas, S.J. *Wilderness Kingdom Indian Life in the Rocky Mountains: 1840–1847.* Ed. by Joseph P. Donnelly, S. J. Chicago, 1967.

Ralph, Julian. *Our Great West.* New York, 1893.

Raufer, Maria Ilma. *Black Robes and Indians on the Last Frontier.* Milwaukee, 1966.

Ray, Verne F. *Cultural Relations in the Plateau of Northwestern America. Publications of the Frederick Webb Hodge Anniversary Publication Fund of the Southwest Museum, III.* Los Angeles, 1939.

——. *Cultural Element Distribution: XXII Plateau. University of California Publication,* Vol. VIII, No. 2, 1942.

Richmond, Gerald M., and others. "The Cordilleran Ice Sheet of the Northern Rocky Mountains, and Related Quaternary History of the Columbia Plateau, in *The Quaternary of the United States.* Princeton, New Jersey, 1965.

Ritz, Philip. *Settlement of the Great Northern Interior.* San Francisco, 1878.

Ross, Alexander. *Adventures of the First Settlers on the Oregon or Columbia River.* London, 1849.

——. *The Fur Hunters of the Far West.* Ed. by Kenneth A. Spaulding. Norman, 1956.

Roy, Prodipto, and Della M. Walker. *Assimilation of the Spokane Indians.* Institute of Agricultural Sciences, *Bulletin 628.* Washington State University, Pullman, Washington, 1961.

Ruby, Robert H., and John A. Brown. *Half-Sun on the Columbia: A Biography of Chief Moses.* Norman, 1965.

Ruth, Kent. *Great Day in the West: Forts, Posts, and Rendezvous Beyond the Mississippi.* Norman, 1963.

Saum, Lewis O. *The Fur Trader and the Indian.* Seattle, 1965.

Schoenberg, Wilfred P., S. J. *A Chronicle of Catholic History of the Pacific Northwest 1743–1960.* Spokane, 1962.

Schoolcraft, Henry R. *Information Respecting the History, Condition and Prospects of the Indian Tribes of the United States.* Philadelphia, 1853.

Simpson, Sir George. *Narrative of a Journey Round the World, During the Years 1841, 1842.* 2 vols. London, 1847.

Smalley, Eugene V. *History of the Northern Pacific Railroad.* New York, 1883.

Spier, Leslie. *The Prophet Dance of the Northwest and its Derivatives: The Source of the Ghost Dance. General Series in Anthropology Number I.* Menasha, Wisconsin, 1935.

——. *Tribal Distribution in Washington. General Series in Anthropology Number 3.* Menasha, Wisconsin, 1936.

Splawn, A. J. *Ka-Mi-akin The Last Hero of the Yakimas.* Portland, Oregon, 1917.

Stevens, Hazard. *The Life of General Isaac Ingalls Stevens.* 2 vols. Boston, 1900.

Sutherland, Thomas A. *Howard's Campaign Against the Nez Perce Indians, 1877.* Portland, Oregon, 1878.

Swan, James G. *The Northwest Coast: Or Three Years' Residence in Washington Territory.* New York, 1857.

Townsend, John K. *Narrative of Journey across the Rocky Mountains, to the Columbia River.* In Vol. XXI, Reuben Gold Thwaites, ed., *Early Western Travels.* Cleveland, 1905.

Trimble, William J. *The Mining Advance into the Inland Empire, a Comparative Study of the Beginning of the Mining Industry in Idaho and Montana, Eastern Washington and Oregon, and the Southern Interior of British Columbia, and of Institutions and Laws Based on That Industry. Bulletin 638.* University of Wisconsin, Madison, Wisconsin, 1914.

Victor, Frances Fuller. *The Early Indian Wars of Oregon.* Salem, Oregon, 1894.

Wilkes, Charles, U.S.N. *Narrative of the United States Exploring Expedition During the Years 1838, 1839, 1840, 1841, 1842.* 5 vols. Philadelphia, 1845.

Wilkinson, Ernest L. *Appellant's Reply Brief in the United States Court of Claims Appeals Docket No. 5–62,* Washington, n.d.

———. *Petitioner's Proposed Findings of Fact and Brief Before the Indian Claims Commission Docket No. 331,* Washington, n.d.

———. *Reply to Defendant's Objection to Petitioner's Proposed Findings of Fact, Objections to Defendant's Proposed Findings of Fact, and Reply Brief Before the Indian Claims Commission Docket No. 331,* Washington, n.d.

Williams, Howell. *Crater Lake: The Story of its Origin.* Berkeley, 1961.

Wyeth, John B. *Oregon: or, a Short History of a Long Journey from the Atlantic Ocean to the Region of the Pacific, by Land.* In Vol. XXI, Reuben Gold Thwaites, ed., *Early Western Travels.* Cleveland, 1905.

Young, F. G., ed. *The Correspondence and Journals of Captain Nathaniel J. Wyeth 1831–6.* Eugene, Oregon, 1899.

ARTICLES

Anonymous. "Indian Commission. Heathen Red Men Asking for Christian Light," *Spirit of Missions*. Vol. XXXVIII, No. 10 (October, 1873).

———. "Last of the Spokane Tribe." *Northwest Magazine*. Vol. XI, No. 1 (January, 1893).

———. "Monthly Record of Current Events," *Harpers New Monthly Magazine*, Vol. XVIII, No. 103 (December, 1858).

———. "Obituary of Father Joseph M. Caruana, S. J.," *America*, Vol. X, No. 7, (November, 1913).

———. "Shall We Help Them? And Who Will Be Their Missionary?" *Spirit of Missions*, Vol. XXXVIII. No. 12 (December, 1873).

Barnum, Francis A., S. J. "The last of the Old Indian-Missionaries— Father Joseph Joset, A Sketch From Notes Gleaned from the Missionary by Father Barnum," *Woodstock Letters*, Vol. XXX, No. 2 (1901).

Barry, J. Neilson. "Pickering's Journey to Fort Colville in 1841," *Washington Historical Quarterly*, Vol. XX, No. 1 (January, 1929).

Beall, Thomas B. "Pioneer Reminiscences," *Washington Historical Quarterly*, Vol. VIII, No. 2 (April, 1917).

Bell, Beth. "In and around Spokane," *Northwest Magazine*, Vol. XIII, No. 9 (September, 1895).

Brode, Howard S., ed. "Diary of Dr. A. J. Thibodo," *Pacific Northwest Quarterly*, Vol. XXXI, No. 3 (July, 1940).

Browman, David L., and David A. Munsell. "Columbia Plateau Prehistory: Cultural Development and Impinging Influences," *American Antiquity*, Vol. XXIV, No. 3 (July, 1969), 249.

Campbell, John V. "The Sinclair Party—An Emigration Overland Along the Old Hudson Bay Company Route from Manitoba to the Spokane Country in 1854," *Washington Historical Quarterly*, Vol. VII, No. 3 (July, 1916).

Canis, George F. "Steptoe's Indian Battle in 1858," *Washington Historian*, Vol. I, No. 4 (July, 1900).

Cataldo, Joseph, S. J. "North Indian Missions," *Letters and Notices*, No. XXV (September, 1868).

Clark, Robert C. "The Archives of the Hudson's Bay Company," *Pacific Northwest Quarterly*, Vol. XXIX, No. 1 (January, 1938).

Coan, C. F. "The Adoption of the Reservation Policy in the Pacific

Northwest, 1853–1855," *Oregon Historical Quarterly*, Vol. XXIII, No. 1 (March, 1922).

Dee, Henry Drummond, "An Irishman in the Fur Trade: The Life and Journals of John Work," *The British Columbia Historical Quarterly*, Vol. VII, No. 4 (January, 1943).

Eel[l]s, Reverend Myron. "The First Book Written in the State of Washington," *The Washington Historian*, Vol. I, No. 4 (July, 1900).

Elliott, T. C. "David Thompson's Journeys in the Spokane Country," *Washington Historical Quarterly*, Vol. VIII, No. 3 (July, 1917).

———. "Journal of John Work, June–October, 1825," *Washington Historical Quarterly*, Vol. V, No. 2 (April, 1914).

———. "Journal of John Work, September 7th–December 14th, 1825." *Washington Historical Quarterly*, Vol. V, No. 3 (July, 1914).

———. "Journal of John Work, December 15th, 1925, to June 12th, 1826," *Washington Historical Quarterly*, Vol. V, No. 4 (October, 1914).

———. "The Fur Trade in the Columbia River Basin Prior to 1811," *Oregon Historical Quarterly*, Vol. XV, No. 4 (December, 1914).

Foote, E. Barnard. "An Indian Burying-Ground," *The West Shore*, Vol. XIV, No. 9 (September, 1888).

Gray, William H. "The Unpublished Journal of William H. Gray from December 1836 to October 1837," *Whitman College Quarterly*, Vol. XVI, No. 6 (June, 1913).

Haines, Francis. "Where Did the Plains Indians Get Their Horses?" *American Anthropologist*, Vol. XL, No. 1 (January–March, 1938); Vol. XL, No. 3 (July–September, 1938).

———. "How the Indian Got the Horse," *American Heritage*, Vol. XV, No. 2 (February, 1964).

Haller, Theodore N. "Life and Public Services of Colonel Granville O. Haller," *Washington Historian*, Vol. I, No. 3 (April, 1900).

Jones, Arthur. "Minnie-Wah-Wah," *The Overland Monthly*, Vol. XXIII, No. 134 (February, 1894).

Kelley, John F. "The Steptoe Disaster," *The Pacific Northwesterner*, Vol. I, No. 1 (Winter, 1956–57).

Kingston, C. S. "Spokane House State Park in Retrospect," *Pacific Northwest Quarterly*, Vol. XXXIX, No. 3 (July, 1948).

Lewis, William S. "The Daughter of Angus MacDonald," *Washington Historical Quarterly*, Vol. XIII, No. 2 (April, 1922).

———. "The First Militia Companies in Eastern Washington Territory," *Washington Historical Quarterly*, Vol. XI, No. 4 (October, 1920).

Lyman, H. S. "Indian War Recollections," *Oregon Native Son*, Vol. I, No. 4 (August, 1899).

———. "Reminiscences of Louis Labonte," *Oregon Historical Quarterly*, Vol. I, No. 1 (March, 1900).

Monroe, M. Orion. "A Critical Discussion of the Site of Camp Washington," *Washington Historical Quarterly*, Vol. VII, No. 1 (January, 1916).

Morison, Samuel Eliot. "New England and the Opening of the Columbia River Salmon Trade, 1830," *Oregon Historical Quarterly*, Vol. XXVIII, No. 2 (June, 1927).

Nute, Grace Lee. "A Botanist at Fort Colville," *The Beaver*, Outfit 277 (September, 1946).

Oliphant, J. Orin. "George Simpson and Oregon Missions," *Pacific Historical Quarterly*, Vol. VI, No. 3 (September, 1937).

Osborne, Douglas. "Archaeological Occurrences of Pronghorn Antelope, Bison, and Horse in the Columbia Plateau," *The Scientific Monthly*, Vol. LXXVII, No. 5 (November, 1953).

———, and others. "Archaeological Investigations in the Chief Joseph Reservoir," *American Antiquity*, Vol. XVII, No. 4 (1952).

Partoll, Albert J. "Angus McDonald, Frontier Fur Trader," *Pacific Northwest Quarterly*, Vol. XLII, No. 2 (April, 1951).

Peltier, Jerome A. "Neglected Spokane House," *The Pacific Northwesterner*, Vol. V, No. 3 (Summer, 1961).

Phillips, Paul C., and W. S. Lewis. "The Oregon Mission as Shown in the Walker Letters 1839–1851, Elkaneh Walker to Reverend David Green, January 23, 1843." *University of Montana, Historical Reprints Sources of Northwest History*, No. 13.

Pipes, Nellie B. "John Mix Stanley, Indian Painter," *Oregon Historical Quarterly*, Vol. XXXIII, No. 3 (September, 1932).

Point, Nicholas, S. J. "Recollections of the Rocky Mountains," *Woodstock Letters*, Vol. XII, No. 2 (1883).

Ray, Verne F. "Native Villages and Groupings of the Columbia Basin," *Pacific Northwest Quarterly*, Vol. XXVII, No. 2 (April, 1936).

———. "The Bluejay Character in the Plateau Spirit Dance," *Ameri-*

can *Anthropologist*, Vol. XXXIX, No. 4 (October–December, 1937).

——, *et al.* "Tribal Distributions in Eastern Oregon and Adjacent Regions," *American Anthropologist*, Vol. XL, No. 3 (July–September, 1938).

Smalley, E. V. "Spokane Falls, the Rapidly Growing Business and Manufacturing Metropolis of Eastern Washington," *Northwest Magazine*, Vol. V, No. 10 (October, 1887).

Smith, Allan H. "An Ethnohistorical Analysis of David Thompson's 1809–1811 Journeys in the Lower Pend Oreille Valley, Northeastern Washington," *Ethnohistory*, Vol. VIII, No. 4 (Fall, 1961).

Smith, John E. "A Pioneer of the Spokane Country," *Washington Historical Quarterly*, Vol. VII, No. 4 (October, 1916).

Todd, Ronald, ed. "Notes and Documents Letters of Governor Isaac I. Stevens, 1857–1858," *Pacific Northwest Quarterly*, Vol. XXXI, No. 3 (October, 1940).

Van Ree, L., S.J. "The Spokane Indians, Sketch of the Work of Our Fathers," *Woodstock Letters*, Vol. XVIII, No. 3 (1889).

Welty, Raymond L. "The Indian Policy of the Army 1860–1870," *The Cavalry Journal*, Vol. XXXVI, No. 148 (July, 1927).

Wheeler, Richard. "The First Flag-Raising on Iwo Jima," *American Heritage*, Vol. XV, No. 4 (June, 1964).

Winder, C. S. "Captain C. S. Winder's Account of a Battle With the Indians," *Maryland Historical Magazine*, Vol. XXXV (1940).

Wissler, Clark. "The Influence of the Horse in the Development of Plains Culture," *American Anthropologist*, Vol. XVI, No. 1 (January–March, 1914).

Wood, C. E. S. "Famous Indians: Portraits of Some Indian Chiefs," *The Century Magazine*, n.s. Vol. XXIV, No. 3 (1893).

Miscellaneous Items

Catalogue Pictures of Indians and Indian Life By Paul Kane, Property of E. B. Osler Esq., M. P., Toronto [n.d.].

Dubuar Scrapbooks [newspaper clippings and articles], University of Washington Library, Seattle.

Eells, Cushing, letters of February 25, 1840, in *Missionary Herald*, Vol. XXXVI, No. 11 (November, 1840); March 1, 1841, *Missionary Herald*, Vol. XXIX, No. 2 (February, 1843); March 23, 1844, *Missionary Herald*, Vol. XL, No. 11 (November, 1844).

Missionary Herald, Vol. XXX, No. 6 (June, 1934); Vol. XXXIII, No. 3 (March, 1837).

Smith, Rev. Asa Bowen, letter of, August 27, 1839, in *Missionary Herald*, Vol. XXXVI, No. 8 (August, 1840).

Spalding, Henry H., letter of, September 4, 1837, in *Missionary Herald*, Vol. XXXIV, No. 10 (October, 1838).

Spokane, Booklet in Eastern Washington Historical Society, Spokane, Washington.

The Oregonian, and Indian's Advocate, Vol. I, No. 7 (April, 1839); Vol. I, No. 10 (July, 1839).

The Spokane Indian Mission, publication of the Women's National Indian Association, Philadelphia [n.d.].

Index

Index

Fort Lee: 79
Fort Nez Percés: 49–50
Fort Okanogan: 194
Fort Omaha: 219
Fort Sherman: 218
Fort Simcoe: 115, 121, 124
Fort Spokane (Hudson's Bay Company Fur post): 55, 61, 64
Fort Spokane (military post): 178, 194, 199, 215, 216, 229, 256–57, 260, 264, 265, 271, 290
Fort Spokane (Pacific Fur Company post): 41–42, 47
Fort Spokane Boarding School: 216, 220 ff., 224
Fort Spokane Sanatorium: 228–29, 231
Fort Taylor: 126
Fort Umpqua: 119
Fort Vancouver (Hudson's Bay Company Fur post): 61–62, 120
Fort Vancouver (military post): 90, 95, 119–20, 143, 144
Fort Walla Walla (Hudson's Bay Company Fur post): 62, 64, 77
Fort Walla Walla (military post): 108–109, 114, 121, 124–26, 138–42, 144
Fort Waters: 79
Fort William: 40
Four Lakes, Wash.: 26, 129, 131
Fourth of July celebration: 209, 259
Fox boys (students): 215
Fox, Henry: 231
Francis (Flathead chief): 144
Fraser River: 53
Frazier, Ben: 214
Freeland, F. B.: 233
Freeman (fur trapper): 41, 52
French-Canadian (fur company employees): 40, 57, 64–65, 85
French-Scottish (fur company employees): 194
Friedlander, Sam: 276
Friezie (Spokane Indian): 175
Fruitland, Wash.: 287
Frush, Charles W.: 115, 117
Funeral customs: see burials
Fur trade: 40–43, 51, 154

Gabbert, Archie D.: 251
Galbraith, Glenn: 292
Gallegos, Lucille Boyd: 285

Gambling: 16, 26, 70, 75, 76, 146, 187, 191, 198, 229, 274, 308–309
Garden City, Wash., Council: 254
Garfielde, Selucius: 157n.
Garnett, Major Robert: 121
Garry, Albert: 212
Garry, Alice: 276
Garry, Joseph: 291
Garry, Nellie: 194–95, 201
Garry, Spokane: 47, 59–63, 69–70, 86, 88, 90–91, 98, 100, 102–106, 109–10, 116, 124, 129, 134–35, 138–39, 143–47, 149, 151–54, 158–60, 163–64, 167, 169, 170–71, 173, 175, 179, 187, 189–91, 194–97, 200–201, 276
Garry, Thomas: 189
Gaston, Lieutenant: 112, 126, 129
Gazzoli, Gregory, S.J.: 163
Geary, E. R.: 145
Gengros (settler): 194
Geology: volcanic ash fall, 3, 32; Spokane area land forms, 4–5
Gibbon, General John: 216
Gibbs, George: 83, 92
Gibson, M.J.: 238
Giordi, Joseph, S.J.: 163, 167–68
Glatt, Eugene, S.J.: 308
Glover, J. M.: 166, 170, 173, 180
Goethals, George W.: 212
Gold discovery: 83–84, 92, 104, 149, 170
Gonzaga College: 187
Graham, James A.: 120
Grand Coulee Dam: 15, 279–80, 290
Grand Ronde River: 91
Grant, Mr. (settler): 173
Grant, President Ulysses S.: 163
Gray, William H.: 62–63
Great Northern Railway: 265
Great Plains: 5, 46, 120, 150
Greenwood Cemetery (Spokane, Wash.): 31
Greer, Major (of Wright's command): 130, 136
Gregg, Lieutenant (of Wright's command): 130, 136
Grist mill: 146, 152, 166, 173–74
Guns: 116, 120, 123, 130–31, 135; Mississippi Yager rifles, 109; howitzers, 111
Gwydir, Rickard: 186, 197

337

Lumber mill: 227, 255, 305

McChesney, Dr. Charles E.: 262
McClellan, Captain George: 84, 86–88
McCoy (settler): 194
McCoy, Isabella: 250–51
McCoy, Millie Morrell: 251
McCoy, Robert: 262
McCoy Lake: 255
McDermott, Fred: 248
McDonald, Angus: 85, 89, 93–94, 97, 102–103
McDonald, Archibald: 64, 74
McDonald, Finan: 37–38, 40, 48, 50, 52
McDowell, Malcom: 272
McKay, Alex: 142
McKay, Douglas: 282, 284
McKee, Dr. Mary H.: 224
MacKenzie, Alexander: 34 n.
McKenzie, Donald: 50
McMillan, James: 40
McNickle, Mable: 243
MacTavish, John George: 40
Magone, Major Joseph: 80
Marriage: 68–69, 71, 186–87, 229, 257–58; mixed, 53, 149, 194, 230 n.
Marshall, John: 277
Martin (attorney): 237–38
Mason, C. H.: 94
Masses (Spokane Indian): 197
Medical Lake, W.T.: 173
Mellon, Otis: 245, 249–50
Merritt, E. B.: 273
Messiah Dance: 199
Methodist Church: 77 n.
Mexican muleteers: 126, 132
Meyer, D. S.: 279
Meyer, Harvey K.: 278
Meyers, John S.: 224
Midnite Mine Inc.: 281–83 & n., 284–85
Miles, Wash.: 263
Milkapsi (Coeur d'Alene chief): 123
Miller, Elmo: 290 n.
Milroy, R. H.: 157, 162
Mining and minerals: 95, 115, 242; Indian depredations, 94; on Spokane reservation, 221, 274, on Colville reservation, 239; reservation leases, 274; *see also* gold discovery *and* uranium

Miocene era: 5
Missoula, Montana: 242
Missouri River: 37, 92, 97
Moffat, the Reverend Walter: 307
Moisturm (Kalispel chief): 139
Monoghan, James: 182 n.
Montour, George: 101–103, 105, 117, 145
Montour, Nicholas: 41
Mooney, James: 29
Moore, Benjamin: 223 n.
Moore, Frank W.: 289
Morgan, Thomas: 202, 225
Morrison, Charles F.: 228, 244–45
Morrison, Eleanor: 228
Moses (Columbia chief): 78, 94–95, 135, 139, 168, 170, 176, 179, 187, 217
Moses (Spokane Indian): 181
Moses, Annie: 273 n.
Moses, Cole: 250
Mosquetquat (Spokane chief): 4
Mouat, Gavin C.: 196
Mount Mazama: 3 n.
Mount Surabachi: 310
Moxnoose (Spokane chief): 4
Mullen, Dr. James: 145
Mullan, Captain John: 114, 120 n., 127, 135, 140, 147, 202
Mulligan (attorney): 237–38

Nahutumhalko (Spokane chief): 60
National Board of Missions of the United Presbyterian Church: 216
National Congress of American Indians: 283
National Indian Congress: 259, 275–76
Neah Bay, Wash.: 215
Nesmith, Colonel J. W.: 107, 117, 119
Nespelem Indians: 12, 15
Nespelem River: 260
Nespelem Valley: 162
Nespelem, Wash.: 260, 264
New England: 62
New Deal: 277
Newman, George H.: 206
Newmann (merchant): 252
Newmont Mining Corporation: 283, 286
New York City: 142–43
Nez Percé Indians: 15, 21, 24–25, 31, 44, 52, 55, 60–62, 80, 85, 90–92,